When Minds Meet

This extraordinary volume offers a sampling of Lewis Aron's most important contributions to psychoanalysis.

One of the founders of relational thinking, Aron was an internationally recognized psychoanalyst, sought after teacher, lecturer, and the Director of the New York University Postdoctoral Program in Psychotherapy and Psychoanalysis. His pioneering work introduced and revolutionized the concepts of mutuality, the analyst's subjectivity, and the paradigm of mutual vulnerability in the analytic setting. During the last few years of his life, Aron was exploring the ethical considerations of writing psychoanalytic case histories and the importance of self-reflection and skepticism not only for analysts with their patients, but also as a stance towards the field of psychoanalysis itself. Aron is known for his singular, highly compelling teaching and writing style and for an unparalleled ability to convey complex, often comparative theoretical concepts in a uniquely inviting and approachable way. The reader will encounter both seminal papers on the vision and method of contemporary clinical practice, as well as cutting-edge newer writing from the years just before his death. Edited and with a foreword by Galit Atlas, each chapter is preceded by a new introduction by some of the most important thinkers in our field: Jessica Benjamin, Michael Eigen Jay Greenberg, Adrienne Harris, Stephen Hartman, Steven Kuchuck, Thomas Ogden, Joyce Slochower, Donnel Stern, Merav Roth, Chana Ullman, and Aron himself.

This book will make an important addition to the libraries of experienced clinicians and psychoanalytic scholars already familiar with Aron's work, as well as students, newer professionals or anyone seeking an introduction to relational psychoanalysis and one of its most stunning, vibrant voices.

Galit Atlas is on the faculty of the NYU Postdoctoral Program in Psychotherapy and Psychoanalysis. She is the author of *The Enigma of Desire: Sex, Longing and Belonging in Psychoanalysis* (Routledge, 2015) and *Dramatic Dialogues* (co-authored with Lewis Aron, Routledge, 2017). She is a faculty member at the Four Year Adult and National Training Programs at the National Institute for the Psychotherapies (NIP). She serves on the editorial board of *Psychoanalytic Perspectives* and is a psychoanalyst and clinical supervisor in private practice in New York City.

RELATIONAL PERSPECTIVES BOOK SERIES

ADRIENNE HARRIS,
STEVEN KUCHUCK & EYAL ROZMARIN
Series Editors

STEPHEN MITCHELL
Founding Editor

LEWIS ARON
Editor Emeritus

The Relational Perspectives Book Series (RPBS) publishes books that grow out of or contribute to the relational tradition in contemporary psychoanalysis. The term *relational psychoanalysis* was first used by Greenberg and Mitchell[1] to bridge the traditions of interpersonal relations, as developed within interpersonal psychoanalysis and object relations, as developed within contemporary British theory. But, under the seminal work of the late Stephen A. Mitchell, the term *relational psychoanalysis* grew and began to accrue to itself many other influences and developments. Various tributaries—interpersonal psychoanalysis, object relations theory, self psychology, empirical infancy research, feminism, queer theory, sociocultural studies and

---

1 Greenberg, J. & Mitchell, S. (1983). *Object relations in psychoanalytic theory.* Cambridge, MA: Harvard University Press.

elements of contemporary Freudian and Kleinian thought—flow into this tradition, which understands relational configurations between self and others, both real and fantasied, as the primary subject of psychoanalytic investigation.

We refer to the relational tradition, rather than to a relational school, to highlight that we are identifying a trend, a tendency within contemporary psychoanalysis, not a more formally organized or coherent school or system of beliefs. Our use of the term *relational* signifies a dimension of theory and practice that has become salient across the wide spectrum of contemporary psychoanalysis. Now under the editorial supervision of Adrienne Harris, Steven Kuchuck and Eyal Rozmarin, the Relational Perspectives Book Series originated in 1990 under the editorial eye of the late Stephen A. Mitchell. Mitchell was the most prolific and influential of the originators of the relational tradition. Committed to dialogue among psychoanalysts, he abhorred the authoritarianism that dictated adherence to a rigid set of beliefs or technical restrictions. He championed open discussion, comparative and integrative approaches, and promoted new voices across the generations. Mitchell was later joined by the late Lewis Aron, also a visionary and influential writer, teacher and leading thinker in relational psychoanalysis.

Included in the Relational Perspectives Book Series are authors and works that come from within the relational tradition, those that extend and develop that tradition, and works that critique relational approaches or compare and contrast them with alternative points of view. The series includes our most distinguished senior psychoanalysts, along with younger contributors who bring fresh vision. Our aim is to enable a deepening of relational thinking while reaching across disciplinary and social boundaries in order to foster an inclusive and international literature.

A full list of titles in this series is available at https://www.routledge.com/mentalhealth/series/LEARPBS.

"This welcome book will bring both satisfaction and pain to all of us who have long admired the work of Lew Aron. Reading his words, we can still hear his enthusiastic yet measured voice; witnessing his posthumous engagement with the other fine minds represented here, we again mourn his loss. More than a festschrift, this book captures Dr. Aron's remarkable professional journey, insatiable intellect, and big heart."

Nancy McWilliams, Rutgers Graduate School of Applied & Professional Psychology

"The experience of reading *When Minds Meet* is reminiscent of listening to a concerto in which a solo instrument is answered and highlighted by an orchestra. Here, the soloist is Lewis Aron whose pioneering work is answered by an orchestra of commentaries written by a selection of highly distinguished psychoanalysts. The sounds they produce together give life to novel and unforgettable melodies that will continue to resonate in readers' minds long after they have put the book down..."

Antonino Ferro, M.D. Training and Supervising Analyst in the Italian Psychoanalytic Association, APsaA and IPA

When Minds Meet: The Work of Lewis Aron

Edited and with a Foreword by Galit Atlas

LONDON AND NEW YORK

First published 2021
by Routledge
2 Park Square, Milton Park, Abingdon, Oxon OX14 4RN

and by Routledge
52 Vanderbilt Avenue, New York, NY 10017

Routledge is an imprint of the Taylor & Francis Group, an informa business

© 2021 selection and editorial matter, Galit Atlas, individual chapters, the contributors

The right of Galit Atlas to be identified as the author of the editorial material, and of the authors for their individual chapters, has been asserted in accordance with sections 77 and 78 of the Copyright, Designs and Patents Act 1988.

All rights reserved. No part of this book may be reprinted or reproduced or utilized in any form or by any electronic, mechanical, or other means, now known or hereafter invented, including photocopying and recording, or in any information storage or retrieval system, without permission in writing from the publishers.

Trademark notice: Product or corporate names may be trademarks or registered trademarks and are used only for identification and explanation without intent to infringe.

British Library Cataloguing-in-Publication Data
A catalogue record for this book is available from the British Library

Library of Congress Cataloging-in-Publication Data
Names: Aron, Lewis, author. | Atlas, Galit, editor, writer of foreword.
Title: When minds meet : the work of Lewis Aron / edited and with a foreword by Galit Atlas.
Description: Abingdon, Oxon ; New York, NY : Routledge, 2021. | Includes bibliographical references and index.
Identifiers: LCCN 2020027918 (print) | LCCN 2020027919 (ebook) | ISBN 9780367622107 (hardback) | ISBN 9780367622121 (paperback) | ISBN 9781003108368 (ebook)
Subjects: LCSH: Object relations (Psychoanalysis) | Interpersonal psychotherapy. | Transactional analysis. | Psychoanalysis--Methodology.
Classification: LCC BF175.5.O24 A76 2021 (print) | LCC BF175.5.O24 (ebook) | DDC 150.19/5--dc23
LC record available at https://lccn.loc.gov/2020027918
LC ebook record available at https://lccn.loc.gov/2020027919

ISBN: 978-0-367-62210-7 (hbk)
ISBN: 978-0-367-62212-1 (pbk)
ISBN: 978-1-003-10836-8 (ebk)

Typeset in Times New Roman
by KnowledgeWorks Global Ltd.

Dedicated to Benjamin, Raphael, Kirya, Emma, Yali and Mia

Table of Contents

Author biographies xiii
Foreword xviii
Acknowledgments xxiv
Permissions xxv

PART I
Psychoanalytic vision 1

1 Dreams, narrative, and the psychoanalytic method (1989) 3
 INTRODUCTION BY LEWIS ARON

2 Working toward operational thought: Piagetian theory and psychoanalytic method (1993) 23
 INTRODUCTION BY ADRIENNE HARRIS

3 The internalized primal scene (1995) 48
 INTRODUCTION BY STEPHEN HARTMAN

4 God's influence on my psychoanalytic vision and values (2004) 89
 INTRODUCTION BY MICHAEL EIGEN

PART II
Clinical choices and relational practice — 105

5 Interpretation as expression of the analyst's subjectivity (1992) — 107
   INTRODUCTION BY THOMAS OGDEN

6 The patient's experience of the analyst's subjectivity (1991) — 141
   INTRODUCTION BY STEVEN KUCHUCK

7 Self-reflexivity and the therapeutic action of psychoanalysis (2000) — 164
   INTRODUCTION BY CHANA ULLMAN

8 Clinical choices and the relational matrix (1999) — 186
   INTRODUCTION BY DONNEL B. STERN

9 "With you I'm born again": themes and fantasies of birth and the family circumstances surrounding birth as these are mutually evoked in patient and analyst (2014) — 217
   INTRODUCTION BY MERAV ROTH

PART III
The ethics of clinical practice — 243

10 Mutual vulnerability: an ethic of clinical practice (2016) — 245
   INTRODUCTION BY JESSICA BENJAMIN

11 Beyond tolerance in psychoanalytic communities: reflexive skepticism and critical pluralism (2017) — 269
   INTRODUCTION BY JOYCE SLOCHOWER

12 Ethical considerations in psychoanalytic writing revisited (2016) — 285
   INTRODUCTION BY JAY GREENBERG

References — *316*
Index — *345*

Author biographies

Lewis Aron (1952–2019) was an internationally recognized psychoanalyst, sought after teacher, lecturer, and the Director of the New York University Postdoctoral Program in Psychotherapy and Psychoanalysis. He was a past President of the Division of Psychoanalysis (39) APA; founding President of the International Association for Relational Psychoanalysis and Psychotherapy (IARPP); and founding President of the Division of Psychologist-Psychoanalysts of NYSPA. Aron was also the co-founder and co-chair of the Sándor Ferenczi Center at the New School for Social Research, and Adjunct Professor, School of Psychology, Interdisciplinary Center (IDC) Herzliya, Israel; a co-founder of Psychoanalytic Dialogues; and the co-editor of the Relational Perspectives Book Series. He is the author and editor of numerous articles and books, including *A Meetings of Minds*, *A Psychotherapy for the People* (co-authored with Karen Starr), and *Dramatic Dialogue* (co-authored with Galit Atlas).

Galit Atlas is on the faculty at NYU Postdoctoral Program in Psychotherapy and Psychoanalysis, and faculty at the Four Year Adult and National Training Programs at NIP. She is the author of *The Enigma of Desire: Sex, Longing and Belonging in Psychoanalysis* (Routledge, 2015) and *Dramatic Dialogues* (co-authored with Lewis Aron, Routledge, 2017). Her next book, *The Secrets of Others*, will be published in Spring, 2021. Atlas serves on the editorial board of *Psychoanalytic Perspectives* and is the author of articles and book chapters that focus primarily on gender and sexuality. Her *New York Times* article, "A Tale of Two Twins," was the winner of a 2016 Gradiva Award. Atlas is a psychoanalyst and clinical supervisor in private practice in New York City.

Jessica Benjamin is the author of *The Bonds of Love* (1988), *Like Subjects, Love Objects* (1995), *Shadow of the Other* (1998), and *Beyond Doer and Done To: Recognition Theory, Intersubjectivity and the Third* (2018). She is a supervising faculty member of the New York University Postdoctoral Psychology Program in Psychotherapy and Psychoanalysis and at the Stephen Mitchell Center for Relational Studies in New York where she practices as an analyst. In 2015, she was awarded the Hans Kilian prize at the University of the Ruhr in Bochum, Germany, the largest European award for work that joins psychoanalysis with the humanities. From 2004 to 2010, she initiated and directed "The Acknowledgement Project" in Gaza involving Israeli and Palestinian mental health practitioners and has continued since then her interest in the area of collective trauma and acknowledgment.

Michael Eigen is the author of 29 books and many papers. He has been giving a private seminar on Winnicott, Bion, Lacan, and his own work for over 45 years and teaches in the New York University Postdoctoral Program in Psychotherapy and Psychoanalysis and the National Psychological Association for Psychoanalysis. He has been the Editor of *The Psychoanalytic Review*, Director of Educational Training at the Institute for Expressive Analysis, and started a training program for working with creative people at the New York Center for Psychoanalytic Training. He was given the Lifetime Achievement Award by the National Association for the Advancement of Psychoanalysis.

Jay Greenberg is a Training and Supervising Analyst, William Alanson White Institute; Editor, *The Psychoanalytic Quarterly*; former Editor for North America, *International Journal of Psychoanalysis*; and former Editor, *Contemporary Psychoanalysis*. He is the co-author with Stephen Mitchell, *Object Relations in Psychoanalytic Theory*; author: *Oedipus and Beyond: A Clinical Theory*; and author of more than 80 papers on aspects of psychoanalytic history, theory, and technique. He was the recipient in 2015 of the Mary S. Sigourney Award for Outstanding Achievement in Psychoanalysis.

Adrienne Harris is a Faculty and Supervisor at New York University Postdoctoral Program in Psychotherapy and Psychoanalysis. She is on the faculty and is a supervisor at the Psychoanalytic Institute of Northern California. She is an Editor at *Psychoanalytic Dialogues* and *Studies in Gender and Sexuality*. In 2009, She, Lewis Aron, and Jeremy Safran established the Sandor Ferenczi Center at the New School University. She, Lew Aron, Eyal Rozmarin, and Steven Kuchuck co-edit the RPBS. She is an editor of the *IPA* e-journal *psychoanalysis today*. As in so much of his work, he takes you on a voyage you did not expect but surely would not have missed.

Stephen Hartman is a Training Chair at the Psychoanalytic Institute of Northern California and is a faculty member on the Relational track at the New York University Postdoctoral Program in Psychotherapy and Psychoanalysis. He is an executive editor of *Psychoanalytic Dialogues* and a co-editor of *Studies in Gender and Sexuality*. Stephen is the author of several articles and book chapters that address object relations theory from the standpoint of emerging technologies, the socio-politics of a collectivist psychoanalytic frame, sexuality, and gender in an intersectional matrix, and the interface of digital culture and the practice of psychoanalysis. His most recent work on *the social primal scene* (in press) is greatly indebted to Lew Aron's groundbreaking exploration of *The Internalized Primal Scene*.

Steven Kuchuck is a Co-Editor, RPBS, President of the International Association for Relational Psychoanalysis and Psychotherapy (IARPP), Senior Consulting Editor (formerly Editor-in-Chief) of the journal *Psychoanalytic Perspectives,* and Board Member, supervisor, faculty at NIP, and faculty/supervisor at the NIP National Training Program, Stephen Mitchell Relational Study Center, faculty at NYU Postdoctoral Program in Psychotherapy and Psychoanalysis, and other institutes. Dr. Kuchuck's teaching and writing focus primarily on the clinical impact of the therapist's subjectivity. In 2015 and 2016 he won the Gradiva Award for best psychoanalytic book: *Clinical Implications of the Psychoanalyst's Life Experience: When the Personal Becomes Professional* and *The Legacy of Sandor Ferenczi: From Ghost to Ancestor* (co-edited with Adrienne Harris).

Thomas Ogden is a Personal and Supervising Analyst of the Psychoanalytic Institute of Northern California. He has published 12 books on psychoanalytic theory and practice, most recently *Reclaiming Unlived Life*; *Creative Readings: Essays on Seminal Analytic Works*; and *Rediscovering Psychoanalysis*. In addition, he has published two novels, *The Parts Left Out* and *The Hands of Gravity and Chance*. He received the 2012 Sigourney Award.

Merav Roth is a Clinical Psychologist and a Training Psychoanalyst, Teacher, and Supervisor at the Israeli Psychoanalytic Society; a cultural researcher from a psychoanalytic perspective; former founder and chair of the postgraduate Klein studies and of the interdisciplinary Doctoral studies of psychoanalysis in the psychotherapy program, Sackler School of Medicine, Tel Aviv University; and the current chair of the psychotherapy program in Sackler School of Medicine, Tel Aviv University; editor and writer of introduction and prefaces, with J. Durban, of *Melanie Klein: Essential Papers II* (2013). Among various publications in psychoanalysis and in culture studies, Roth is the author of *A Psychoanalytic Perspective on Reading Literature: Reading the Reader* (Routledge, 2020).

Donnel B. Stern is a Training and Supervising Analyst at the William Alanson White Institute in New York City; Clinical Consultant and Adjunct Clinical Professor of Psychology at the NYU Postdoctoral Program in Psychoanalysis and Psychotherapy; and Faculty, New York Psychoanalytic Institute. He is Founder and Editor of a book series at Routledge, Psychoanalysis in a New Key, and the former Editor-in-Chief of *Contemporary Psychoanalysis*. He has co-edited many books and authored four, most recently *The Infinity of the Unsaid: Unformulated Experience, Language, and the Nonverbal* (2018) and *Relational Freedom: Emergent Properties of the Interpersonal Field* (2015). He serves on numerous journal editorial boards and is in private practice in New York City.

Joyce Slochower is a Professor Emerita of Psychology at Hunter College and the Graduate Center, CUNY. Joyce is faculty and supervisor at the NYU Postdoctoral Program, the Steven Mitchell Center, the National Training Program of NIP (all in New York), Philadelphia Center for Relational Studies in Philadelphia, and the Psychoanalytic

Institute of Northern California in San Francisco. In addition to over 90 articles, second editions of *Holding and Psychoanalysis: A Relational Perspective* (1996) and *Psychoanalytic Collisions* (2006) were released in 2014. She is the co-editor, with Lewis Aron and Sue Grand, of *De-idealizing Relational Theory: A Critique from Within* and *De-centering Relational Theory: A Comparative Critique*.

Chana Ullman is a Clinical Psychologist, a Training Psychoanalyst, and Faculty at the Tel Aviv Institute of Contemporary Psychoanalysis. Dr. Ullman is faculty and supervisor at the relational track, the school of Psychotherapy, Sackler school of Medicine at Tel-Aviv University, and faculty at the doctoral program of Psychoanalysis at Tel Aviv University. Dr. Ullman is past-president of the International Association of Relational Psychoanalysis and Psychotherapy. She is the author of the book *The Transformed Self: The Psychology of Religious Conversion* (1989) and of numerous publications regarding witnessing, political context, and the relational perspective on psychoanalytic process. She lives and practices in Rehovot, Israel.

Foreword

Galit Atlas

Lew and I started working on this collection of his articles in February 2018, in retrospect exactly a year before his death on February 28th, 2019, at the age of 66 years old. Our first step was to choose the chapters for this volume. Given the breadth of his publishing history, the difficult part for us was to pare down the 112 published papers to 12 chapters. Lew's original plan was to write a short introduction to each chapter. He began with the one on dreams, a paper that he presented for the first time in 1987, after he graduated from NYU Postdoctoral Program in Psychotherapy and Psychoanalysis, a program he later directed for 21 years.[1] Lew expressed his gratitude to his mentors and colleagues who had encouraged him to publish that paper, which he believed launched his career. Unfortunately, he never completed the introduction to that chapter, the first in this collection. I decided to publish his incomplete introduction the way it is, and in the spirit of Lew's original vision for this book, I invited a number of colleagues who worked closely with him to write the introductions to the rest of the chapters.

Inspired by Lew's teaching style, I would like to reflect here on the chapters in this book and on Lew's thinking, as they connect to his personal as well as professional history.

Anyone who knew Lewis Aron was familiar with his compelling teaching and writing style as well as with his unparalleled ability to convey complex, often comparative theoretical concepts in a uniquely inviting and approachable way. One of Lew's main focuses, as Steven Kuchuck describes in his introduction to Chapter 6, was on the way one's personal dynamics influenced his or her theoretical formulations and practice technique. Lew believed that theory doesn't exist in a vacuum but rather must be understood within a historical, political, and sociological context. Therefore, he made sure to know everything about the theory he was planning to teach. Lew strove to master his field of study. As a young man, he had a black belt in martial arts, and for many years he practiced the guitar every single day. He believed in hard work and dedication and therefore thoroughly prepared for every talk he gave, studied for every class he taught, practiced even for presentation he gave many times before. As Don Stern mentions in his introduction to Chapter 8, Lew was interested in every school of psychoanalysis, and it was not a myth; he indeed read every journal and psychoanalytic book that was published. He would sit every day, for hours, yellow marker in hand, immersing himself in reading and preparing for teaching. His weekly private study groups included about a 150 students. Lew believed teaching was the best way to learn. He aspired to be "Talmid Chacham," a Hebrew title given to a Torah scholar who studied day and night to become skilled in Jewish law. Teaching was what Lew loved most and what he insisted on doing until the last weeks of his life, when he became too sick to get out of bed. "When I stop teaching you'll know that I'm about to die," he told me. Three weeks after he made the decision to stop meeting with his study groups, he passed away.

Lew dived very deeply into the lives of the people whose theories he taught. I remember when he was teaching the work of Harold Searles: He thoroughly studied Searles's biography and read every paper he had written or that was written about him. Not long before Searles's death, Lew contacted him, and Searles gave him some unpublished videos and papers that Lew then used in his teaching. After Searles' death in 2015, Lew got in touch with his family. He met with his daughter, Sandra Dickinson, and learned more about the family's history. When teaching Searles, Lew spoke about Harold, the little boy who used to model clothes for his father's clothing store and who ended up being a performer, demonstrating controversial therapy techniques on stage. In his teaching and in the chapter Lew wrote for our co-authored book *Dramatic Dialogue,* Lew discussed the sadomasochistic dynamic Searles reenacted on the stage and connected it with the biographical details he had learned about him. This was the way Lew used to think and teach every topic: from inside the mind and life of the person.

Inspired by Lew's interest in integrating a theory with social context and the theorist's personal history, I would like to briefly explore the person of Lew and how it influenced his thinking.

Lewis (Eliezer) Aron was an only child to his parents, Gertrud and Rubin. From a very young age, Lew called his parents by their nicknames: Gitt and Ruby. Ruby was a butcher, and Lew often described the way he used to visit him at work and how his father would go to the back of the store, choose and then cook for him the best piece of meat he could find. Lew felt that his father always gave him the best part of himself. He loved his father deeply and described him as traumatized from World War II, where he had fought the Japanese in the battle in central Burma and was awarded a good conduct medal. His father was a warrior and Lew identified with him.

His mother, Gitt, had lost her mother when she was 12 years old. Her mother had been sick for a few years, and Gitt was her caretaker. Lew used to say that his mother never got over that loss and especially never recovered from the years of taking care of her dying mother. After her mother passed away, Gitt was the one to take care of her father. Lew often described his mother as a talented pianist[2] who had given up on her own career to care for her father (his grandfather lived with them until the day he died). Later on, she transferred that dedication to Lewis, her only son, whom she greatly admired. Lew described the relationship between his mother and her father and subsequently between his mother and him, as one of the reasons he was initially so drawn to the Oedipal complex and to the many configurations of the Primal Scene, a concept Stephen Hartman will elaborate on in his introduction to Chapter 3.

Lew was very attached to his mother, and throughout his life he struggled to separate and differentiate from her. He reenacted that dynamic with the historical figures he taught—he identified with them, immersed himself in them—but then always rebelled against and differentiated himself from them. This cycle was played out over and over: identifying with his ancestors, followed by a wish to differentiate and break apart from them, and then reuniting with them. We can easily recognize that cycle in his internal relationship with Freud's legacy, which he admired and mastered, but then rebelled against and came back to again and again. This was the way Lew connected with every theorist he taught, and his students often commented on the love and hate relationships he demonstrated with those figures: While he clearly admired them, he was also renown as the critic of those very same people. In a similar way, and as Joyce Slochower describes in the introduction to Chapter 11, Lew was encouraging critique from within. His last book project (2018), with Sue Grand and Joyce Slochower, was editing *De-Idealizing Relational Theory* and *Decentering Relational Theory*, in which the three co-editors invited relational thinkers to critique relational psychoanalysis. Lew believed that self-reflection and self-critique were the essence of healthy development.

A similar cycle played out in Lew's relationship with Judaism as well. Lew was raised in a religious Jewish household. In his introduction to Chapter 4, Michel Eigen discusses Lew's religious beliefs as an influence on his psychoanalytic vision and values. As a teenager, Lew studied in a Yeshivah in Jerusalem and had a very special connection to Israel and later on to the Israeli psychoanalytic community, as is noted in Chana Ullman's introduction to Chapter 7 and Merav Roth's introduction to Chapter 9.[3]

While his family was religious, as Lew grew up and tried to separate from his mother, he pushed himself to become more and more orthodox. His mother followed him and turned more religious herself, until at some point Lew decided to rebel against religion and became secular. He often mentioned that his psychoanalytic journey was similar. As a student, Lew entered a Freudian analysis, looked for the most Freudian supervisors, and tried to be even more orthodox than they were, but then he reached a point where he rebelled against classical theory and joined his friend and mentor Stephen Mitchell in pushing against psychoanalytic orthodoxy. For Lew and many others, as Adrienne Harris describes in her introduction to Chapter 2, the relational turn was both an evolution and a revolution; it went against and simultaneously was a development born out of classical psychoanalysis. In the last 10 years of his life, and especially after his mother's death, Lew went back both to reading Freud and to Judaism. He opened a few reading groups on Freud, and he started studying the Torah again.

Lew loved being an only child. He used to say that he never regretted not having siblings but that as a child he didn't have mutual relationships; the closest people to him were his parents and his grandfather, who all looked up to him and in some ways lived through him. "Because of my childhood, mutuality doesn't come naturally to me," Lew said, "I find hierarchical relationships like being a son, or a father, a teacher or a mentor, much more simple." In his theory, Lew challenged hierarchies as he was reflecting on his childhood experience, often stating that what people write about is what they struggle with most.

In his first book, *A Meeting of Minds*, and as Thomas Ogden discusses in his introduction to Chapter 5, Lew emphasized the difference between symmetrical and mutual relationships. Mutuality implies reciprocation, sharing together and unity through interchange. It emphasizes what the patient and the analyst have in common or between them. Symmetry, in contrast, implies equality or similarity, a correspondence in form or arrangement. Lew argued that the analytic relationship is not a symmetrical one, in the same way that a parent-child relationship is not symmetrical, but that mutuality is necessary for psychological growth. As Jessica Benjamin emphasizes in her introduction to Chapter 10, for Lew, mutual vulnerability became the heart of psychoanalytic theory and practice and an essential part of broader moral, social, philosophical, and human concerns.

As an analyst and Talmudic scholar, Lew believed in dialogues and debates. He used to say that when reading Winnicott, for example, one has to read him as if he is arguing with Klein. When reading Mitchell, he should be seen as debating drive theory, Sullivan, and Fairbairn. Theory, he believed, must be understood as part of an ongoing conversation, an endless dialogue. Lew was one of those people who lived the theory he believed in, and his teaching style was very much in the spirit of the discussion and debate he theorized. His goal as a teacher, a supervisor, and a writer was not so much to teach his students the right theory, but rather to help them struggle and ask the hard questions. The intellectual exploration he encouraged and engaged in always ended up being a personal inquiry. In the same way, Lew believed that the essence of clinical work is that there is never only one answer. As Jay Greenberg so well articulates in his introduction to Chapter 12, Lew was unique in his investment in exploring difficult issues without demanding closure.

Sitting in his office with students, Lew often said that he could picture among them Freud, Jung, Ferenczi, Klein, Winnicott, and

Bion, and furthermore he could imagine what each of their arguments would be, who would argue with whom. Lew would joke that it doesn't matter which of those figures were dead and which were alive, because we tend to argue mostly with those who are not with us. That was surely true for Lew, who constantly dialogued with the dead.

Steve Mitchell was Lew's closest friend, and his sudden death in 2000 was a traumatic event that Lew tried to process for years. Steve died on December 21st, Lew's birthday. Steve called Lew that same morning to wish him happy birthday and asked if he would read and give him feedback on the first draft of *Can Love Last?* Lew told him that he couldn't think of anything better to do on his birthday, and they agreed to speak again later that night, when Lew finished reading the book. A few hours after they spoke, Steve died from a heart attack. Lew was heartbroken.

Lew often mentioned how much he missed Steve, and it was comforting for him to imagine their reunion: a study group after Lew's death, with his best friends Steve Mitchell, Jeremy Safran, and with Freud and Ferenczi, Searles and Loewald, drinking bourbon and arguing amongst themselves. One of the hopes I have in editing this book is to keep alive the dialogue that Lew loved so much—a dialogue that will last and last.

Notes

1 Spyros Orfanos, the man Lew called his brother, worked closely with him as the clinic director at NYU Postdoctoral Program in Psychotherapy and Psychoanalysis.
2 Lew was also a musician and played guitar in the band Sig with his friends and colleagues Steven Knoblauch, Steve Solow, Andrew Tatarsky, John Shaw, Frank Bosco, and Victoria Mierlak.
3 *A Psychotherapy for the People*, a book Lew co-authored with Karen Starr, presents an important historical framing of psychoanalysis as it is related to the trauma of the Holocaust and anti-Semitism, as well as issues around race, homophobia, and misogyny. Lew worked with Jill Salberg on topics of psychoanalysis and Judaism, and with Libby Henik he edited the Contemporary Psychoanalysis and Judaism Book Series.

Acknowledgments

I would like to thank all the contributors to this collection: Adrienne Harris, Thomas Ogden, Jessica Benjamin, Merav Roth, Chana Ullman, Jay Greenberg, Donnel Stern, Stephen Hartman, Joyce Slochower, Michael Eigen, Nancy McWilliams, and Antonino Ferro.

A special thanks to Steven Kuchuck for his contribution, edits, and continuous support.

To Bob Miller for everything he is for me.

Much gratitude to Kristopher Spring, Spyros Orfanos, Barbra Locker, Velleda Ceccoli, Jill Salberg, Kate Dove, Carina and Robert Grossmark, Marie and Lowell Hoffman, Melanie Suchet, David Goodman, Jonathan Slavin, Miki Rahmani, Colette Linnihan, Steven Knoblauch, Noga Davidson, Marie Saba, and Ezzy Waldman.

A thank you to Kate Hawes and Hanna Wright from Routledge.

A special thank you to Andrea Recarte for the beautiful cover image of Lew.

To Benjamin, Raphi, and Kirya Ades-Aron, and to Emma, Yali, and Mia Koch.

To my parents, Shoshi and Yaccov Atlas.

To Keren, Ashi, and Anat.

I'm grateful to the NYU Postdoc community, which Lew was so proud of and who have been a constant source of support.

And to Lew, whom I miss so much.

Permissions

Chapter 1: Aron, L. (1989). Dreams, narrative, and the psychoanalytic method. *Contemporary Psychoanalysis, 25*(1), 108–127. Reprinted by permission of William Alanson White Institute of Psychiatry, Psychoanalysis & Psychology and the William Alanson White Psychoanalytic Society, www.wawhite.org.

Chapter 3: Aron, L. (1995). The internalized primal scene. *Psychoanalytic Dialogues, 5*(2), 195–237. Reprinted by permission of Taylor & Francis Ltd, http://www.tandfonline.com.

Chapter 4: Aron, L. (2004). God's influence on my psychoanalytic vision and values. *Psychoanalytic Psychology, 21*(3), 442–451. Reprinted by permission of APA

Chapter 5: Aron, L. (1992). Interpretation as expression of the analyst's subjectivity. *Psychoanalytic Dialogues, 2*(4), 475–507. Reprinted by permission of Taylor & Francis Ltd, http://www.tandfonline.com.

Chapter 6: Aron, L. (1991). The patient's experience of the analyst's subjectivity. *Psychoanalytic Dialogues, 1*(1), 29–51. Reprinted by permission of Taylor & Francis Ltd, http://www.tandfonline.com.

Chapter 7: Aron, L. (2000). Self-reflexivity and the therapeutic action of psychoanalysis. *Psychoanalytic Psychology, 17*(4), 667–689. Reprinted by permission of APA.

Chapter 8: Aron, L. (1999). Clinical choices and the relational matrix. *Psychoanalytic Dialogues, 9*(1), 1–29. Reprinted by permission of Taylor & Francis Ltd, http://www.tandfonline.com.

Chapter 9: Aron, L. (2014). "With you I'm born again": Themes and fantasies of birth and the family circumstances surrounding birth as these are mutually evoked in patient and analyst. *Psychoanalytic Dialogues, 24*(3), 341–357. Reprinted by permission of Taylor & Francis Ltd, http://www.tandfonline.com.

Chapter 10: Aron, L. (2016). Mutual vulnerability: An ethic of clinical practice. In D. M. Goodman & E. R. Severson (Eds.), *The ethical turn* (pp. 19-40). London: Routledge. Reprinted by Permission of William James College.

Chapter 11: Aron, L. (2017). Beyond tolerance in psychoanalytic communities: Reflexive skepticism and critical pluralism. *Psychoanalytic Perspectives, 14*(3), 271–282. Reprinted by permission of National Institute for the Psychotherapies, www.nipinst.org.

Chapter 12: Aron, L. (2016). Ethical considerations in psychoanalytic writing revisited. *Psychoanalytic Perspectives, 13*(3), 267–290. Reprinted by permission of National Institute for the Psychotherapies, www.nipinst.org.

Part I

Psychoanalytic vision

Chapter 1

Dreams, narrative, and the psychoanalytic method (1989)

Introduction by Lewis Aron

This chapter was first presented when I was a recent graduate of the New York University Postdoctoral Program in Psychotherapy & Psychoanalysis at their annual weekend retreat, "The Postdoc Weekend" in 1987, along with a warmly engaging and encouraging discussion by Ben Lapkin. It was my first psychoanalytic presentation and one could not find a more welcoming and hearteningly receptive audience of colleagues. Such a boosting experience is particularly suited to launch a professional career. I then presented the chapter at the Spring Meeting of the Division of Psychoanalysis (39) of the American Psychological Association in San Francisco in 1988, where Harriette Kaley offered a deeply appreciative, stimulating, and clinically useful discussion. In those years, I was working as a supervising psychologist at the Roosevelt Hospital in NYC. The psychology department at Roosevelt was in those years an ideal teaching center that provided the time and resources for thinking, scholarship, and research as well as it was a first-rate teaching faculty. I had worked on the clinical use of dreams with Lee Caligor, who was from the William Alanson White Institute, and who had written a book on dreams with Rollo May, and taught an interpersonal and existential approach to dreams. Lee was a close friend of Philip Bromberg, who also taught at Roosevelt, and he gave a copy of my chapter to Phil, who enthusiastically, but without telling me, showed it to his friend, Art Feiner, then the Editor of *Contemporary Psychoanalysis*. The next day Art contacted me to offer to publish it in the journal.

Aron, L. (1989). Dreams, narrative, and the psychoanalytic method.

Contemporary Psychoanalysis, 25(1), 108–126.

"I had a dream. You always write down dreams. This one is disgusting! I was in a restaurant and I ordered a certain dish made up of certain types of meats, delicacies, kidney, prosciutto, sautéed in urine. I thought it was disgusting, but they said try it, and I did, and I liked it. I thought it was gruesome. I heard that dreams are wish fulfillments; is that true?"

Mrs. D. is an attractive, married, woman in her early thirties. She has been in psychoanalytic treatment for three years sorting out a chaotic and horrendous life history. Raised by a strict, puritanical, rigid Catholic mother who could tolerate no disagreements or any attempts at autonomy or disobedience and by a distant, working class, sometimes alcoholic father who was prone to physically abuse her brothers and to sexually abuse her. While the specifics of the sexual abuse remain unclear, there now seems little doubt that she was repeatedly abused between the ages of five and eight.

A younger sister, having dropped out of college, returned home following a dramatic suicide attempt. Mother now spends much of her time taking care of this daughter. From a young age, Mrs. D. attempted to defy her mother, to challenge her views on religion, and to struggle for some measure of autonomy. Her experience has been consistent: mother loves, nurtures, and protects at times of weakness, neediness, and compliancy. She becomes cold and distant with the least sign of strength and independence.

In her early 20s Mrs. D. married an Asian professional. Her family was outraged. But her marriage has deteriorated as her husband would like to have a child, and Mrs. D. has not, or has not felt ready. Three "accidental" pregnancies have been terminated by abortion. It was her concerns about the repeated abortions and her sense that not wanting children might be indicative of underlying problems, and finally her sister's suicide attempt, which precipitated her decision to enter treatment.

The dream (introduced above) occurred in the third year of treatment, on a week in which she had made an appointment to begin marital counseling with her husband. I had made the referral to a male therapist after much discussion with the patient about her marital concerns.

Mrs. D. is a psychologically unsophisticated patient who has recently begun to read psychologically oriented self-help books. When she introduced the reported dream by noting my interest in dreams, I took this to be the first association to the dream. Was she attempting to cater to me, to serve me a dish, and would it be a delicacy or something less appetizing? When she bracketed the dream with a reference to wish fulfillment, I thought, how sensitive of her to tune into my area of interest. How could she have known I was looking for just such a dream "specimen"?

My first response to the dream was simply to wait in silence. The manifest theme of the dream, the dream story which I had been told, had a clearly organized structure. This was a story of being told to do something, to swallow something, and of being disgusted but enjoying it. This simple theme resonated with my knowledge about this patient and in particular with my experience in the transference-countertransference. What was it she was serving me? More to the point, what was it she felt that I was trying to shove down her throat? Mrs. D.'s dream and its analysis will be further reviewed after an examination of some theoretical issues.

Dreams have a special significance for all psychoanalysts and to some they are still regarded as the most important source of material provided by patients. For many years, psychoanalysis was identified with dream analysis, and dreams were exploited by analysts as "the royal road" to the unconscious. For Freud (1900), dream analysis revealed hidden and disguised childhood sexual wishes. Through the method of free association, the analyst could unearth the buried but preserved infantile past and bring to consciousness the derivatives of the drives.

Freud recognized and described the dramatic quality and composition of dreams. He elaborated that they have plots, characters, settings, beginnings, middles, and endings. Freud believed that the narrative coherence of dreams argued against their being considered the product of random neurological processes. In clinical work with dreams, however, Freud argued that analysts "should disregard the apparent coherence between a dream's constituents as an unessential illusion" (Freud, 1900, p. 449). For classical psychoanalytic theory, dreaming is both meaningful and motivated, but the meaning and motivation are to be found *not* in the manifest content, but in the dreamer's associations.

Freudian technique has always been cautious and reserved about the clinical use of manifest content. Attention to manifest content was thought to lead the analyst astray and to divert attention from the unconscious depths. However, from the beginning of the history of psychoanalysis there have always been some dissenting opinions regarding manifest content. Some early analytic writers suggested that the manifest content itself be viewed as an important communication.

As early as 1916, Jung focused attention on thematic aspects of dream structure. He suggested looking at dreams as forms of drama (1916, p. 266) and thought that most dreams had a discernible structure to which the analyst could attend as an aid to interpretation. The dream structure included the exposition (consisting of the identified characters, the setting, and the initial problem), the development of the plot, the climax of the action or the culmination, and the solution or final result. It was because of Jung's interest in narrative themes and dream structure that he recognized the potential for studying dreams in series.

While controversy has continued, there seems to be a growing consensus among analysts on the value of manifest content (Panel, 1984). Erikson's (1954) examination of the Irma dream alerted analysts to the clinical usefulness of manifest content. Pulver (1987) recently described how analysts condemn the interpretation of the manifest dream while they belie that position in their clinical behavior. He points out how psychoanalytic training texts emphasize the dangers of working from manifest content, but that many analysts are convinced of its great value. Pulver outlines many ways in which the manifest dream contributes to our understanding of the dreamer.

Kohut's description of self-state dreams has once again brought the controversy regarding the clinical use of manifest content to the center of analytic debate. Kohut (1977) described the existence of two types of dreams, structural-conflict dreams and self-state dreams. Structural-conflict dreams are described in the terms of classical theory. According to Kohut, they are dreams which express verbalizable latent content. They are the dreams of "guilty man," and they are interpreted along the traditional lines of drive and defense. The analyst follows associations, which lead to latent dream thoughts derived from conflict between id, ego, and superego. Self-state dreams are those in which the meaning of the dream can be understood with only a knowledge of the dreamer, but with little associative activity, on the basis of manifest content alone. These dreams are attempts to bind the nonverbal tensions of traumatic states with the aid of verbalizable dream imagery. They are adaptive attempts to master the anxiety generated by a disturbing change in the state of the self.[1]

Kohut's approach has once again brought up the controversial question of how much to pay attention to the manifest theme of the dream and how much to rely on a detailed pursue of the patient's associations to dream elements. Kohut advised that with self-state dreams "free associations do not lead to unconscious hidden layers of the mind; at best they provide us with further imagery which remains on the same level as the manifest content of the dream" (Kohut, 1977, p. 109). Kohut (1977) argues that urging a patient to free associate to a dream, that is to break it up into its parts and to associate to each component, can be a disorganizing experience to some patients. This type of analysis can feel to fragile patients as if they themselves are being taken apart. Self-psychologists believe that it is not necessary to pursue the patient's associations, day residue, or the various dream details. The dream is understood directly, from manifest content, as a portrayal of the dreamer's dread of threats to the integrity of the self. More traditional analysts have expressed concern that an approach which relies on manifest content is superficial, and that it may lead to interpreting the dream material in accordance with preconceived ideas about the patient or in line with prior theoretical convictions. Attending to the patient's associations more rigorously serves to keep the analyst in touch with the meaning of the dream to the patient, and it allows the patient to play a more active role in the psychoanalytic process.

Slap and Trunnell (1987) criticized the self-psychology literature for not providing associations to dreams. They felt that this reflects the self-psychologist's conviction that these data do not contribute to the understanding of dreams. Because these data are not reported, any attempt to validate the concept of self-state dreams is made difficult.

Why has there been so much controversy about the clinical value of manifest content? To understand the debate, we need to examine the place of the dream in Freud's theoretical model. Psychoanalytic dream theory and the technique of dream interpretation developed in such intricate connection with psychoanalytic theory and technique as a whole that dream interpretation became the Shibboleth of classical psychoanalysis. Freud's discovery of the psychoanalytic method and his own self-analysis centered on the investigation of his own dreams. In *The Interpretation of Dreams* (1900), Freud presented his theory of dreams embedded in a general theory of mind, a theory of the structure of neurosis, and a theory of psychoanalytic methodology. What characterizes the Freudian point of view is that the manifest dream is seen as a facade whose purpose is to conceal and disguise and *not* to reveal the inner psychological life of the dreamer.

Freud explained the phenomena of dreaming in terms of the topographic theory. The dream work took place in the system Ucs, and was governed by the laws of the primary process. Freud considered the distinction between primary and secondary process thought to be among his most important contributions. He considered these two modes of thought to be antagonistic. Primary process thought was associated with the unconscious and was characterized by symbolization, displacement, and condensation. It tended to be visual rather than verbal and to disregard the laws of syntax, time, and place. In contrast, secondary process thought was characterized by logic and rationality and tended to be verbal and associated with the ego.

It has largely been assumed that Freud considered dreams to be brought about through the primary process exclusively. Any aspect of dreams that reflected more organized thought reflected secondary process thinking tacked onto the dream as part of secondary revision. At times Freud did write as if secondary revision did its work after the dream "has already, in a certain sense, been completed" (Freud, 1900, p. 313). But later, in the same work, Freud's position vacillated, and he wrote:

> We must assume rather that from the very first the demands of this second factor constitute one of the conditions which the dream must satisfy and that this condition, like those laid down by condensation, the censorship imposed by resistance, and representability, operates simultaneously in a conductive, and selective sense upon the mass of material present in the dream-thoughts.
> (p. 499)

But in the very next sentence Freud again depreciates the organized aspect of the dream by saying that of the conditions involved in the formation of dreams, secondary revision is "the least cogent."

Why did Freud wish to minimize the importance of secondary revision and of the organized quality of dreams, and why have analysts since Freud continued to disparage the organized narrative quality of dreams? Because Freud used dreams as his talking-point in describing the functioning of mind, the method of free association and the topographic theory, he emphasized a certain view of the dream. Freud was determined to use dreams to prove the topographic model of the mind, the primary process functioning of the unconscious, the importance of infantile sexuality, as well as the usefulness of the free-association method. Even after the development of structural theory, Freud continued to view dreams in much the same way.

Free association is the technical term for the method used to uncover the hidden meaning of the dream. In dream interpretation, the dream must first be broken up into its component parts, that is, it must be "analyzed." The method is very specific in breaking down the dream into its parts and not treating it as a whole. "Our first step in the employment of this procedure teaches us that what we must take as the object of our attention is not the dream as a whole but the separate portions of its content" (Freud, 1900, p. 103). The assumption is that the free associations to the various details will ultimately converge on a common theme.

> The dreamer's associations begin by diverging widely from the manifest elements, so that a great number of subjects and ranges of ideas are touched on, after which, a second series of associations quickly *converge* from these on to the dream-thoughts that are being looked for.
>
> (Freud, 1923, p. 110)

In describing Freud's position that the dream needs to be analyzed into its components to be interpreted, I am referring to an aspect of method and not to technique. By method I mean a mode of pursuit, a way of approaching the dream, in contrast to technique which refers to practical details. Freud was capable of great flexibility regarding the technique of analyzing a dream as can be seen in his description of "several technical procedures" (Freud, 1923, p. 109). However, from a methodological viewpoint, he argued the need to take the dream one piece at a time and to disregard its apparent coherence. Freud described his method as employing interpretation *"en detail* and not *en masse* ... it regards dreams from the very first as being of a composite character, as being conglomerates of psychical formations" (Freud, 1900, p. 104).

It can be seen that to focus on manifest content was not only to be seen as superficial and missing the psychic depths, but more importantly it represented a challenge to the psychoanalytic "method" of investigation. Freud insisted that the dream be broken up into its parts and *not* treated as a whole. He was adamant about this because he needed to be certain that the insights into the unconscious would not be lost or trivialized. Freud anticipated, quite correctly, that if the dream were not broken up into its constituents, if it were taken as a whole, as a story, that the distinction between primary and secondary process would break down.

Seeing the manifest content of the dream as resulting from secondary elaboration which occurs after the dream is completed has enormous clinical consequences. The manifest dream story is then seen *not* as the "real" dream, but as an added on afterthought. It is seen as nothing but a false impression, a concocted story to disguise and mislead. This view of manifest content is in accord with the dichotomies that Freud was constructing at this early point in the history of psychoanalysis. Thus, manifest hides latent, conscious conceals unconscious, surface buries the depths, defense distorts wish, and present reenacts the past. It can quickly be seen why anyone focusing on the manifest dream story would be suspected of heresy. Clearly, to focus on manifest content was to be neglecting the unconscious, drives, the psychic depths, the nature of primary process thought, the past, and in particular infantile sexuality. A focus on manifest content would clearly mark anyone as a revisionist. This was especially true since Jung did focus on manifest content and also did dissent in regard to sexuality and other basic psychoanalytic tenets.

In my view, this aspect of the history of the development of psychoanalytic theory has had a stultifying effect on progress in dream theory and in the clinical technique of dream interpretation. Specifically, it has led to a false polarization between work with dream associations and attention to the manifest dream theme. Classical analysts have tended to neglect the coherently organized dream narrative. This is a result of the broader trend to neglect and minimize all of the more organized, structured, developmentally mature aspects of dreams. Any organized aspect of a dream is dismissed as due to the results of secondary elaboration or secondary revision, but not really a part of the dream. It is as if it could be assumed that the "real" dream is a result of primary process and that all of the seemingly organized aspects of dreams are added on after the fact.

I have been describing Freudian dream theory as it emerged in the context of the topographic theory. Arlow and Brenner (1964) set out to revise dream theory in accordance with the structural point of view. They argue that the dream, like all other thoughts, is the result of an interaction of the workings of all three psychic structures: id, ego, and superego. Since the dreamer is asleep during dreaming, this compromise formation is effected by the regressed state of the ego and superego, and only a small role is played by the claims of external reality. This leaves a relatively large part to be played by infantile, wish-fulfilling fantasies. The dream is therefore largely influenced by id wishes and by the regressive alterations of the ego and superego.

Arlow and Brenner are very clear in arguing that dreams are constructed from both primary and secondary process mentation simultaneously. According to the topographic theory the dream is created in the system Ucs., that is, according to the primary process. How, they argue, can this be when we know that dreams are also the result of the censor and the need for secondary revision? They conclude that the topographic theory does not fit the facts. Structural theory explains the dream work as an interplay among id, ego, and superego. Thus, it postulates that ego functions, including defensive and integrative functions, participate in the dream work throughout.

Despite this recognition, Arlow and Brenner (1964) continue to emphasize the regressed quality of dreams. They write:

> despite many exceptions, dreams are not as a rule harmonized and integrated with respect to their various component parts to nearly the same degree as we expect ordinary waking thoughts, or even daydreams, to be. The dreamer, like the child, is less concerned with unity and consistency than is the waking adult, even though, as Freud noted, the integrative function of the ego plays a part in dream formation.
>
> (p. 125)

From a methodological point of view, they continue to disregard the manifest theme of the dream, although Brenner (1976) acknowledges that a psychoanalyst may know enough about a patient so as to be able to understand a dream even without associations.

The trend in much of the contemporary psychoanalytic literature has been to stress the adaptive and communicative functions of dreaming. Fosshage (1987) is the most recent of many analysts who propose revising psychoanalytic dream theory in order to highlight the adaptive, regulatory, and organizing functions of dreaming. Once again, it can be seen in his work, that in order to view dreams as primarily adaptive, one needs to reexamine the nature of primary process thought. In contrast to Freud, Fosshage defines primary process not as a primitive form of mentation, but as a form of cognition which uses visual and sensory images in the service of integrative and synthetic functioning. Once dreams are viewed as serving adaptive, self-regulatory functions, then there is no theoretical reason to insist on the ubiquitous operation of disguise and defense in dreams, and therefore the distinction between manifest and latent content breaks down. As a result, Fosshage ends up advocating the abandonment of the free-association method. He writes:

> To view dreaming as a form of mentation positions us in the clinical setting to listen to the major themes or meanings communicated, as we would with waking mentation. Just as persistent attempts to isolate elements in the patient's waking mentation for associational purposes would detour and disrupt the patient's waking communication, so it does in approaching the dream.
>
> (p. 306)

For many classical analysts, despite the contributions of structural theory and ego-psychology, the primary impetus for dreaming remains the infantile drive or wish seeking discharge or gratification. The focus remains on the regressed and primitive qualities of the dream. It is for these reasons that classical analysis has always been skeptical toward any view of dreams, which sees them as problem-solving or in any way too much like waking thought. For if dreams are seen to be more organized and developmentally more complex, then we can no longer equate dreams with the unconscious, the primary process, the psychic depths, or the primitive, bestial core of man. The distinction between manifest and latent content is necessitated by a theory of drive and defense (Brenneis, 1975), and the associations are required to translate the manifest dream into latent dream thoughts. For classical analysts, a methodological shift of attention to the manifest content endangers the most fundamental Freudian principles.

On the other hand, when revisionist analysts have tried to focus on and make use of manifest content, these attempts have typically gone hand in hand with an abandonment of the free-association method. Thus, beginning with Jung, his focus on the whole dream gestalt was accompanied by an abandonment of the method of free association and a reliance on his own method of "amplification." Similarly, the previous discussion of Kohut's innovations has demonstrated that his focus on the manifest content led him away from the free-association method, and the most recent work of Fosshage (1987) suggests the abandonment of the free-association method. An examination of the views of other major revisionists will clarify how an emphasis on manifest content was accompanied by a neglect or dismissal of the free-association method.

Sullivan was critical of the free-association method and replaced it with the detailed inquiry, and correlated with this shift he too relied considerably on manifest content. Sullivan was most interested in the dream as a "relatively valid parataxic operation for the relief of insoluble problems of living" (1953, p. 342). He gave dreams considerable attention as diagnostic and prognostic indicators in psychotherapy. But my impression, derived from Sullivan's clinical vignettes, is that he was impatient with the careful disciplined exploration of dream details. At least with the difficult patients that he treated, he considered that the free-association method led to obsessional details, which obscure what is most central and significant in the dream. Sullivan's technique with dreams consisted of paraphrasing the main theme or point of the dream, as he could extrapolate it from the manifest content, back to the patient, and then he would ask for associations.

> The psychiatrist clears up as much as he can of what is irrelevant and obscuring in the reported dream, presents what he seems to hear in terms of a dramatic picture of some important problem of the patient's; and then propounds the riddle: "What does that bring to mind?"
>
> (p. 338)

In a critique of the role of associations in dream interpretation, Fromm (1980) emphasized reliance on manifest content and attacked the free-association method. In as much as Fromm shifts the emphasis from how the dream conceals to how the dream reveals, he sees pursuing associations as a distraction. Referring to Freud's interpretations of his own dreams, Fromm wrote:

> By heaping up association upon association which end up in practically nothing, he succeeds in covering up the awareness of the meaning of the dream ... Freud's method of endless associations is an expression of resistance against the understanding of the meaning of his dreams.
>
> (p. 79)

Stolorow (1978) observed that many analysts make use of both manifest content and free associations when working with dreams. He suggested that in addition to focusing on the "molecular" approach, which breaks the dream down into its elements that analysts focus on the "molar" approach, which examines the distinctive manifest dream themes. He specifically recommended that analysts make use of these themes as the starting points for free association.

Rycroft (1979) in an attempt to integrate Freudian and Jungian approaches to dream interpretation advocated approaching the dream as a whole as well as associating to its details. He rejected the supposed opposition between primary and secondary process thinking. Instead he saw the two modes of functioning as complementary to each other. As a result, he proposed an alternative view of dreams as imaginative activity occurring during sleep. This view focuses on dreams *not* as primitive and regressive, but as creative and progressive.

I agree with a view of dreaming which emphasizes its adaptive, integrative, creative, communicative, and self-regulatory functions, and I value what can be learned clinically from the manifest content in and of itself. Nevertheless, I strongly disagree with a neglect or abandonment of the free-association method, as well as to the de-emphasis of the role of psychic conflict that often accompanies this shift. I will return to this methodological critique after a discussion of the role of narrative in dreams and in psychoanalysis.

Freud's utilization of an archaeological metaphor for psychoanalysis in which the buried, repressed, infantile, sexual, but still alive past must be unearthed by the psychoanalytic method, has been challenged in recent years. It has been argued that therapy is not accomplished through discovery of the traumatic past, but rather that what matters is the construction of a life in the form of a narrative. In the following section of the chapter, I would like to describe story making, the narrative function of mind, as an important element in the construction of one's sense of self, and in the creation of dream narratives.

Psychoanalysis has been described as a hermeneutic discipline in which the analyst helps the patient to construct a self-consistent, coherent, and comprehensive story of their life (Schafer, 1983; Spence, 1982). The analyst engages the patient in the task of putting thoughts into words and through the analytic dialogue a plausible life-historical narrative is constructed. This process serves an organizing function in that the narrative creates order and meaningfulness out of the confusion of the patient's life. The history of the patient continues to evolve as it is told and the analytic process must be self-reflective enabling the continual revisions of histories previously developed. This revision of psychoanalysis is interesting in that it speaks to contemporary concerns about narrative that could not exist but for the sensibility that Freud's original conceptualizations helped bring into being (Brunner, 1986).

The creation of a life historical narrative is not unique to the analytic experience. The continual creation and revision of a life story is an ongoing process in which we all engage. It is a basic function of the mind which serves to maintain identity and the coherence of the self. People maintain ongoing internal dialogues in which they construct continually revised narratives of their lives. These are internal, largely unconscious, autobiographies, mediated through language, and forming our sense of identity. The self is thus a personal myth (Kris, 1956), a continually evolving theory, fantasy, or belief about one's own person (Grossman, 1982).

This view of the self as a story, theory, or myth places great emphasis on language and internal dialogue. Much of the theory of the self and of self and object representations has relied on visual and spatial metaphors such as self-image, shape of the self, or self-boundaries.

I am not arguing that non-verbal or pre-verbal factors are unimportant. On the contrary, to paraphrase Freud, the self is first and foremost a bodily self. But with the development of language and the internalization of words and symbolic thought, the self that can be studied by the psychoanalytic method is forever transformed into a narrated verbal self.

The narrative quality of the manifest dream is a reflection of the mind's capacity and tendency to integrate, synthesize, and create order, both in wakefulness and in sleep. The narrative story-like quality of dreams is a result of an inherent organizing property of the mind, which functions in the realm of language by constructing narratives. As described earlier, story making, the narrative function of the mind, is an important element in the construction of one's sense of self. It is this same tendency of our mind which creates stories of our life which also creates our dream narratives, and therefore the same organizing themes would be expected to appear. The principal schemas and strategies with which we organize our experience and from which we create our internal autobiographies will be reflected in the themes and narrative constructions of our dreams. An exploration of the thematic aspects of dream structure reveals clues as to patients' typical and characteristic patterns of organizing narratives of themselves in relation to others.

Foulkes (1985) carefully investigated the phenomenology and structure of manifest dreams. He described dreams as mental acts organized both at a momentary level and on a sequential level. Dreams cohere in the form of a narrative or story in the same manner as does much of our waking experience. It is true that at times the narrative organization breaks down in dramatic ways, however most transitions in dreams preserve either the characters or the setting or both. Furthermore, a careful study of the development of children's dreams revealed that this organization in dreams is a developmental achievement (Foulkes, 1982). Developmental evidence suggests that the kind of narrative organization found in dreams emerges in development only at the point where children's waking thought shows internally regulated coherency. These studies indicate that dreams are generally coherent, organized, narrative stories. Dream imagery is generally well formed, and sequentially dreams are well ordered. It would seem that dreams are deliberately planned mental activity.

This is not to argue that all dreams are simply understood, coherently organized, well-told stories; clearly they are not. I am only suggesting that psychoanalysts have overemphasized their disorganized, regressive, and disguised qualities to the exclusion of their more organized and coherent thematic aspects.

The thrust of much recent experimental and laboratory work on dreams has been to view dreaming as serving an adaptive function. This is consistent with the trend in contemporary psychoanalysis which emphasizes the organizing, self-maintaining, and communicative function of dreams. Much research points to the role of dreaming in the transfer of newly acquired information into the permanent memory structure (Palombo, 1978). In dreaming we assimilate new information to our established sense of self and accommodate our self to newly acquired information. Thus, the very purpose of the dream is information processing serving the maintenance, organization, preservation, and growth of the self.

I now return to Mrs. D.'s dream. Her spontaneous associations concerned looking for a job and going on interviews. Generally, the interviewers were men and Mrs. D. was concerned that they would not hire her because of their fear that she would soon become pregnant and leave the position. She would be silently outraged if an interviewer asked her if she had or planned to have children. Her associations led to thoughts of marital difficulties and to her feeling that she could not communicate with her husband. She tried to speak with him, but he just "erected" a barrier. She twice remarked that it was similar to her communication with her mother.

I inquired in some detail regarding associations to the elements of the dream. She elaborated that the dish was served to her in a Teflon frying pan, the cheap and nonstick type. Mrs. D. likes to go to restaurants, but her husband often takes her out when he knows that she wants to discuss a controversial issue; he is aware that she will not bring up problems in public. Mrs. D. also had thoughts about their sexual difficulties. They discussed their conflict about having children at the marital session. She was surprised that her husband had been responsive to the idea of treatment. But will he "stick" with it?

She described that the urine was sizzling and bubbling like a liquor which had been poured on. The meat was glazed with what seemed like a smooth coat of oil. One piece of meat in particular stood out, it was of a deep reddish color and shiny like oil. The dish was sweet. "I never order fried meats, ham steak, or kidney. I never eat organ meats, plus urine is disgusting. Like my marriage, it's awful, I can't believe it." Because her husband wants children he refused to have anything to do with birth control. Mrs. D. resented this and as a result they have had little sex. I said that eating disgusting organ meats with urine might refer to oral sex. She laughed and said that this was embarrassing, but that this had been on her mind. "I think he likes it but I don't. It's distasteful, disgusting, it's something he really likes and enjoys, probably very important to him, but he denies it." I asked who "they" were in the dream who told her to try it. She said it was a waiter in a white coat. She thought that the image of the white coat was more of a doctor than of a waiter. She wonders if she's more sexually repressed than she knows. "I'm not doing what everyone else does, I'm not a connoisseur."

Together we explored these themes in relation to her current concerns about her life and her treatment. Her husband buys her off, cheaply, with a dinner, from truly saying how she feels. "A male doctor convinces you to do something that you find disgusting, and when you do try it you are repulsed but find you like the sweet taste. Is there a doctor here trying to force something down your throat? Is the new doctor, the marital counselor, also going to try to persuade you to do what you find objectionable?" I found myself wondering whether I was really neutral about her choice of whether or not to have children. Do I really believe that if she were healthy, if her analysis were successful, she would opt to have a child? Am I trying to secretly and subtly persuade her of this? Am I trying to cover my true intentions with slippery oil to disguise what I really want her to swallow? I discussed her perceptions of me and my attitudes in regard to this. Is there perhaps a wish to be persuaded by me that sex, oral sex, men, babies, and pregnancy are not so bad or disgusting? Does she want me to try to help her to try new experiences which frighten and repulse her? Would she like to be more of a gourmet, more sophisticated, and not as parochial, conservative, and narrow-minded as her mother?

I asked her to consider whether it might be that she would like to see both me and the marital counselor as trying to convince her to do disgusting things, to be insensitive to her feelings, and to try to serve her offensive and repugnant ideas. She might want this so that she could react with outrage and abhorrence and feel justified in returning to her mother and her mother's views of men. Other questions that were raised included whether my interventions were being viewed as attempts at sexual seduction. Or was she seducing me, by presenting such a rich dream specimen into ignoring her hostility and cynicism, so that I would not notice how "pissed off" she truly was? Another approach to this dream, by way of amplification, was to wonder if she had thought to ask to see a menu, to actively participate in the decision-making, rather than to go along with the waiter's recommendation?

For Freudians, things are never as they seem. Philosophically, they are interested in the reality behind appearances. The surface is viewed as a deception covering a deeper buried core truth. This is inherent in the distinction between manifest and latent content, which is a distinction required by a theory of drive and defense. From this perspective, a dream can never mean what it seems to say. For interpersonalists (Levenson, 1985), the issue is not the search for the truth behind appearances, but rather the search for the truth inherent in appearances. "For the Freudians, the key question is, what does it truly mean? For the interpersonalist, the question is, what's going on around here?" (p. 53). It is in a similar spirit that Basescu (1987) remarks that dream interpretation, in the traditional sense, does not play a large role in the work of most interpersonal analysts. It is not that dreams are neglected, but rather that there is no attempt to decipher them. They are treated as communications rather than as puzzles, so that the analyst asks what does the dream say rather than what does it mean.

The method of free association seems ideally suited to the goal of excavating the buried, hidden, and disguised latent content. But where the classical model encourages getting behind, under, or beneath the surface by taking apart, "analyzing," deciphering, the manifest appearance, the interpersonal model seeks the expansion of experience by meticulously focusing on the surface. The interpersonalist holds a magnifying glass over the surface in an attempt to see the most subtle nuances of experience.

We have seen that a variety of revisionist positions have in common an exclusive focus on manifest content and a disregard of associations or at least a neglect of the careful, disciplined perusal of associations to specific dream elements. In my opinion, an over-reliance on manifest content shifts the balance of the analytic work too much onto the analyst, and the patient may feel left out of the interpretive process. By learning to free associate to the dream, the patient learns to take an active part in the analysis. Furthermore, the systematic search for associations leads into directions that could not have been guessed at by the analyst without these.

At the other extreme, is the classical approach which neglects the manifest content, dismissing it as just a misleading story superimposed on the real dream as part of secondary revision. I am also critical of this approach in that it neglects the value of the thematic and structured aspects of dream narrative.

Freud described how associations diverge from the specific elements of the manifest content and later converge crystallizing into clear latent dream thoughts. His writing leaves unclear whether this convergence occurs spontaneously or whether it is a result of active interventions on the part of the analyst. By leaving this point vague, Freud avoids the recognition that at some point in the procedure the analyst imposes order on the material. How is the analyst to choose a focus from among the numerous directions in which associations may lead? In what way does the analyst decide when and how to organize the patient's associations? I have found it helpful clinically to maintain a balance between following associations in whatever direction they may lead and returning to the manifest theme story of the dream. My experience confirms Palombo's observation that "The manifest dream is the point of convergence for the multiple associative strands that radiate from it" (1984, p. 405). It is by moving back and forth from associations to manifest theme, from analysis to synthesis, that the diverging associations ultimately converge allowing the analyst and patient jointly to construct a meaningful dream interpretation.

A variety of technical options exist for the contemporary psychoanalyst. In addition to the many techniques suggested by Freud (1923), it has been suggested that the analyst ask the patient if any memories come to mind in relation to each of the dreams components (Palombo, 1984). The analyst may begin by asking what the patient felt during the dream (Bonime, 1962). It would be in the spirit of Gill's recent writings (1982) for the analyst to ask the patient to help the analyst see any connection between the dream and what is going on in the treatment. In this way the analyst may choose to focus the exploration of the dream around the past, the extra-transferential present, or on the transference in the here-and-now. The analyst may choose to ask for associations to specific dream elements as well as for associations to the central dream theme as suggested by Stolorow (1978). This may help to construct interpretive narratives which are more plausible to the patient and which can more readily be incorporated into the psychoanalytic life narrative being created jointly in the analysis. To ask the patient what comes to mind about the dream theme can be less threatening and less disorganizing because not only may the patient feel less taken apart, but in addition the dream story has a way of capturing the patient's imagination in a most compelling way. While I agree with Fosshage's (1987) suggestion to elucidate and amplify the meanings of the dream images, affects, and themes, I cannot agree with his abandonment of the free-association method, or with his de-emphasis of the central role of conflict in psychic life.

I would also suggest, as illustrated in my use of Mrs. D.'s dream, that the analyst can use the dream themes to monitor not only the patient's transferences, but also the patient's perceptions of and fantasies about the analyst's counter transferences. This is an area too often neglected in analytic work, and it is particularly important to be alert for these attitudes because they are often not directly voiced by patients (Gill, 1982).

Dreams are exceptional in the clinical situation specifically because as stories, they lie at an optimal distance between daily waking reality and life concerns on the one hand and between unconscious fantasy, autistic, indescribable thoughts and chaotic images on the other. The dream narrative is organized, communicable, describable, and to a great extent cohesive and coherent. Yet, dreams are also our most private, personal, and revealing communications. The dream is a story, the function of which is synthesis. It weaves together a subplot of our lives, and its integration with the rest of our autobiography results in a further consolidation of self. In Winnicott's (1971a) language, dreams are "transitional phenomena" and as such they can express our deepest concerns with a playful lightness and paradoxically with a vivid and profound urgency. Dreams, which may seem most trivial, provide the distance, which allows the most serious issues to be explored. Yet even the most difficult issues, when approached through a dream narrative, can be worked and played with creatively and can thus provide a sense of hope.

Note

1 Kohut had drawn attention to the similarity between his view of self-state dreams and Freud's (1920) description of traumatic dreams. One can read Freud as dealing with the problem of the cohesion of the self in the language of prestructural theory and the economic point of view. "Binding," from this perspective, refers in economic terms, to the need for cohesion.

Chapter 2

Working toward operational thought: Piagetian theory and psychoanalytic method (1993)

Introduction by Adrienne Harris

Like many writing these introductions to Lewis Aron's Collected Papers, I wish so deeply that Lew and I were sitting down to a conversation about the issues and themes in this chapter. To be sure, and maybe ironically, Lew and I would be meeting to talk about Piaget and Psychoanalysis as much younger selves. The chapter was built on work and writing he was doing at Roosevelt Hospital. Relational theory is coming into a complex visibility—sometimes critiqued, sometimes admired, feared, and wished for. In this period in the early 1990s, Lew and I are growing into analytic identities, relational novitiates, eager theory makers, pulling a variety of theorists inside psychoanalysis and outside, into the webs and fabrics Stephen Mitchell and a wonderful group of colleagues were weaving and constructing.

It is eerie for me to start into this chapter of Lew's and immediately find old and current comrades. I was at Rutgers and so a colleague of Melvin Feffer's when he was writing about Piaget and radicalizing the constructivist approach Piaget had created. And we might remember that Piaget's complex relation to psychoanalysis includes having had an analysis with Sabina Spielrein, herself a complex thinking working across disciplines of psychology, linguistics, and psychoanalysis.

Lew thanks Susan Coates his colleague at Roosevelt, and in reading that, I remember all the ways Susan was leading us into gender's complexity and how powerful I felt her influence in writing *Gender as Soft Assembly*. Lew's introduction to the essay conjured up a history and a time in our shared history when many new integrations and evolutions were occurring: opening the space for relational work, discovering Ferenczi, and many others in our history.

It is a moment when developmentalists and clinical psychoanalysts are talking and thinking together, and this essay of Lew's makes a deep case for the engagement of cognitive and analytic theory. Above all, as we can see in this project, Lew is opening and deepening his theoretical interests. Over and over again, via different routes and entry points, he will pursue his understanding that thinking and feeling is interactional, intersubjective, made in the complex encounter of at least two people.

Here, he engages with the cognitive developmental thought of Jean Piaget and engages Piaget in his own thinking about the complex transactions and interactions in the evolution of the thinking subject. This thinking subject thinks, feels, loves, triangulates. Lew will bring his reader from an examination of Piaget's theory to his thoughts about the primal scene, surely a developmental problem of all children.

In this chapter, Lew unpacks the content and the radical constructivism of Piaget's theory in elaborating how thought emerges from interaction, from interaction at the level of sensation and action, and that even as capacities evolve, they are always entwined with earlier forms. The chapter is primarily focused on the earliest level—preoperational thought—in which Lew shows how useful Piaget's focus would be to thinking about the thought processes of patients. The preoperational stage has, as Lew walks us through the theory, certain key features: egocentrism, centration/focus, reversibility, and transformation. He shows by theoretical deconstruction and by clinical exploration how deeply these processes operate in clinical material. How, Lew is asking, does a patient struggle toward and sometimes react violently against the capacity for complexity, for the simultaneity of different experiences?

A contemporary reader of this chapter will feel many evocations of Bion's ideas of alpha work, his theory of thinking in which the transaction of mother and child in a dialectical system from beta elements (sensation) transformed in to alpha structures. Like Bion, Piaget's fundamental metaphors for thinking involved digestion and transformation across thinkers. Lew's elaborations of Piaget allow us to see another vision of it taking two thinkers for one person to hold a thought. Assimilation and accommodation—the two mechanisms Piaget identified in thinking's evolution—are the mechanisms of alpha work.

I cannot resist thinking of Piaget's own complex history in regard to psychoanalysis. With his analyst, Sabina Spielrein, he was doing his groundbreaking work in Geneva on the evolution of thought. Spielrein, he notes in a footnote, worked with the thought and language of younger children, and in her early papers, we see the complex transactions of meaning she found in sound and words and verbal exchanges.

In bringing Piaget's model for thinking to bear on psychoanalytic work and theory, Lew, as always, casts a wide net. He sees in Piaget's dialectical method of engaged dyadic transaction of matters of technique the complexity of transference and its interweave with countertransference. He brings us close to Levenson's models of technique, with the work of Searles and Bach. As in so much of his work, he takes you on a voyage you did not expect but surely would not have missed.

Aron, L. (1993). Working toward operational thought: Piagetian theory and psychoanalytic method.
Contemporary Psychoanalysis, 29(2), 289–313.

One of the greatest problems of psychoanalytic theorizing is the tendency to deal with the complexities and ambiguities of psychic life by simplifying, dichotomizing, and splitting, by resorting to "either-or" instead of "both-and" solutions. One manifestation of this is the splitting of two areas of scholarship, which if studied together could enrich each other. This has been the case in the tendency to isolate the study of the cognitive and the study of the affective. Even sophisticated psychoanalysts and cognitive theorists have made the mistake of identifying Piaget with the cognitive and psychoanalysis with the affective and in so doing have unnecessarily and unfortunately perpetuated the splitting and isolation of these two worlds of scholarship. Often, Piaget is considered as an interesting theorist for child therapists or for cognitive theorists or for those interested in child development or structuralist philosophy, but of limited usefulness for the clinical analyst working with adults. In contrast, I have found Piaget's concepts to be very helpful clinically and very clarifying in understanding the ways in which the analytic process leads to structural change.[1]

In this chapter, I review Piaget's discussion of the limitations of preoperational thought and of the processes involved in attaining operational thought. Understanding the processes described by Piaget is helpful to the clinical analyst because these processes entail the capacity to hold two ideas in mind at once. I will draw parallels between the move from preoperational to operational thought, the move from splitting to integration, and the move from the paranoid-schizoid position to the depressive position. Each of these developments requires a period of working through in which two ideas are kept in mind at once. I use the Piagetian framework as a vehicle to explore some of the similarities between the classical free association method and the Sullivanian detailed inquiry. This chapter will utilize Piaget's concepts to describe some clinical implications for working toward synthesis and integration of the self and of the object, as well as for the development of subjectivity, intersubjectivity, ambivalence, symbolization, and a sense of continuous history. Intersubjectivity, intentionality, integration, historical continuity, and cohesion are all interrelated aspects of the depressive position (as this has come to be understood by contemporary Kleinian analysts) (see, especially, Ogden, 1986, 1989, 1991) and in this chapter will be related to the establishment of operational thought.[2]

F. Scott Fitzgerald (1936) wrote: "The test of a first-rate intelligence is the ability to hold two opposed ideas in the mind at the same time, and still retain the ability to function. One should, for example, be able to see that things are hopeless and yet be determined to make them otherwise" (p. 69). The integration of a cohesive self requires the capacity to tolerate, if not to resolve, discrepancies. Only when two contrary ideas can be thought about simultaneously can comparison and contrast be made between them. It is the capacity for symbolic thought which makes it possible to bring to mind more than one idea at a time. Before the attainment of the semiotic function (with the differentiation of the symbol and the symbolized), incompatible notions can co-exist without mutual influence. That is to say that at this earlier stage, ideas may be fused but not yet integrated.

A central aspect of what is worked toward in psychoanalysis (Aron, 1991a) is the capacity to hold two contrasting ideas in mind simultaneously. It is only when both sides of a conflict can be entertained in mind simultaneously that the patient can find new and better ways of resolving the formerly unconscious and etiologically neurotogenic conflicts. Whereas classical theory describes the goal of psychoanalysis in terms of the lifting of repressions and the resolution of conflict, relational theories conceptualize the goal in terms of integrating formerly split-off aspects of the self and of objects. For example, a patient needs to recognize that the analyst, who frustrates the patient by ending the session on time, by expecting to be paid, or by leaving for vacations, is the same person who gratifies the patient by listening patiently and by being reliably available and concerned. Similarly, when the focus is put on disturbances in the attainment of a cohesive self, then the patient is seen as needing to integrate contrasting aspects of self into a whole integrated unit. This may entail, for example, the integration of split-off grandiose and idealized aspects of the self, together with tendencies toward self-denigration and low self-esteem. Clearly, the integration involved in moving beyond splitting operations requires the development of the capacity to keep two contrasting ideas in mind simultaneously. It is this synthetic-integrative function of the ego that provides the essential basis for mental complexity. Nunberg's (1931) classic paper on the synthetic unction of the ego established that failure of the synthetic function was at the basis of all mental symptom formation. He had put the synthetic function on a biological basis by arguing that it was a manifestation of Eros, the drive to bind together. Thus, the importance of integration has been central to all major psychoanalytic thinkers. The idea that the normal mind seeks integration and synthesis and that neurotic pathology is a result of the breakdown of this synthesis can be traced back to Freud's early writings and specifically to his discussion of the pathogenic effects of "incompatible ideas" (Freud, 1894).

Melanie Klein too placed the movement toward integration at the center of her theoretical model seeing disintegration as a manifestation of the death instinct and integration as an expression of the life instinct. The shift from disintegration to integration is represented in Kleinian theory by the movement from the paranoid-schizoid to the depressive position that occurs when love prevails over hatred. Much of the discussion in this chapter may be understood as an attempt to clarify this dialectical movement between the paranoid-schizoid and depressive positions in the terms of Piagetian theory. It needs to be emphasized that one of the advantages of contemporary Kleinian thinking is that it does not regard these positions as discontinuous or linear stages. Instead, the positions are viewed as fundamental psychological modes of organizing experience that mutually create, preserve, and negate each other dialectically. While there is a chronological, sequential relationship between the positions (as there are for Piaget's developmental periods), the positions also operate simultaneously and dialectically (see Ogden, 1991).

The limitations of preoperational thought

Preoperational thought (which emerges at about age two with the development of language and symbolic thought) is a considerable advance over sensori-motor intelligence because actions are internalized using symbolic functions. Preoperational thought is limited, however, compared to the logical operations to come in later periods, in that preoperational thought is still not liberated from perception (Piaget & Inhelder, 1969). I will discuss four of the characteristics of preoperational thought which serve as obstacles to the attainment of logical thinking.[3]

The characteristics of preoperational thought to be discussed— egocentrism, centration, transformations, and reversibility—are closely related and interdependent. Preoperational thought is dominated by each of these characteristics, and as cognitive development proceeds they gradually subside in unison, with changes in one characteristic each modifying the others in turn.

Egocentrism

Egocentrism, in Piagetian theory, always refers to some lack of differentiation. All new cognitive developments entail some egocentrism as a byproduct of development, and therefore in each developmental period, the child is egocentric in some way. Infants, for example, are radically egocentric with respect to sensori-motor actions in their inability to differentiate internal sensations and perceptions from external objects, and in their inability to differentiate his/her own actions from the independent existence of objects upon which they act. The adolescent too is egocentric in quite a different way. Adolescents are egocentric in their inability to differentiate the objects of their own thoughts from the objects toward which the thoughts of others are directed. This is why each adolescent can believe that everyone is so concerned about his/her behavior and appearance (Elkind, 1974).

In the preoperational period, egocentrism refers to the child's inability to take the role of, or see the viewpoint of, another. This is clearly reflected in preoperational children's language where they make little effort to adapt their communication to the needs of their listeners. Preoperational children are egocentric with respect to representations and so they cannot reflect on their own thoughts; therefore, they always believe that their logic is correct and see no need to justify their arguments.

Piaget believes that it is only through repeated social interactions (particularly arguments, disagreements, and confrontations) that children learn to take the viewpoint of the other and so begin to think about their own thoughts and question their own logic. This may be surprising to many people who believe that Piaget placed exclusive emphasis on the child's learning from the experience of manipulating physical objects. However, as Flavell (1963) notes, when it comes to the question of the mechanism by which the child ultimately frees him or herself from the grip of egocentrism, Piaget argues that it is social interaction (particularly with peers) which is the "principle liberating factor."

Centering and decentering

Preoperational children tend to *center* or focus on one aspect or feature of a stimulus and to ignore other aspects or features. The child fixes his/her attention on a limited perceptual aspect of the stimulus and seems unable to explore other aspects of the stimulus. The child is unable to *decenter*, that is, to take into account other aspects of the object being investigated. The child cannot decenter and thereby take into account two or more aspects of the event simultaneously. This leads to a superficial assimilation of the stimulus being studied in which only the most perceptually striking features are considered by the child. This leads to distortions in reasoning since in centering on limited aspects of the perceptual field the child distorts information and draws false conclusions.

A well-known example of centration occurs when a preoperational child observes a liquid poured from a short wide container to a tall narrow container. The child tends to believe that there is more liquid in one container than the other. The child focuses on whichever stimulus feature is more perceptually striking. If the child centers on height, then he or she will conclude that there is more liquid in the tall container. If the child centers on width, then he or she will conclude that there is more liquid in the wide container. What the preoperational child is unable to do is to *decenter* by considering both height and width simultaneously, and thus reason that greater height compensates for less width and that greater width compensates for less height. The child's centration thus interferes with reasoning and with the capacity for establishing conservation.

States and transformations

The preoperational child, while observing a sequence of changes or successive states, focuses exclusively on the elements of the sequence or the successive states or configurations, rather than on the transformations by which one state or configuration is changed into another. Preoperational thought is static and immobile. The child does not focus on the process of transformation from one state to another but limits his/her attention to each in-between state as it occurs. In a well-known Piagetian experiment, when children are asked to observe and then draw a bar being dropped from a vertical to a horizontal position, they typically are able to draw only the initial and final positions of the bar. They cannot attend to or draw the transformations or successive movements of the bar.

Reversibility and irreversibility

The single most important characteristic of preoperational thought is its irreversibility and, for Piaget, reversibility is the most clearly defined characteristic of intelligence. Reversibility refers to the ability to follow a line of reasoning back to where it started, for example, moving from conclusions to premises. A simple or a very complex procedure may be involved in retracing the steps of a logical operation back to the starting point. An example would be a child who is asked to compare two rows of checkers. He/She agrees that each row has the same number of checkers. One of the rows is lengthened. The child no longer agrees that there are the same number of checkers in each row. He/She cannot retain the equivalence of number in the face of perceptual change. Part of the child's problem is that he/she cannot *reverse* the operation of lengthening the row of checkers.

The interdependence of the characteristics of preoperational thought

During the later part of the preoperational period, the child undergoes a transition during which all of the limitations of preoperational thought gradually give way to the capacity for logical concrete operations. The process by which this change comes about involves the gradual modification of each of the previously described characteristics of preoperational thought. These characteristics are closely related and interlocking components of the child's system of thought. As children move from centering on static states toward attending to and comprehending transformations, his/her thinking becomes increasingly reversible and conceptualization becomes more mature. Egocentricity is modified as the child can attend to the transformation involved in shifting (decentering) from his/her static position to the perspective of the other and can reverse this transformation to take alternative perspectives. As Flavell (1963) puts it:

> The rigid, static, and irreversible structures typical of preoperational thought organization begin, in Piaget's phrasing, to "thaw out" and become more flexible, mobile, and above all decentered and reversible in their operation. The child of this transitional phase, having first centered on a single, distorting facet of a display, gradually becomes able to decenter and take account of other, correcting aspects.
>
> (p. 163)

The decline of egocentricity is both a necessary prerequisite to the attainment of the capacity to decenter, to attend to transformations, and reversibility and is a consequence of these changes. The deterioration of egocentricity both permits and requires the child to decenter, attend to transformations, and reverse. On the other hand, as children can decenter, attend to transformations, and reverse their thinking, they become increasingly able to take into account two contrasting points of view simultaneously.

If you and I are looking at a design from two different angles, in order for me to take your point of view, while simultaneously holding on to my own perspective, I need to be able to attend to both my position in relation to the design as well as yours. I need to be able to imagine moving from my position to yours so that I can imagine the perspective of the design from the various transitional positions. Furthermore, I need to be able to reverse this transition mentally so that I can imagine returning to my own point of view and regaining my own perspective. Thinking about how a young child struggles with figuring out which is your right or left hand when you are facing him/her illustrates the difficulties involved in this process.

The limitations of preoperational thought and psychopathology

Piaget's descriptions of the limitations of preoperational thought are extremely useful in understanding various elements of psychopathology along the entire spectrum from mild, neurotic symptoms to severe psychopathology (Feffer, 1967, 1970; Greenspan, 1979). Beyond this, Piaget's concepts are remarkably useful in explicating the nature of analytic change. This should not be surprising since both Piaget and psychoanalysis are interested in studying changes in internal psychic structures.

Consider the following illustration: A male patient comes into treatment complaining about how critical his wife is and how she is always attempting to control his life. He reports that for many years, as a teen and young adult, he was too dependent on his mother, but now he prides himself on not letting her opinions influence him. The man has had difficulty in relationships with women because he feels that no matter how hard he tries to please them they are always demanding more than he can give. The man is given three names of therapists to choose from, two of whom are men and the third a woman. He says that he chose the woman because she is convenient. In the course of the initial consultations with this female analyst, he asked many questions about how he should proceed, and what is the best way for him to get better. He then states that he does not want to come to treatment more than once a week because he does not want to need the therapist too much. When asked about this, he says, in a way that makes it seem that he believes it is the most obvious thing in the world that he would not want to be dependent. After all, one of the reasons he sought treatment in the first place was that he felt he was overly influenced by others, so what good could it possibly do for him to now become more dependent on the therapist. In another moment he demands that the therapist should be more active and more directive, give more direct advice, help, or make specific suggestions. "If you are just going to be quiet and sit and listen, then what good are you. I might as well stay home, save my money, and talk to the wall." The patient moves back and forth between dependent and counterdependent positions, oscillating between two sides of an intense conflict, seemingly with little or no recognition that he has expressed contradictory wishes. His statements make it sound as if independence is a virtue and dependence is a fatal flaw. And of course, this is just what the patient believes.

Certainly, this is not true, and the therapist needs to remember that the capacity to allow oneself to be dependent on another is a critical achievement. (While we all start out being dependent that is not done with either awareness or intentionality.) Without the ability to depend on another, a person would be isolated and incapable of mutual give and take. You cannot learn from another if you are unable to depend on them at least momentarily. On the other hand, being overly dependent has clear disadvantages in that one is incapable of functioning autonomously. The solution to this dilemma, that is the resolution of neurotic conflict regarding issues of dependence and independence, is not for patients to become more dependent or more independent, and more importantly, it is not to reach some midpoint, or balance, being not too dependent and not too independent. The solution is to develop the capacity to be both highly dependent and highly independent in a flexible way, depending on the individual and unique situation and context. People need to be able to be both dependent and independent based on the specific circumstances. To recognize this requires the capacity to maintain both perspectives in mind at once. One needs to see both the advantages and disadvantages of both dependence and independence.

What we need to do to resolve conflict or to heal a psychic split is, in Piagetian terms, to simultaneously decenter from our immediate perception of the situation in order to attend to a contrasting dimension of experience. In the above example, the patient is either centered on being trapped, controlled, influenced, and taken over, or he is centered on feeling needy, wanting a response, demanding advice, and expecting care. He is not able to see these two dimensions of experience as being related to each other and as being different aspects of one problem.

Working through egocentricity and working toward decentering

How does psychoanalysis work? How does the analyst help the patient to decenter and attend to both sides of a conflict simultaneously? While there are many explanations and a plethora of theoretical approaches to answer these questions, I believe that in practice there are some underlying principles which all analysts follow regardless of theoretical orientation. I will compare two contrasting approaches that are different from each other in order to show their underlying commonality. I will describe the classical (Freudian) free-association model and then compare it to the interpersonal (Sullivanian) method of detailed inquiry.

Toward the end of a session, early on in her analysis, a patient describes an embarrassing and painful memory of watching her mother yell and scream at her father in a busy supermarket. She begins to describe, with some intensity of feeling, her anger at her mother. After a momentary pause, she goes on to justify the mother's behavior in light of various provocations. She begins to say that the mother never meant any harm, and then she sighs and complains that she feels like she's not making herself or the situation at all clear. The analyst points out that just as she began to express some anger at her mother, she seems to have shifted over to excusing and justifying her mother's behavior, and that immediately after she does this, she begins to criticize herself. I would like to consider this ordinary piece of analytic work in order to show how this intervention fosters working toward the capacity for operational thought.

The free association method allows both the patient and the analyst a view of the patient's mental functioning (see Aron, 1990a). Arlow (1987) writes that, "the stream of the patient's free associations is the record of the vicissitudes of the analysand's intrapsychic conflicts" (p. 70). The analyst aids the patient in being able to observe the flow of his or her associations and to become aware of any interferences in the flow of these associations. In this way, the patient becomes increasingly familiar with the nature of his or her resistances. This gives patients access to the way their minds work in the analytic situation; in particular, they become aware of their own conflictedness. In the above example, the analyst intends for the patient to become aware that something has interrupted the flow of her thoughts and communications about her anger at her mother. The analyst would like the patient to see that instead of going on to express her anger at mother, she defended mother. In this way she defends herself from awareness of her own anger. Why would the patient stop herself from feeling angry? The analyst would want to explore the nature of the danger that leads the patient to inhibit her expression of anger. One danger that that analyst will pay particular attention to is the patient's fears regarding the analyst's reactions to this material. Then, the analyst would want to show that not only does she defend her mother, but she becomes critical of herself, and so expresses anger at herself instead of at her mother. Instead of accusing her mother, she accuses herself and defends mother. Furthermore, she criticizes herself before her analyst has the chance.

For my purposes here, I will leave aside the genetic and dynamic aspects of this material, as well as the transference-countertransference implications. I would like to focus on the structural elements. The patient has shifted from a view of mother as the villain to a view of mother as victim. Both of these are views that this patient has of her mother. However, the patient is not able to hold these two views of mother in mind simultaneously. Instead, she shifts momentarily from one view to the other, that is, she decenters sequentially but not simultaneously (Feffer, 1967, 1970). This is not a serious form of "splitting" because the two views are not kept rigidly apart, and the patient does have access to both views with just a bit of help from the analyst. However, the patient's conflicts lead her to alternate between the two views, rather than to hold both of them in mind together and make use of both dimensions of her knowledge of her mother. I believe that the analogy of the preoperational child who centers on either the length of the flask or the width, but not on both dimensions at once, is apt.

How does the analyst's comment foster a more complex view? The analyst asks the patient to step out of her experience for a moment and to observe and reflect on what she just said. He encourages her to reverse her mental operations, that is, to go backward over her thought processes and see that her defense of her mother is the converse of her anger at mother, and that her anger at herself is an inverse of her anger at her mother. The analyst has encouraged the patient to reverse her thinking and therefore to discover that anger at self has replaced anger at mother.

However, this ability to reverse her thinking can only occur when the patient has been led to attend to the transformations in her thinking. It is not enough to speculate with patients about reversal of affects or about "turning their anger at themselves." Here, the analyst has helped the patient to attend to the transformations in her thinking, so that the discovery of reversal occurs in the context of the detailed and personal discovery of the way her own mind works (see Gray, 1973).

The method of free association permits patients to acquire a detailed and personal understanding of the working of their own minds. By attending to transformations, patients learn to reverse their mental operations, and this leads to the capacity to decenter, to attend simultaneously to different dimensions of the same event. In the above illustration, the patient observes the flow from one thought to the next and thus becomes aware of the transformations, and then can see the reversals from anger at mother to anger at self, and then can, at least momentarily, hold onto two views of mother at once. For at least a brief time, the patient can see herself as angry at mother and can see herself as wishing to defend mother, simultaneously. All of this leads to a decrease in egocentricity as the patient can gradually observe her associations, at the same moment, from both her own point of view, and from the viewpoint of others, for instance, from the perspective of her analyst.

It is not just the classical free association method that works in a way that can be described using Piagetian principles. The interpersonal method of the detailed inquiry (Sullivan, 1954) can be thought of in a similar way. For the interpersonalist, much that is considered unconscious is really "unformulated experience" (Stern, 1989). Analysts draw patients' attention to various events in their lives to which they have only selectively attended (out of anxiety) and that have therefore remained unformulated. For Sullivan, dissociation and selective inattention are among the most common security operations. Because these solutions to the problem of anxiety were problematic and disruptive, Sullivan's therapeutic inquiry was designed to study them through participant-observation between therapist and patient. The analyst attempts to help patients focus on these events through inquiry into the details of their lives. The analyst's questions press the patient for further data. According to Levenson (1988), it is just this forcing of data, brought about by the inquiry, the deconstruction of the patient's text, which is the driving force behind the analytic work. It is the press for ever more data that causes anxiety and promotes the transference. Levenson argues, along lines similar to those put forth here, that the common denominator among analysts using the free association method and those using the detailed inquiry is that despite different metapsychologies, they both "elicit sufficient data, under sufficient pressure" (p. 15) to facilitate a psychoanalytic process. For Levenson, forcing the data leads to a deconstruction of the patient's narrative, which creates "a chaotic flux of meanings, from which new meanings may emerge, forged in a transferential crucible of considerable tension" (p. 12). In agreement with Levenson, I am emphasizing that it is the non-theory-specific aspects of the analytic process that are most important in leading to change.

In describing her clinical supervision with Sullivan, Pearce (1950) highlights Sullivan's use of the detailed inquiry.

> Most of the content of his therapy was in fact directed towards inquiry into the actual procedure of who said what to whom in some particular situation which was under observation for its anxiety provoking characteristics and into what else might have been going on other than what the patient assumed was going on.
> (p. 2)

Consider the following vignette provided by Zucker (1967) as an illustration of the detailed inquiry. A patient reports that she went to her friend's home. "It was quite an evening. We had dinner. And talked quite a bit. After a while I realized I wasn't really involved. Of course, I joined the conversation a number of times. But I knew I was really detached, thinking about other things" (p. 42). Zucker considers, and would encourage the therapist to ask the patient, any and all of the following questions: Are you this way in other situations? When did you first notice this sort of thing? What other things were you thinking about? What was being talked about? Who does the "we" refer to? Who was actually there? What did you actually say? Zucker suggests that the patient's summaries and impressions do not provide the necessary detail for the therapist to develop his or her own sense of the situation. Furthermore, the person's summary might not accurately reflect what actually happened.

While this method is strikingly different and both theoretically and practically incompatible with the traditional free association method,

I would like to emphasize that in at least one respect they may both further a similar process in the patient. In the above illustration, the therapist's questions are aimed at "gaps" in the patient's narrative. There are bits of information that have been omitted, and the inquiry is aimed at these gaps in the patient's account. These questions force the patient to observe their thoughts and attend to the gaps in their communications. Tenzer (1984) writes, "An important part of working through is the stimulation of curiosity with respect to contradictions so that cognitive gaps come into relief" (p. 425). The above patient, as suggested by Zucker, might mention that the evening's talk was about politics, a topic that she felt she knew little about. This might lead to her recognition that her thoughts became "detached" and focused on other things because of her insecurities and fears of exposure and humiliation. Leaving aside for the present purposes the dynamic meanings of the content and even references to the transference, the patient learns a method to figure out what is going on in her mind, in her communications with her therapist, and in her behavior with others. But how does one look for that which is missing? Stern (1990) answers that "the analyst pursues an awareness of absence by focusing the most detailed attention on what is present" (p. 460). The patient is led to notice gaps by looking at the details of what she has reported. Her report of detachment follows immediately after the thoughts of trying to enter the conversation. By attending to the transformations in the communications the gaps are filled in which allows for a reversal of the mental operations. Instead of focusing either on her detachment or on her wishes for involvement and connectedness, she can decenter and observe the transformations between these states and the reversals from one to the other.

Competence, performance, and anxiety

The analytic process requires the active, observing, intellectual activity of both patient and analyst, and this goes on in conjunction with and in the context of the ongoing, affectively laden, person-to-person relationship, that constitutes the analytic situation. Even if it is agreed that much analytic work aims at enhancing the analysand's capacity for self-observation, it still may be argued that surely most adult patients have reached at least the concrete operational stage of development and that the development of operational thought would not have to be facilitated by the analyst. However, adults may behave at a preoperational level even after they have achieved concrete operations. How is this to be explained in Piagetian terms? How does Piagetian theory deal with what psychoanalysts would refer to as "regression"? To explain how someone who has achieved operational thought functions as if they have not, Piagetians make the distinction between competence and performance (Flavell & Wohlwill, 1969). Competence refers to the formal, logical, abstract forms of development, while performance represents the process by which competence actually gets utilized in real situations. Structures are not immediately and universally reflected in performance, which means that in various situations, a person may not perform at his or her highest level of structural development, and there may be a tension between cognitive structures and their behavioral manifestations at the level of performance. The Piagetian concept of "decalage" refers to the observation that while an individual may be generally characterized by a particular cognitive structure, that individual will not necessarily be able to perform within that structure for all tasks. Among the conditions that could account for the discrepancy between competence and performance are affective factors such as anxiety and depression. The distinction between competence and performance and the related concept of "decalage" explains what may look like regression in cognitive operations (Bearison, 1974).

It is interesting to contrast this Piagetian explanation for apparent regressions with Kleinian ideas about ongoing fluctuations between the paranoid-schizoid and depressive positions. Unlike Piaget who emphasizes a linear developmental progression in cognitive operations, for Kleinians the paranoid-schizoid and depressive positions are related to each other both diachronically and synchronically, that is, there is a progressive developmental relationship between them that moves from the primitive to the mature, however, the positions are also thought to interact simultaneously in dialectical relation to each other. Whether conceptualized in the Piagetian terms of fluctuations in performance due to anxiety, or whether conceptualized in the Kleinian terms of movements back and forth between the positions, either way the implication is that one would expect to see fluctuations in the predominant mode of functioning of both the patient and the analyst (Ogden, 1991). As we will see this has profound clinical consequences.

The role of self and object relations

A 29-year-old, male obsessional attorney is in analysis with a female analyst who raises her fee after two years of treatment. The fee had originally been low because the patient began treatment when he first began to work. In the sessions following being told of the fee increase the patient reports many feelings, reactions, and fantasies. At first, he sees himself as the victim, being taken advantage of by the greedy and conniving therapist. "You feel that you can get away with it with me because I need you so much. You know that my family is wealthy and will help out with the money. I knew that I shouldn't have told you the truth about my family's finances, but here I am trying to be open and truthful and saying whatever comes to my mind." The patient goes on to complain about a computer that he bought which has been giving him problems. He bought it at a discount store and now he can't get good service and they won't return it. "Real thieves!"

However, the patient goes on to say that sometimes he feels he is still paying too low a fee. "In fact, I should be paying your full fee. After all I'm working and my family does have lots of money. Why aren't you charging me your full fee? Maybe I didn't tell you the full story? I'm wondering if I kept something back. But I'm afraid to talk about money because if I do you'll realize how much I have, and you'll feel the need to raise your fee, because you'll feel that I've been taking advantage of you." The patient goes on with much more of this, but these few remarks capture the flavor of his associations. The analyst interprets that the patient feels all relationships involve victimization, the only question is whether he will be the victim or the victimizer, and he moves back and forth between these two roles. "You are ripping me off, concealing information, and taking advantage of me, and I am a gullible sap who can't look out for myself," or "I am greedily and mercilessly milking you for all you're worth, while hiding it behind the appearance of giving you a discounted fee, and you are a helpless and dependent victim who can't defend yourself or even protest effectively."

I am not proposing a new technique or procedure, but simply illustrating the ways in which our ordinary analytic method facilitates the analysand's use of higher level cognitive operations. In this example, the analyst's interpretation enables the analysand to observe the oscillating currents in his associations. He becomes aware of the back and forth, momentary shifts between his identification of himself and of the analyst, alternately, as victim and victimizer. By attending to the transformations, the shifts from one self-depiction to the other and from one object representation to the next, the patient begins to notice the reversals in transference-countertransference configurations, between identifications and projections. Ultimately, this allows him to *decenter* his perceptions so that he can hold both of these ideas in mind at once. He can simultaneously look at *both* himself and the analyst as both victim and victimized. This leads to a decrease in egocentricity in the sense that he can see the encounter from outside of his own point of view. The decrease in egocentricity, in turn, facilitates greater ability to attend to transformations and to be able to reverse thought, kicking in progressively more sophisticated cycles of self-other observation.

This is far from an intellectualized exercise aimed at teaching cognitive operations. It is an intense, affectively loaded encounter between patient and therapist, in which the patient and the analyst oscillate between affective interpersonal experience and reflective observation of self, other, and interaction. Patient and analyst are interacting participants who through the joint processes of projection and identification enact fluctuating, alternating, and dynamically isolated roles and reciprocals. Gradually, with the reconciliation of these complementary dimensions, equilibrium is attained in which the patient moves from role dimensions which were experienced as antagonistic polarities, to the simultaneous mutual regulation of complementary viewpoints which allows for coordination between the opposing roles and therefore self and object constancy (the hallmarks of the depressive position).

As the patient alternates among enactments of varying self-representations and identifications, the analyst will find him or herself changing in his or her responsiveness to the patient. The therapist needs to maintain a free-floating responsiveness (Sandler, 1976), remaining open to the wide range of roles that may be actualized, and feelings and self-states that may be elicited. The analyst then, in containing all of these countertransference reactions, integrates for the patient all of these diverse self and object relational configurations. That is, the analyst's capacity to integrate helps the patient to develop an integrated sense of him or herself as he/she deals with the analyst. Elaborating on Searles (1959), I am suggesting that the decentering and consequent integration of self and object relational experience needs to occur intersubjectively, with the analyst integrating the fragmented role relations so that this can ultimately develop intrapsychically in the patient. To illustrate with the above example, the analyst may need to feel that she is being ripped off and victimized, she then may become defensive and begin to feel that she should demand a higher fee, as she begins to feel this, and even enact it, she may begin to feel greedy and guilty. It may very well be the analyst who has to decenter, attend to transformations, reverse her thinking, and thus better integrate her image of herself and of her patient as whole people, before she is able to help her patient integrate such a whole sense of self and other. However, as stated previously, it is not that the analyst is seen as having attained these higher capacities once and for all and now has to teach these skills to the patient, rather, the analyst too is thought of as fluctuating in her or his performance of concrete operations. The analyst, like the patient, moves back and forth between functioning predominantly in the paranoid-schizoid and the depressive position. It may be that it is the analyst's own struggles in gaining, loosing, and regaining the capacity for integration that allows the analysand to gradually function with greater flexibility.

The Oedipus complex and intersubjectivity

The oedipal stage of development occurs near the beginning of the Piagetian period of concrete operations. [4]In order for the Oedipus complex to be successfully negotiated, the child must attain the capacity for operational thought. However, in order to fully develop concrete operational thought, the child must become involved in the complex three-person psychology of the oedipal period. Greenspan (1979) has discussed the relationship between the psychodynamics of the oedipal stage and the cognitive developments of the concrete operational period. Rather than review this in detail here, I want to build on Greenspan's work and contribute to the discussion from a slightly different perspective. Concrete operational thought entails the capacity for seriation and classification. Both seriation and classification emerge out of the child's increasing ability to attend to transformations, reverse thought, decenter, and decrease egocentricity. French psychoanalysis has consistently emphasized the critical psychic achievement of the differentiation between the sexes and between the generations that comes with the resolution of the Oedipus complex (see Chasseguet-Smirgel, 1991). As Greenspan has noted, the differences between the generations is a seriation task, in that it involves an understanding of the relations between bigger than and smaller than. Similarly, understanding the difference between the sexes is a task involving classification. Thus, to understand one's place in the system of relations that constitute one's family, a person needs to have at least the rudimentary capacity for concrete operational thought.

Melanie Klein (1945) and contemporary Kleinians following her (Segal, 1989) have linked the Oedipus complex to the depressive position. I believe that Greenspan's (1979) contribution linking the Oedipus complex to the development of concrete operations can be expanded and enriched considerably by linking both the Oedipus complex and concrete operations to the depressive position. The attainment of the depressive position, like the attainment of concrete operations, entails the capacity to hold two contrasting dimensions of experience in mind at once. It is this achievement that allows for the discovery of ambivalence and concern, the differentiation of the symbol from the symbolized, of internal from external reality, and the capacity for intersubjectivity.

Elsewhere (Aron, 1991b) I have argued for the importance of the internalized primal scene as a fundamental structure in the establishment of one's sense of self and of internal object relations, and I have referred to its role in the establishment of intersubjectivity. Prior to the oedipal stage the child lives in a two-person world. The child relates to both the mother and to the father, and the child relates to each of them differently, that is, he or she has a separate and unique relationship with each parent. However, the child relates to only one parent at a time, even if alternating from one to the other in momentary glances. It is only with the oedipal stage of triadic object relations that the child perceives that he or she is part of a system of relations which includes a separate relation between the parents from which the child is excluded. Britton (1989) uses the term "triangular space" to describe the internalization of this relation.

> The closure of the oedipal triangle by the recognition of the link joining the parents provides a limiting boundary for the internal world. It creates what I call a "triangular space"—i.e., a space bounded by the three persons of the oedipal situation and all their potential relationships. It includes, therefore, the possibility of being a participant in a relationship and observed by a third person as well as being an observer of a relationship between two people.
> (p. 86)

The Oedipus complex entails not just the child's viewing of the parental relationship as an excluded outsider, rather it entails the myriad phantasies of the child in which the entire system of family relations is experimented with and internalized. The little boy or girl is at one moment the small, excluded, child barred from the gratifications of adult sexuality, and at another moment is the phantasied rival of the father for mother's love, and at the next moment is loving father and seeking a separate, private, and exclusive relationship with him. The child alternates between seeing him or herself as outside of a two-person relationship, him or herself as the observer, and inside a two-person relation being observed by a third. Thus, it is in the oedipal stage that the child first alternates between observation and participation. This oscillating function, the capacity to move back and forth smoothly between experiencing and observing, can only come about with the attainment of concrete operations because it requires maintaining two perspectives in mind at once. It is clinically important because the oscillating function becomes the basis upon which a person can participate in an analysis.

Similarly, the child alternates between loving and hating each parent. The same parent who is the object of desire at one moment is the rival at the next moment. Thus, each parent alternates playing the role of subject and object, and likewise, the child alternates in his or her self-perception as subject of desire and as object of desire. In order to resolve the Oedipus complex the child needs to utilize concrete operational thought, which includes the capacity for conservation of relations. Through the same processes of transformations, reversals, and decentration that we have been discussing throughout this chapter, the child comes to recognize that the self who loves the father is the same self who wants to displace him for mother's affection. The child similarly comes to see that it is the same self that loves mother and hates father who also loves father and hates mother, and also that mother who is loved is the same person as mother who is hated.

From the standpoint of the development of intersubjectivity, it is critical that in reversing the configurations of the oedipal triangle, the child comes to identify the self-as-subject with the self-as-object and the other-as-subject with the other-as-object. Children are confronted with a multitude of tasks around establishing self and object constancy. They need to establish a sense of self as a center for action and thought, and they need to view this self in the context of other selves as an object among other objects (Bach, 1985). Similarly, they need to establish a sense of the other as a separate center of subjectivity as well as a view of the other as the object of their own subjectivity (Benjamin, 1988). These developments are of central importance to psychoanalysts since the analytic process consists of introspection and reflective self-awareness as well as of awareness of the self's interpersonal relations. Thus, a person needs to develop a cohesive sense of self as a subjective-self, a separate center of subjectivity, of self-as-agent, an experiencing ego, and the person needs to be aware of and be able to reflect upon him or herself as an object of his or her own investigation, as well as of him or herself as an object of the wishes and intentions of others. Each of these two dimensions of self needs to be attained and integrated into one seamless whole self. This requires a decentered, reversible, and transformational capacity. Where the analysand has not achieved these distinct senses of self or their integration, for example, in the "narcissistic neuroses," the goal of analysis becomes to help them achieve them. A dramatic example of the failure to develop this integration is provided by Guntrip (1969), who tells of a schizoid woman who would punch herself, thus perpetuating the beatings of her mother. When Guntrip once said to her that she must feel terrified being hit like that, she stopped and stared and said, "I'm not being hit, I'm the one that's doing the hitting" (p. 191).

Guntrip (1969) responded to R. D. Laing's criticism that "object-relations theory" should more properly address "persons" rather than "objects" by arguing that actually we might speak of "personal or ego or subject-relations theory" (p. 388). However, Guntrip argues that once it is recognized that psychodynamics is the study of persons, egos, or subjects, there still needs to be room in the theory for Buber's "I-It" relations, for the study of people's relations to themselves and to others as objects as well as subjects. As psychoanalytic theorists, we need to maintain a balance or tension between studying people experiences of themselves and of others as both subjects and as objects (as functioning in both the paranoid-schizoid and depressive positions) rather than collapsing our theory toward one or the other.

I am arguing that the development of intersubjectivity should not be thought of as a pre-oedipal phenomena occurring only in the earliest mother-infant dialogue. Rather, the capacity for intersubjective relations is an ongoing developmental task that transcends any single psychosexual stage, but that a critical nodal point in its development takes place around oedipal issues in conjunction with the attainment of concrete operations and the depressive position.[5] In the course of the psychoanalytic process, the analysand (and the analyst as well) moves back and forth between the paranoid-schizoid and depressive positions, between experiences of self-as-subject and as self-as-object. Similarly, they alternate between experiencing the other as an impersonal object and as a separate center of subjective experience, as a separate person. As they learn to attend to the transformations between these experiences, and reverse their thinking from one mode to the other, they become increasingly decentered, less stuck in rigid and static perceptions of themselves and of others. These developments decrease egocentricity, which in turn allows for greater and greater capacities for reflective self-awareness and increased awareness of interpersonal relations between self and others.

I want to conclude by noting that psychoanalytic theorists of varying schools of thought each tend to center on one dimension of human experience at the expense of others. Thus, one theorist centers on the vicissitudes of instinctual drive, while another focuses on the experience of self, another on the phenomenology of the object, and yet another on interpersonal interaction. Or, one group of theorists centers on the self as autonomous and cohesive, while another focuses on the self as permeable and in-relation-to-the-other. Or, yet again, one group of theorists focuses on the analyst as confronter, interpreter, and penetrating investigator, while another centers on the analyst as empathic container, holding environment, and reflecting mirror. Whole schools of psychoanalysis rise and fall on the basis of elevating one dimension of human experience over others. One split, in particular, that this chapter has tried to heal is the unfortunate tendency to isolate Piagetian theory, identified as a theory of cognition, from psychoanalytic theory, identified as a theory of affect. As theorists and practitioners, we need to attend to the transformations that occur in the development of our theories, to reverse our perspectives, to decenter from any single dimension, and to thus become less egocentric in our psychoanalytic perspectives.

Notes

1 This work may be seen as an extension and elaboration of ideas first suggested by Feffer (1967, 1970), who applied Piaget's cognitive approach, and particularly the concept of decentering, to the interpersonal sphere, Greenspan (1979) who very thoroughly and systematically compared Piaget's psychology and dynamic psychology, and Tenzer (1983, 1984) who related Piaget's concepts specifically to working through in psychoanalysis. Fast (1992) has led the way in battling the identification of Piaget with the cognitive and psychoanalysis with the affective. For an overview of work relating Piagetian theory to dynamic psychology and psychoanalysis see Rosen (1985), and for a fascinating critique of the literature on Piaget and psychotherapy, see Friedman (1988).
2 Since this chapter explores the implications of the move from preoperational thought to operational thought, I am concerned predominantly with patients who have already successfully achieved the capacity for symbolization and who have established a fairly well-developed sense of self. My clinical examples are therefore drawn more from patients who are more neurotic than psychotic, and more likely functioning predominantly in the depressive rather than in the paranoid-schizoid mode.
3 For a more detailed review of Piagetian theory, see Flavell (1963).
4 The Oedipus complex as a developmental achievement may be understood independently of one's acceptance or rejection of Freudian metapsychology, in general, or drive theory, in particular. For a fascinating discussion, see Greenberg (1991).
5 Although he was speaking within the framework of a cognitive-social psychology, much of this was outlined by Feffer (1970) and is consistent with a self-object relations approach to understanding transference-countertransference integrations.

Chapter 3

The internalized primal scene (1995)

Introduction by Stephen Hartman

Quirky, expansive, meta, and luxuriant, Lew Aron's 1995 essay "The Internalized Primal Scene" is something of a cult classic in psychoanalysis. It may not be Aron's most frequently taught or cited article, but the paper's passionate readers grow wide-eyed whenever Aron's sprawling treatise on gender's multiplicity is made mention. Like cult film classics, Aron's essay peppers a display of future trends with references to conventions past. Ideas that were yet to be current in psychoanalysis jump off Aron's page like a bonanza of shooting stars—redolent of the primal scene's vim and vigor. Virtually impactful, the paper is also stunningly meticulous in historical detail. Aron illustrates how psychoanalytic theories sustained polarities in gender that denuded transference of its irreverent potential. By contrast, he offers a version of the primal scene that is multidimensional, nonlinear, and social. Aron's primal scene is no clichéd snapshot of Junior barging in on Dad (and mom) because a psychoanalysis of that ilk thrives on binaries that, Aron insisted, it is our job to psychoanalyze.

Aron's primal scene trains our lens on the multitude of potential objects, some phantasmatic in origin—others social in provenance, some atemporal—others fixed in time that populate sexual encounter. This unruly firmament of images and characters—some narcissistically fused, others intersubjectively related—jostle in the register of gender and sexuality to proffer a plethora of internal *and external* object relational patterns to mind. Aron's precocious text sneaks a peek at the mash-up of individual and *groupal* objects that will fuel a psychoanalytic revival of the *collective unconscious* twenty years hence while he traverses a Freudian and Kleinian landscape that relational pundits too hastily left behind.

Originally written to celebrate the contribution of relational feminists to the queering of gender, Aron gleans that: "we need both a notion of gender identity and a notion of gender multiplicity; more broadly, we need an emphasis on people both as unified, stable, cohesive subjects and as multiple, fragmented, and different from moment to moment" (1995, p. 195). That's where the fun begins. Aron takes us on a sweeping ride into a complex galaxy of theoretical controversies and clinical dilemmas, more than I can possibly count here. Suffice it to say that the essay maps a moment in psychoanalytic time while charting constellations that are still in formation.

The generous didactic essay nonetheless packs a sturdy political punch. Aron takes issue with psychoanalytic depictions of patients' "wish to have it all" and then repurposes heternormative theories of psychic bisexuality to prize what we now call *gender fluidity*: the capacity to hold two contrasting ideas in mind (and body) simultaneously. Along the way, Aron deconstructs shibboleths in psychoanalytic theory that fetishize completeness and wholeness and that locate heterosexuality "in too privileged a position" (p. 213) for meaning to be newly made. In their place, Aron proposes a simple paradox to be found in every primal scene: We have a variety of phantasy systems; each posits multiple versions of a life to be led; these combine in a coherence we call "identity"; identity and multiplicity (in a facilitative environment) re-combine or assemble (anticipating Harris) as social and psychic need-be; the resulting "pastiche," in what might be best thought of (after Winnicott) as an act of creativity, furnishes the child with the raw material "to integrate both himself or herself and the other as simultaneously both subject and object" (p. 218). Trauma disrupts this latent capacity "to maintain an ongoing dialectic between one's identity and one's multiplicity, including one's gendered identity and one's multi-gendered multiplicity" (p. 219). When psychoanalysts rank patients' objects according to the gender binary, they interpellate their patients hailing them to obedient spell states (Guralnik, 2019) that harken what I have called (after Aron) *the social primal scene* (Hartman, 2020).

For me, the key to the essay's generativity can be found in Aron's assertion (inspired by R. D. Laing, 1972) that the child internalizes a complex network of perceived relationships rather than a smattering of objects *per se*. This implies (with a nod to Dimen) that children "internalize structures based on the field of forces by which they are surrounded" (p. 215). Identity becomes a complex read of psychic and social structures, the unrepresented and the overdetermined, the individual and the groupal, the historical and the historicizing. In this regard, Aron's paper (roughly contemporary with the Laplanche's (1997) elaboration of the *fundamental anthropological situation* and an interesting contrast to it) locates the social in the originary bricolage of the unconscious, staging a collectivist impulse in the space where *primal seduction* hails the subject to elaborate difference.

Reading Aron's ode to the primal scene recalls a visit to a crowded planetarium: vertiginous and immersive, alone while among, dreamlike yet awake. And like the primal scene, it renders how we as a lineage of readers locate ourselves in space and time. That psychoanalysis embedded sexuality in a Milky Way of gendered (and raced) polarities, Aron concludes with characteristic zeal, is our legacy to bear but it may be a useful—even necessary step toward greater integrity: "for it helps us to organize our experience until such time as *we* are ready for greater complexity" (1995, p. 234, italics added).

Aron, L. (1995). The internalized primal scene.
Psychoanalytic Dialogues, 5(2), 195–237.

Psychoanalysis is a complex system of thought in which any one proposition is in some respect systematically related to all other propositions. One cannot tamper with one aspect of an integrated system without thinking through the effect of that change on the rest of the system. This means that, to write a psychoanalytic paper even about a specific and limited aspect of psychoanalysis, the writer needs to rethink all of psychoanalysis. Clearly, at least for most of us, this is impossible. Nevertheless, my experience is that when writing a paper, I need to spend time thinking through the topic as if I were going to rethink all of psychoanalysis. I need to allow myself the phantasy that I can play with the entire system of psychoanalysis and not just with an isolated piece of it. In essence, I believe that it is only by allowing myself the grandiose phantasy that I can recreate psychoanalysis that I can allow myself to begin to think through the issues involved in any one paper. Conflicts relating to the regulation of grandiosity are often responsible for the difficulty that so many analysts have in writing papers. To control these narcissistic conflicts it is tempting to inhibit one's grandiosity, and in eliminating access to one's omnipotent and omniscient phantasies, people deprive themselves of an important prerequisite to the creative process (see Eigen, 1993).

Of course, this first inspirational and manic phase of the creative process must lead to a second phase, more dominated by secondary process, judgment, and reality testing, in which the author views the paper more objectively and from the point of view of the audience. It is important to emphasize that the first phase, which is dominated by primary process, grandiosity, and omnipotence, is just as important as the second phase, which seems so much more reasonable, healthy, and mature. We come to the realization that it is not necessary to overcome, give up, or abandon our omnipotent phantasies, but, rather, that we need to appreciate them, celebrate them, and integrate them into our overall sense of self. One omnipotent phantasy, in particular, that has been considered pathogenic and that, it has been argued, requires renunciation is the "bisexual" wish to be both sexes. To refer to the desire to *be* both sexes as "bisexual" is traditional in the history of psychoanalytic theory. This, however, is seriously problematic terminology, for one thing because it overlooks the desire to *have* both sexes. It would be somewhat more accurate to say "bigendered" in referring to identifications with people of two distinct genders. Perhaps "multigendered" identifications are more accurate if we consider that the number of genders in any given cultural system varies (Dimen, 1991). Indeed, as Butler (1990) argues, since both sex and gender are culturally constituted the difference between them collapses and there is no reason that either sex or gender need be limited to two.

Kubie (1974) emphasized the importance of what he called the drive to become both sexes, and he provided abundant data to support his view that human beings seem almost invariably to want to be both sexes because one of the deepest desires of girls and boys alike is to identify with and become both parents: with the stronger parent so as to acquire strength, and with the weaker parent out of sympathy and the wish to provide consolation. Regrettably, Kubie emphasized the problems with psychic bisexuality and neglected the positive contributions. He argued that the drive to become both sexes is one of the most self-destructive of human motives. Since it can never be satisfied, he believed, it leads to depression, frustration, and rage. He demonstrated that neuroses, inhibitions, psychoses, and interpersonal difficulties all stem from the drive to become both sexes.

I argue, in contrast, that the omnipotent with "to have it all," to fulfill symbolically the phantasy of being both sexes, can be used constructively and needs to be appreciated as a valuable human motive. Just as narcissism was studied by analysts and recognized as of central importance but for a long time was viewed pejoratively, so too bisexuality, and particularly the grandiose, omnipotent wish to be both sexes, has long been recognized but much underappreciated. Similarly, the primal scene, and Klein's (1929) related notion of the combined parent figure, was thought of as a pathogenic event and phantasy (Blum, 1979; Fenichel, 1945) but was not seen as a valuable and constructive organizing structure. I am proposing that our understanding of the pathogenic significance of narcissism and grandiosity, to the wish to be both sexes and to the internalization of the primal scene be supplemented by a more affirmative approach. The internalization of the primal scene is made possible by, and in turn permits, at increasingly higher levels of development, the capacity to hold two contrasting ideas in mind simultaneously. This psychic achievement becomes possible with, and contributes to, the capacity for symbolic thought, for sustaining ambiguity, and for creativity (Aron, 1993; Britton, 1989). Benjamin (1988) and Ghent (1992) have described the historically longstanding tendency among psychoanalysts to polarize concepts, to employ either-or thinking, and to resort to reductionism. This has led to theoretical divergences, to the proliferation of the many schools of psychoanalysis, and to continual schisms. A more sophisticated contemporary psychoanalytic theory must be able to sustain paradox, that is, in Winnicott's (1971a) terms, to allow paradox to be tolerated, respected, and left unresolved.

I use Melanie Klein's (1929) notion of the combined parent figure and the classical concept of the primal scene as metaphors that illuminate the capacity to hold two contrasting ideas in mind at once without either fusing them or splitting them apart. The relational-perspectivist epistemological stance that I advocate (see Aron, 1992a, 1992b) does not contradict the analyst's use of theory or metapsychology as an orienting framework that guides analytic listening and the formulation of interpretations. On the contrary, a perspectivist (Levenson, 1972), constructivist (Hoffman, 1991, 1992), or narrative (Schafer, 1992) approach highlights that the analyst always organizes the raw material in accordance with certain presuppositions, whether or not these are articulated. My intention is to play with metaphors and images that I have found helpful in understanding psychic life. I do not intend to reify the notions that I present or to convey that these models are universal. Rather, I believe that the analyst's theories reflect aspects of his or her subjectivity; metapsychological constructs are the analyst's personal imaginings, and it is essential that the analytic process includes the analysis of the impact of the analyst's subjectivity on the process.

Contemporary psychoanalytic theorizing has been dominated by what Loewald (1979) referred to as "the waning of the Oedipus complex." It is my impression that many analysts working from within relational traditions have neglected the metaphor of the primal scene; in moving away from a drive-discharge model and in focusing on preoedipal phenomena, they have moved away from the sexual and oedipal imagery that dominated psychoanalysis for half a century. Nonetheless, the primal scene is an important and clinically rich metaphor to be utilized by analysts independent of their commitment to a drive-discharge metapsychology. A relational approach does not have to ignore or minimize the importance of childhood sexuality in general or the significance of the Oedipus complex in particular. In fact, a relational approach can add depth and complexity to our understanding of these central psychoanalytic notions.[1]

Psychic bisexuality

Contemporary psychoanalytic, postmodernist, and feminist thinking regarding gender has led to a radical critique of Freud's theory of gender development: Freud's phallocentric and patriarchical bias has been attacked; postmodernist thought has destabilized the question of gender differences. Essentialist notions, such as that masculinity can be equated with activity and femininity with passivity, have been challenged. Gender is not seen as biologically given or natural, and therefore obvious and immutable, but rather as constructed. The notion of "natural" sexual differences obscures the social opposition of men and women by attributing these differences to the "facts" of nature. Moreover, although this critique is not aimed directly at Freud but rather at post-Freudian theoretical elaborations, the significance of a core or unitary gender identity has been challenged. Goldner (1991) has argued that Freud collapsed the distinction between sex, sexuality, and gender and thus reductively viewed the differences between men and women as natural and constitutionally based. In contrast, it is now being argued that exclusive and consistent gender identity is a result of the suppression of the natural similarities between men and women (Rubin, 1975). The very construct of "gender identity" serves as a "socially instituted normative ideal" that "pathologizes any gender-incongruent act, state, impulse, or mood" (Goldner, 1991, pp. 254–255). The current argument is that no trait is automatically or biologically given according to sex and that, therefore, all characteristics can occur in people of both sexes. The repudiation of certain traits as incongruent with a person's sex is an unnecessary limitation and causes a pathological outcome. Less radically, Benjamin (1988), while not arguing that the category of gender be eliminated, suggests that, along with a conviction of gender identity, people should be able to integrate and express both male and female aspects of self as these are culturally defined (p. 113).

Irene Fast's (1984, 1990) differentiation model of gender development proposes that children's primary identifications, both with their mothers and with their fathers, provide a developmental base for bisexuality. For Fast (1990), however, unlike for Freud, "the meanings of masculinity and femininity are not constitutionally determined, but are functions of children's experiences and their cognitive organizations" (p. 111). Fast proposes an early developmental period before children become aware of sex differences. This period is both undifferentiated and overinclusive with regard to gender awareness. During this phase, children maintain a narcissistic sense that all sex and gender possibilities are open to them. Only after the recognition of sex differences at about 18–24 months of life does the child renounce "early gender-indiscriminate aspects of self and gender inappropriate identifications" (p. 111). Awareness of the differences between the sexes requires the recognition of limits that are associated with feelings of loss, denial, envy, and demands for restitution. This growth toward a gender-differentiated identity is only one of a group of differentiations out of narcissism and egocentricism. The differentiation model suggests that the wish for "bisexual completeness" (1984, p. 146) occurs in both boys and girls. Not only do girls envy boys their penis, but boys envy girls the ability to bear babies.

Fast's term "bisexual completeness" is confusing because it conflates two different kinds of wishes: one, the wish to have both types of sex organs, vagina and breast and a penis, and two, the choice of love object, the wish to love both a man and a woman. It also may refer to the wish to have traits culturally associated with each sex, that is, it may refer to the wish to be both active and passive, penetrating and receptive. This aspect of the wish may better be referred to as the wish to be bigendered. Can we discuss the wish to be both penetrating and receptive without relating this to the wish to express male and female qualities, identifications, traits, and organs? How can we discuss the relationship between maleness-femaleness and various traits (i.e., active-passive) without essentializing gender differences? We should note in Fast's argument the continued asymmetry regarding gender, with envy of a body part conceptually compared to envy of a bodily function. This asymmetry is a further result of the confusion inherent in the expression "bisexual completeness," and it follows from the complex and confusing use of the term bisexuality in Freud's (1923) work. Does the child's wishes for both types of body parts, both types of functions, both types of characteristics, or both types of love objects? Butler (1990) exposed the ambiguity surrounding desire for the love object in Freud's concept of psychic bisexuality. According to Freud, while a boy loves and desires both mother and father, the boy's love of the father is seen as feminine. Butler elaborates:

> The conceptualization of bisexuality in terms of dispositions, feminine and masculine, which have heterosexual aims as their intentional correlates, suggests that for Freud bisexuality is the coincidence of two heterosexual desires within a single psyche. The masculine disposition is, in effect, never oriented toward the father as an object of sexual love, and neither is the feminine disposition oriented towards the mother.... Hence, within Freud's thesis of primary bisexuality, there is no homosexuality, and only opposites attract.
>
> (pp. 60–61)

Paradoxically, according to Butler, Freud's concept of bisexuality eliminates homosexuality from the normative developmental scene. I mention this here only to explicate how problematic the notion of bisexuality is in Freudian theory.

Fast (1984) puts forth a developmental model that emphasizes the need to progress through developmental stages from undifferentiated states of narcissism and egocentricity to more differentiated states in which one renounces the wish for bisexual completeness, accepts the limitations inherent in being of only one sex, and commits oneself to one's own sexual identity. She views a variety of pathological developments including neurosis and perversion as due in part to the failure to move beyond the early narcissistic stage.

The approach that I am advocating here considers narcissism, and particularly the illusion of omnipotence and "bisexual completeness," not as something that needs to be overcome, abandoned, or renounced, but rather as something to be integrated with other, more differentiated positions. I believe that the phantasy of "bisexual completeness" continues to exist in everyone and plays a major fundamental and constructive role in creativity and in our capacity to think and symbolize. Thus, psychic "bisexuality" is but one aspect of narcissism and omnipotence in human development. The traditional term "bisexual" here refers to the unconscious wish to have it all, both male and female organs, identifications, love objects, and culturally designated gender traits. The difference between Fast's position and mine is one of emphasis: She stresses the need to move beyond narcissism, I focus on the need to move not exactly toward integration but, rather, toward an acceptance and celebration of multiplicity. Yes, we psychoanalysts have made a big point about the need to accept the facts of life, the differences between the sexes and the generations, but perhaps we also need to acknowledge how important it is not to maintain such sharp distinctions all the time.

The "bisexual" phantasy involves having it all, to identify with and to desire both mother and father and to allow the masculine and feminine "sides" of our personalities to engage each other, to conjoin. Masculine and feminine can refer only to what culture construes as characteristic of each gender. We do not actually have male or female "sides" to our personality, any more than certain traits are essentially male or female. But there is a common, if not universal, phantasy, often consciously believed or even reified in theory, of aspects of ourselves as male or female. Tolerating the contradictions of a bigendered self requires the acceptance and tolerance of one's grandiosity and omnipotence. Here we come to a significant paradox: while we need a core gender identity to maintain the boundaries of our gender, we also need to preserve a multigendered self that preserves the fluidity of our multifarious identifications. Early identifications need to be reintegrated on a higher level following a period of oedipal exclusivity. Ogden (1989) concluded that "the development of a healthy gender identity is a reflection of the creation of a dialectical interplay between masculine and feminine identities ... in healthy masculinity and healthy femininity each depends upon, and is created by the other" (pp. 138–139).

Postmodernist or poststructuralist thought has questioned the very existence of a unitary, cohesive, singular, essentially unique identity. Poststructuralism deconstructs and decenters the human subject and insists that an individual is socially and historically constituted. It is from this postmodernist perspective that Dimen (1991) and Goldner (1991) have challenged the notion of a unitary gender identity as anything other than a simplified version of a self from which opposing tendencies have been split off and repressed: "a universal, false-self system generated in compliance with the rule of the two-gender system" (Goldner, 1991, p. 259). The postmodernists insist on each of our "multiplicities" and view our "identities" with suspicion. Sympathetic critics (Flax, 1990), however, have argued that postmodernists have erred by not distinguishing between a "core self" and a "unitary self." Flax proposes that "those who celebrate or call for a 'decentered' self seem self-deceptively naive and unaware of the basic cohesion within themselves that makes the fragmentation of experiences something other than a terrifying slide into psychosis" (pp. 218–219). Similarly, Rivera (1989) concluded that the idea of personality integration or unification is necessary but that personality integration prescribes

> not the silencing of different voices with different points of view—but the growing ability to call all those voices "I," to disidentify with any one of them as the whole story, and to recognize that the construction of personal identity is a complex continuing affair in which we are inscribed in culture in a myriad of contradictory ways.
> (p. 28)

I am suggesting, in agreement with Flax and Rivera, that, instead of abandoning the notion of identity, as the postmodernists would have us do, we need both it and the idea of multiplicity. Identity emphasizes a person's sense of continuity, constancy, synthesis, and integration. Postmodernism is correctly concerned with the way in which identity obscures differences within and between human beings. While people certainly need a cohesive and integrated sense of self, they also need to accept, tolerate, and even enjoy confusion, contradiction, flux, lack of integration, and even chaos in their sense of who they are. They need to accept their own internal differences, their lack of continuity, their multiplicity, their capacity to be different people at different times, in different social and interpersonal contexts. Thus, rather than abandon "identity," I am suggesting that we maintain both identity and multiplicity or difference. In terms of gender identity, it seems to me, as it does to Benjamin (1988), that we need not eliminate gender as a category (although its meaning is thrown into question) but rather recognize the need for both gender identity and "gender multiplicity" (Dimen, 1991, p. 349) within each of us.

Whatever it may mean to us to be masculine or feminine, our conceptions of ourselves as masculine and feminine draw on our internalizations of and identifications with our parents. In some ways it makes no sense to continue speaking in terms of feeling masculine or feminine or to speak of male or female traits, because to do so is to essentialize the nature of a given trait as well as masculinity and femininity. Nevertheless, in our culture there is the common phantasy or belief, conscious or unconscious, that a particular trait or attribute is male or female. Thus, for example, it is common (although, I believe mistaken), even in contemporary theoretical discussions, to consider relational attributes to be female and autonomy to be male. If we think of ourselves as having moments of masculinity, moments of femininity, and moments that are gender free (see Dimen, 1991, who raises and questions this idea), then, whatever masculinity or femininity may mean to us personally, these moments are modeled on our experience of each of our parents' own internal, multiple, phantastic male—female relationships. This relational experience is captured in the constellation of phantasies that constitute the primal scene. To understand the internal structure of the multigendered sense of self, we may understand the interaction between our various traits, characteristics, and identifications as patterned and structured on the basis of our internalizations of primal scene experience.

The primal scene

Freud (1905) believed that the observation of parental intercourse could be traumatic and that the child inevitably conceives of the sexual act as sadistic. The child's character is shaped on the basis of identifications formed with one or both participants in the primal scene. Freud (1918) argued that even if the child did not actually witness the primal scene, he or she would develop and elaborate primal phantasies of the scene derived from hereditary phylogenetic influences.

In his review and reconsideration of the primal scene, Esman (1973) concluded that, indeed, the primal scene is a universal element in mental life. He, however, found no evidence to support the belief that observation of the primal scene is inevitably traumatic or pathogenic. Furthermore, he argued that conceiving of the primal scene as sadistic is not inevitable and seems to be based on other elements in the parents' behavior, such as their overt expression of violence and aggression.

One of the difficulties with the concept of the primal scene is that its meaning and referents are unclear. It sometimes refers to the actual observation of parental sexual intercourse, sometimes to the phantasy of parental sexual intercourse, and sometimes to the wide area of the child's knowledge and phantasy regarding sexuality. As Blum (1979) has noted, just as the primal scene inevitably elicits reactions of rejection, exclusion, and intrusion on a personal level, so too, on a theoretical level, there is confusion about the scope and boundaries of the concept. McDougall (1980) uses the term primal scene "to connote the child's total store of unconscious knowledge and personal mythology concerning the human sexual relation, particularly that of his parents" (p. 56). Louise J. Kaplan (1991) has written that

> when little children fantasize about what their parents are doing in bed, they play imaginatively with being one parent or the other in that imaginary, misperceived, and fantastic scene of sexual intercourse. Any infantile fantasy of the parents' sexual intercourse is referred to nowadays as a primal scene fantasy.... The primal scene is a fantasy that represents a child's (or adult's) distorted impression and personal mythology concerning human sexual relations.
> (p. 60)

According to classical theory there are many reasons why the primal scene can be traumatic. One well-known cause is that, because of the child's immature cognition and because of the projection of jealous rage, the child imagines the sexual act as an aggressive one, as an aggressive and dangerous battle. Another explanation is that the primal scene is traumatic narcissistically because of the child's shame and humiliation at being excluded from the parental dyad. A less commonly recognized aspect of what can make the primal scene traumatic is that, looking at the sexual scenario, the child does not know for the moment with whom to identify. Inasmuch as both partners to the scene are seen as in the pursuit of pleasure, it is plausible for the oedipal witness to be inclined to identify with both parties to the scene, male and female. According to classical theory, it is the confusion that results from the wish to identify with both parents that intensifies castration anxiety and penis envy and leads to the splitting or repression of bisexuality and the extreme stereotyping of identity along gender lines.[2]

The concept of the primal scene needs not be interpreted as the child's literal viewing of sexual intercourse between the parents. It may be understood as the total of the child's experience, elaboration, and personal mythology of the interaction and relationship between the parents, which is often best symbolized by the child's image of the parents in sexual intercourse or in some form of pregenital sexual activity. From this perspective, the nature and quality of the primal scene phantasies reflect, in symbolized form, the child's perceptions, understandings, and experience of the parental relationship and interaction. This is consistent with the findings of Esman (1973).

Why would the relationship between the child's parents, which is so complex and multidimensional, be so universally symbolized by the phantasies of the combined parent figure and the primal scene? For classical theorists the answer is obvious, because for them experience is largely determined by libidinal phase dominance. For classical analysts, drive theory provides a rationale that explains the centrality of sexuality. Mitchell (1988a), however, has elaborated several alternative explanations that explain the centrality of sexual experience for most people as being not a result of the internal pressure of biological drives but, rather, an expression of interactive and relational meanings.

Mitchell suggests four reasons why sexuality takes on centrality as an organizer of childhood experience. First, because bodily sensations, processes, and events dominate the child's early experience, bodily events are drawn on and elaborated imaginatively in order to construct and represent a view of the world and of the important people in it. Second, since sexuality involves both an interpenetration of bodies and desires, as well as contact with the bodies, boundaries and openings, it is ideally suited to represent longings, conflicts, and negotiations in the relations between self and others. Third, bodily, and especially sexual, experience entails powerful surges that are used to express the dynamics of conflict and interpersonally generated affect.

> Fourth, the very privacy, secrecy, and exclusion in one's experience of one's parent's sexuality make it perfectly designed to take on meanings concerning a division of interpersonal realms, the accessible vs. the inaccessible, the visible vs. the shadowy, surface vs. depth. Sexuality takes on all the intensity of passionate struggles to make contact, to engage, to overcome isolation and exclusion.
>
> (p. 103)

The meaning and function of the primal scene certainly concerns sexuality, but it also concerns much more. The primal scene is one of the primary psychic organizers linking narcissism and object relations (Ikonen & Rechardt, 1984). The child wishes to share in and participate in the world of the adults. The child's wish to be included represents both a wish for relationship with the parents (an object-relational need) and an attempt to maintain self-esteem (a narcissistic need). It is both a narcissistic injury to be excluded from the couple's activities and a relational deprivation in being cast out of the parents' interaction. If the primal scene phantasies are worked through in the context of a supportive family environment, then the primal scene does not inevitably have to be pathological or traumatic. Rather, the primal scene serves as an internal structure regulating both narcissism and object relations. As long ago as 1928, Margaret Mead suggested that even repeated primal scene exposure, under certain cultural conditions, might foster sexual and social development in the context of that culture. Analysts have generally rejected this idea, however, and at most they have conceded that an individual might master the primal scene trauma, thus making some "use of adversity" (Blum, 1979). I suggest that we think of reactions to the primal scene as varying from the more malignant to the more benign.

In the classical psychoanalytic tradition, the primal scene is thought of as "the quintessential oedipal drama" (Blum, 1979, p. 30), although the child may regressively experience the primal scene along preoedipal lines. Therefore, the primal scene is thought of as involving three people: the mother, the father, and the child in an interaction of three whole objects, and it is thought to involve genital sexuality. In contrast, for Klein (1928) the oedipal situation begins in relation to part-objects and its content is pregenital. In this way Kleinian theory relates oedipal issues and whole-object relations to pregenital issues and to part-object relations. Klein's concept of the combined parent figure (too often neglected in the US) serves a transitional function emphasizing the continual interaction of oedipal and preoedipal issues, whole-object and part-object relations, and movements between the paranoid-schizoid and depressive positions. While borrowing heavily from Klein, I recontextualize Kleinian theory by disembedding her clinical ideas from her metapsychology and resetting her concepts into a frame of reference that considers the impact of the personality and character structure of the actual parents, as well as the context of the family system, on the child's development.

The combined parent figure

In her description of infantile anxiety situations, Klein (1929) concluded that the earliest anxiety situation of all referred to the consequences of the child's sadistic attacks on the mother's body, which implied a struggle with father's penis, thought to be inside the mother. This led to the fear of retaliation by the "united parents" (p. 213), who are seen as "extremely cruel and much dreaded assailants." Klein suggested that the boy's later (oedipal) fear of castration by father is a modification of this earlier and more basic fear.

One of an infant's most profound experiences is the wish to penetrate the mother's body, to explore it, to take possession of the contents, and then to destroy the contents out of anger, frustration, and jealousy. These phantasies lead to the terror that the mother and the objects contained inside of her will retaliate. The phantasy of the combined parent figure is that the parent's sexual organs are locked together permanently in violent sexual intercourse. This is the earliest and most primitive version of the primal scene and of the oedipal situation. When frustrated, the infant feels that the father and mother enjoy all the desired pleasurable objects the infant feels deprived of. The intercourse is viewed in pregenital terms, as a constant sharing of good foods and good feces; an "everlasting mutual gratification of an oral, anal and genital nature" (Klein, 1952a, p. 55).

Thus, the child's phantasy of the primal scene comes to include the notion that the parents are involved in ongoing feeding, beating, cutting up, biting to pieces, messing each other, and controlling each other, as well as genital phantasies of penetrating, cutting, caring for, and protecting each other (Klein, 1927; see also Hinshelwood, 1989). Because of the continual operation of internalization, the infant establishes the combined parent figure inside of himself or herself. The combined parent figure may be symbolized by the young child as a monster, "the beast with two backs," and it is this terrifying figure which forms the core of children's fears of monsters, nightmares, and other terrifying delusions of persecution (Segal, 1964).

In her more mature papers, Klein (1957) emphasized that the strength of the combined parent figure was determined in large measure by the intensity of envy. In severe psychopathology, such as the psychoses, the inability to disentangle the relation of the father from the relation to the mother, owing to the intensity of the envy, plays an important role in generating confusional states. [3]In pathology, the combined parent figure operates in a way that is detrimental to both object relations and sexual development. In contrast, in healthy development, the imago of the combined parent figure loses strength; there is a more realistic relation to the parents, who are now seen as separate whole objects related to each other in a happy way (Klein, 1952a). Even after the parents are more fully differentiated, however, jealousy and envy may lead the child to regress to the image of the combined parent figure as a defense. In this case, the combined parent figure serves to deny the relationship between the parents as separate individuals and also to deny the recognition of sexual intercourse (Segal, 1964).

Klein (1952b) suggested that in the transference the analyst comes to represent not only each parent individually and parts of each parent (part-objects), but also both parents combined as one figure. I believe that this observation is of great significance in the clinical situation and that its consequences have not yet been sufficiently explored.

In outlining a theory of thinking, Bion (1962a, 1962b) described how conceptions are born as a result of the mating or satisfying conjunction of preconceptions and realizations. In this lies the basis for the Kleinian view that thinking is modeled on sexual intercourse. Meltzer (1973) extended Bion's approach by describing creativity as a function of the further mating between previously formed conceptions. The personality is structured on the basis of the internalization of the parents in sexual intercourse. These internal copulating parents provide a sense of Godlike omnipotence, from which emerges the inspiration for constructive and creative activity. According to Meltzer, one of the essential developments of the depressive position is that the primitive part-object combined parent figure is reconstructed along more realistic lines in terms of whole objects of mother and father. Meltzer emphasizes that the reconstituted combined internal object becomes the basis for personal creativity. Creativity, in the realms of sexuality, the intellect, or aesthetics, is the product of identification with the internal whole-object parents in pleasurable and restorative sexual intercourse.

Meltzer's point is a radical one because for Klein the emphasis was always on the combined parent figure as frightening and dangerous. Meltzer's contribution expands on the idea, only hinted at by Klein (1952a, p. 79n), that the combined parent figure gradually develops and matures. For Meltzer, it evolves in the mind to encompass whole objects; it is not seen as dangerous and destructive but, rather, as a model of a productive interaction.

Although he does not directly refer to Klein's notion of the combined parent figure, Ogden (1989) has elaborated a point of view regarding the primal scene that is based on Kleinian theory. Ogden proposes that primal scene phantasies do not simply express the highly charged sexual and aggressive aspects of parental intercourse. Rather, primal scene phantasies are pivotal organizers of internal and external object relations. Ogden proposes a developmental line of primal scene phantasy in which there are early preoedipal phantasies of part-objects engaged in mysterious sexuality intermingled with battle and violence. For Ogden, these primitive primal scene phantasies operate in the paranoid-schizoid mode, and therefore the observing child has no reflective awareness. The child is caught up in the scene but has little sense of being removed from it. The child in this mode is unable to see himself or herself as the author or interpreter of his or her own experience, and therefore thoughts and feelings seem just to happen to the child, with symbols being experienced concretely.

Ogden contrasts this early and primitive version of the primal scene (which I believe is equivalent to Klein's concept of the combined parent figure) with the developmentally later and more differentiated version of the primal scene. The latter occurs in the context of the depressive position. In this mode, the child is aware of herself or himself as a separate subject in interaction with whole and external objects. The achievement of whole-object relations, and the concomitant establishment of the individual's subjectivity, allows for the experience of the primal scene on the oedipal level. Now the child is an interpreting subject in a world of whole objects (separate persons with their own subjectivities); the child can form identifications with each parent and also take each parent as a love object. In the depressive mode, the child can maintain awareness of his or her own subjectivity and of the separateness of the other; he or she maintains a symbolic relation with the primal scene and is therefore not threatened with merger and the loss of identity.

I am suggesting, then, that the phantasies that constitute the combined parent figures become transformed as the child develops the capacity for whole-object relations and establishes a separate sense of self with the capacity for symbolization. In other words, as children move from functioning predominantly in the paranoid-schizoid mode to functioning predominantly in the depressive mode, the internal imago of the combined parent figure becomes transformed into the image of their parents as separate whole objects in a mutually gratifying interaction with each other. Now, with a sense of themselves as separate and with the capacity for symbolic thought, children can elaborate that group of phantasies which constitutes the primal scene. Insofar as the child is further along in psychosexual development, the primal scene takes on a more predominantly phallic-oedipal cast. Inasmuch as it is a transformation of earlier preoedipal phantasies, it will, however, forever be subject to interpretation along preoedipal lines. The combined parent figure represents a fusion of elements whose qualities are not clearly distinguished and whose union produces a sense of chaos (Britton, 1989). The combined parent figure is a symbol, a symbolic equation (Segal, 1957), that functions in the paranoid-schizoid mode. With the working through of the depressive position, there is a differentiation of the elements that make up the combined parent figure. The parents emerge as whole, separate people and are appreciated as separate centers of subjectivity. It is in this context that the primal scene proper develops, and in this context, the primal scene represents the integration of previously inchoate aspects of the parents in some meaningful interaction with each other and in relation to the self. There is, then, a sequence, following the orthogenetic principle of development (Werner, 1957) from relative lack of differentiation or fusion to increasing differentiation, articulation, and hierarchic integration.

Following Ogden's (1986, 1989) extension of Kleinian theory (especially as elaborated by Bion), I, however, view both the paranoid-schizoid and depressive modes each as being enduring and fundamental components of all psychological states. This is to say that the development of mind is not simply linear. Klein's positions, unlike stages, are not developmental phases, but "synchronic dimensions of experience" (Ogden, 1989) or, as Ghent (1992) has put it, "paradoxical dimensions of experience." From this perspective, one never renounces, gives up, or abandons old positions (see Aron, 1991a). Instead, there is a continual movement back and forth between the two positions, a "dialectical interplay of synchronic modes" (Ogden, 1989, p. 18). Similarly, it is not as if the primal scene, with the implication of separate whole-object relations and an observing subject, replaces the earlier combined parent figure, with its implication of fused or undifferentiated object relations. Rather, both the combined parent figure and the primal scene continue to operate synchronically as crucial dimensions of experience. Recent developmental research and theory (e.g., Stern, 1985) suggests that infants have some sense of self and other much earlier than was previously thought. Therefore, there are problems with positing relations with part-objects as earlier than relations with whole objects. Instead of viewing the move from the combined parent figure to the primal scene as a progressive developmental sequence, it makes more sense to view them as two alternate phantasy systems, each of which has versions ranging from the more primitive to the more mature. The dialectical relationship between the paranoid-schizoid and depressive positions serves as a theoretical framework to highlight the necessity of maintaining a view of the person as both unified and multiple, stable and in flux, identical and different.

The internalization of the primal scene is central psychologically in that it regulates self and object relations as well as relations between our phantasies of masculine and feminine selves. However, it also requires, and enhances, the capacity to tolerate feelings of omnipotence and grandiosity. For what could be more grandiose than the notion that one can both be and love both genders? Furthermore, containing the primal scene requires the capacity to tolerate the manic excitement, chaos, and confusion of the highly charged scene, without attacking the parental imagoes or splitting them apart. One implication of this is that in order to hold two contrasting ideas in mind at once, to sustain the contradiction, ambiguity, and paradox that is necessary for the creative process and for higher level conceptualization, people need to be able to tolerate and even enjoy their own grandiosity, omnipotence, and manic excitement without, of course, being carried away with these beliefs to the point of actual conviction.

I have one strong reservation regarding this formulation. Suggesting that the origins of thought and creativity can be traced back to an internalized model of the primal scene is appealing, for it suggests a phantasy that underlies sexuality both as procreation and as creativity. Creativity, however, has many other developmental sources and equally suitable metaphors. Bion's (1962a, 1962b) focus on satisfying conjunctions giving birth to conceptions and Meltzer's (1973) explanation of creativity as based on the model of sexual intercourse places heterosexual intercourse in too privileged a position. The Kleinian notion of the combined parent figure is useful precisely because it does not privilege heterosexual intercourse but rather allows for, and even suggests, all sorts of sexual and aggressive arrangements: heterosexual and homosexual combinations and also nongenital sexuality. Within the metaphor of the combined parent figure, the child has not yet sorted out the idea that fathers are men and have penises and mothers are women and have vaginas, and therefore the phantasies that constitute the combined parent figure are not exclusively heterosexual or genital. Thus, this is a better model to use as a basis for creativity and thought than the traditional primal scene. The danger in using only the metaphor of the more "mature" primal scene is that it may be taken to refer not to desire but to procreation, and nonprocreative sexuality, including foreplay; oral, anal, and other varieties of intercourse and sexual practice disappear, along with homosexuality, as alternative models of creativity.

The Kleinian tradition has, moreover, used the metaphor of the combined parent figure to highlight the continual importance of aggression in psychic life (and in the clinical situation). It needs to be emphasized that the model suggested here is not a cleaned-up or wholesome version of the primal scene, that is, that parents with a nice healthy relationship produce children with clean, wholesome primal scenes/ideas. As metaphors, the combined parent figure and the primal scene remind us of all kinds of sexuality and not only with whole separate objects but also with part-objects and confused objects. These metaphors evoke the dark side of sexuality—the aggression, the power, the destructiveness—as well as the creativity. The dark side, all varieties of sexuality, power, and aggression, plays a significant role in creativity, which should not be conceptualized as the exclusive result of mature, healthy, clean, procreative heterosexuality.[4] To continue to use the primal scene as a central metaphor in psychoanalytic theory and clinical practice, while benefiting from the advances made in social and critical theory, gender studies, and feminist thought, psychoanalysis needs to stretch and broaden the primal scene concept beyond the privileging of normative heterosexual genitality to include a whole range of pregenital polymorphous sensualities.

In my expanded vision, the primal scene becomes an example of pastiche, in which varying styles, often from different epochs, are combined, although not integrated, with effects that are both shocking and fascinating, encouraging a plurality of perspectives and a fragmentation of experience. Such a pastiche represents "a free-floating, crazy-quilt, collage, hodgepodge patchwork of ideas or views. It includes elements of opposites such as old and new. It denies regularity, logic, or symmetry; it glories in contradiction and confusion" (Rosenau, 1992, p. xiii). This revisioning of the primal scene evokes not so much stable heterosexuality as an unstable, chaotic process and flux, sameness, difference, and multiplicity.

The combined parent figure and the internalization of relations

Relatively little use has been made of Klein's concept of the combined parent figure especially outside the circle of Kleinian analysts, even though the combined parent figure is a particularly important contribution. One implication of the idea of the combined parent figure is that the child internalizes not just the mother or the father but also internalizes a representation of the perceived relationship between the parents: Not only are representations of others formed in the internal world, but also relational configurations between self and other are internalized. Thus, Sutherland (1963), in developing Fairbairn's contributions, posited that the basic representational unit consists of a self-representation, an object representation, and an affective state linking the two. Kernberg (1980) has been at the forefront of developing this approach. However, implied in the notion of the combined parent figure is that it is more than the relationship between self and other that is internalized to form a basic elementary structure of mind. It is not only the self and object that are internalized, but, rather, the individual internalizes the systems of perceived relations among others. This means that the child comes to internalize not only a representation of mother as an individual, and not only the relation between mother and child, but that the child is capable of internalizing the relationship between the mother and the father. This emendation of psychoanalytic theory opens up the possibility that children internalize a complex network of perceived relationships. It implies that individuals internalize structures based on the field of forces by which they are surrounded.

That patterns of relationship, rather than objects per se, are internalized is a view first proposed by R. D. Laing (1972).[5] Although Laing did not acknowledge Klein, one can clearly hear her influence in the following:

> The family as a system is *internalized*.... Parents are internalized as close or apart, together or separate, near or distant, loving, fighting, etc., each other and self. Mother and father may be merged as a sort of fused parental matrix or be broken down into segments that transect the usual personal partitions. Their sexual relation

as envisaged by the child holds a sort of nuclear position in every internal "family".... The family is not an introjected object, but an introjected set of relations.

(pp. 4–6)

My emphasis on the internalization of the primal scene attempts to use the concrete metaphors of psychoanalytic clinical experience as a way of grounding the abstract notion that it is systems of relations that are internalized.

Prior to the oedipal stage, the child lives in a two-person world. The child relates to both the mother and the father and to each of them differently; that is, he or she has a separate and unique relationship with each parent. But the child relates to only one parent at a time, even if alternating from one to the other in momentary glances. It is only with the oedipal stage of triadic object relations that the child perceives that he or she is part of a system of relations that includes a separate relation between the parents from which the child is excluded. In discussing what I am calling the internalized primal scene, Britton (1989) suggests that it creates a "triangular space," which allows for the possibility of being a participant in a relationship and observed by a third person and of being an observer of a relationship between two other people.

> The closure of the oedipal triangle by the recognition of the link joining the parents provides a limiting boundary for the internal world. It creates what I call a "triangular space"—i.e., a space bounded by the three persons of the oedipal situation and all their potential relationships. It includes, therefore, the possibility of being a participant in a relationship and observed by a third person as well as being an observer of a relationship between two people.
>
> (p. 86)

The Oedipus complex entails not just the child's viewing the parental relationship as an excluded outsider; it entails the myriad phantasies of the child in which the entire system of family relations is experimented with and internalized. The little boy or girl is at one moment the small, excluded child barred from the gratifications of adult sexuality, at another moment is the phantasied rival of the father for mother's love, and at the next moment loves father and seeks a separate, private, and exclusive relationship with him. The child alternates between seeing himself or herself as outside of a two-person relationship as the observer, or as inside a two-person relation being observed by a third. Thus, it is in the oedipal stage that the child first alternates between observation and participation. This fact is clinically important because the oscillating function becomes the basis on which a person can participate in an analysis.

I believe that the internalization of the primal scene and the creation of an internal "triangular space" is the basis for the integration of the sense of self as both a subject and an object (see Bach, 1985) and therefore for the development of intersubjectivity. In a simple version of the Oedipus complex, the focus is on the child's desire in relation to one parent and the child's anger and fear in relation to the other parent; thus, the parents are the objects of the child's subjectivity. In the full development of the Oedipus complex and particularly in the drama of the primal scene, however, the focus shifts to the mutual desire of the parents for each other and the child's feelings of exclusion from their intersubjective dyad (see Kaplan, 1991, p. 62). Thus, in conceptualizing the later development of the primal scene, there is an assumed capacity for intersubjectivity, and the internalization of the primal scene facilitates this evolving capacity on increasingly higher levels.

From the standpoint of the development of intersubjectivity, it is critical that, in reversing the configurations of the oedipal triangle, the child comes to identify the self-as-subject with the self-as-object and to identify the other-as-subject with the other-as-object. Children are confronted with a multitude of tasks around establishing self and object constancy. They need to establish a sense of self as a center for action and thought, and they need to view this self in the context of other selves as an object among other objects (Bach, 1985). Similarly, they need to establish a sense of the other as a separate center of subjectivity as well as a view of the other as the object of their own subjectivity (Benjamin, 1988). These developments are of central importance to psychoanalysts since the analytic process consists of introspection and reflective self-awareness as well as of awareness of the self's interpersonal relations. Thus, a person needs to develop a cohesive sense of self as a subjective-self, a separate center of subjectivity; of self-as-agent, an experiencing ego. And the person needs to be aware of, and be able to reflect on, himself or herself as an object of his or her own investigation and of himself or herself as an object of the wishes and intentions of others. These dimensions of self need to be integrated and yet multiple; there should be a sense of both identity and multiplicity. If an analysand has not achieved and integrated these distinct senses of self, for example in the "narcissistic neuroses," the goal of analysis becomes to help the analysands achieve them. A dramatic example of the failure to develop this integration is provided by Guntrip (1969), who tells of a schizoid woman who would punch herself, thus reenacting the beatings of her mother. When Guntrip said to her that she must feel terrified being hit like that, she stopped and stared and said, "I'm not being hit, I'm the one that's doing the hitting" (p. 191).

Guntrip responded to Laing's (cited in Guntrip) criticism that object relations theory should more properly address "persons" rather than "objects" by arguing that actually we might speak of "personal or ego or subject-relations theory" (Guntrip, 1969, p. 388). However, Guntrip argued that, once it is recognized that psychodynamics is the study of persons, egos, or subjects, there still needs to be room in the theory for Buber's (cited in Guntrip) "I-It" relations, for the study of people's relations to themselves and to others as objects as well as subjects. As psychoanalytic theorists, we need to maintain a balance or tension between studying people's experiences of themselves and studying their experiences of others as subjects and as objects (as functioning in both the paranoid-schizoid and depressive positions) rather than collapsing our theory toward one or the other.

I am suggesting that it is in the primal scene that the child learns to integrate both himself or herself and the other as simultaneously both subject and object. The development of intersubjectivity should not be seen as an early or exclusively preoedipal development, for example, one tied to the anal-rapproachment subphase, to be studied in isolation from later oedipal issues. Rather, I am suggesting that the establishment of subjectivity and of intersubjectivity continues to evolve with oedipal development and both facilitate the transformation from the combined parent figure to the primal scene and are, in turn, greatly facilitated by this transformation (see Aron, 1993).

In the move from the paranoid-schizoid position to the depressive position, a person integrates a sense of himself or herself and of the other as both subject and object. It is only then that the person can envision both parents as two whole, separate people, each with his or her own subjectivity and objectivity, each meaningfully related to the other in ways that exclude the child, and each meaningfully related to the child in ways that exclude the other parent. Only then can the child identify with each parent, internalize this complex set of relations, and thus integrate a sense of self as bigendered. With the internalization of the combined parents and the transformation of this imago into the primal scene, which occurs with the shift from the paranoid-schizoid to the depressive position, the individual consolidates a sense of self as bigendered, a self that is constituted by different, opposing, and contradictory self-representations, all of which exist in dynamic interaction with each other. When we say that the primal scene is traumatic, we mean that this consolidation of one's subjectivity with one's objectivity has been disrupted, that is, that one's cohesive sense of self has become unbound. Conversely, trauma may leave someone rigidly identified with a single sense of self, an identity that is incapable of change and flexibility. Trauma disrupts the capacity to maintain an ongoing dialectic between one's identity and one's multiplicity, including one's gendered identity and one's multigendered multiplicity. This view highlights the ways in which the paranoid-schizoid position and the depressive position each continue to exert a constructive force on mental life. The paranoid-schizoid position contributes the capacity that we each should have for multiplicity, difference, and discontinuity, while the depressive position contributes the capacity for integration and identity. Both are critical for development.[6]

We have come to see how a contemporary psychoanalytic theory needs to contain contradiction and respect paradox in addressing issues of oedipal and preoedipal stages, part-objects and whole objects, paranoid-schizoid modes and depressive modes, intrapsychic and intersubjective realms, phantasies of masculine and feminine selves, a sense of self and other, each viewed as both subject and as object. Psychoanalytic theory and practice needs to avoid the dual errors, first, of condensing these realms or collapsing them one into another so that only one aspect is highlighted. This is the error of premature synthesis, which is modeled on the combined parent figure, which collapses what should be two distinct elements. It needs to avoid the other error of splitting off contradictions and ambiguities, separating them from each other so that they are thought to apply to different developmental stages or different diagnostic groups. This error is modeled on attacks on the primal scene, which attempt to separate the parents and keep them apart, away from interacting with each other.

Fusion, splitting, and integration of gender in relation to the analyst

The relevance of the internalized primal scene for the clinical psychoanalytic situation was anticipated early on by Harold Searles (1966–1967), who wrote that

> the acceptance of the parents-in-intercourse marks an unprecedently deep integration of the young person's identifications with his father on the one hand and with his mother on the other hand. This landmark in identity development is seen in projected form, in the context of the developing transference relationship in analysis, in those rare but deeply significant instances when the patient reacts to the analyst as being both parents simultaneously, engaged in sexual intercourse with one another.
>
> (p. 59)

An analyst may be experienced in the transference as a combined parent figure or as representing both parents in the primal scene. Therefore, much of the analytic interaction may be viewed as representing attacks on the combined parents as represented by the analyst.

Attacks on the analyst's mind and body, and especially the splitting of the analyst's gender into male and female components, is engaged in by patients and by analysts alike and is even embodied in our theories and metapsychologies. O'Shaughnessy (1989) has described this form of splitting, which she refers to as "fracturing," as representing an attack on the heterosexual properties of the parental couple. It is only by integrating or tolerating the multiplicity of all of the split-off parts of ourselves, both in practice and in our theoretical constructions, specifically those elements that we fantasize to be male and female, that we can function effectively and creatively as psychoanalysts. This requires both patient and analyst to function on the basis of an internalized primal scene. The primal scene symbolizes two contrasting ideas that can be held together in the mind, can interact with each other, and do not become fused, on one hand (as in the combined parent figure), or split apart or fractured, on the other.

According to the Kleinian theory of part-object functions, at the deepest levels of the mind the infant experiences each of the mother's functions as if performed by separate objects. Thus feeding, cleaning, and holding give rise to the experience of separate part-object: the holding mother, the feeding mother, and so on. So, too, in the relation to the analyst, on the deepest and most unconscious levels the patient regards each separate function of the analyst as a concretely separate part-object analyst. There may be a feeding-breast analyst, an evacuating-breast analyst, a fecal-penis penetrating analyst, and so forth (Meltzer, 1973). These various part objects are seen as combined and integrated into one whole person in the depressive mode but as either split apart or fused in the paranoid-schizoid mode.

Thus (as described by Hinshelwood, 1989, p. 65), the analyst may be experienced by the patient as empathic; and yet another aspect of the analyst, for example, a more firm and penetrating side, may be split off and projected onto others or it may be introjected and identified with (Lipton, 1977). A patient may describe experiencing me as warm and supportive during a particular session but at that same moment feel that I am not capable of helping him or her because I am not smart enough or insightful enough. Frequently, such split aspects of the analyst's mind are experienced in gender terms, as male or female aspects of the analyst, and are equated with maternal and paternal aspects of the analyst, which the patient then needs to keep separate. Integrating these parts of the analyst's mind may be resisted and fiercely attacked by the patient and by the analyst as well. Conversely, a feeling and intuitive side of the analyst may be felt to be missing if the analyst is seen as functioning through his or her intellect. That side may be projected into someone else whom the patient talks about, in which case it emerges in the patient's associations through projection and displacement; or the patient may attribute the feminine aspects to him or herself through identification (Lipton, 1977). In this case, the patient may see himself or herself as being more sensitive and emotional, while the analyst is experienced as cold and intellectualized.

The associative material exposes the use of identification and introjective mechanisms subsequent to the initial splitting of the analyst.

One way of viewing these common clinical events is to understand them as enacting attacks on the primal scene in which the two sides of the analyst have come to represent the two parents. The patient cannot tolerate the parents' functioning together as a couple and so attacks the symbolic parental intercourse. A more confusing situation arises when, instead of splitting the two aspects of the analyst and keeping them apart, the patient defensively fuses the disparate analytic functions. This fusion, modeled on the combined parent figure, results in frightening confusional states and a paranoid mistrust of the analyst. For example, at these times the patient may see the analyst as persecuting and loving simultaneously, not in rapid oscillation as in some forms of splitting. During moments of the clinical encounter in which this has occurred, I have understood the usefulness or affirmative aspects of splitting, which provides order and controls chaos until such time as integration is possible.

Contemporary analysts understand that a transference is never simply a "mother transference" or simply a "father transference" but always is overdetermined and multilayered. Inasmuch as the patient experiences the analyst as containing both maternal and paternal objects, the patient may become interested in the analyst's internal conflicts.

Consider the following two-part scenario. In the first, the patient realizes that our time is almost up and that shortly we will have to stop. He says to me, "Of course, you will end right on time, you always do. That's because you always follow the rules. You do whatever he says [pointing to a picture of Freud hanging on my office wall]. You are more concerned with the rules than you are with me." On another occasion, this patient struggled with the sense of obligation he felt to say everything that came to his mind. He again pointed to the Freud portrait and said, "He said so," implying that Freud had ordered this harsh requirement. My sense was that I was being experienced as less demanding and more permissive. In this instance, my patient split his image of me in two. One side was identified with me, and the other was split off and projected onto Freud.

In the first scenario, I end the session because I love Freud and my profession, psychoanalysis, more than I love my patient and so am ending the session on time because I love someone else more than I love him. Here, what might be viewed on a preoedipal level as a conflict between the patient and me about whether I would be seen as frustrating or gratifying was transformed into an oedipal scenario in which the conflict was between three of us: my patient, me, and Freud (or my profession). My patient experienced himself as excluded from my marriage to my profession, which he experienced concretely as my relationship with an internal object, Freud. Now, let me add that I do not dismiss all of this as my patient's projection or displacement of internal conflict onto me. I do have a strong love for and commitment to my profession, which is connected for me with Freud; and my patient also correctly observes that I am committed to certain structures of the treatment that transcend his individual, momentary needs, although, clearly, I hope that they meet his needs in the long run. Each analyst has a different relationship with Freud, with his or her profession, and each analyst has a different internal relationship to structures, rules, and procedures. The patient does not merely project in a vacuum but also responds to who the analyst is as a person and to the analyst's internal relations.

In the second scenario, the patient is more clear about his sense of my being in conflict. He has moved a bit closer to articulating his sense that my professional marriage is in trouble. Here he says that it is Freud who is stern and harsh and requires him to say everything. I am really more understanding and would be more permissive if I could. So, if he pushes hard enough, maybe he can get me to relax the rules, break with my passive submission to my lover, and side with my patient. Does he believe that I am in some conflict about requiring him to say everything? In fact I am. Although I do not tell my patients that I require them to say everything that comes to mind, I do nevertheless expect them to do just that to whatever degree they can. That is, I do not evoke the fundamental rule in the traditional authoritarian manner, but I do work with patients to free associate. This is an area of some conflict for me as it seems to be for many contemporary analysts (see Lichtenberg & Galler, 1987). My patient, once again, is not projecting onto a blank screen. When he says to me, "He [Freud] says so," he is accurate that Freud, not I, said so. He has accurately picked up on something that I feel conflicted about.

One can see in this vignette how my patient sees me as united with my lover against him; we act in concert to exclude him. Or do we? Am I not really the good parent, who does not really want to abandon him at the end of the session or force him to speak? Is it not only because of my love for someone else that I betray him? And perhaps it is a particular type of love, a "passive-homosexual-love" (to use, for the moment, a classical, but highly problematic, category). Could it be that my patient experiences me as a wimp who submits passively to my lover's greater strength and authority? What does he imagine about my relationship with my spouse? What has he observed about me so far in the analysis that may give him clues about my relationships and my tendency to be bossed around or to submit? Indeed, he has picked up on one area where I have not submitted to Freud but where I have remained in some conflict. I believe that patients often do pick up on areas of conflict in the analyst. Patients are highly motivated to penetrate the analyst's inner world, and in doing so, they especially are likely to be sensitive to the analyst's conflicts. This is a critical area of analytic inquiry inasmuch as it opens the door to the patient's experience of the analyst's subjectivity (Aron, 1991b, 1992b) and offers an entrance to memories of the patient's experience of the parents' inner worlds or character structures. Furthermore, because the analyst represents both mother and father, the analysis of the patient's experience of the analyst's subjectivity also provides a window on the patient's experience of the relation between the parents, especially where they were in conflict.

When the patient alludes to my marriage to my profession, should I assume that it is a heterosexual marriage? Since my patient has referred to my love and commitment to Freud, should I suspect that he has the phantasy that my love is homosexual? We should not be too quick to conclude that in the transference the analyst is either the mother or the father, male or female. Am I the permissive mother, who submits to the cruel father? Am I the gentle aspect of the mother submitting to a strict aspect of the mother, who is identified with her own father (or mother)? Am I the father submitting to his own internal father (or mother)? In my own "unconscious phantasy" do I not view my profession as both masculine and feminine, male and female, in whatever sense I personally give to masculinity and femininity? And do I not experience myself as both masculine and feminine, and, therefore, inasmuch as I love my profession, is not that love bisexual?

In a classic and wonderfully imaginative paper on the analytic situation, Lewin (1955) suggested that the couch is connected with sleep and its maternal implications and that the analyst is at times experienced as the preoedipal father, who, with his loud-noised interpretations, wakes the patient from his sleep at mother's breast. When the analyst ends the session, he (even if "he" is "she") is the father who is forcefully waking the patient from sleep with mother (couch). For Lewin, however, the analyst both induces sleep through the couch and the free association method that encourages regression and wakes the patient up through transference interpretations. Each transference interpretation says, "Wake up, stop dreaming. I'm not your mother!" Here is another example in which the analyst is split along the lines of gender, with one side being identified with the analyst as a person and the other with the analytic situation (the couch). Bollas (1987) made a similar point when he suggested that the couch provides a "cot-like" (p. 258) experience that, when oedipal issues are active, can allow a patient to feel that he or she is "being held by the mother whilst talking to the father about being his child" (p. 259).

We can see here how helpful it is that the patient can split the analyst in this way. Imagine how terrifying and confusing it would be if the patient could not do this. The patient would experience the analyst as simultaneously trying to put him or her to sleep and trying to wake him or her up. The effect might be comparable (using Lewin's analogy of psychoanalysis and anesthesia) to an overdose of amphetamines and barbiturates taken together. The combined parent figure would be a terrifying one, with the patient feeling split apart. Splitting, however, allows the patient to organize his or her experience so that it is coherent, although simplified. Ultimately, the patient can move beyond splitting and recognize that it is indeed the analyst who is encouraging both sleep and wakefulness, regression and progression. In the vignette just described, splitting was constructive and progressive in that my patient was able to organize his experience of me as both frustrating and gratifying without its leading to his being confused or disorganized. Of course, it is also defensive in that it simplifies his experience of me at a time when he could not tolerate ambivalence.

In addition, Lewin gives fixed meaning to certain symbols. Thus, the couch is equated with sleep, and sleep is equated with the mother. It should be clearer today than it was when Lewin wrote that fathers also put children to sleep and that mothers also wake them up. While there may still be a strong trend to connect sleep with the mother, this is because women still mother (Chodorow, 1978; Dinnerstein, 1976). It would not necessarily be this way if parenting were shared or, for example, in a family constituted by two male homosexual parents. My point, again, is that we cannot be too quick to assume fixed essential meanings connected with male and female, masculine and feminine, or maternal and paternal.

I want to emphasize that it is not only the patient who may fracture the analyst along gender lines; analysts are prone to splitting in this way as well, and patient and analyst may easily miss these dynamic interactions because of their mutual difficulties. It is not that patients fracture the analyst simply along gender lines but that patient and analyst co-participate (Wolstein, 1981) in constructing these transference-countertransference integrations.

Most commonly, the splitting of gender is followed by primitive idealization of one object and denigration, devaluation, and contempt of the other, and these positive and negative evaluations may or may not remain stable. For example, at one moment, the analyst's penetrating qualities may be admired and idealized. The patient feels that the analyst has "the tools" to break through his or her resistances and "uncover" the patient's secrets and "expose" the patient's weaknesses. At these times, the patient may devalue and ridicule anyone who is regarded as maternal, more understanding or empathic. The patient may dismiss a more understanding person as someone "who just takes a lot of crap" and who does not have the strength to stand up to abuse. This is the devaluation of what the Kleinians have called the "toilet-breast analyst." At other times, the patient may be contemptuous of the phallic qualities of the analyst. The patient may express that the interpretations are worthless, irrelevant, or disgusting and that they reflect the analyst's own dirty mind. The analyst is seen as the devalued, denigrated, paternal fecal-phallus. At these times the patient may admire a friend who seems to have an analyst who is understanding, nurturant, empathic, and warm. The feeding-breast analyst at these times is idealized and longed for. My point is that to arbitrarily link a particular trait with one gender is to engage in a form of splitting. To believe that empathizing is feminine or that to be intellectually penetrating is masculine is to split off each of our complex and multiple capacities. Terms like "toilet-breast analyst" or "phallic-penetrating interpretations" should be used only to capture metaphorically the way in which certain functions are experienced unconsciously; they should not be taken to imply that we believe that these functions are intrinsically male or female.

Consider the way in which the dichotomy thought–affect is linked to male–female. The common isolation of thought and affect in patients can be thought of as a form of fracturing in which thought, which is often associated in our culture with masculinity, is kept separate from affect, which is more often connected to femininity. From this perspective, a typical obsessional defense is seen not simply as a psychic deficit, but also as an active keeping apart of mother and father because of the danger represented by their intercourse. Schafer (1983) illustrates this by describing a patient who, by keeping his thoughts and feelings apart, was unconsciously keeping his parents apart and saving himself "from the extreme violence of a primal scene involving parents at war with one another in the bedroom" (p. 201). In addition, Schafer points out that transference and resistance may be usefully viewed as enactments of primal scene voyeurism and exhibitionism (p. 230). In my view, patient and analyst coparticipating in the transference-countertransference, resistance–counterresistance interactions may each alternate in identifications with the two parent imagoes. I need to stress, though, that it is not analytic theory (or at least it should not be) that claims that thinking is male and feeling is female; rather, in our culture this is a common conscious and unconscious belief, which itself needs to be subject to analysis.

A clinical vignette that illustrates how obsessional defenses can also be seen in terms of the primal scene concerns a male patient who was involved in a relationship with a woman who was herself plagued with severe obsessive-compulsive symptoms. The patient's parents had fought with each other violently, and he was exposed to violent and sexual scenes throughout childhood. He saw his father as an angry and sadistic man who would demean and humiliate him. His father taught him about sex by taking out his own penis and showing his preadolescent son what an erection was. He viewed his mother as good natured but weak and unable to stand up to her husband to protect herself or her son. The patient saw his girlfriend as his mother and his father combined. She was seen as the sweet and innocent victim of her obsessive-compulsive illness. The "illness" was viewed as the enemy, harsh, and brutalizing, while she was viewed as the pathetic victim. At times the patient would literally become terrified of the girlfriend when she seemed out of control of her symptoms, for example, when she attempted to keep certain items from touching other items in their house. She seemed to him at these moments like a monster, running wildly and furiously around the house. He would describe her at these moments as "fucking crazy," and in the analysis, it seemed useful to depict his view of her at these times in terms and images of her enacting a rageful primal scene.

The very act of thinking may take on the meaning of intercourse, since thinking requires the bringing together of different ideas in mind. Britton (1989) provides a wonderful example. A patient of his who could not tolerate any attempt on his part to use his analytic function shouted, "Stop that fucking thinking!" For this patient, the analyst's thinking was experienced as a form of internal intercourse that corresponded to parental intercourse, which she experienced as threatening her very existence. Similarly, Feldman (1989) observed that, with the working through of the Oedipus complex, the patient internalizes a model of intercourse (an internal primal scene) that is experienced as a creative activity. When the healthy, creative, and loving aspects of the primal scene outweigh its aggressive, hateful, and frightening dimensions, and when this is internalized as a structure, this serves as a model of identification for allowing thoughts and ideas, as well as thoughts and feelings, to interact in a kind of healthy, fruitful, and creative intercourse. I repeat my earlier statement that the combined parent figure and the primal scene both continue to operate synchronically and that creativity may emerge on the basis of homosexual as well as heterosexual primal scenes and may be inspired by pregenital and aggressive sexuality and by genital and oedipal sexual imagery. The frightening, aggressive, and hateful dimensions of the primal scene are essential to many creative productions.

Another example of the way in which a person's male and female identifications may be split is presented by McLaughlin (1987). In noting patients' body, hand, and foot positions on the couch during the course of analyses, McLaughlin reported that typically patients link their right hands and arms to spoken content relating to themselves as doers or agents, to father, and to masculinity, assertiveness, and dominance; and they link their left hands and arms to content connected to mother, femaleness, homosexuality, and themselves as passive recipients. In one patient, whom McLaughlin observed carefully, this gradual splitting of body movements, in which the patient moved one hand while speaking of mother and the other hand while speaking of father, gradually changed. As the patient became more comfortable blending his identifications with both parents, he began to move his hands in a more back-and-forth hand interplay. I would speculate that the back-and-forth hand movements were connected to the working through of primal-scene material. This illustration underscores just how deeply entrenched the splitting of gender may be in our minds as well as in our bodies.

Psychoanalytic schools and the splitting of gender

In the history of psychoanalysis there has been a significant shift in the functions and attributes assigned the analyst, and this shift has taken place along the lines of gender. In its early days, psychoanalysis portrayed the analyst's functioning in the image of the phallus. The analyst was thought of as the fearless and adventurous male who seeks to uncover, expose, and penetrate the feminine "unconscious." The analyst needs to be sharp and insightful, brave and intrepid, fearless in "his" "pursuit" of the unconscious. The male, phallic quality of the analyst's functioning was captured in Isakower's (1963) well-known metaphor of "the analyzing instrument." Although Isakower did not intend his meaning, the idea of the analyst functioning as a penetrating, phallic instrument was reinforced by the one-sided emphasis within classical analysis on interpretation, rather than relationship, as the exclusive agent of structural change.

By contrast, must of contemporary psychoanalytic theory uses distinctively feminine imagery in its attempt to capture the functioning of the psychoanalyst. It was first in the writings of Ferenczi (1932) and of Rank (1926) that psychoanalysts were first alerted to the importance of the mother–infant relationship and of the importance of the mother transference. Especially since the work of Melanie Klein and, following her, Winnicott (1971a) in Britain and Kohut (1971) in America, analysts have shifted their gendered metaphors. Analysts now think in terms of "holding environments" and of "mirroring" their patients' affect states; of "containing" their thoughts through maternal-like "reverie" (Bion, 1962a); of being "good-enough analysts" modeled on "good-enough mothers" (Winnicott, 1971a). Instead of thinking of themselves as penetrating, they think of themselves as reflecting. Instead of confronting, they think of empathizing. The imagery has generally shifted from the penetrating phallus to the relational matrix or womb.

Melanie Klein (following Ferenczi and Rank) shifted the focus of the analysis of the transference from that of the patriarchically determined oedipal-father transference to the preoedipal mother transference (Sayers, 1989). Klein increasingly made the maternal transference the central means of treatment, although she continually interpreted the transference in terms of the analyst as good and bad, mother and father. Freud (1931) himself indicated that psychoanalysis would have to wait for female analysts to investigate female sexuality because women would make more "suitable mother-substitutes" (p. 227). Freud himself was uncomfortable being placed in the role of mother in his patients' transferences. He wrote to the poet H. D. (1933), "I do not like to be the mother in the transference, it always surprises and shocks me a little. I feel so very masculine" (pp. 146–147). It is therefore not surprising that Freud would have discovered more about the paternal oedipal transference and that it would have taken the work of later analysts to open up for examination the importance of the maternal. Now that both paternal and maternal transferences have been brought to light, however, contemporary analysts need to have access to their bisexuality—to phantasies of themselves as male and female and to themselves as male and female, with both heterosexual and homosexual desires—access to their own internal mothers and fathers, in order to make optimal use of the analytic process.

Whole schools of psychoanalysis tend to be characterized, by their proponents as well as their opponents, along gender-stereotyped lines. For instance, the ongoing debates between Kernbergians and Kohutians have the quality of contrasts between the paternal and the maternal. To make my point briefly, I will oversimplify. For Kohutian enthusiasts, the maternal, empathic, holding qualities of the analyst are idealized and thought to be curative, whereas they view Kernberg's tough, firm, interpretive, and confrontive approach as unnecessarily aggressive—the angry, phallic-aggressive father. For Kernberg influenced analysts, these same stereotypically male functions are idealized. Thus, they see it as curative to be firm, confronting of primitive defenses, relentless in pursuing the interpretations of the meaning of interpretations. They are likely to disparage the self-psychologists' maternalistic emphasis on reflection, mirroring, holding, and empathy. The extreme polarization of these two approaches represents the outcome of our tendency to split or fracture the interaction between masculinity and femininity. Of course, it is critical to keep in mind that viewing empathy as feminine and viewing assertiveness as masculine is itself a symptom of cultural splitting.

Another example of our tendency to polarize theory along gender lines can be seen in the work of some recent feminist therapists. I am referring to a trend within feminist theorizing arising out of and influenced by Gilligan (1982) and Miller (1987) and developed at The Stone Center, Wellesley College. The orientation being developed has been referred to as "self-in-relation" theory. Miller has highlighted the ways in which women are constituted by qualities of affiliativeness, relatedness, empathy, and nurturance, all of which are devalued in the dominant male culture. There is a tendency among these theorists toward a polarized view of male and female development. The danger here is that psychology can be fractured, split between the masculine and the feminine, such that men are seen as developing a sense of self-in-opposition and women a sense of self-in-relation. It is this splitting that leads Gilligan's and Miller's followers to idealize the "feminine" attributes of nurturance and empathy and to devalue "male" attributes such as agency, assertiveness, and boundedness.[7]

While it may be that, under present social-cultural arrangements in which women mother, girls are destined to be more relational and boys to strive for autonomy (Chodorow, 1978; Dinnerstein, 1976), nevertheless, this does not imply that relatedness is essentially female and autonomy male. As Hare-Mustin (1986) has persuasively argued, it may well be that women's concerns with relationship results from their having less power in our society rather than from any essential psychological difference between men and women. By conflating traits such as autonomy with masculinity and relatedness with femininity, theorists essentialize the differences between the sexes and construe these traits in mutually exclusive terms. By such stereotyping, they simplify human psychology and thus also privilege and essentialize heterosexuality since the two mutually exclusive genders then essentially need each other. In contrast, I am arguing that no trait is essentially, naturally, or specifically male or female but that, under present social and cultural arrangements, they are thought to be so, both consciously and especially unconsciously. Rather than split off aspects of ourselves that according to these dichotomies are gender incongruent, we need to find ways to integrate them or, perhaps better said, to contain these multiplicities within our identities.

Sayers (1991) argues against the exclusively mother-centered trend in post-Freudian psychoanalysis inasmuch as these revisionist theories minimize the ways in which psychic life is shaped by patriarchical authority and sexual difference through the Oedipus complex. She asserts, as I have, that analysts today often experience themselves in maternal terms. I believe that a more complex feminist psychology, such as those proposed by Benjamin (1988, 1991, 1992), Chodorow (1989), Dimen (1991), Goldner (1991), and Harris (1991), considers that the establishment of both autonomy, independence, and agency and relatedness, empathy, and attachment are lifelong problems for men and for women. As psychoanalysts, we need to guard against the ubiquitous temptation to fracture our multigendered self in our clinical work and in our theoretical conceptualizations.

It is tempting to argue, in line with Jung's (1953) early androgyny theory, that we psychoanalysts need to have access to both our masculine and feminine dimensions or qualities, our anima and animus. Chasseguet-Smirgel (1984) has proposed an approach somewhat along these lines. The analyst's maternal dimension forms the background of the analytic work, while the setting of the analysis forms the boundary representing the paternal. The analysis is thus dependent on the analyst's capacity to experience both maternal and paternal identifications. "For it is clear that the analyst's 'maternal aptitude,' his femininity, must also have its limits. Are they not to be found in the analyst's masculinity, in identification with the father, whether the analyst is a man or a woman, which enables the child to cut his tie to his mother and to turn toward reality?" (p. 175). But this argument essentializes the qualities of the masculine and the feminine. Why, for example, is limit-setting assumed to be, and encouraged to be, masculine and paternal? Articulating the goal in terms of androgyny reproduces, reifies, and perpetuates the very gender polarization that contemporary feminists have attempted to critique. The point is not just that individual analysts or analytic theories need access to both masculine and feminine qualities, although as masculine and feminine qualities have been defined by our culture they certainly do, but, rather, that we must throw open to question what we might even mean by either masculine or feminine. Emphasizing that the analyst needs a complementarity between masculine and feminine qualities not only essentializes what is masculine and what is feminine, but in emphasizing the need to conjoin the male and the female it also implies the "naturalness" of heterosexuality (Bem, 1993). Since my focus on the primal scene may be seen as a move in that direction, it is important to keep in mind that I have attempted to reconceptualize and revision the primal scene along the lines of a pastiche or collage with elements of both the heterosexual and the homosexual.

In line with the postmodern emphasis on deconstructing dichotomies, this chapter has emphasized the deconstruction, or, rather, the psychoanalysis, of such polarized concepts as male-female, masculine-feminine, heterosexual-homosexual, father-mother, genital-pregenital, oedipal-preoedipal, identity-multiplicity, paranoid-schizoid depressive position, drive theory-relational theory, and even patient-analyst. Our tendency to split the world in these artificial ways is understandable and, as I have been arguing, is even useful and necessary, for it helps us to organize our experience until such time as we are ready for greater complexity. We cannot, however, afford to get stuck in either-or thinking; rather, we must value both splitting (either-or thinking) and integration (both-and thinking), making room for both identity and multiplicity.

Notes

1 For a fascinating exposition of the Oedipus complex from a relational perspective, see Greenberg (1991).
2 I am indebted to Donald Kaplan for this understanding of the traumatic effect of the primal scene.

3 Not only are the differences between the mother and the father blurred, but envy also leads to attacks on the good object and therefore leads to confusion between the good and bad object and between self and other.
4 Because I am trying to stress the affirmative side of the primal scene, I have not paid enough attention in this essay to what happens when children observe a more destructive relationship between the parents.
5 I am indebted to Virginia Goldner (1991) for highlighting Laing's ideas on the internalization of relational systems.
6 Ultimately, the necessity for and our capacity for unity, integration, cohesiveness or identity, as well as for multiplicity and difference, may be related to Freud's (1940) broadest dual-instinct theory of Eros and Thanatos as forces that bind together and undo connections.
7 This critique of the "self-in-relation" school has developed in collaboration with Jessica Benjamin; see Benjamin (1992).

Chapter 4

God's influence on my psychoanalytic vision and values (2004)

Introduction by Michael Eigen

This is a masterful and caring chapter introducing and exploring the kind of God that informs Dr. Aron's life and practice. Dr. Aron stays close to the God of relationship, an intersubjective, interactive field of being and experience. He nods to and respects the philosopher god of reason, rationality over feeling. Next to Aristotle's god of active reason, intuition, feeling, sensation were second-class citizens to be transcended. But we now sense that reason itself must be transcended for how reason is used is crucial. Affective attitudes inform thinking, and thinking and feeling inform each other, neither superior nor inferior. Rather, how they work together and partner each other is part of our gift and challenge.

Dr. Aron salvages complexities of Freud's attitude toward spiritual experience and begins to share his own sense of our psycho-spiritual beings. His main focus is on relational aspects of the Jewish God, and we gain a deepening sense of a lifelong dialogue he has had with his God: "The author uses his own experience as an example of the subtle ways in which religious ideas may influence psychoanalytic practice." A sense grows as to how many disciplines and capacities can feed and enhance each other rather than give way to mutual depreciation.

This is a chapter filled with relevant scholarship zeroing in on doors and windows that open fuller appreciation of experience. Psychoanalytic science and spirituality meet and partner each other in the center of the author's life. Here is a man who lives and breathes psychoanalysis and lives and breathes the living God in undogmatic search for better and fuller ways to be with each other and with oneself. It is no accident that Dr. Aron was also a musician, loving to play guitar in a way that gave expression to our musical psyche, the psycho-spiritual psyche of psychoanalysis and of life.

I personally have not come upon an author who is supported by and learns from the array of analytic workers he explores together with the range and depth of writers on Judaism and the Jewish God's relationships with humanity, for example, Freud, Fenichel, Hartmann, Beebe, Lachman, Ghent, Ogden, Mitchell together with Buber, Heschel, Rizzuto, Schorsch, Finkelstein, Soloveitchik, Gillman, Talmud, and figures like the Baal Shem Tov and Rabbi Luria. Intertwining becomes seamless and enhancing, while differences enrich.

Dr. Aron emphasizes mutuality in the covenant between God and people, *between* a key word for Buber and Winnicott. Qualities of meeting and failing to meet are part of the core of our lives, a *between* that sanctifies the therapy relationship in immediate, full, and down-to-earth ways.

Here are a few quotes from this chapter for flavor:

> The tradition in which I grew up led me to imagine an ongoing internal experience of conversing with God. Praising, beseeching, thanking, complaining, questioning, challenging, and even arguing with God is simply expected. Prayer presupposes an intimate personal experience with God.
>
> According to the Talmud, if we strive to hallow our lives here on earth, we will be bathed with a burst of holiness from above. Jewish daily liturgy expresses an ongoing theme of reciprocal love and a mutual and dynamic relationship between God and humanity.
>
> What does it mean, what could it possibly mean, to think of a human being as having an intersubjective relationship with God? Is God a subject to be engaged? An interpersonal relationship with God?

Dr. Aron valorizes mutual dependency not as weakness but a strength, part of our way of being together in a caring and mutually enhancing way. God laughs and cries with us, and we laugh and cry with each other. Sacrifice is part of relationship, and it is no accident that it is a ripple of the word *sacred*.

It is part of a challenge that never ends to grow ways to support our experience and make it more productive. Both Kaballah and psychoanalysis are, in part, engaged in repair of what is broken or learning to sustain and work with our broken beings and hearts. Rabbi Nachman says that nothing is more whole than a broken heart, and God's heart is part of it. So often we link with each other in our brokenness and reparative tendencies. We search out how to be with ourselves and others, a creative work endlessly open to further possibilities. We discover rhythms of moving toward-away, opening-closing, and opening again. We discover wellsprings of devotion through which we learn how to live. Dr. Aron writes, "We are partners with God in creation, revelation, and redemption." Repair and discovery, for we not only modulate what is broken but are transformed by the new.

Dr. Aron ends his wonderful confession and exploration with the words, "Psychoanalysis may be envisioned as a religious practice, a form of worship, in which contact is made with the Almighty through immersion in the richness and depth of the inner life and in communion with the Other." A practice that does not end with our lives. Others continue it far into the future.

Dr. Aron sometimes would quote Halevi, a Jewish poet saying, "I go out to meet You and find You coming towards me." Buber wrote, "All real living is meeting." Something worth dwelling with in all its fragments and incompleteness.

Years ago, resonating with aspects of Rebbe Schneerson, I wrote, "The wound that never heals meets the fire that never goes out." And at this moment I think of and feel the spark, the flame, the light that ran through Lew's life, a light many have felt and shared. A shared light that we feel today, this moment. And the next.

Aron, L. (2004). God's influence on my psychoanalytic vision and values.

Psychoanalytic Psychology, 21(3), 442–451.

Freud asserted that psychoanalysis did not necessitate any values other than those of science, which it embraced. Hartmann (1960) recognized that psychoanalysis endorsed "health values." Under the influence of feminism, constructivism, and postmodernism, analysts have become more willing to acknowledge the role of individual and societal values in analytic theory and practice. Despite this relatively recent recognition of the institutional values of psychoanalysis, there has been little talk about the influence of God. Speaking of values is still safer than speaking of religion directly.

The effort to talk openly and directly about religious differences and the implications for psychoanalysis is enormously complicated and filled with a variety of dangers. Years ago, a book about psychoanalysis and money was titled *The Last Taboo* (Krueger, 1986). I think it is more accurate to say that religion generally, and God in particular, have remained taboo among analysts. And feelings about God run strong. Some people, upon hearing of this symposium, have directly confronted me with their outrage. "Why are you bringing God into a professional meeting? If I want to hear about God I can go to my church or synagogue; why bring God into a psychoanalytic forum?"

Religious conflict, repression, and deep fears about religion pervade the history of psychoanalysis. Freud was concerned, even preoccupied, with the "danger" involved in the psychoanalytic movement "becoming a Jewish national affair" (Klein, 1985, p. xviii). Although Peter Gay (1989) may be correct that in many respects Freud was "A Godless Jew," Philip Reiff makes the stronger point that "despite his irreligion," Freud's cultural Jewishness "was more binding than religious orthodoxy" (Gilman, 1993, p. 7). It was Freud's worry that psychoanalysis would be seen as a "Jewish science" that led him to choose a non-Jew, Jung, to lead the movement as his successor. Ironically, Jung would later publicly stress the differences between a Jewish and an Aryan psychology and would privately disparage the "essentially corrosive nature" of Freud and Adler's "Jewish gospel" (p. 223). Can four analysts of different religious traditions or persuasions come together to discuss the impact of God on their psychoanalytic thinking without the discussion degenerating into religious reductionism and hostility?

But religious belief is taboo among psychoanalysts not only because of the psychology of religious, ethnic, and racial differences and its role in psychoanalytic history. It has also resulted from Freud's view of religion as an illusion—I am tempted to say the mother of all illusions, but to stay consistent with Freud's imagery it would be better to say the father of all illusions. Here is a single but poignant illustration: Listen to Otto Fenichel, from his 1939 classic *Problems of Psychoanalytic Technique*, a text that influenced the theory and practice of psychoanalysis for decades, even to our own day:

> It has been said that religious people in analysis remain uninfluenced in their religious philosophies since analysis itself is supposed to be philosophically neutral. I consider this not to be correct. Repeatedly I have seen that with the analysis of the sexual anxieties and with maturing of the personality, the attachment to religion has ended.
>
> (p. 89)

Is it really any wonder that it would have taken until now for analysts to gather together to discuss the impact of their religious backgrounds and to acknowledge the influence of God on their psychoanalytic vision and values? To examine the place of their own "God representations," to use Ana-Mar-'a Rizzuto's (1979) term, as influences in their psychoanalytic thinking and practice?

Freud's Enlightenment ideal of science saw it as liberating the individual from the illusion of religion. Psychoanalysis offered Truth as replacement for regressive fantasy. Religious belief was "a lost cause," a "childhood neurosis" (Freud, 1961b, p. 53), and Freud paid homage only to "Our god Logos—Reason" (p. 54).

But as modern psychoanalytic thinkers and philosophers of science have pointed out, "a more contemporary and nuanced view of science challenges any strict dichotomy between natural science and all other fields, including psychoanalysis and religion" (Jones, quoted in Spezzano & Gargiulo, 1997, p. x). Freud's worship of the god Reason is ironically not supported by the contemporary empirical sciences, which challenge a unitary conception of rationality. Both science and rationality on the one hand and religion and spirituality on the other are more complex and multidimensional than Freud envisioned (Spezzano & Gargiulo, 1997).

Stephen Mitchell's (1993a) presentation of relational psychoanalysis offered a strong critique of the dichotomizations of fantasy and reality, illusion and rationality, religion and science. For him, "What is inspiring about psychoanalysis today is not the renunciation of illusion in the hope of joining a common, progressively realistic knowledge and control, but rather the hope of fashioning a personal reality that feels authentic and enriching" (p. 21). With its goal as the enhancement and revitalization of human experience, and in its primary concern with felt meaning, significance, purpose, and value, the sharp division between religion and psychoanalysis diminishes.

In accord with this shift in our view of science and rationality, our contemporary epistemology gives greater recognition to the subjectivity of the scientist and of the psychoanalyst. Freud was intent to eliminate "the subjective factor" (letter of January 4, 1928, cited in Grubrich-Simitis, 1986, p. 271), as he called it. For psychoanalysis to be an objective science the uniqueness of the individual analyst was not to matter. In its most extreme form this became the doctrine of the interchangeability of the analyst—as long as the analyst was well trained and well analyzed, it shouldn't matter who the analyst is as a person. Sander Gilman (1993) has persuasively demonstrated that Freud's goal was to universalize racist characterizations of Jews such that the scientist-analyst was to observe with a neutral, universal gaze and not with a unique, idiosyncratic, and Jewish one. Medical ideology in Vienna especially stressed the central role of the physician as objective scientist and the neutral role of the scientist-diagnostician.

As we pay greater attention to the subjectivity of the analyst, and to the patient's experience of the analyst's subjectivity, we now expect analysts to attend to their countertransference and to report on their own responsiveness in presenting case material (Aron, 1996c). The analyst's personal experience is now generally taken for granted as relevant analytic data. Our clinical sensibility, across most schools of psychoanalysis, leaves much more room for the analyst as an observing participant (Hirsch & Aron, 1991).

In this chapter, I examine one very specific aspect of my own religious background to illustrate the role that it has played in my own psychoanalytic vision. I discuss only one dimension of my religious experience, but an important one, namely, the nature of my own relationship to and dialogue with God.

Let me emphasize some of what I am *not* doing. I am not suggesting that analysts should or must believe in God, nor am I promoting any particular religious view or claiming that one religious perspective is more closely tied to psychoanalysis. I am simply demonstrating the way in which my relation to God has affected my own values and how these have become a part of my psychoanalytic identity. I assume that other analysts have been shaped and influenced by their own experience with God, and I am suggesting that an examination and comparison of these influences would be productive. And, yes, like Rizzuto (1979), I do assume that all of us form some God representations, whether or not we believe in God. If we are atheists, then there is some particular God or gods that we have chosen to reject. Who this God is that we do not believe in may be just as significant an influence on our values as a God that we choose to worship.

There are many aspects of my Jewish heritage—aside from God—that have influenced my psychoanalytic approach. Many of these have been discussed by others who have examined various aspects of Judaism and psychoanalysis, but these have generally not taken up in any direct way the analyst's personal relation to God. They have focused on a wide range of other topics, such as Freud's Jewish background and identity, the Jewish origins of the psychoanalytic movement, Freud's identification with Moses, Freud's relation to the B'nai Brith, Freud's dream theories and parallels from the Talmud, the psychoanalytic meanings of Jewish rituals, Freud and rabbinic hermeneutics, psychoanalytic interpretation of stories from the Hebrew Bible, psychoanalytic memory and forgetting and Jewish memory and forgetting, Freud as an embodiment of Jewish Viennese emancipatory thinking, Freud as reacting to his father's Haskalah (Jewish Enlightenment) vision, Freud and the Jewish mystical tradition, or Freud's Jewish anxieties. This literature is vast, and I mention these topics just to give a glimpse of the range of subject matters covered. Two recent examples of excellent scholarship are Daniel Rothenberg's (1997) study of psychic space and time in the underlying structure of Judaism and psychoanalysis and Stephen Friedlander's (1997) examination of language and death in these two discourses. But of all of these and many, many more, I would certainly single out, along with Harold Bloom, the subject of psychoanalysis and interpretation. As Bloom (1987) wrote, "Freud's most profound Jewishness, voluntary and involuntary, was his consuming passion for interpretation" (p. 52). As Bakan (1958) persuasively argued, Freud applied to the study of individual behavior the traditional Jewish methodological principle of interpretation in which every letter of the Torah was assumed to be meaningful and subject to multiple understandings. The role of interpretation in Judaism and psychoanalysis can be explored endlessly, and I hope to contribute to this topic at a later date. But in this chapter my area of exploration will have to be more limited. I'm only going to focus on God.

In my own psychoanalytic research, I have given a great deal of attention to an examination of the dimensions of mutuality and symmetry. My book *A Meeting of Minds* (Aron, 1996c) is organized around the theme of the different aspects of mutuality that can be conceptualized between patient and analyst. I explore mutual recognition, mutual regulation, mutual resistances, mutual generation of data, mutual empathy, mutual regression, mutual participation and enactment, mutual construction of interpretation, and so on. Mutuality implies reciprocation, sharing together, community, and unity through interchange. I differentiate mutuality, which emphasizes what patient and analyst have in common or between them, from symmetry, which implies correspondence in form or arrangement. Symmetry implies a degree of similarity and equality. I argue throughout the book that psychoanalysis is best viewed as in many respects mutual but asymmetrical because of the significant differences between patient and analyst in role, function, and responsibility. This contrast between mutuality and asymmetry was not original, but I like to think that my contribution was to sustain a detailed examination of these concepts as they have shaped contemporary psychoanalytic thinking and practice.

During the time that I worked on these ideas for my book, I was not attending to their reverberation with my religious beliefs, background, or values although I did give considerable attention to Martin Buber's (1923/1970) relational philosophy of I-Thou. What I would like to do is to review some of the ideas about God with which I grew up and that continue to speak to me spiritually. I am interested in examining the influence of my "God representations" on my own psychoanalytic conceptualization. I present themes and images that have been meaningful to me personally. I recognize that others, even others who have been raised within the same Jewish tradition, have different visions and relate to God differently than I do. In particular, I recognize that women's experiences within the tradition may have been quite different than my own. It should be added that just as my religious background has affected my psychoanalytic vision, so too, my psychoanalytic experience has influenced my spiritual values and ideals. Consider the centrality of the theme of mutuality and asymmetry in the following reflections on Jewish belief.

The Jewish tradition, as I understand it, is radically relational in its assumption of a mutual and intersubjective relationship between God and humanity. The Brit, or covenant, between God and Israel is the core foundation of the Jewish faith. A covenantal relationship requires mutuality, not symmetry or equality, for it is clearly hierarchical, but nevertheless it must be a two-way street, a reciprocal agreement. Revelation necessitates give-and-take, a creative tension between the giving of Torah, God's teaching or law, and the receiving of Torah, and the Brit (the covenant) implies Judaism's foundations in this mutual relation. Rabbi Joseph Soloveitchik (known simply as "The Rav," a leading figure of modern Jewish philosophy) described the covenant as resting on "free negotiation, mutual assumption of duties and full recognition of the equal rights of both parties concerned" (1992, p. 29). Chancellor Ismar Schorsch of the Jewish Theological Seminary writes, "Reciprocity holds the key to eternity for each of us," citing as a proof-text, "If my light will be in your hand, your light will be in My hand" (Shemot Rabbah 36:3). Elsewhere he quotes Leviticus: "You shall not profane My holy name, that I may be sanctified in the midst of the Israelite people—I the Lord who sanctify you" (22:32). The verse depicts a reciprocal relationship between God and Israel in which sanctification operates bidirectionally. The nation has an obligation to bring credit to God even as God sanctifies it. Holiness is a reciprocal relationship. According to the Talmud, if we strive to hallow our lives here on earth, we will be bathed with a burst of holiness from above.

Jewish daily liturgy expresses an ongoing theme of reciprocal love and a mutual and dynamic relationship between God and humanity. Our prayer "With abounding love you have loved us" is reciprocated with "and you shall love your God." Jews wear ritual bindings, tefillin, encasing the pronouncement, "Here O' Israel, the Lord our God, the Lord alone," and reciprocally, in the rabbinic imagination, the Talmud asserts that God dons tefillin proclaiming "who is like thy people Israel, one people on earth."

Rabbi Louis Finkelstein, who was Chancellor of the Jewish Theological Seminary from 1934 to 1972, used to say that when he prayed, he talked to God, but when he studied, God talked to him. The tradition in which I grew up led me to imagine an ongoing internal experience of conversing with God. Praising, beseeching, thanking, complaining, questioning, challenging, and even arguing with God is simply expected. Prayer presupposes an intimate personal experience with God. As young children we repeatedly hear the bible story of Abraham audaciously arguing with God over Sodom, even going so far as to challenge God's morality: "Shall not the judge of all the earth deal justly?" (Genesis 18:22). The very name Israel means "one who struggles with God" and was given to Jacob after he wrestled with a divine being (Genesis 32:29). Jews are taught to grapple with God, to question and confront God, and to maintain an ongoing dialogue with God.

What does it mean, what could it possibly mean, to think of a human being as having an intersubjective relationship with God? Is God a subject to be engaged? An interpersonal relationship with God? But certainly God is not a person, and isn't it sacrilegious to attribute to God such personal attributes? In what sense can we think of ourselves as God's partners, God's lovers? Rabbi Neil Gillman (1992) elegantly reviews the Jewish literature that so pervasively, in spite of philosophical objections, portrays a personal God. Our tradition does indeed affirm an intersubjective relationship, an I-Thou relationship, between God and humanity, between God and Israel, and even between God and the individual. God does seem dependent on our recognition, subject to our affirmation. This is not the God of the rationalist philosophers; the God of the Rambam (Maimonidees), following Aristotle, is abstract, transcendent, unmoved, and certainly beyond the need of anyone, but his is only one of many authentically Jewish conceptions of the Divinity, and important as it is, according to Gillman, the rationalistic view needs to be held in tension with a more personal view of God. It should also be noted that Maimonidees himself paradoxically preaches a moral ideal of continuous fellowship with God (Soloveitchik, 2002, p. 93).

In the Western philosophical tradition, dependency is considered a weakness, a sign of inadequacy, incompleteness, femininity, and neediness, and so to think of God as reliant on people is to reveal God's limitation and hence to deny God's omnipotence. For the rationalists, an all-powerful God must be depicted as abstract, autonomous, independent, above it all, and alone. But if we value relation and engagement and view it as an ideal state to be connected and attached, then we may challenge the conventional assessment and instead regard God's need for humanity as one aspect of omnipotence rather than as a limitation or deficit.

Throughout the Jewish tradition God is portrayed as caring about all human beings. The Creator of the Universe is also, paradoxically, Kel Malei Rachamim, the Lord Full of Compassion. The Torah repeatedly uses metaphors of God and Israel as husband and wife, parent and child, even depicting the relationship as between lovers and soul mates. Song of Songs is interpreted by the rabbis allegorically as an erotic love song between God and the people. The relationship between the lovers in Songs is egalitarian antipatriarchal, and the mutuality of their desire is the recurrent theme. What could more poetically characterize mutuality than "Ani ledodi ve'dodi li"—I am for my beloved and my beloved for me? Ilana Pardes (1992) argues that "for once the relationship of God and His bride relies on mutual courting, mutual attraction, and mutual admiration" (p. 127). Pardes then cites a Midrash that celebrates Song in which their hymn to God is answered by a hymn to them. Thus God praises Israel, saying [Songs I: 15]: "Behold thou art fair, my love; behold thou art fair"; and Israel responds with a paean to Him: "Behold, Thou art fair, my Beloved, yea, pleasant" (Pardes, 1992, p. 127).

In our literature, God is moved, feels emotions, negotiates, becomes enraged, shows compassion, appears vulnerable and ambivalent. Often frustrated are God's dreams for humanity and for the world that God created. Abraham Heschel (1959) designated "the divine pathos" (p. 116) as the key to the Jewish worldview. For Heschel, God cares and reaches out, yet is frustrated and vulnerable. God even laughs and cries with us. Our rabbis portray God weeping after the destruction of the temple, and by contrast, in Psalms, in an image that some find disturbing, God laughs at the destruction of our enemies. The Talmud (Baba Meziah) famously depicts God laughing with joy at the rabbis' triumph as they overrule celestial authority in the interpretation of law, for "the Torah is not in heaven!" When the people crossed the sea escaping the Egyptians they sang the Song of the Sea. The Baal Shem Tov, the founder of Chasidism, taught that when Israel sang, this caused God to join in and sing the song with the people.

Reciprocity may be seen in the Bible's naming of the holiday of Passover. The designation of the holiday as Passover reflects a human point of view, in which we celebrate God's passing over the Israelites during the tenth plague. God, on the other hand, refers to the holiday as the Feast of Unleavened Bread, a name that reflects God's recognition of Israel's haste and sacrifice in following God into the uncharted wilderness.

The theme of mutuality between God and the Jewish people is most fully developed in the literature of Jewish mysticism and particularly in 16th century Lurianic Kabbalah. In the Kabbalistic myth, at the center of creation is humankind, who, through proper acts and devotion, the fulfillment of both ritual and social-ethical commandments, can repair the world, *tikkun olam*. In the theosophy of the Kabbalah, God creates the world through *zimzum*, God contracts or withdraws himself to make room for creation. Homiletically, zimzum, the self-limitation of God, is understood by many Kabbalists as the foundation of free will, as if God's self-contraction is necessary to make room for human freedom. With the Shevirat ha-Kelim ("breaking of the vessels") there is a failure of the divine emanation to be contained, resulting in the descent of divine sparks, which need to be rescued and returned to their source. Through the performance of commandments with the proper intention (*kavanah*), we gather the divine sparks and hence contribute to cosmic restoration and reintegration. Restating this insight, Rabbi Soloveitchik (1984) said that it is as if "the creator spoiled reality so that mortals might set it right" (p. 148). God does not unilaterally liberate Israel from Egypt, but rather in Kabbalistic thought, it is as if the liberation is mutually necessary because God, as well as the world and humanity, needs to be mended, repaired, liberated, and redeemed. The central image here is that of two partners sharing in the task of repairing the world, tikkun olam. We are partners with God in creation, revelation, and redemption.

The medieval sage Nachmanides asked why the Ten Commandments begin with God's proclamation "I am the Lord your God who took you out of the Land of Egypt" instead of asserting "I am the One who created heaven and earth." Levi Yitzchak of Berditchev, who was one of the most beloved figures of the Hasidim, answered this question in the following way: To say that God created the universe is abstract and philosophical. Such an assertion places God as the first of all firsts, the prime mover, abstract and distant; it speaks of God as an idea, a principle—God as transcendent. By beginning with the declaration that God took us out of Egypt, God is revealed as showing love, intimacy, and involvement—God as immanent in our lives and our history. God's commandments are in fact part of a deal. Like the Hittite vassal treaties on which the structure of the Decalogue may be modeled, the Brit enacts a mutual understanding, a bilateral agreement with reciprocal responsibilities. I did this for you, and so you do these commandments for me. I am with you so you be with me; "You must be holy, for I, the Lord your God, am holy." Because we are to imitate God's holy ways, there are implications regarding mutuality for our human interpersonal relations as well. To mention a single instance, perhaps if we imagine God as reliant on us for support and reparation, we might feel less shame about our own vulnerability and dependence on others.

Following the existential tradition of Martin Buber, who emphasized the primacy of the I-Thou relationship, others have highlighted that in all relationships there are moments of intimacy and moments of withdrawal. Irving Greenberg emphasizes the alternating movements of presence and absence, faith and denial. "Faith, then, is never a permanent acquisition but rather a momentary achievement, all too easily dispelled. Atheism is a legitimate stage in the dynamic of faith" (Greenberg, cited in Gillman, 2000, p. 453). In our relationship with God, along with the gift of human freedom, we must endure the vicissitudes of all relationships and live in an unpredictable and sometimes cruel and pernicious world. We all undoubtedly recall moments when it seems as if God's face has been hidden from us or, as Martin Buber (1957) referred to it, moments where there seems to be an "eclipse of God." At these times we remember that God too is waiting to resume our partnership. As it is written, "Turn back to me—said the Lord of Hosts—and I will turn back to you" (Zechariah 1:3).

We have seen that in the Jewish tradition, God turns with us, waits with us, sings, prays, and rejoices with us, laughs, cries, and mourns with us. All too often in Jewish history, it seems that God must be crying with us. Perhaps even through our suffering, we may experience God's seeming absence and abandonment, our confrontation with nothingness, as a summons from God in the form of a catastrophic revelation, a "call out of the whirlwind" (Soloveitchik, 2003).

Our souls cry out in longing for God, but in Heschel's (1976) classic phrase, likewise, God is "in search of man." Mutuality and intersubjectivity can take place only between two subjects who count on one another, seek each other, recognize each other, let each other down, negate each other, and repair and mend the inevitable disruptions of the alliance. The feeling that God is absent is no less a legitimate religious experience than the sense of divine presence. Relationships are by their nature conflicted, mercurial, and inconsistent; the presence of the other is subject to ebb and flow. There are moments of faith and moments of doubt or outright disbelief, but both faith and doubt participate in one's ongoing internal dialogue. In my conversation with God I can say, "I don't believe in you. You don't exist, you can't exist, you make no sense, you are absurd, my rational mind denies you." Still, my conversation with God goes on. I would think of this relationship with God in terms of ongoing regulation, disruption and repair, and heightened affective moments (Beebe & Lachmann, 2002).

For the purposes of this essay, I have emphasized mutuality and taken asymmetry for granted, but of course mutuality is only one side of a complex dialectic process. If the story of Abraham standing up to God in regard to Sodom illustrates the mutuality of their relationship, then the Akeda, the binding of Isaac, depicting Abraham's silent submission to God's will, is perhaps the quintessential exemplar of asymmetry. The asymmetry is inherent in our transience and nothingness in relation to the Creator; the mutuality derives from our dignity as human beings who are created in the image of the divine, allowing us to commune with God. In the words of Rabbi Soloveitchik (2003),

> In God, man finds both affirmation of himself as a great being, and a ruthless, inconsiderate negation of himself as nothing. This is the main, the dominant theme of Judaism.... Finding God is, on the one hand, the greatest victory which man may obtain and, on the other hand, the most humiliating, tormenting defeat which the human being experiences.... In a word, the dialectical movement of surging forward and falling back is the way of life ordained by God for the Jew.
>
> (p. 108)

And here I want to add a brief tribute to the memory of Mannie Ghent, who, among his many other contributions, did so much to champion a legitimate place for spirituality in psychoanalysis. Although Mannie took his influence for what he called "surrender" from the eastern Buddhist traditions, there is a striking, almost uncanny similarity to the Rav's dialectic approach as seen in his emphasis on the total surrender of body and soul, the need to maintain dignity in defeat, the universal alternation between surging forward and conquering versus withdrawal and defeat, opposing suffering and yet accepting mortality. Ghent (2002) concluded his most recent article,

> Every day in our practice we pay homage to, and stand back in awe of, the marvels of the human mind caught up in the struggle to heal and transcend itself, while holding back in fear, jousting with itself in dread of walking through the valley of the shadow of death.
>
> (p. 804)

Judaism places great emphasis on the value of life. God proclaims in Deuteronomy (30:19), "I have put before you life and death, blessing and curse. Choose life" (Hebrew-English Tanach, Philadelphia, 1999). This utterance embodies two cardinal values (choice and life) that are also fundamental to psychoanalysis. An existential dimension of psychoanalysis champions agency that is developed through making choices, exercising our will, our authorship of our own lives (see my discussion of rank, will, and agency in Aron, 1996c). The ultimate value of psychoanalysis is for the analysand to choose life, to choose vitality, meaning, and authenticity (see Ogden, 1995). Freud was right in spirit in his recognition that psychoanalysis sides with the life over the death instincts. As psychoanalysts, we should recognize that some of our cherished ideals are central to religious traditions and that in analyzing forms of aliveness and deadness, and thus in helping our patients to choose life, we are performing a sacred task.

The relational emphases on mutuality and asymmetry have structural parallels in Jewish theological formulations with which I live. I present these to you simply as an illustration of the influence of one select aspect of the analyst's subjectivity on psychoanalytic values and ideals. I do want to end with one final point. Analysts have too often played God. We have acted as if we were omnipotent and all knowing, aloof and above it all. I hope that I have in some way indicated my belief that being deeply engaged with God, imitating God's ways, may paradoxically help keep us from playing God. Michael Eigen (1998), drawing on his own study of Judaism and Kabbalah, described psychoanalysis as a form of prayer. Indeed, psychoanalysis may be envisioned as a religious practice, a form of worship, in which contact is made with the Almighty through immersion in the richness and depth of the inner life and in communion with the other.

Part II

Clinical choices and relational practice

Chapter 5

Interpretation as expression of the analyst's subjectivity (1992)

Introduction by Thomas Ogden

In this pivotal chapter, Lewis Aron proposes that the analyst's interpretations communicate to the patient important qualities of the subjectivity of the analyst, and recognizing and making use of this aspect of experience contributes to the mutative effect of psychoanalysis. In addressing the analyst's communication of his or her subjectivity in the analytic experience, he indirectly addresses the larger question: What is relational (or interpersonal) psychoanalysis? The words Aron uses in the title of this chapter are significant in this regard. The word *"interpretation"* is used very differently from the way it is used by classical Freudians, Kleinians, British Independents, and other analytic groups, all of which use the term to refer to the analyst's verbalization of his or her understanding of the *unconscious meaning* of the patient's thoughts, feelings, fantasies, dreams, associations, acting in and acting out, and so on. Aron, in his chapter on the analyst's interpretations, uses the term *unconscious* only once. The virtual absence of the term *unconscious* reflects an important aspect of the thinking of relational psychoanalysts.

The term *subjectivity*, also used in the title of the chapter, replaces such terms as *intrapsychic* and *internal world*, which are widely used in psychoanalysis to refer to the unconscious aspect of the mind. Instead of using the term *intrapsychic*, Aron uses the term *subjectivity*, a concept that transcends the division of the mind into conscious and unconscious elements.

Aron makes it clear that "relational psychoanalysis" is not a unitary entity. It is not a school of psychoanalysis, as is the Kleinian school or the school of self-psychology or the school of Freudian ego psychology. The term *relational* is more adverb than adjective in that it describes a quality of the experience of *engaging in clinical analytic work*. It refers to a quality of being in the lived relationship with the patient. It spans a wide variety of approaches along a spectrum of symmetry/asymmetry, that is, a spectrum of similarity or difference between the role and function of the patient and that of the analyst. At one extreme is Ferenczi's failed "mutual analysis" experiment in which he and the patient each took the role of analyst to the other. At the other end of the spectrum lie doctrinal techniques, which are not unique creations of each patient and analyst, but sets of rules passed down from one generation of analysts to the next. Aron locates himself at a place on the symmetry/asymmetry spectrum in which it is clear that the analyst has responsibility for the analytic frame, for the conduct of the analysis within the bounds of rules laid down by the analyst, for instance, what sorts of behavior are tolerated. At the same time, for the analysis to be effective, the interaction of patient and analyst must be reciprocal in the sense that each is responding to the other and changed by the experience. It is psychological change that derives less from *arriving at understandings* than it derives from *experiencing a relationship in which there is genuine responsiveness to who the other is*, a responsiveness that brings with it affirmation of the full depth and breadth of the other's subjectivity, the other's humanity.

Aron emphasizes that the role the analyst takes with the patient must not be contrived, and instead, must be allowed to develop in response to what is naturally occurring in the session. He is loath to talk with the patient about his feeling states and prefers to allow his subjectivity to be communicated in the form of the way he speaks and what he says about the patient's responses to him. The role of the analyst is that of reflecting and understanding the patient's communications and responding to them in a way that communicate something of his own subjectivity.

While Aron's "relational-perspectivist" analysis places a premium on mutual recognition, analysis inevitably involves enactments that have the effect of limiting the freedom of both patient and analyst to be fully alive as subjects. In the tradition of Winnicott, Aron suggests that the most therapeutic aspect of the psychoanalytic experience may not be the periods in which analyst and patient are sensitively responsive to one another. Rather, what is therapeutic may lie in the experience of patient and analyst reestablishing reciprocal mutuality following failures or lapses on the part of the analyst.

It seems to me that Aron, in this chapter, does not view "relational-perspectivist" psychoanalysis as a school of psychoanalysis that is interested in developing a theory of mind, such as Freud's conception of the conscious and unconscious mind mediated by the repression barrier or Klein's conception of an internal object world comprised of unconscious phantasies that are psychic representations of instinctual pressures. Neither does relational-perspectivist psychoanalysis constitute a general psychology. Rather, it is a body of thought focused primarily on clinical phenomena. Aron, in his conception of relational-perspectivist psychoanalysis, describes a clinical sensibility in which the act of *experiencing relationships of mutual recognition* in the analytic setting serve as a principal medium in which psychological growth may occur.

Aron, L. (1992). Interpretation as expression of the analyst's subjectivity.
Psychoanalytic Dialogues, 2(4), 475–507.

Interpretation[1] is a complex, intersubjective process that develops conjointly between patient and analyst. For Freud (1900, p. 96), to interpret (*Deutung*) was to assign meaning (*Bedeutung*) to the patient's material. In this chapter I propose a shift from the traditional view of interpretation as conveying information about the mind of the patient from the analyst to the patient to a view of interpretation as a bipersonal and reciprocal communication process, a mutual meaning-making process. A contemporary reinterpretation of the nature of psychoanalytic interpretation demands a deconstruction of several fundamental psychoanalytic terms, concepts, and principles. Therefore, this chapter will examine the data of psychoanalysis, the method of psychoanalysis (particularly the free association method), and the extent of symmetry and mutuality between patient and analyst.

The data of interpretation

From the point of view of traditional psychoanalysis an interpretation is an explanation[2] that conveys knowledge about the patient's psychic life from the analyst to the patient (Lowenstein, 1951). From within this perspective everything that the patient says is to be regarded as an association. The patient never interprets, because by definition an interpretation conveys knowledge from the analyst to the patient. When a patient insightfully explains an aspect of his or her own behavior, it may seem as if the patient has interpreted his own behavior, but the analyst is to regard even this as a further association, manifest content, which itself needs interpretation. Inversely, the analyst, from a traditional point of view (whether Freudian or Kleinian), should never be associating, that is, speaking his or her mind freely, but rather the analyst should be only interpreting. That is, the analyst may make other interventions, like clarifying or confronting, but these interventions are preparatory to the interpretation and should be kept to a minimum, subordinated to the primacy of interpretation as the mode of conveying knowledge to the patient. From this highly asymmetrical perspective, Etchegoyen (1991) states that what distinguishes the psychoanalytic field is that the observational data come from the patient and that the analyst "abstains rigorously from offering any data.... The aim of the analytic situation is to create a field of observation where the data are offered exclusively by the patient" (p. 502).

Etchegoyen, himself a Kleinian, has recently written what is bound to become a classic text on psychoanalytic technique that integrates the world's literature, drawn from four languages on the subject (although unfortunately excluding the American interpersonal literature). He is conveying the international consensus opinion among psychoanalysts when he suggests that the analyst's task is to interpret, that is, to explain the patient's behavior and associations; it is not to add any new data. Therefore, if the patient has a particular impact on the analyst, if for instance, the patient always confuses the analyst, then for the analyst to tell the patient this, that is, to communicate the countertransference reaction directly, would be to provide the patient not with an explanation, but rather with a new piece of data that itself is in need of an explanation. Etchegoyen's position is that this is contrary to the analytic method. Similarly, to tell a patient how you arrived at a particular interpretation, even if it revealed nothing personal about the analyst's life, would not be an explanation of the patient's data, but would rather provide the patient with further data of the analyst's, that is, it would provide the patient with aspects of the analyst's thought processes and in this sense would be self-revealing.

It is particularly interesting to note Etchegoyen's asymmetrical position because he is aware of the intersubjective and mutual nature of the analytic situation. He recognizes as valid, for example, the Barangers' (1966) claim that the analytic situation is a bipersonal field. Nevertheless, for Etchegoyen and most traditional analysts, even if the analytic situation is seen as an interpersonal field, that is, as mutual and reciprocal, and even if the object of investigation is the field itself, rather than the patient per se, the method of studying the field is asymmetrical, being limited to the analyst's acquiring data from the patient, rather than the two participant-observers' sharing data with each other and then coparticipating in interpreting this mutually arrived at data.

My objection to Etchegoyen is that in sharpening the distinction between interpretation and data generation (association), he obscures the recognition that every interpretation by the analyst inevitably contains aspects of the analyst's subjectivity. In my view, even when the analyst attempts to interpret without revealing any personal associative material, something personal nevertheless emerges in the course of interpreting if the interpretation is to be related and meaningful. Only the most hackneyed and barren of interpretations could be so (secondary) "processed" that it would be a rational bit of information devoid of the humanity and subjectivity of the analyst. I would like to contrast the traditional asymmetric approach with the most daring experiment in the history of psychoanalysis investigating the use of a symmetrical approach.

Ferenczi's mutual/symmetrical analysis

In the late 1920s and early 1930s, Sandor Ferenczi began his experiments with mutual analysis as part of his overall experimental program of technique, which was focusing on relaxation and indulgence. Ferenczi was considered to be the best clinical analyst of his day, and his practice included work with the most difficult cases. He was considered the analyst of last resort, and his patients typically had years of analysis previous to beginning their work with him. Ferenczi was committed to the principle that an analyst should not give up on the patient and dismiss the patient as unanalyzable. Instead the analyst should continue the analysis as long as the patient was willing to come for analysis, and instead of blaming the patient's resistances, the analyst should consider that it is his or her own technique or personal limitations that are interfering in the analysis.

If the resistances were at least potentially to be found in the analyst, however, then it followed that the analyst needed to resolve his or her own resistances before he or she could successfully analyze the patient. Therefore, Ferenczi was the strongest advocate of what he termed the second fundamental rule of analysis, namely, that the analyst's own training analysis should be even deeper than the analysis of non-analysts, going right down to rock bottom, as he used to say (Ferenczi, 1993, p. 158). Given the limitation of his own training analysis with Freud, however, and given the limitations of conducting a self-analysis, Ferenczi began to experiment with allowing his patients to analyze him. It was clear to Ferenczi that his patients observed a great deal about him and that to deny these observations would be to repeat a major trauma of childhood in which the parents deny disturbing aspects of what their children notice about what is going on around them (Ferenczi, 1933). He therefore, courageously, and at the cost of much personal conflict, agony, shame, and humiliation, began his experiments with mutual analysis, which he documented in his *Clinical Diary* (Ferenczi, 1932).

Ferenczi's procedure was literally that his patients analyzed him. They would have back-to-back sessions in which they alternated free-associating and interpreting to each other. I will not elaborate on this further here (see Aron & Harris, 1993 ; Ragen & Aron, 2013) except to say that the *Clinical Diary* that documents these experiments is among the most fascinating, but also disturbing, texts in the history of psychoanalysis. According to Ferenczi's *Clinical Diary*, however, his experiments with mutual analysis became endangered because of practical difficulties. Most important, the problem of confidentiality became impossible to resolve because Ferenczi, faced with the requirement to free-associate to each patient, would have to reveal the private confidences of other patients. Furthermore, since some of his patients were themselves analysts to others, in applying mutual analysis they would be revealing personal details about Ferenczi to their own patients, who would also be their analysts. One can easily see how the whole procedure would break down. In studying the diary, however, I have been puzzled that Ferenczi attributed the breakdown of his experiments to such a practical difficulty. I believe that his experiments broke down for more fundamental and consequential reasons. It seems to me that the practical dilemma of confidentiality is only symbolic of what went wrong in the experiments. In my view, Ferenczi was on the right track in proposing mutual analysis, but he erred in that mutual analysis became symmetrical analysis. Not only did Ferenczi encourage his patients to analyze him when they observed something about him as the analyst, but he literally became the patient's patient. The roles were completely shared, and the boundaries between patient and analyst completely abandoned. Where Ferenczi attributed the breakdown of the experiments to problems with confidentiality, I think that this was his recognition and acknowledgment of the difficulties posed by symmetry. As psychoanalysis is increasingly conceptualized as a mutual endeavor, as a "two-person psychology" (Aron, 1990) or as a "bipersonal field," questions arise regarding how mutual or symmetrical an analysis can or should be. How many of the analyst's associations can be revealed or should be revealed to the patient? What are the necessary and appropriate boundaries and divisions of labor between patient and analyst? I believe that the major benefits of Ferenczi's mutual analysis can be retained, but that analysis can be conducted within a relatively asymmetrical frame, and it is to this distinction between symmetry and mutuality that I will now turn.

Mutuality and symmetry in psychoanalysis

This chapter, which examines interpretation as an expression of the analyst's subjectivity, builds on an earlier article (Aron, 1991b) that explored the patient's experience of the analyst's subjectivity. I emphasized, following Gill (1982) and Hoffman (1983), that as one aspect of the analysis of transference, it was important for the analyst to examine and make explicit a patient's perceptions of the analyst's subjectivity. I wrote that the analyst's establishment of his or her own subjectivity in the analytic situation was essential and yet problematic. Here, I will argue that the optimal way for the analyst to establish himself or herself as a subject is through the use of interpretations, which, while being explicitly about the patient, carry a great deal of implicit data about the subjectivity of the analyst.

In choosing to emphasize the patient's experience of the analyst's subjectivity and in implementing this technically, the analyst provides the patient with further opportunity to observe, experience, think, fantasize, and make inferences about the person of the analyst. Each and every intervention, as well as each and every lack of intervention, reveals something to the patient about the psychology of the analyst, his or her interests, concerns, motivations, blind spots, sensitive points, or whatever. Since patients seek to connect with their analysts and also anxiously need to guard against their analysts, they are strongly motivated to observe their analysts and probe beneath their facade, to learn about their analysts as people. Anonymity is never an option for an analyst. You can sit, but never hide, behind the couch! The patient's perceptions and observations of the analyst are relevant even if the analyst does not recognize himself or herself in the patient's descriptions. This is to say that the analyst is not in a unique position to judge the accuracy of the patient's observations. It is this relativistic and intersubjective approach to clinical psychoanalysis that I have been referring to as "relational-perspectivism"[3] (Aron, 1992a, p. 189).

Burke (1992) has read my earlier paper as suggesting that I promote a technical strategy of anonymity. He concludes this, in spite of his citing me approvingly as highlighting the extent to which self-revelation is inevitable. Burke may have confused my generally cautious stance with a technical prescription of anonymity. As I stated earlier, inadvertent self-revelation is inevitable, and in addition, I do believe that there are many times when a direct expression of the analyst's experience is useful. To be specific, I believe that it is often useful to share one's associations with a patient when the analyst's associations provide data that are absent from, and yet directly relevant to, the patient's associations. Often I find that revealing my own associations occurs in explaining to a patient how it was that I came to formulate a particular interpretation. What I believe to be particularly problematic are self-revelations in which the analyst states what she or he feels about a patient in a way that closes off further discussion, for example, saying to a patient, "Yes, you are right, I was annoyed when I said that!" or "No, I'm not aware of feeling impatient with you." These types of self-revelation are troublesome, not because they reveal too much of the analyst, but rather because they imply too much certainty on the analyst's part and minimize the extent to which the analyst too has an unconscious, and hence they discourage further exploration by the patient (see Hoffman, 1983, and see my later discussion of Bollas). Of course, if the analyst is careful to emphasize that there may be more that he or she is feeling that is out of awareness, then this may serve as an invitation to the patient to speculate about the analyst or to come forth with further observations, and in this manner it may prove useful. The critical issue seems to be whether or not the analyst's interventions invite or discourage further elaboration, correction, observation, and association from the patient.

Throughout his paper, Burke (1992) opposes the principle of mutuality to the principle of asymmetry and suggests, for example, that the principle of mutuality leads the analyst to more frequent self-revelations and the principle of asymmetry leads the analyst to less frequent self-revelations. I believe that this mistakenly collapses two dimensions of the analytic interaction into one. One dimension refers to symmetry-asymmetry, and the other refers to mutuality-lack of mutuality. Burke defines "asymmetry" as referring to the dimension of how similar or dissimilar the experience of the participants is, and he defines "mutuality" in terms of how shared or reciprocal the quality of the therapeutic interaction is. I believe that this definition is imprecise and confusing and that it led to his soon collapsing these two dimensions into one and therefore opposing mutuality to asymmetry.

I prefer to define symmetry-asymmetry as a dimension referring to the similarity or dissimilarity of the patient's and analyst's roles and functions in the analytic process; that is, symmetry-asymmetry refers to the division of responsibility within the interaction. By roles and functions I mean to include such things as free-associating, interpreting, confronting resistances, establishing ground rules. I think of mutuality-lack of mutuality as a dimension referring to how reciprocal the interaction and the experience of the interaction are; that is, do the two participants mutually and reciprocally influence each other and experience that they influence each other bidirectionally? Mutuality-lack of mutuality refers not so much to behaviors as to the way in which the relationship is conceptualized. For example, the lack-of-mutuality position conceives of transference as influencing countertransference, while the mutuality position conceives of transference and countertransference as reciprocally creating and defining each other. Therefore, in my view, an analyst may have a position that emphasizes mutuality, recognizing the reciprocal influence that patient and analyst have on each other, and yet this analyst may take a technical position that emphasizes either symmetry or asymmetry. Similarly, an analyst may work from a position that views the interaction as more typically one-directional and conceptualizes it more as a "one-person psychology," for instance, believing that most of the time the transference arises independently of the analyst's contribution. This analyst may still choose to construct an analytic situation that is either symmetrical or asymmetrical. For example, such an analyst may be more or less active or self-revelatory.

It now may be clear what I meant when I suggested (Aron, 1991b) that the analytic situation is mutual but asymmetrical. I conceive of the analytic relationship as fully mutual, and on the dimension of mutuality-lack of mutuality, I would place myself, as well as Burke, at the extreme end of the mutuality dimension. (I believe that this is what Burke meant when he included both of our positions as being broadly interpersonal.) We differ, however, in where we stand on the symmetry-asymmetry dimension. It is here that Burke seems to me to be somewhat closer to the symmetry pole, while I think of myself as leaning closer to the asymmetry pole, although not at the extreme end of that pole. Since in my conceptualization these are dimensions, rather than categories, one does not have to choose sides.

The conceptualization of mutuality and asymmetry as falling on two different dimensions has heuristic appeal in understanding similarities and differences between various theorists and clinicians and serves to clarify the meanings of both my previous work as well as Burke's. Rather than conclude, as Burke does, that I promote asymmetry as contrasted with mutuality, my schematization clarifies that I propose radical mutuality with a moderate degree of asymmetry. In spite of Burke's misreading of my position as suggesting a technical strategy of anonymity, his conclusions regarding therapeutic strategy are quite similar to those I proposed earlier, namely, that each analyst-patient pair needs to work out a unique way of managing the dynamic tension between the analyst's participation and nonintrusiveness (Aron, 1991b, p. 43).

I situate myself as leaning toward the asymmetry pole of the symmetry-asymmetry dimension in that I believe that analysts should be cautious in regard to self-revelations, for they are always complicated and problematic; however, everything that the analyst says or does not say is complicated and problematic. What is critical is not whether the analyst chooses to reveal something at a particular moment to a patient, but, rather, the analyst's skill at utilizing this in the service of the analytic process. Is the analyst or, more accurately put, is the particular analyst-patient dyad able to make use of the analyst's self-revelation in the service of clarifying and explicating the nature of their interaction? In other words, does this intervention lead to further analysis of the transference-countertransference? A discussion of some of the technical developments emerging out of the Winnicottian tradition in the British independent group, particularly as developed in detail by Christopher Bollas, will clarify some of the controversy regarding symmetry and asymmetry, interpretation, and self-revelation.

Winnicott on interpretation

Winnicott's contributions to the theory of interpretation and analytic process, and especially the way in which his ideas have been developed further by analysts within the British independent group, provide an alternative to the traditional asymmetrical model presented by Etchegoyen.[4]

Winnicott was highly critical of, as well as very respectful and appreciative of, both of the two prevailing psychoanalytic methods, the Freudian and the Kleinian, and much of his writing can be read as a critique of these techniques (see Phillips, 1988). Winnicott evolved a point of view that shifted the emphasis of the psychoanalytic process from knowledge and insight to intersubjective recognition and acceptance of spontaneity and play, and therefore of true self. He gradually and subtly transformed the method of psychoanalysis from one that emphasized the patient's internalization of the analyst's reason, rationality, and insight to one that was based on the patient's "use of the object" analyst for the expression of true self.

Since Winnicott did not spell out the implications of his contributions for psychoanalytic technique, it is necessary to extract technical suggestions from his more general writings. Drawing on the imaginative and creative elaboration of his ideas by Christopher Bollas (1987, 1989) and the careful biographical exogenesis of his writing by Adam Phillips (1988), I will describe three Winnicottian metaphors that shed light on Winnicott's attitude toward interpretation.

Winnicott (1941) described his use of a spatula in evaluating children. He observed a mother-infant pair at his desk, where he left a shiny spoon. He observed how the infant hesitated before reaching for the spatula and noted how the infant first checked back and forth from mother's face to Winnicott's face before picking it up. Gradually the child took the spatula, played with it, held it, bit on it, sucked it, threw it on the floor, and got down on the floor to play with it. Here Winnicott provides us with one metaphor for an interpretation. The analyst needs to provide the patient with an interpretation and observe the way in which this exciting piece of information is accepted by the patient. The interpretation, like the shiny spatula, excites the patient's greed, and the patient wants more and more from the analyst. Following this metaphor, we would expect the patient to hesitate, to take time to decide whether it is safe to accept the interpretation. Resistance is not a reluctance or refusal to accept new knowledge, but rather "a period of hesitation," a slow coming to realization. Attempting to force a patient to accept an interpretation is like trying to shove the spoon down the infant's mouth. With the metaphor of the spatula, Winnicott shifts the focus from the analyst as the active purveyor of carefully constructed interpretations to the patient as the active participant who takes what the analyst has to offer and reshapes it and recreates it in accord with his or her own needs.

A second metaphor (and the overarching concept) that depicts Winnicott's (1951) attitude toward interpretation is that of the transitional object. A parent may place a variety of items into the infant's crib and hope that the infant selects one particular item or another as a transitional object, but the parent cannot choose which item the infant will select. Winnicott implies that so it is with interpretations. The analyst puts out lots of interpretations, but you cannot select which of them your patient will accept or cling to. Furthermore, the interpretation may be useful not because it provides new information, but rather because it represents a link with the analyst. The interpretation can be carried around and sucked on when the analyst is away. The patient can play with the interpretation, cling to it, incorporate it, love it, modify it, attack it, discard it, transform it, or throw it back at the analyst.

It is with the third metaphor that we can see the full development of Winnicott's attitudes toward interpretations. The model of the squiggle game, a therapeutic technique that Winnicott developed for use with older children, is relevant as a model of the kind of interaction that Winnicott might have advocated with patients generally. In the squiggle game, Winnicott (1971a) plays with his patients freely and spontaneously. Winnicott would draw a line on a piece of paper, and the child would have to turn the line into something. Then, the child would draw a line, and Winnicott would have to complete it. Whose squiggle is it? Is it the child's or Winnicott's? Like the transitional object, it does not belong inside or outside, to Winnicott or the patient. Like an interpretation, in Winnicott's view, it does not come from the analyst or from the patient, but rather it emerges from the transitional space between them.

When Winnicott squiggles his line, he does it spontaneously. He has the patient in mind; however, he does not deliberately or intentionally plan his squiggles. On the contrary, they express his spontaneity; they are reflections of true self, spontaneous gestures. He does not necessarily know what will come out when he begins to draw. If he did, it would feel contrived and false. Similarly, by the end of his life, Winnicott advocated that the analytic process be thought of as an expression of play between analyst and patient. Grolnick (1990), in describing the analytic process as a form of squiggling with adults, wrote:

> Squiggling, bilateral mutual play, is at another realm of discourse than standard free associative technique.... The radical nature of the squiggling technique is that it involves the sharing of reactive imagery in order to foster the associative and symbol building capacities.
>
> (p. 157, 163)

Winnicott fundamentally altered our understanding of the meaning and function of interpretation. Where analysts had previously focused on gaining understanding, Winnicott insisted that the analyst must be able to tolerate not knowing. He saw the need to interpret and understand as frequently rooted in the analyst's anxiety and need to do something for the patient. Winnicott shifted our focus from viewing the analyst as active and in control in being the interpreter to a view that emphasized the patient as actively taking in from the analyst what was most useful and reshaping it to meet his or her own needs. The analyst was encouraged to tolerate not knowing, in the sense of having outside objective and certain knowledge, and instead the analyst was encouraged to offer spontaneous and authentic responsiveness, with the point of interpreting being to show the patient that the analyst was fully alive and imperfect. Winnicott's conceptualization of transitional phenomena destroys the sharp distinction between interpretation and free association or data generation, which are central for classical technique, and in this respect Winnicottian technique moves increasingly in the direction of symmetry.

Interpretation and self-expression: the British independent group

British independent group analysts, following Winnicott as well as Balint (1968), have reconceptualized interpretation as a fundamentally relational event. Klauber (1981) emphasized that an analyst needs to be both authentic and spontaneous, not only for his or her own sake, but in order for the patient to "use" him or her. In arguing for the analyst's spontaneity, Klauber was explicitly attacking the notion that an interpretation should always be filtered through the analyst's secondary process thought. Klauber argued that a patient knows much more about the analyst than had been recognized, and he understood the nature of therapeutic action as emanating from this "mutual participation in analytic understanding" (p. 46) in which interpretation leads to deep emotional contact between the participants, which is healing.

Lomas (1987) points out the limits of interpretation when interpretations are stripped of the analyst's emotional responsiveness. He encourages analysts to "try to reveal their true feelings as far as possible" (p. 132), with the rationale that in disclosing countertransference responses, the analyst increases the patient's insight into the ways in which he or she may unwittingly affect those around them. Lomas is critical of the blank screen approach, anonymity, and abstinence in that they tend to conceal interpersonal reality and lead to "mystification," and instead he recommends revealing oneself openly and honestly so that the patient is in a better position to understand where his or her projections depart from reality.

Symington (1983) highlighted that interpretations not only need to be authentic and spontaneous, but also were markers of a change in the relationship between the patient and the analyst. Rather than thinking of the interpretation only as leading to change in the patient, it was more accurate to view the interpretation as the expression of a change that had already occurred. If an interpretation is thought of as more than just conveying information, but rather is seen as the carrier of the relationship, then the relationship would have had to change in order for the analyst to be able to interpret in a way that he or she could not have interpreted before.

> The inner act of freedom in the analyst causes a therapeutic shift in the patient and new insight, learning and development in the analyst. The interpretation is essential in that it gives expression to the shift that has already occurred and makes it available to consciousness. The point though is that the essential agent of change is the inner act of the analyst and that this inner act is perceived by the patient and causes change.
>
> (p. 286)

Expressive uses of countertransference

In a creative and highly articulate extension of the Winnicottian tradition, Bollas (1987, 1989) has suggested that the analyst needs to establish himself or herself as a subject in the analytic field. In order to accomplish this, he cautiously advocates that there are moments in the clinical situation when countertransference disclosure is indicated, and by countertransference disclosure Bollas means a disclosure of mental content, psychic process, emotional reality, or self-state that is congruent with the character of the analyst, meaning that it is authentic. Bollas argues that inasmuch as patients utilize projective identification, they place into their analysts dissociated aspects of themselves. Analysts also become "mediums for the psychosomatic processing of the patient's psyche-soma" (1989, p. 59). Therefore, much of the data that needs to be processed analytically exists within the analyst, rather than within the patient, and the analytic work needs to take place predominantly in the analyst. Bollas recommends a method entitled "the dialectics of difference," in which the analyst reveals more of himself or herself than is traditionally sanctioned. The analyst is encouraged to describe to the patient how he or she arrived at a particular interpretation, rather than just making the interpretation in the finished form of secondary process.

In advocating these procedures, Bollas suggests caution and is careful to clarify that all of this requires discipline. Bollas, however, like Winnicott before him, underplays the extent to which these technical suggestions mark a fundamental break with the classic analytic method. Bollas's recommendations represent a radical change in technique because in revealing his inner process, Bollas is sharing with the patient his own associations, and in doing so he is promoting increased symmetry between patient and analyst. He is no longer the representative of rationality and reality as in the classical model, but now reveals his own psychic reality. The implication of Bollas's recommendations is that the analyst actually contributes data and not just explanation of data; the analyst takes on a function that previously was thought to be the prerogative of patients.

Bollas's procedure calls on the analyst to free-associate with the patient. The analyst's associations are thought of as "musings" that may be freely shared with the patient, so that patient and analyst are squiggling together. As an example, the analyst may share his or her own associations to a patient's dream as a way of facilitating the associative process in the patient. Interestingly, analysts writing from within a more radical interpersonal tradition, with an emphasis on increased symmetry as well as mutuality, have considered not only sharing associations to a patient's dreams, but even relating one's own dreams to the patient (Tauber, 1954). Here we can see the contrasting technical implications of varying positions along the symmetry-asymmetry axis.

Bollas encourages the analyst to differ with himself. He may say that he disagrees with a prior interpretation that he made. In doing this, Bollas not only brings into the analytic situation his own psychic reality, but, in particular, introduces attenuated aspects of his own psychic conflict. Bollas highlights those moments in which his patients disagree with him, and this paves the way for him to disagree with the patient and thus confront the patient with alternative perspectives. It seems to me that in establishing this dialectic of difference, Bollas makes it easier for patients to acknowledge their own psychic conflict since they are not forced into a position in which they are the only one in the room experiencing conflict. By sharing his own associations with patients, Bollas inevitably is led to share some of his own conflicts with them. In shifting from a method in which all of the relevant data of study are contributed by the patient to one in which data are contributed for analysis by both participants, Bollas has modified the classical setup, in which it was only the patient who was seen as presenting psychic reality while the analyst represented external reality, reason, secondary process, and rationality. In introducing the analyst as a subject in the analytic field, with his or her own associations, psychic reality, and conflict, Bollas has made the analytic situation not only more mutual, but also more symmetrical, in that the division of roles that is kept so sharp in the classical model is left less absolute. While Bollas's contribution is clearly in the Winnicottian tradition, Bollas is more explicit about his recommendations for clinical psychoanalytic technique than Winnicott was, and therefore, although he presents himself as part of the psychoanalytic mainstream, the radical nature of his contributions is more obvious.

Mutuality with asymmetry

After advocating procedures that emphasize expressive uses of the countertransference and the dialectics of difference, Bollas (1987, 1989) asks how we can share our associations with our patients and not have this become an intrusion into what should be the patient's space. How can we prevent this procedure from constituting "a subtle takeover of the patient's psychic life with the analyst's" (1989, p. 69)? Bollas defers a full consideration of the technical issues, but he answers briefly:

> The analyst's reporting of his thoughts and associations must be momentary and set against the background of the patient's discourse and the silence that creates the analytic screen. A

continuous, incessant flow of the analyst's thoughts or observations would not be appropriate...So, although there will be occasions when the analyst will elaborate associations, it is important for the analyst to stop in order to create a boundary around the association.

(p. 69)

In my earlier paper, I (1991) argued along similar lines that analysts may abandon traditional anonymity only to substitute imposing their subjectivity on patients and thus deprive patients of the opportunity to search out, uncover, and find the analyst as a separate subject, in their own way and at their own rate... Focusing exclusively on the presence of the analyst does not permit the patient temporarily to put the analyst into the background and indulge in the experience of being left alone in the presence of the analyst.

(p. 42)

In his discussion of my chapter, Hoffman (1991) similarly stressed the "importance of the asymmetrical arrangement as a means of ensuring that the patient's experience remains the center of attention" (p. 92). I concluded then, and I continue to believe, that the analytic relationship needs to be mutual and yet asymmetrical (see Baranger & Baranger, 1966; Hoffman, 1991; Wachtel, 1986 for similar proposals). Some degree of asymmetry is a necessary, although certainly insufficient, condition for analysis. The optimal balance or tension between participation and nonintrusiveness, between symmetry and asymmetry, cannot be established in advance by a standard set of rules or by a "model technique," but rather must emerge from the analytic work between a particular patient and a particular analyst and will likely change even from moment to moment within a given analysis.

Relational perspectives on the analyst's self-expression

Relational theorists have reconceptualized the nature of analytic change and especially the interaction among insight, structural change, and the analytic relationship and have given an emphasis to the ways in which interpretations are themselves "complex relational events" (Mitchell, 1988a, p. 295). Winnicott thought of interpretation not as the provision of new understanding so much as the analyst's recognition and acceptance of the patient's self through the analyst's own spontaneous, playful, and authentic participation with the patient. We have explored some of the contributions that have emerged in the tradition of the British independent group along these lines. Similarly, Kohut (1984) shifted the focus of our interpretive efforts from explanation to understanding and proposed that new experience with the analyst as self-object is as important as explanation. So, too, Loewald (1960), writing from within the Freudian tradition, has advanced the belief that interpretations convey the analyst's love and respect for the individuality of the patient and for the patient's individual development. The analyst functions, like the parent in development, by being a contemporary, real, emotionally related object, who can offer the patient the opportunity to form new and better personal integrations.

The interpersonal tradition provides yet a different perspective on the nature of interpretation in its emphasis on interpretation as an interpersonal participation by the analyst. The interpersonal approach views the analyst as a "participant-observer" (Sullivan, 1953) or "co-participant" (Wolstein, 1981) functioning within an interpersonal field, and the "detailed inquiry" (Sullivan, 1954) is a "collaborative inquiry" (Chrzanowski, 1980) in which the analyst is as free to provide data as the patient. Since the analyst is free to provide data and not just interpretation, interpersonal analysts suggest that the analyst may at times share her or his own associations and experiences with the patient even before the analyst knows their meaning or significance (Ehrenberg, 1984). This procedure is suggested in the hope that by discussing the analyst's experience with the patient, some meaning or significance will be established.

From a contemporary interpersonal perspective (Levenson, 1972), transference-countertransference interactions are mutually constructed and are never just talked about, but always enacted as they are being discussed. The analyst must recognize her or his participation in the enactment and work her or his way out of it either through further inquiry or through interpretation. Even in "accurately" interpreting a transference-countertransference enactment, however, and in thus working one's way out of an interaction, the analyst may well be participating in or enacting another interaction. Therefore, what may be an interpretation (a working one's way out) of one transference-countertransference enactment may be a participation in (being pulled into) another enactment (Gill, 1983). Speech always serves more purposes than simply to communicate; speech always serves in addition as a form of action. When we speak, we act on the person spoken to. The implication of this position is that interpretation cannot be seen as simply in the service of communicating information or knowledge to the patient; rather, interpretation is itself an interpersonal act. Interpretation is one form, and for some it is the form, by which analysts participate in the interaction with their patients.

I have referred to the analyst's being caught up in, or pulled into, the relation to the patient, that is, the analyst's enacting a role-responsiveness (Sandler, 1976) in response to the patient. Gill (1983) and, earlier, Levenson (1972, p. 174) described this in terms of participating and working one's way out of participation through understanding. Burke (1992) correctly identifies Gill as capturing the essence of the asymmetry position in this way of describing the analytic process, and he clarifies that this is a highly controversial proposition. Burke points out that Gill, Hoffman, and I, each supporting an asymmetric position, make it seem that the analyst's participation should always be unwitting or involuntary, that is, that the analyst is pulled into participation inadvertently and then attempts deliberately to work out of the interaction through understanding. In contrast, according to Burke, analysts working from the position of mutuality (in my scheme this would be from the position of symmetry) would make room for thinking of the analyst as deliberately working his or her way into the interaction, as well as attempting always to be working one's way out of it.

I do not believe that Gill's, Hoffman's, or my own position rules out the analyst's spontaneous expression or participation with the patient. Rather (and it is precisely for this reason that I prefer to think in terms of dimensions rather than categories), I believe that we each emphasize the necessity for relative asymmetry, and on balance we emphasize the hazards of too much self-expression on the analyst's part. For the analyst deliberately to work his or her way into an interaction with a patient, as Burke proposes, would be to interfere with whatever kind of interaction the patient is attempting to create. The only legitimate interaction that the analyst should be trying to work his or her way into is that of understanding the meanings of the interaction. Of course, inadvertently, the analyst will be pulled into other interactions or enactments, and in addition to "being pulled in," the analyst, out of his or her own interpersonal patterns, will unwittingly attempt to push the patient into particular patterns of enactment. It should be clear that both patient and analyst must be conceptualized as pushing and pulling each other if the conceptualization is to be mutual or intersubjective. The analyst's goal, however, is to understand these patterns with the patient, and while recognizing the inevitability of participating and enacting and even welcoming this development as the necessary next step in the progress of the analysis, the analyst should not be participating, that is, taking on any particular role, purposefully or deliberately. Participating should be done inadvertently, as much as possible as a response to the patient, rather than as a deliberate provocation or suggestive interpersonal influence. Viewing the analyst's participation as inevitable is a description, rather than a prescription of analytic activity (Greenberg, 1981). Sandler's term role-responsiveness captures this attitude well in its emphasis on the analyst's participating in response to the patient's relational demands, rather than out of some therapeutic strategy, and this differentiates it from the role-playing associated with Alexander's corrective emotional experience (Alexander & French, 1946).

Another argument, supporting asymmetry while recognizing the subjective dimensions of interpretation, is offered by Smith (1990), who put forth the thesis that all mutative interpretations are first enacted in the countertransference and that therapists gain awareness of the nature of the transference through these enactments. In other words, often, and perhaps regularly, we do not know the "correct" interpretation until after we make an interpretation. It is only by interpreting, which is our analytic form of participation, that we can recognize the nature of the interaction that we are involved in with the patient. Smith, however, in contrast to the radical interpersonalists, while acknowledging that "actual neutrality is a fiction" (p. 100), does not conclude that neutrality should be abandoned. Instead, he argues that paradoxically, "the less possible it is to be neutral in fact, the more crucial it is to strive toward it" (p. 101). Smith's position, in my schema, is one that recognizes mutuality, but advocates strict asymmetry, in contrast, on the one hand, to Burke (1992), Ehrenberg (1984), and Ferenczi (1932), who are advocating both mutuality and a high degree of symmetry, and, on the other hand, to Bollas (1987, 1989), Hoffman (in press), and myself, who advocate mutuality and a moderate degree of asymmetry. Interestingly, I disagree with Burke, who considers Bollas to advocate the principle of mutuality and not the principle of asymmetry. In my reading of Bollas, especially in the quotation just cited, he advocates both mutuality and relative asymmetry.

To round out this comparison of relational perspectives on the nature of interpretation, I would like to highlight the contributions of Baranger and Baranger (1966), who write from within a Kleinian metapsychological orientation. The Barangers note that both the patient and the analyst tend to repeat past problematic patterns of relations in their contemporary interpersonal life. Therefore, for the Barangers the analyst's interpretations serve to modify the analyst's relation to the patient as well as the patient's relation to the analyst. Put simply, the interpretation, in reducing the pathology of the bipersonal field, serves to cure the analyst as much as the patient. Nevertheless, the Barangers consider their clinical work to emphasize the asymmetry between patient and analyst. Etchegoyen (1991) has legitimately questioned in what respects the Barangers' position remains asymmetrical.

Case illustrations

The following illustrations serve as points of departure for a discussion of interpretation that highlights some of the subtleties and the complexities of clinical psychoanalytic practice utilizing the dimensions of mutuality-lack of mutuality and symmetry-asymmetry as an organizing framework. Following the discussion of case material, I conclude with my own thoughts synthesizing a variety of relational perspectives on interpretation as expression of the analyst's subjectivity.

From Hoffman

Hoffman (1992) suggests that supervisees may report that they are struggling in their work with patients because they would like to tell the patient X but they are afraid of Y. At these moments Hoffman says that he often suggests to supervisees that they tell the patient just that, that is, that they tell the patient, I want to tell you X but I am afraid of Y. Hoffman gives a number of examples that take this form. In one the supervisee is encouraged to say something like the following. "I am pulled to see your point of view or to take your side in this conflict that you describe with your friend; however, I have to admit I also feel some sympathy with this other person because similar things have happened between us and I have felt that I was in their position." In a similar example Hoffman suggests an intervention along the following lines: "I am inclined to give you the reassurance that you want because it seems that is what you need; however, I worry that in doing that I am perpetuating your dependency when it really is not necessary." Without knowing more about these hypothetical cases, we are really not in any position to decide how useful we might think this intervention would be. My point here, however, is that in line with Bollas's suggestions, Hoffman is here revealing his own, or encouraging his supervisee to reveal his or her own, subjectivity. More specifically, I do not think it is an accident, although Hoffman is not explicit about this, that what is revealed in particular is an aspect of conflict in the analyst (however, see Hoffman's discussion of the patient's perception of conflict in the analyst, 1983, p. 420). As described above in discussing Bollas (1987, 1989), once the analyst takes the step of introducing the data of his or her own experience, then the analyst is revealing aspects of his or her own psychic reality, and naturally enough that will include a focus on the analyst's conflicts. When Bollas disagrees with himself, establishing a dialectics of difference, he is revealing his own conflictedness. I believe that in moderation this is most useful in that it demonstrates to the patient that his or her psychic reality is not the only one in the room and, further, that it educates the patient about the ways in which an analyst thinks about psychic reality, namely, in terms of conflict (see Mitchell, 1988a, regarding the centrality of conflict in relational theories). Of course, the impact of the analyst's modeling is a form of suggestion that itself needs to be brought into the analysis at appropriate moments.

The following example highlights the therapeutic power of the analyst's interpretation containing aspects of the analyst's subjectivity and, in particular, aspects of the analyst's psychic conflict.

From Casement

In what has become a well-known and frequently cited teaching case, Casement (1982) presented his dilemma with a patient who was demanding that he allow her to hold his hand during one phase of her analysis. This patient had been scalded when she was an infant, and at 17 months she required surgery, which was performed under local anesthesia. During the surgery the patient's mother fainted, and the patient panicked when her mother's hand slipped away from hers. At first, Casement offered to consider the patient's request, but after thinking about it over the weekend, he told her that he thought it would be a mistake because it would sidestep her re-experience of the childhood trauma and that therefore in giving her his hand, he would be failing her as her analyst. The patient's response was to feel that in taking back his original offer, he had repeated the original trauma; that is, he gave her his hand and then withdrew it from her. She inferred from this that he could not stand to remain in touch with her emotional reliving of the traumatic experience. In reaction to this feeling of abandonment, the patient developed a psychotic transference reaction and expressed that she was fully suicidal.

Casement's paper describes the persistent and highly sensitive analytic work that he did with this patient and that ultimately led to her emergence from this despondent state.

This case has been discussed by Fox (1984), who emphasizes that the principle of abstinence requires that a balance be maintained between frustration and gratification in the form of emotional availability. According to Fox, Casement was correct that if he held the patient's hand, he would have been providing a corrective emotional experience. Fox, however, believes that in Casement's initially considering to hold her hand and not immediately refusing, Casement was providing the optimal balance between frustration and emotional availability.

I would like to highlight a different aspect of Casement's technique. Following the development of her psychotic transference, the patient became suicidal and hopeless about the treatment and felt that she could not go on with the analysis. She lost any sense of her analyst as not really being her mother or the surgeon. At this point Casement (1982) offered the following interpretation:

> You are making me experience in myself the sense of despair, and the impossibility of going on, that you are feeling. I am aware of being in what feels to me like a total paradox. In one sense I am feeling that it is impossible to reach you just now, and yet in another sense I feel that my telling you this may be the only way that I can reach you...Similarly I feel as if it could be impossible to go on, and yet I feel that the only way that I can help you through this is by my being prepared to tolerate what you are making me feel, and going on.
>
> (p. 283)

It was this interpretation that Casement depicts as the turning point in the patient's recovery from psychosis and suicidal despair. This is similar to the famous case in which Winnicott (1960) tells a depressed patient that he (Winnicott) is hopeless about the treatment and yet willing to continue, and for the first time the patient feels hope.

Casement's extremely lucid and engaging case presentation raises highly controversial issues concerning psychoanalytic technique. I want to emphasize the way that his interpretations contain and convey a great deal of his personal subjectivity and, in particular, the way that they express his own conflict about his relationship with the patient. In my view, it is only when he conveys explicitly to her his own struggle, hope, and despair about ever reaching her and, in so doing, sharing his psychic reality with her that she is able to emerge from the psychotic transference. It seems to me that what was therapeutic in this case was not that Casement walked the tightrope of abstinence, as Fox would have it, but rather that he fully engaged the patient by sharing with her his own psychic reality in the form of an interpretation that clarified both his own and the patient's psychic functioning as well as the intersubjective engagement that had developed between them.

From Etchegoyen

Etchegoyen (1991) describes an incident in which he moved his residence into an apartment on the same floor as his consulting room and his wife moved the doormat from in front of the former office to the front of his home. A female patient of his, whom he describes as coming out of a long period of confusion, told him that she thought she must be crazy because she had seen the old doormat in front of the other apartment. Etchegoyen interprets to the patient that she thought that the doormat had come from his former office and that she believed that it was as if he had purposely moved the doormat so as to let her know where he lived. He added that in telling him that she thought she must be crazy, she was communicating her belief that he had gone crazy; since she generally saw him as rigid, she knew that it would not be his style to leave the doormat where it would be spotted, so for him to do such a thing, he must have gone mad. Etchegoyen observes that following the interpretation, the patient's anxiety decreases as if by "enchantment," and furthermore the analyst feels calmer. The patient then says that she had noticed the doormat the very first day of the move and now concluded that his wife had probably moved it there without his noticing. Etchegoyen concludes that it is only a short step from this to the primal scene. I want to examine this vignette further.

Etchegoyen reveals to us, his readers, but not to his patient, that it was in fact his doormat and that his wife had moved it to his home doorway. He tells us that he was actually conflicted about this. He first wanted to tell his wife not to do this because a patient might notice and so find out where he lived, but then he thought that this was taking analytic reserve to the extreme. Etchegoyen deliberately does not reveal any of this to the patient, nor does he confirm or disconfirm that it is in fact his doormat. This is consistent with his belief, learned from Strachey (1934), that the best way to reestablish a patient's contact with reality is not for the analyst himself or herself to offer reality to the patient. Furthermore, it is in accord with his strictly maintained position that the analytic situation must be asymmetrical. When the analyst, however, says to his patient that she had the thought that he wanted her to know where he lived and when the analyst tells us that he is aware of being conflicted about putting the mat there because a patient might know where he lives, this raises interesting questions. Is it not possible that he had some conflict about this patient's knowing where he lived and that part of him wanted her to know? When he so quickly interprets that she thought that he wanted her to know and when this interpretation is made so quickly with relatively little data from the patient (at least few data are provided to the reader), is it not possible that the patient would hear this as confirmation that the analyst did have some conflict about this? How else would the analyst come to this conclusion so quickly, unless he resonated with the patient's conflict? As Singer (1968) says, "It takes one to know one, and in his correct interpretation the therapist reveals that he is one" (p. 369).

What am I suggesting that the analyst might have done differently? Am I suggesting that he reveal his conflict to the patient? Yes and no! In some ways I believe that the analyst has already revealed quite a bit in his creative and precipitant interpretation. I believe that subtly he has provided some data that at least make it plausible to the patient to believe that the analyst was conflicted about wanting her to know where he lived. Furthermore, her associations reveal that she believes she notices things about her analyst that he does not notice, in that she says she noticed the doormat but the analyst probably did not.

The master analyst from Buenos Aires is being consistent with his Kleinian technique when he interprets so quickly and so certainly. I am suggesting that he might have either waited to acquire more information or inquired along the following lines. If the patient thought that she saw the analyst's doormat, what was her idea about how it got there? If she believed that the analyst had wanted her to know where he lived, how did she explain that to herself? What has she noticed about him that leads her to think he would want her to know where he lives? Why did she wait before mentioning the doormat when she had noticed it right away? Has she noticed anything else about him that she believes he has not noticed? Once the analyst makes the interpretation as Etchegoyen did, there needs to be a follow-up inquiry into the way in which the patient experienced the interpretation. I am suggesting that the patient may very well have taken the interpretation as confirmation of her belief that the analyst was conflicted about wanting her to know where he lived.

The analyst concludes that it is only a short step from here to the primal scene, but why jump so quickly to the primal scene? What does the patient imagine about the analyst and his wife that she believes the analyst wants her to know where he lives? Or, that she imagines that his wife wants her to know where they live? Rather than move to the primal scene, I would first want thoroughly to explore the patient's beliefs, fantasies, observations, and inferences about the analyst in the here and now.

The analyst might tell the patient that she had the thought that the analyst was conflicted about wanting her to know where he lived. How different it is if the analyst tells the patient that she had the fantasy that the analyst was conflicted about this or if he says that she had noticed that the analyst was conflicted about this. The subtleties matter, not just the words, but the tone of voice and attitude. In my view, what is critical is not whether the analyst acknowledges some subjective state explicitly or not, but rather whether it is done in a way that furthers the analytic inquiry or in a way that shuts it down. If the analyst reveals something about himself or herself with a tone of certainty and authority, then this may serve to close off further inquiry rather than opening it up. On the other hand, the analyst may reveal some aspect of his subjective reality in a way that allows room for the patient to accept it, modify it, challenge it, or move beyond it.

From Aron

A young, attractive, married, female patient told me that it seemed to her that in the past week I had become more aloof than is my usual stance. She wondered if anything was wrong or what was going on in me. She did not refer to it, but I remembered that in the prior week there had been some banter back and forth between us in the context of highly charged sexual material in her associations. I thought that she was right; it did feel to me that I had pulled back from her following this exchange in an attempt not to get caught up in a seductive or flirtatious enactment. I did not share my thoughts with the patient but simply listened. She went on to tell me that a supervisor of hers at work had recently asked her if she had any single sisters to whom she could introduce him. He knew that she was married, but he had often flirted with her. This was the closest he had ever come to telling her directly that he was interested in someone like her. Following his asking her about her sisters, my patient noticed that he had not spoken with her for a few days. I told the patient that she believed that I had become uncomfortable with the intensity of our closeness, particularly when we were talking about such hot sexual material. She must have figured that I had pulled away out of my own discomfort, which I was conflicted about flirting with her. She agreed and went on to discuss her own conflicts about her temptations to have an affair and her embarrassment about expressing her sexual feelings to me.

This was a "good" patient; by this I mean that she was compliant and protective of me, in that she did not feel the need to push me further. She could have said, "Well, are you conflicted about your sexual feelings toward me?" "Have you backed away from me because you were afraid of your own temptations?" It is my belief that it was not necessary to reveal my own thoughts and feelings about this any further with this patient, at this time. In my interpretation to her I revealed enough, namely, that I was comfortable enough with these sexual feelings that I could risk talking about them with her. I believe that she knew that I could not have made that interpretation, in the way that I made it, unless I had experienced such feelings to at least some degree. This example also serves to illustrate the way in which making the interpretation serves to cure the analyst in the sense that in making the interpretation, I repositioned myself in relation to the patient; that is, in interpreting, I freed myself up with the patient so that I did not have to resort to such a distant, defensive posture.

What if she were not such a cooperative patient? If she had pushed me further and asked what I had felt or if I might ever feel such a conflict about her, rather than resorting to silence and evasiveness, I might have said or implied that I would fully expect to have a wide variety of thoughts and feelings toward my patients as well as conflicts about them, just as I would expect that they would have a wide variety of thoughts and feelings and conflicts about me. If she pushed further and asked, "Well, if you have feelings like that toward me, will you tell me?" I could only say, "First of all I might not have to tell you because you might know; in fact you might notice some of these things about me before I do." And, finally, I could only say, "I will tell you whatever I think will further the analysis." Here is the asymmetry. It is the patient who must attempt to tell all. The patient has to try to free-associate. The analyst may or may not associate based on his or her own clinical judgment of what is in the patient's interests or, more accurately, the interests of the analytic process. Finally, it is legitimate to ask whether I should have confronted her with her not asking me directly whether I had pulled away from her out of my own anxiety. By not demanding a response, she was being a traditionally "good" or compliant patient and in that way protecting the analyst as well as herself. Should this not be brought to her attention?

Beginning with Ferenczi (1932), analysts have recognized that patients may serve, at least to some extent, as their analysts, interpreting the analyst's countertransference (Hoffman, 1983). Searles (1975) has continually emphasized the ways in which the patient can serve as therapist to the analyst. It is important, however, to recognize that an interpretation, if it is intersubjectively constituted, must have consequences for both partners in the dialogue. That is, an interpretation has an impact on the one giving it as well as on the one receiving it. That is one reason, when a patient interprets to the analyst, it may be of benefit not only to the analyst but to the patient as well, and vice versa. Hoffman (1983) clarified that "at the very moment that he interprets, the analyst often extricates himself as much as he extricates the patient from transference-countertransference enactment" (p. 415) and that interpretations are effective partly because they have a "reflective impact" (p. 415) on the interpreter himself or herself. All interpretations are at least implicitly self-interpretive (Singer, 1968). Thus, interpretation is a complex, intersubjective, and mutual process that benefits both the interpreter and the one to whom it is intended. The following clinical material illustrates these points.

A patient was working for the first few years of his analysis on the issue of his conflicts regarding opening up and expressing feelings, both in general and to the analyst specifically. As would be expected, he was much concerned with his bodily orifices and with the dangers of fluids and bodily contents leaking outward. Thus, he was much concerned with his bowel movements, constipation, and diarrhea, as well as being self-conscious about sneezing, coughing, crying, sweating, vomiting, and spitting. All of this was analyzed and was related to his conflicts regarding holding in his inner thoughts and feelings and not letting out any feelings, particularly toward his analyst. All of this emerged repeatedly and was gone over again and again, but it was only with the following incident that it took on new meaning.

At one point while the patient was discussing his fear of letting his anger show, the analyst coughed, but coughed quietly, stifling the full extent of the cough. The patient, who was on the couch, first reacted to this by saying that he thought he had heard the analyst laugh, and he assumed that the analyst was laughing at him because of his continued inability to express himself. The analyst inquired as to why the patient thought that the analyst would be glad to humiliate him. The patient then said that another thought had suddenly crossed his mind: perhaps the analyst had coughed, but it sounded like a laugh because the analyst had stifled the cough. But why the analyst would stifle his cough, he wondered, unless the analyst was just like himself, holding in his expressiveness. The analyst said, "So I would want to laugh at you and humiliate you in order to distance myself from you and hold myself above you, so that I could avoid recognizing how similar we are and deny to myself and to you that I struggle with similar conflicts."

The analyst benefited enormously from this interaction in that he stopped inhibiting himself and felt freer from this moment on in his own self-expression with this patient. In the course of the continuing analytic work the patient noticed the increased freedom and spontaneity in the analyst, and the patient's contribution to this change was recognized and acknowledged by both patient and analyst. This led to greater insight by the patient into his own tendency toward inhibition and to increased openness and spontaneity on his part in relation to the analyst.

Gill (1987) has demonstrated that for an analyst to recognize that a patient views him or her in a particular way and for the analyst to consider this a plausible experience on the patient's part, the analyst has to see how his or her participation in the interaction lends plausibility to such an experience on the patient's part. Therefore, in listening to patients, the analyst, utilizing a relational-perspectivist approach, is continually learning about himself or herself as well as about his or her patient, and the analyst's interpretations implicitly or explicitly acknowledge this intersubjective dimension. Inasmuch as the analyst recognizes his or her own participation in creating the plausibility of the patient's perception, the analyst's interpretations come to include this aspect of the interaction and consequently reposition the analyst vis-à-vis the patient, and in doing so they lead to new interpersonal integrations and therefore to change in both patient and analyst.

Interpretation as expression of the analyst's subjectivity

In this chapter I have drawn on numerous psychoanalytic theorists in order to reexamine the nature of interpretation from a relational perspective. I am in agreement with Mitchell (1988a) that there is a great deal unifying the variety of relational approaches, in spite of their widely divergent metapsychologies, in their reconceptualization of the nature of interpretation.

The relational-perspectivist approach views the analyst as a co-participant with the patient in a mutually and reciprocally constructed transference-countertransference integration. The analyst inevitably participates by enacting a variety of relational patterns with the patient. What makes analysis unique is the analyst's commitment to reflection and inquiry so that the analyst is always attempting to understand and concomitantly free himself or herself from the enactment, while recognizing that this interpretive act of freedom is in itself a participation in another cycle of enactment. An interpretation is an interpersonal participation. It is an observation from within the interaction rather than from outside it.

> An interpretation is a *complex relational event*, not primarily because it alters something inside the patient, not because it releases a stalled developmental process, but because it says something very important about where the analyst stands vis-à-vis the patient, about what sort of relatedness is possible between the two of them.
>
> (Mitchell, 1988a, p. 295)

Interpretation is the principal process by which analysts position and reposition themselves interpersonally in relation to their patients, and in this sense interpretations contain aspects of the analyst's subjectivity, which are made available for use by the patient. Inasmuch as the analyst has captured aspects of the patient's psychic life in a particular interpretation and insofar as the interpretation also expresses aspects of the analyst's subjectivity, interpretation is best thought of as the quintessential container and purveyor of intersubjectivity between patient and analyst.

Viewing interpretation as an intersubjective process, rather than as an act on the part of the analyst, has the advantage of focusing attention on the interpersonal context in which interpretations are co-constructed and on both the patient's and analyst's mutual responses to interpretations. Furthermore, viewing interpretation as a process, rather than as an act, highlights the way in which interpretation complements, proceeds in tandem with, and is itself one aspect of psychoanalytic inquiry.

The interpretive process, which includes the interventions that prepare for interpretations as well as the follow-ups to interpretations and especially the exploration and inquiry that are essential to the interpretive process, is the form by which analysts and patients participate with each other in the analytic endeavor. Inasmuch as they are interpersonal acts of participation, it is through interpretations that the patient, as well as the analyst, comes to know where the analyst stands in relation to the patient, and it is through interpretations that the analyst best conveys his or her interest in, capacity to understand, and respect for the individuality of the patient. Just as insight may be thought of as a marker of change intrapsychically, so, too, interpretation may be thought of as a signal of change intersubjectively. Interpretations should be thought of as both markers of change and facilitators of change in the relationship between patient and analyst, which means that they serve to clarify and cumulatively to cure the patient, the analyst, and the interactional field that exists between them. The analyst's interpretation serves as an expression of the analyst's subjectivity and furthers the intersubjective and mutual, although asymmetrical, analytic process.

Notes

1 In this chapter, I use the term *interpretation* broadly to include much of the process of interpersonal exploration and inquiry. Some writers (see Bromberg, 1985) have objected to the broadening of the term *interpretation* on the grounds that extending the term obscures the extent to which

it was originally embedded in the structural model of conflict. In its more traditional and positivist context, it was thought that interpretations had to be "exact" in order to resolve the particular underlying, pathogenic intrapsychic conflict. I believe that an analyst may interpret with a sense of conviction even while eschewing certainty and abandoning positivist, epistemological presuppositions. Also, in its focus on the interpretive process, this chapter does not consider the noninterpretive factors that play an important role in a broader theory of therapeutic action. Much of this is to be elaborated in a forthcoming work by the author.

2 The German *Deutung* is closer to the English term *explanation* than to *interpretation* (see Laplanche & Pontalis, 1973, p. 228).

3 I prefer the term *relational-perspectivism* over Hoffman's term *social-constructivism*, because the term *social* carries too much of the baggage of "social psychology" in connoting a behavioral or superficial level of analysis. Thus, it was characteristic of the classical critique of the early interpersonalists that they were denigrated as promoting a form of "social" psychology. The terms *perspectivism* and *constructivism* are often used interchangeably; however, see the debate between Hoffman and Orange, this issue. Perspectivism emphasizes that everyone has his or her own plausible perspective on reality, that all knowledge is perspectival, and that there are always other perspectives than one's own. Along these lines, I have come to think of psychoanalytic "neutrality" as the analyst's openness to new perspectives, a commitment to take other perspectives seriously, and a refusal to view any interpretation as complete or any meaning as exhaustive.

4 This chapter is not intended to be a systematic or sequential historical review of the literature regarding interpretation. I prefer to move back and forth between a variety of theoretical positions, all of which are active and influential in contemporary psychoanalytic practice. My aim is to allow the positions to talk to each other and inform each other, rather than portray psychoanalysis as having moved in a progressively linear direction. I also recognize that this is not a balanced presentation. For example, I am highlighting the contributions of the British independents and only mentioning minimally the recent Kleinian contributions. Similarly, there is a wealth of recent writing from Freudians that is relevant to my thesis. I hope to elaborate further on the recent Kleinian and Freudian contributions in a forthcoming work.

Chapter 6

The patient's experience of the analyst's subjectivity (1991)

Introduction by Steven Kuchuck

My mind first met Lewis Aron's about 17 years ago. My heart was quick to follow. Like many who were classically trained and practicing for years, I had only recently discovered a way out of disillusionment and the creeping approach of potential burnout through the hope of Relational psychoanalysis. As luck would have it, I somehow found Lew's first authored book (1996/2001), a central part of that liberation process for me. It completely revolutionized my approach to understanding and practicing psychoanalysis, and therefore, I don't think it's an overstatement to say that in a number of ways both professionally and personally, it changed my life. I soon became one of Lew's students, and we began a long, rich professional and eventually personal relationship. Over time, we collaborated on numerous professional projects, and I later joined Lew as one of the co-editors of the Relational Perspectives Book Series. When he and my dear friend Galit Atlas became life partners, our relationship deepened further.

As those who knew him can attest to, Lew embodied the intertwining nature of personal and professional, working and living his life with love, passion, and generativity. Perhaps it's no surprise then that a singular through line in his teaching and writing is his curiosity about subjectivity. Perhaps it goes without saying that all clinicians are interested in our patients' subjectivities. Historically, of course, the interest in our own personality was mainly about how to analyze away its influence on the treatment (see this chapter). But Aron was among the very first to shine a light on the crucial importance of actively considering the analyst's subjectivity, and how that directly impacts clinical work. As early as his first published papers, he considered the importance of examining the analyst's personality to be an integral part of contemporary theory and practice.

By the time he wrote "The Patient's Experience of the Analyst's Subjectivity," Lew's exploration of the nature and impact of the analyst's psyche had become much more sophisticated and would remain a central component of his writing for the rest of his professional life. By the end of his long, distinguished, but tragically abbreviated career, he had spent three decades exploring specific ways in which the clinician's subjectivity both enhances and impedes therapeutic action as well as noting the significant barriers to how much we can know ourselves. We must therefore, he wrote, rely on our patients (this chapter and others) as well as our colleagues (2017) to more fully understand our impact, blind spots, and limitations as practitioners and theoreticians. In later years and up until the end of his life, he expanded his focus to include an investigation of the subjectivities of central figures in psychoanalysis and how these personal dynamics influenced theoretical formulations. Those biographical researches included but were not limited to Sigmund Freud, Sandor Ferenczi, Harold Searles, Carl Jung, Hans Loewald, and others.

In the following chapter, Aron develops this central thesis: Patients seek to deeply explore and know their therapists' psyches similar to the ways in which the developing child longs to know the parents' mind. It is only by probing the analyst's (initially parents') mind that the patient (child) can more deeply learn about his or her own mind, its impact on others, can better understand interpersonal dynamics in and outside of the consultation room, and can gain a fuller understanding of the parents' impact on the patient's psyche. Aron elaborates on the theoretical underpinnings of this premise and provides a detailed, practice-focused explanation of how to help patients explore their analyst's subjectivity, as well as the positive and negative implications of attempting to foreground the presence of the analyst in this way.

As he explains, any exploration of the analyst's mind will inevitably lead to a certain amount of inadvertent and possibly deliberate self-disclosure on the part of the analyst or at least a consideration of the latter. Aron therefore engages in a fuller discussion of self-disclosure and related (though distinct) concepts of mutuality and asymmetry, ideas that are initially introduced in this chapter and later elaborated in his first book (1996c) and other writing. Additionally, Aron notes that although important and even necessary, helping patients to more fully explore our subjective selves presents a tremendous challenge for most analysts. Those drawn to this profession, he states, are conflicted about being seen and known. "Why else," he asks, "would people choose a profession in which they spend their lives listening ... while they themselves remain relatively silent and hidden? The recognition that analysts ... are never invisible and, ... that patients seek to know their analysts raise profound anxieties..." (pp. 43–44). Ever the teacher, here he attempts to impart something profound and for many of us, resonant, about our own subjectivity.

In the text that follows, we see trademarks of Aron's teaching and writing. He is always interested in both the theoretical and clinical and moves adeptly between each. As mentioned throughout this introduction, he is deeply concerned with elements of the analyst's subjectivity and, I would add, the clinician's overall relationship to her or his patients—he is indeed the consummate relationalist. He is fully committed to intellectual and theoretical rigor while remaining remarkably accessible in his prose. In fact, I maintain that Lew was one of the clearest, most compelling writers and gifted editors our field has produced. I believe that readers will see evidence of that in the following pages and indeed throughout this entire volume.

Aron, L. (1991). The patient's experience of the analyst's subjectivity.

Psychoanalytic Dialogues, 1(1), 9–51.

The purpose of this chapter is to highlight the clinical centrality of examining the patient's experience of the analyst's subjectivity in the psychoanalytic situation. Although many cultural, social, and scientific developments have contributed to a relational view of the psychoanalytic process, I believe that the shift to an intersubjective perspective has emerged predominantly out of our accumulated clinical experience in psychoanalytic work with patients. I would like to begin by noting some developments in two areas not directly related to clinical psychoanalysis: feminist thought and infancy research. My purpose is not to base clinical theory on the grounds of laboratory research nor to rest it on the movement to rectify social inequities; rather, because the implications of an intersubjective view are being clearly spelled out in these areas, they provide an illustration of what I mean by intersubjectivity.

Only with the recent development of feminist psychoanalytic criticism has it become apparent that psychology and psychoanalysis have contributed to and perpetuated a distorted view of motherhood (Balbus, 1982; Benjamin, 1988; Chodorow, 1978; Dinnerstein, 1976. In all of our theories of development, the mother has been portrayed as the object of the infan6t's drives and as the fulfiller of the baby's needs. We have been slow to recognize or acknowledge the mother as a subject in her own right. In discussing the prevalent psychological descriptions of motherhood, Benjamin (1988) recently wrote:

> The mother is the baby's first object of attachment, and later, the object of desire. She is provider, interlocutor, caregiver, contingent reinforcer, significant other, empathic understanable, and mirror. She is also a secure presence to walk away from, a setter of limits, an optimal frustrator, a shockingly real outside otherness. She is external reality—but she is rarely regarded as another subject with a purpose apart from her existence for her child.
>
> (p. 24)

Benjamin has argued that the child must come to recognize the mother as a separate other who has her own inner world and her own experiences and who is her own center of initiative and an agent of her own desire. This expanding capacity on the part of the child represents an important, and previously unrecognized, developmental achievement. Benjamin has proposed that the capacity for recognition and intersubjective relatedness is an achievement that is best conceptualized in terms of a separate developmental line, and she has begun to articulate the complex vicissitudes involved in this advance. This developmental achievement is radically different from that which has previously been described in the literature. The traditional notion of "object constancy" is limited to the recognition of the mother as a separate "object." What is being emphasized from an intersubjective perspective is the child's need to recognize mother as a separate subject, a need that is a developmental advance beyond viewing mother only as a separate object. Dinnerstein (1976) anticipated this when she wrote, "Every 'I' first emerges in relation to an 'It' which is not at all clearly an 'I.' The separate 'I'ness of the other person is a discovery, an insight achieved over time" (p. 106).

Intersubjectivity refers to the developmentally achieved capacity to recognize another person as a separate center of subjective experience. Stern's (1985) description of the developmental progression of the sense of self has begun to draw attention to the domain of intersubjective relatedness in which the nature of relatedness expands to include the recognition of subjective mental states in the other as well as in oneself. Recent theorizing about the construction of internal representations of self and others (Beebe & Lachmann, 1988a; Lichtenberg, 1983; Stern, 1989) has just begun to consider the child's emerging ability to attribute subjectivity or internal states to others and to explore the ways in which these internal states can be interpersonally communicated.

Winnicott (1954–1955) anticipated the importance of an intersubjective perspective and provided a preliminary hypothesis regarding the establishment of intersubjectivity. He expanded Klein's depressive position to include the development of the capacity for "ruth" (p. 265), which he contrasts to the state of "ruthlessness" that exists prior to the development of the capacity to recognize the other as a separate person. Winnicott (1969) elaborates a theory of "object usage" that describes the process by which the infant destroys the object, finds that the object survives destruction, and therefore is able to surrender omnipotence and recognize the other as a separate person. Other theorists who have been examining the nature and development of intersubjectivity include Stern (1985), Ogden (1986), Kernberg (1987), Stolorow, Brandchaft, and Atwood (1987), and Bollas (1989). It was perhaps Lacan (Miller, 1988) who, in his seminars of the mid-1950s, first discussed the implications of intersubjectivity within the psychoanalytic situation. I will not elaborate here on the developmental aspects of intersubjectivity since my present aim is to discuss intersubjective psychology as it is related to clinical psychoanalysis.

The theory of intersubjectivity has profound implications for psychoanalytic practice and technique as well as for theory. (It should be noted that in my understanding of intersubjectivity I have been influenced by Benjamin [1988] and that my approach to psychoanalytic technique is quite distinct from that being developed by Stolorow et al. [1987].) Just as psychoanalytic theory has focused on the mother exclusively as the object of the infant's needs while ignoring the subjectivity of the mother, so, too, psychoanalysis has considered analysts only as objects while neglecting the subjectivity of analysts as they are experienced by the patient.

The traditional model of the analytic situation maintained the notion of neurotic patients who brought their irrational childhood wishes, defenses, and conflicts into the analysis to be analyzed by relatively mature, healthy, and well-analyzed analysts who would study the patients with scientific objectivity and technical neutrality. The health, rationality, maturity, neutrality, and objectivity of the analyst were idealized, and thus countertransference was viewed as an unfortunate, but hopefully rare, lapse. Within the psychoanalytic situation, this bias, which regarded the patient as sick and the analyst as possessing the cure (Racker, 1968), led to the assumption that it was only the patient who had transferences. Furthermore, it was as if only the patient possessed a "psychic reality" (see McLaughlin, 1981) and the analyst was left as the representative of objective reality. In sum, if the analyst was to be a rational, relatively distant, neutral, anonymous scientist-observer, an "analytic instrument" (Isakower, 1963), then there was little room in the model for the analyst's psychic reality or subjectivity, except as pathological, intrusive countertransference.

As is well known, it is only in the most recent decades that countertransference has been viewed as a topic worthy of study and as potentially valuable in the clinical situation. For Freud (1910a), countertransference reflected a specific disturbance in the analyst elicited in response to the patient's transference and necessitating further analysis of the analyst. Contemporary theorists are more inclined to take a "totalistic" (Kernberg, 1965) approach to countertransference and view it as reflecting all of the analyst's emotional responses to the patient and therefore useful as a clinical tool. Rather than viewing countertransference as a hindrance to the analytic work that should be kept in check or overcome and that should, in any event, be kept to a minimum, most analysts today recognize the ubiquity of analysts' feelings and fantasies regarding patients and hope to utilize their own reactions as a means to understand their patients better. Psychoanalysis has thus broadened its data base to include the subjectivity of the analyst. It has not yet, however, sufficiently considered the patient's experience of the analyst's subjectivity.

In my view, referring to the analyst's total responsiveness with the term *countertransference* is a serious mistake because it perpetuates defining the analyst's experience in terms of the subjectivity of the patient. Thinking of the analyst's experience as "counter" or responsive to the patient's transference encourages the belief that the analyst's experience is reactive rather than subjective, emanating from the center of the analyst's psychic self (McLaughlin, 1981; Wolstein, 1983a). It is not that analysts are never responsive to the pressures that the patients put on them; of course, the analyst does counterrespond to the impact of the patient's behavior. The term *countertransference*, though, obscures the recognition that the analyst is often the initiator of the interactional sequences, and therefore, the term minimizes the impact of the analyst's behavior on the transference.

The relational approach that I am advocating views the patient-analyst relationship as continually established and reestablished through ongoing mutual influence in which both patient and analyst systematically affect, and are affected by, each other. A communication process is established between patient and analyst in which influence flows in both directions. This approach implies a "two-person psychology" or a regulatory-systems conceptualization of the analytic process (Aron, 1990a). The terms *transference* and *countertransference* too easily lend themselves to a model that implies a one-way influence in which the analyst responds in reaction to the patient. The fact that the influence between patient and analyst is not equal does not mean that it is not mutual. Mutual influence does not imply equal influence, and the analytic relationship may be mutual without being symmetrical. This model of the therapeutic relationship has been strongly influenced by the recent conceptualizations of mother-infant mutual influence proposed by Beebe and Lachmann (1988b).

Others have also suggested that we abandon the term *countertransference*. Olinick (1969) suggested the alternative *eccentric responses* in the "psychology of the analyst," but I see no advantage to the pejorative term *eccentric*. Bird (1972) broadened the meaning of the term *transference* and sees it as the basis for all human relationships. He then suggests referring simply to "the analyst's transferences." This strategy, however, leads to terminological confusion, such as in Loewald's (1986,

p. 280) discussion of the importance of analyzing the patient's countertransference to the analyst's transference. McLaughlin (1981) convincingly argues for abandoning the term countertransference. He writes, "The term countertransference particularly cannot accommodate the intrapsychic range and fullness of the analyst's experiences vis-à-vis his patient" (p. 656).

In a seminal chapter, Hoffman (1983) draws together the work of theorists from a wide variety of psychoanalytic schools. These theorists share a radical social and perspectival concept of psychoanalysis that recognizes that patients make plausible inferences regarding aspects of their analysts' experience. Hoffman advances a view of psychoanalytic technique that makes central the analysis of the patient's interpretations of the analyst's experience. In many respects the present chapter may be seen as my efforts to grapple with and elaborate on the implications of Hoffman's contribution. While Hoffman entitles his paper "The Patient as Interpreter of the Analyst's Experience," he continues to refer to the patient's interpretation of the analyst's countertransference. Because of my objections to the implications of the term *countertransference*, I prefer to describe the focus of this chapter in terms of the patient's experience of the analyst's subjectivity.

Racker (1968) was one of the first to make the technical recommendation that "analysis of the patient's fantasies about countertransference, which in the widest sense constitute the causes and consequences of the transference, is an essential part of the analysis of the transferences" (p. 131). Gill (1983) puts it simply and directly, although in my view this point has not received nearly the attention it deserves: "A consequence of the analyst's perspective on himself as a participant in a relationship is that he will devote attention not only to the patient's attitude toward the analyst but also to the patient's view of the analyst's attitude toward the patient" (p. 112).

Since, from a classical perspective, the analyst was viewed as participating with the patient in only a minimal way (Gill, 1983), very little attention was given to the impact of the individual analyst and the impact of the analyst's character. Analysts did not consider that patients would inevitably and persistently seek to connect with their analysts by exploring their own observations and inferences about their analyst's behavior and inner experience.

Wolstein (1983a) has pointed out that resistances are defensive efforts by patients to cope with a particular analyst and that these resistances must therefore be patterned by the patient to accommodate to some aspect of the analyst's unconscious psychology. The point is that the patient could find a specific defense or resistance to be effective only if in some way it was designed to match the personality of the patient's particular analyst. Therefore, the ultimate outcome of successfully analyzing resistances is that patients would learn more not only about their own psychologies but also about the psychology of others in their lives, particularly about the psychology of their analysts. Wolstein (1988) writes:

> Nothing was more natural than for patients to turn the strength of this new awareness and reconstruction toward the psychology of their immediately environing others—especially their psychoanalysts—and describe the perceived aspects of countertransference against which they thought they had gone into resistance.
>
> (p. 9)

The implications of this point are enormous, for it means that as resistances are analyzed, patients not only expose more of their own unconscious but also gain awareness of hitherto unnoticed, dissociated, or repressed aspects of the psychology of their analysts. In spite of extended training analyses, analysts might not be aware of some of what their patients notice. Some of the observations that patients make about their analysts are likely to be unpleasant and anxiety-provoking. Therefore, analysts might back off from exploring the patient's resistances because of their own anxieties and resistances (Gill, 1982; Hoffman, 1983; Racker, 1968).

Of course, it is often argued that patients can and do fantasize about the analyst's psychology and that therefore the successful result of analysis of these fantasies is that patients learn more about their own psychology than about that of their analyst. My point here is that these fantasies are not endogenously determined, drive-determined, autistic creations of patients, nor are they purely the result of expectations derived from past interpersonal experiences. Rather, these fantasies may additionally be seen as patients' attempts to grapple with and grasp, in their own unique and idiosyncratic way, the complex and ambiguous reality of their individual analyst (see Levenson, 1989). Ultimately, an analysis of these fantasies must contribute to a clearer understanding of both the patient's and the analyst's psychologies.

I believe that patients, even very disturbed, withdrawn, or narcissistic patients, are always accommodating to the interpersonal reality of the analyst's character and of the analytic relationship. Patients tune in, consciously and unconsciously, to the analyst's attitudes and feelings toward them, but inasmuch as they believe that these observations touch on sensitive aspects of the analyst's character, patients are likely to communicate these observations only indirectly through allusions to others, as displacements, or through descriptions of these characteristics as aspects of themselves, as identifications (Gill, 1982; Hoffman, 1983; Lipton, 1977). An important aspect of making the unconscious conscious is to bring into awareness and articulate the patient's denied observations, repressed fantasies, and unformulated experiences of the analyst (Hoffman, 1983; Levenson, 1972, 1983; Racker, 1968).

All children observe and study their parents' personalities. They attempt to make contact with their parents by reaching into their parents' inner worlds. The Kleinians have emphasized this point vividly through concrete metaphors of the infant's seeking literally to climb inside and explore the mother's body and to discover all of the objects contained inside. Children imagine with what and with whom their mothers are preoccupied. They have some sense, although they may have never thought about it, as to how their mothers related to their own mothers. There is now empirical research that documents that a mother's internal working model of her relationship with her own mother affects her child's attachment to her (Main, Kaplan, & Cassidy, 1985). The child acquires some sense of the characters who inhabit the mother's and father's inner worlds and of the nature of the relations among these inner objects. Most important, children formulate plausible interpretations of their parents' attitudes and feelings toward the children themselves. Children are powerfully motivated to penetrate to the center of their parents' selves. Pick (1985) states this idea in Kleinian language: "If there is a mouth that seeks a breast as an inborn potential, there is, I believe, a psychological equivalent, i.e. a state of mind which seeks another state of mind" (p. 157).

If, as McDougall (1980) asserts, "a baby's earliest reality is his mother's unconscious" (p. 251), then patients' psychic reality may be said to implicate their analyst's unconscious. Patients have conscious and unconscious beliefs about the analyst's inner world. Patients make use of their observations of their analyst, which are plentiful no matter how anonymous the analyst may attempt to be, to construct a picture of their analyst's character structure. Patients probe, more or less subtly, in an attempt to penetrate the analyst's professional calm and reserve. They do this probing not only because they want to turn the tables on their analyst defensively or angrily but also, like all people, because they want to and need to connect with others, and they want to connect with others where they live emotionally, where they are authentic and fully present, and so they search for information about the other's inner world. An analytic focus on the patient's experience of the analyst's subjectivity opens the door to further explorations of the patient's childhood experiences of the parents' inner world and character structure. Similarly, patients begin to attend to their observations about the characters of others in their lives. This development is an inevitable and essential part of how patients begin to think more psychologically in their analyses. The analytic stance being described considers fantasies and memories not just as carriers of infantile wishes and defenses against these wishes, but as plausible interpretations and representations of the patient's experiences with significant others (Hoffman, 1983). This point was anticipated by Loewald (1970), who wrote, "The analysand in this respect can be compared to the child—who if he can allow himself that freedom—scrutinizes with his unconscious antennae the parent's motivations and moods and in this way may contribute—if the parent or analyst allows himself that freedom—to the latter's self awareness" (p. 280).

In the clinical situation I often ask patients to describe anything that they have observed or noticed about me that may shed light on aspects of our relationship. When, for example, patients say that they think that I am angry at them or jealous of them or acting seductively toward them, I ask them to describe whatever it is that they have noticed that led them to this belief. I find that it is critical for me to ask the question with the genuine belief that I may find out something about myself that I did not previously recognize. Otherwise, it is too easy to dismiss the patients' observations as distortions. Patients are often all too willing and eager to believe that they have projected or displaced these feelings onto their analyst, and they can then go back to viewing their analyst as objective, neutral, or benignly empathic. I encourage patients to tell me anything that they have observed and insist that there must have been some basis in my behavior for their conclusions. I often ask patients to speculate or fantasize about what is going on inside of me, and in particular I focus on what patients have noticed about my internal conflicts.

For instance, a patient said that when he heard my chair move slightly, he thought for a moment that I was going to strike him. I asked the patient to elaborate on what he thought I was feeling, what he thought was the quality and nature of my anger, what he had noticed about me that led him to believe that I was angry in this particular way, and how he imagined that I typically dealt with my anger and frustration. I asked the patient what he thought it was like for me to be so enraged at him and not to be able to express that anger directly, according to his understanding of the "rules" of psychoanalysis and professional decorum. I asked him how he thought I felt about his noticing and confronting me with my disguised anger.

I choose first to explore the patient's most subtle observations of me, which reflect my attitudes toward the patient as well as my character and personal conflicts, in preference to examining either the patient's own projected anger or the displaced anger of others in the patient's current or past life. All of this anger ultimately needs to be explored, but following Gill's (1983) recommendations, I begin with an analysis of the transference in the here and now, focusing on the plausible basis for the patient's reactions. It is important to note that I proceed in this way whether or not I am aware of feeling angry at that point. I assume that the patient may very well have noticed my anger, jealousy, excitement, or whatever before I recognize it in myself.

Inquiry into the patient's experience of the analyst's subjectivity represents one underemphasized aspect of a complex psychoanalytic approach to the analysis of transference. A balance needs to be maintained between focusing on the interpersonal and the intrapsychic, between internal object relations and external object relations. While at times exploring patients' perceptions of the analyst serves to deepen the work, at other times this focus is used defensively, by patient and analyst, to avoid the patient's painful inner experience (see Jacobs, 1986, p. 304 for a clinical illustration of this problem). For each time that I ask patients regarding their experience of me, there are other times that I interpret their focus on the interaction with me as an avoidance of their inner feelings and of looking into themselves.

While asking direct questions about the patient's observations of the analyst is often necessary and productive, the most useful way to elicit the patient's thoughts and feelings about the analyst's attitudes is to analyze the defenses and resistances that make these thoughts and feelings so difficult to verbalize. Asking patients direct questions about their experience of the therapeutic relationship entails the disadvantage that it may appeal to more surface and conscious levels of discourse. The analyst needs to listen to all of the patient's associations for clues as to the patient's experience. Often the patient fears offending the analyst and provoking the analyst's anger by confronting the analyst with aspects of the analyst's character that have been avoided. Patients fear that they are being too personal, crossing over the boundary of what the analyst is willing to let them explore. Patients are especially likely to fear that if they expose the analyst's weaknesses and character flaws, the analyst will retaliate, become depressed, withdrawn, or crumble (Gill, 1982). Implicit in this fear are not only the patient's hostility, projected fears, or simply the need to idealize the analyst but also the patient's perception of the analyst's grandiosity, which would be shattered by the revelation of a flaw. The patient's expectations of the analyst are related to the ways in which the patient's parents actually responded to their children's observations and perceptions of them. How did their parents feel about their children's really getting to know who they were, where they truly lived emotionally? How far were the parents able to let their children penetrate into their inner worlds? Was the grandiosity of the parents such that they could not let their children uncover their weaknesses and vulnerabilities? To return to the rich Kleinian imagery of the infant's attempts in unconscious phantasy to enter into the mother's body, we may wonder whether the violent, destructive phantasies encountered are due only to innate greed and envy or whether they are not also the result of the frustration of being denied access to the core of the parents. Could these phantasies be an accurate reflection of the child's perceptions of the parents' fears of being intimately penetrated and known?

What enables patients to describe their fantasies and perceptions of the analyst is the analyst's openness and intense curiosity about patients' experience of the analyst's subjectivity. The patient will benefit from this process only if the analyst is truly open to the possibility that patients will communicate something *new* about the analyst, something that the patient has picked up about the analyst that the analyst was not aware of before. If, on the other hand, the analyst listens to the patient with the expectation of hearing a transference distortion and is not open to the likelihood and necessity of learning something new about himself or herself, then the analysis is more likely to become derailed or to continue on the basis of compliance and submission to authority.

The recognition of the analyst's subjectivity within the analytic situation raises the problem of the analyst's self-disclosure. The issues involved by the analyst's self-revelations are enormously complex and can only be touched on here. There are, however, a few comments that should be made because they are directly raised by the line of inquiry advocated in this chapter.

When patients are encouraged to verbalize their experiences of the analyst's subjectivity, it is most likely that they will put increased pressure on the analyst to verify or refute their perceptions. It is extremely difficult and frustrating for patients to be encouraged to examine their perceptions of the analyst's subjectivity and then to have their analyst remain relatively "anonymous." Once analysts express interest in the patient's perceptions of their subjectivity, they have tantalized the patient (Little, 1951) and will surely be pressured to disclose more of what is going on inside themselves. Furthermore, the ways in which analysts pursue the inquiry into the patient's perceptions of themselves are inevitably self-revealing. I assume that one reason that analysts have traditionally avoided direct inquiry into the patient's experience of the analyst's subjectivity is that they recognized that pursuing this line of inquiry would unavoidably result in self-disclosure.

Self-revelation is not an option; it is an inevitability. Patients accurately and intuitively read into their analyst's interpretations the analyst's hidden communications (Jacobs, 1986). In unmasking the myth of analytic anonymity, Singer (1977) pointed out that the analyst's interpretations were first and foremost self-revealing remarks.

It cannot be otherwise since the only way we can truly gain insight into another is through our own self-knowledge, and our patients know that fact.

Hoffman (1983) emphasized that patients know that the psychology of the analyst is no less complex than that of themselves. He challenged what he termed "the naive patient fallacy," the notion that the patient accepts at face value the analyst's words and behavior. For analysts simply and directly to say what they are experiencing and feeling may encourage the assumption that they are fully aware of their own motivations and meanings. The analyst's revelations and confessions may tend to close off further exploration of the patient's observations and perceptions. Furthermore, we can never be aware in advance of just what it is that we are revealing about ourselves, and when we think we are deliberately revealing something about ourselves, we may very well be communicating something else altogether. Is it not possible that our patients' perceptions of us are as plausible an interpretation of our behavior as the interpretations we give ourselves? If so, then it is presumptuous for the analyst to expect the patient to take at face value the analyst's self-revelations. Pontalis (cited in Limentani, 1989) asks, "What is more paradoxical than the presupposition that: I see my blind spots, I hear what I am deaf to ... and (furthermore) I am fully conscious of my unconscious" (p. 258).

We hope that we, as analysts, have had the benefit of an intensive analysis of our own, but this in no way ensures that we have easy access to our unconscious or that we are immune from subtly enacting all sorts of pathological interactions with our patients. This recognition has led to our contemporary acceptance of the inevitability of countertransference. Whereas in the past idealized, well-analyzed analysts were thought to have no countertransference problem, today's idealized analysts are thought to be so well analyzed that they have immediate and direct access to their unconscious. It is well to keep in mind that the trouble with self-analysis is in the countertransference! When analysis is viewed as a coparticipation (Wolstein, 1983a) between two people who are both subjects and objects to each other, then the analyst can read the patient's associations for references to the patient's perceptions of the analyst's attitudes toward the patient. This method provides additional data with which analysts can supplement their own self-analysis. In this way the analyst and patient coparticipate in elucidating the nature of the relationship that the two of them have mutually integrated.

Bollas (1989) advocates that analysts need to establish themselves as subjects in the bipersonal analytic field. Bollas encourages analysts to reveal more of their internal analytic process to their patients, for example, describing to a patient how the analyst arrived at a particular interpretation or sharing with the patient the analyst's associations to a patient's dream. He argues that if the analyst's self-disclosure is congruent with who the analyst really is as a person, then the disclosure is unlikely to be taken as a seduction. In establishing themselves as subjects in the analytic situation, analysts make available to the patient some of their own associations and inner processes for the patient to use and analyze. It is important to note that Bollas's revelations have a highly playful and tentative quality in that he does not take his associations or "musings" as containing absolute truth but rather puts them into the analytic field and is prepared to have them used or destroyed by the patient. Furthermore, Bollas is reserved and cautious in his approach because of his awareness that an incessant flow of the analyst's associations could be intrusive, resulting in "a subtle takeover of the analysand's psychic life with the analyst's" (p. 69). Bollas's clinical contributions are enormous, but while I agree that analysts should be available to the patient as a separate subject, the danger with any approach that focuses on analysts' subjectivity is that analysts may insist on asserting their own subjectivity. In the need to establish themselves as separate subjects, analysts may impose this on the patient, thus forcing the patient to assume the role of object. Analyst's imposition of their own subjectivity onto their patients is not "intersubjectivity" it is simply an instrumental relationship in which the subject-object polarities have been reversed.

In my view self-revelations are often useful, particularly those closely tied to the analytic process rather than those relating to details of the analyst's private life outside of the analysis. Personal revelations are, in any event, inevitable, and they are simply enormously complicated and require analysis of how they are experienced by the patient. We as analysts benefit enormously from the analytic efforts of our patients, but we can help them as analysts only if we can discipline ourselves enough to put their analytic interests ahead of our own, at least temporarily.

The major problem for analysts in establishing themselves as subjects in the analytic situation is that because of their own conflicts they may abandon traditional anonymity only to substitute imposing their subjectivity on patients and thus deprive patients of the opportunity to search out, uncover, and find the analyst as a separate subject, in their own way and at their own rate. While a focus on the patient's experience of the analyst needs to be central at certain phases of an analysis, there are other times, and perhaps long intervals, when focusing on perceptions of the analyst is intrusive and disruptive. Focusing exclusively on the presence of the analyst does not permit the patient temporarily to put the analyst into the background and indulge in the experience of being left alone in the presence of the analyst. Analysts' continuous interpretations of all material in terms of the patient-analyst relationship, as well as analysts' deliberate efforts to establish themselves as separate subjects, may be rightfully experienced as an impingement stemming from the analysts' own narcissistic needs. To some degree this outcome is inevitable, and it can be beneficial for a patient to articulate it when it happens.

Winnicott (1971a) has suggested that psychoanalysis occurs in an intermediate state, a transitional space, transitional between the patient's narcissistic withdrawal and full interaction with reality, between self-absorption and object usage, between introspection and attunement to the other, and between relations to a subjective-object and relations to an object, objectively perceived, transitional between fantasy and reality. In my own clinical work, I attempt to maintain an optimal balance between the necessary recognition and confirmation of the patient's experience and the necessary distance to preserve an analytic space that allows the patient to play with interpersonal ambiguity and to struggle with the ongoing lack of closure and resolution. A dynamic tension needs to be preserved between responsiveness and participation on the one hand and nonintrusiveness and space on the other, intermediate between the analyst's presence and absence. My manner of achieving this tension is different with each patient and varies even in the analysis of a single analysand. I believe that each analyst-patient pair needs to work out a unique way of managing this precarious balance. The analysis itself must come to include the self-reflexive examination of the ways in which this procedure becomes established and modified. Analysis, from this perspective, is mutual but asymmetrical, with both patient and analyst functioning as subject and object, as coparticipants, and with the analyst and patient working on the very edge of intimacy. The question of the degree and nature of the analyst's deliberate self-revelation is left open to be resolved within the context of each unique psychoanalytic situation.

In my initial attempts to present these thoughts to varying groups of colleagues and students, I was struck by the overwhelming tendency on the part of my listeners to focus the discussion on the issue of the analyst's self-revelations. I wondered why analysts were so eager to discuss self-revelation when it was not the main point of the chapter. In my view, what is important is not the analyst's deliberate self-disclosure but rather the analysis of the patient's experience of the analyst's subjectivity. The very expression by patients of their perceptions of the analyst leads to the establishment of the analyst as a separate subject in the mind of the patient. So why do analytic audiences focus on self-revelation?

I believe that people who are drawn to analysis as a profession have particularly strong conflicts regarding their desire to be known by another, that is, conflicts concerning intimacy. In more traditional terms these are narcissistic conflicts over voyeurism and exhibitionism. Why else would people choose a profession in which they spend their lives listening and looking into the lives of others while they themselves remain relatively silent and hidden? The recognition that analysts, even those who attempt to be anonymous, are never invisible and, furthermore, the insight that patients seek to "know" their analysts raise profound anxieties for analysts who are struggling with their own longings to be known and defensive temptations to hide.

How is it that psychoanalysis, which is so concerned with individual subjective experience and with the development of the child's experience of the other, for so long neglected the exploration of intersubjectivity? Why has it taken so long for us to recognize that we must develop a conception of the other not only as an object but as a separate subject, as a separate psychic self, as a separate center of experience?

For most of its history psychoanalysis has been dominated by the metapsychology of drive theory. Freud conceived of mind as a closed energy system fueled by biological drives pressing for discharge. This model of mind is based on the notion that there are drives striving for gratification and that the ego regulates, channels, and defends against these drives while attempting to find objects suitable to meet their fulfillment. Within this theoretical framework the other person is "objectified"—seen as the "object" of the drive. Because the focus of the theory is on the vicissitudes of the drives, the role of the other is reduced to that of the object of the drives, and the only relevant variable is whether the person is gratifying or frustrating the drive. The dimension of gratification-frustration becomes the central if not the exclusive characteristic of the object since the object's individual subjectivity is of no relevance in as much as they are an object. Only with the shift in psychoanalysis away from drive theory and toward a relational theory of the development of the self and of "object relations" (that is, of interpersonal relations—conscious and unconscious, real and fantasied, external and internal [Greenberg & Mitchell, 1983]) could psychoanalysis begin to study the other not as an object but as a separate subject (Chodorow, 1989). Adopting a "two-person psychology" or a relational perspective opens up the possibility for the investigation not only of subject-object relations but of subject-subject relations. As Mitchell (1988a) has recently stated, "If the analytic situation is not regarded as one subjectivity and one objectivity, or one subjectivity and one facilitating environment, but two subjectivities—the participation in and inquiry into this interpersonal dialectic becomes a central focus of the work" (p. 38).

It should be clear that it is not only the classical drive/structure metapsychology that narrows our view of people, deprives them of subjectivity, and reduces them to objects. This limitation is true of any asocial, "one-person" psychology. (For a discussion of asocial paradigms, see Hoffman [1983]; for a discussion of one-person psychologies, see Aron [in press].) For example, Kohutian self-psychology provides an important contribution to clinical psychoanalysis in its emphasis on the need for the analyst to be responsive and empathic and in its recognition of the vital experience of emotional attunement in the analytic process. Self-psychology, however, maintains the classical view that who the analyst is as a unique character is irrelevant to the process of the analysis. Kohut (1977) wrote that the patient's transferences were defined by "pre-analytically established internal factors in the analysand's personality structure" (p. 217). The analyst's contribution to the process was limited to making "correct" interpretations on the basis of empathy with the patient. Similarly, Goldberg (1980) has stated:

> Self psychology struggles hard not to be an interpersonal psychology...because it wishes to minimize the input of the analyst into the mix...It is based on the idea of a developmental program (one that may be innate or pre-wired if you wish) that will reconstitute itself under certain conditions.
>
> (p. 387)

In the self-psychological model, the analyst is restricted to being a self-object, focusing only upon what the patient (as subject) needs from the analyst (as object). It is important to recognize that in this respect self-psychology does not differ from the classical model (see Hoffman, 1983). For classical analysts, the function of the psychoanalytic situation, and in particular of free association, "is to ensure that what emerges into the patient's consciousness is as far as possible endogeneously determined" (Arlow, 1980, p. 193). If the analyst is analyzing correctly, the patient's associations are not seen as largely or predominantly determined by the current interpersonal relationship with the analyst. The psychoanalytic situation is thought to represent "a standard, experimental set of conditions" (Arlow, 1986, p. 76) whose purpose is to minimize external stimuli so as to allow the spontaneous unfolding, from within, of derivatives of drive and defense. Both the classical model, with its focus on drive and defense, and the self-psychological model, with its reliance on the notion of a "developmental program," require that the psychoanalytic situation remain free of the contaminants of the analyst's subjectivity so that the patient's transferences can "unfold" in pure form from within. The presuppositions of a one-person psychology demand that the only psychology in the consulting room that should matter is that of the patient. The patient's subjectivity, the patient's transferences, the patient's psychic reality are there to be examined. The person of the analyst is ignored in favor of a conception of an "analyzing instrument," and the subjectivity of the analyst is to be kept out of the equation so as to produce an objective experimental situation. (I recognize that this critique of Kohutian self-psychology may not apply to certain post-Kohutian developments within the self-psychology school.

For a similar but more thorough critique of Kohut's self-psychology as a one-person psychology, see Bromberg [1989] and Ghent [1989].)

Similar objections could be raised regarding the clinical stance taken by psychoanalysts of the British object-relational school and of the American interpersonal school. The metaphors of the analyst as "good enough mother" and "holder" (Winnicott, 1986) or as "container" (Bion, 1970) and "metabolizer" of the patient's pathological contents have been extremely useful inasmuch as they have drawn attention to nonverbal and subtle exchanges and to the ways in which the analyst needs to respond to these "primitive communications." The danger with these metaphors, however, is not only that the patient may be infantilized and deprived of a richer and more complex adult kind of intimacy, as Mitchell (1988b) rightly points out, but that the analyst is similarly instrumentalized and denied subjective existence. Instead of being seen as subjects, the mother and the analyst are transformed into the baby's and the patient's "thinking apparatus" (Bion, 1970). The blank screen has simply been replaced with an empty container, free of the analyst's psychological insides (Hirsch, 1987; Hoffman, 1983; Levenson, 1983). In parallel to this view, Chodorow (1989, p. 253) has recently pointed out that most object-relations theorists still take the point of view of the child, with mother as the object, and do not take seriously the problem of the subjectivity of the mother.

While contemporary interpersonal analysts (Levenson, 1972, 1983; Wolstein, 1983a) emphasize the analyst's personal contributions to the patient's transferences, this emphasis was not true of Sullivan's clinical position. Sullivan saw the therapist as an "expert" on interpersonal relations who would function as a "participant-observer" in conducting the analytic inquiry, and as an expert he assumed that the therapist could avoid being pulled into the patient's interpersonal entanglements (see Hirsch, 1987). Sullivan's interpersonal theory, while interpersonal in its examination of the patient's life, was asocial inasmuch as it neglected the subjectivity of the therapist as inevitably participating in the analytic interaction. Sullivan's description of the principle of participant-observation soon brought attention to the analyst's subjective experience and the patient's perceptions of the analyst's experience, which became the focus of attention for later interpersonal analysts. Historically, Hirsch attributes the contemporary interpersonal focus on the participation of the analyst to the influence of Fromm. I see this clinical movement, which emphasizes the contribution of the analyst's subjectivity, as deriving more from the influence of Thompson in the United States and Balint in England, both of whom were deeply influenced by and attempted to extend the later contributions of Ferenczi. Ferenczi was the first analyst seriously to consider the impact of the analyst's subjectivity within the analytic situation (see Dupont, 1988), and the origins of relational theory and practice can be traced back to the conflict between Freud and Ferenczi.

I will conclude by highlighting eight clinical points:

1. The analytic situation is constituted by the mutual regulation of communication between patient and analyst in which both patient and analyst affect and are affected by each other. The relationship is mutual but asymmetrical.
2. The analyst's subjectivity is an important element in the analytic situation, and the patient's experience of the analyst's subjectivity needs to be made conscious.
3. Patients seek to connect to their analysts, to know them, to probe beneath their professional facade, and to reach their psychic centers much in the way that children seek to connect to and penetrate their parents' inner worlds. This aggressive probing may be mistaken for hostile attempts at destruction.
4. Self-revelation is not a choice for the analyst; it is an inevitable and continuous aspect of the analytic process. As patients resolve their resistances to acknowledging what they perceive interpersonally they inevitably turn their gaze toward their analysts, who need to help them acknowledge their interpersonal experience.
5. Establishing one's own subjectivity in the analytic situation is essential and yet problematic. Deliberate or surplus self-revelations are always highly ambiguous and are enormously complicated. Our own psychologies are as complicated as those of our patients, and our unconsciouses are no less deep. We need to recognize that our own self-awareness is limited and that we are not in a position to judge the accuracy of our patients' perceptions of us. Thus, the idea that we might "validate" or "confirm" our patients' perceptions of us is presumptuous. Furthermore, direct

self-revelation cannot provide a shortcut to, and may even interfere with, the development of the patient's capacity to recognize the analyst's subjectivity.
6. It is often useful to ask patients directly what they have noticed about the analyst, what they think the analyst is feeling or doing, what they think is going on in the analyst, or with what conflict they feel the analyst is struggling. The major way to reach this material, however, is through analysis of the defenses and resistances that inhibit the expression of each patient's experience of the analyst.
7. Focusing exclusively on the presence of the analyst and on establishing the analyst's subjectivity does not permit the patient temporarily to put the analyst into the background and indulge in the experience of being left alone in the presence of the analyst. This focus may be experienced by patients as an impingement that disrupts their encounter with their own subjective experiences. Instead of leading to an intersubjective exchange, analysts' insistence on asserting their own subjectivity creates an instrumental relationship in which the subject-object polarities have simply been reversed.

The exploration of the patient's experience of the analyst's subjectivity represents only one aspect of the analysis of transference. It needs to be seen as one underemphasized component of a detailed and thorough explication and articulation of the therapeutic relationship in all of its aspects.

Chapter 7

Self-reflexivity and the therapeutic action of psychoanalysis (2000)

Introduction by Chana Ullman

I am honored to contribute to this book celebrating the man who represents so much of what we cherish in the relational approach. He was not only an inspiring writer, a mentor, and leader, but a person who exuded generosity, curiosity, and genuine interest in every interaction with him.

I first met Lew in person in 1996 when he was the guest at a conference organized by the Israeli Association of Psychotherapy. For many of us who were then less familiar with the relational approach, Lew gave riveting and unsettling talks. For me, it became clear that I found a professional home. Later that day we had a meal with him. The conversation centered on Psychoanalysis in Israel then dominated by one institute—the classical IPA Jerusalem institute. Some of us described to Lew the problematic power dynamics that this singularity created, and Lew said simply: Why not create another institute? It was a strikingly simple question that moved all of us. Indeed, three years later Steven Mitchell became the head of an advisory committee which helped a group of senior clinical psychologists (headed by Michael Shoshani and Gila Ofer) to create the second institute, Tel Aviv Institute of Contemporary Psychoanalysis, which changed the psychoanalytic landscape in Israel. Reading the paper "Self-Reflexivity and the Therapeutic Action of Psychoanalysis" (2000), I was struck by another insight (or hindsight) about this conversation: This was not only a simple common-sense suggestion, but also a solution grounded in Lew's profound conviction in the value of multiplicity and his extraordinary ability to engage it theoretically and practically.

This chapter on self-reflexivity is a relational reformulation of therapeutic action in psychoanalysis. Lew defines, examines in his Talmudic style, and shapes self-reflexivity as the desirable process and outcome of psychoanalytic therapy, distinguishing it from insight. His stated aim is to ground therapeutic action in the relational meeting of minds. Yet, the references for this chapter span the gamut from Freud, Sterba, Brittan, and Bion, to Benjamin, Bach, and Davies; from William James to Damon and Hart, to Blatt, to Fonagy and Target and research in neuropsychology. The references to classical psychoanalysis and to empirical research are not there to bury them, but to praise them, and offer links to his own relational reformulation. The multiplicity and fruitfulness of links are evident in his definition of self-reflexivity (p. 667). Yet at the same time he remains a founder and a definer of the essence of relational thought.

As in other seminal contributions of his (e.g., *Psychotherapy for the People*, with Starr, 2012, Lew attempts to reshape divisions and produce new links, challenging the binaries shaping psychoanalysis from its inception: scientific research versus clinical knowledge, autonomy versus relationality, inner-world versus reality, "pure" insight versus affective engagement. Similarly, within the clinical exchange, he argues for the playing out of roles within the analyst, who is not locked in a single view. Even in this attempt to reformulate therapeutic action in relational terms he moves between an insider and an outsider position. He stands in the spaces, writing from a position of thirdness.

As insider, he charts for us the innovative ideas within relational thought, as, for example, in spelling out Benjamin's ideas and his work with her on the Third and triangular space. As an outsider, he exposes the larger psychoanalytic and academic context in which his perspective is embedded. This is an attempt to advance relational thought but also to cure Psychoanalysis by transcending binaries, by using the "other" in a Winnicottian sense. In this chapter, he practices what he is about to preach most persuasively in a later chapter ("Beyond Tolerance in Psychoanalytic Communities," 2017), challenging us to go beyond tolerance and respect of differences to a "critical pluralism" where the other perspective is appreciated for what it can uniquely contribute to us. The call is to recognize that the other view of psychoanalysis serves a valuable function that we cannot perform ourselves—it is an opportunity to disturb a balance and prevent stagnation, an opportunity to raise questions not in order to give up our perspective but to reexamine and refine it. Thus, Lew is himself serving a therapeutic function within relational psychoanalysis.

In this chapter on self-reflexivity, Lew is formulating several basic principles of relational psychoanalysis: Multiplicity is a value; the theoretical and the clinical advance by links between different concepts and different self-states; it is both similarities and differences that we need in order to develop, as a theory and as a person. Subjective and objective aspects of selfhood should come together.

I wish to end on a personal note. I was thrilled to read in this paper Lew's extensive use of W. James' distinction between the I and the Me. Long before I became a relational analyst, I was a postdoctoral fellow at the Hebrew university where I researched adolescents' views of the true self, using James' definitions of the I and the Me and the developmental elaborations of these terms. Lew cites Bach (1994), arguing that the child needs to establish a sense of self as an object and a subject, a center for action and thought and in the context of other selves "a thing among other things" (p. 671). My research indeed charted this developmental trajectory during adolescence. Reading this paper, a therapeutic link was therefore created for me between my younger academic self and my current embeddedness within relational psychoanalysis. I wish I could talk with Lew about this.

Aron, L. (2000). Self-Reflexivity and the Therapeutic Action of Psychoanalysis.

Psychoanalytic Psychology, 17(4), 667–689.

Relational psychoanalytic theory, far from eschewing the intrapsychic, is built on the premise that the intrapsychic and the intersubjective are complementary modes of experience and that both are necessary to explain the reciprocal and spiraling influence of interpersonal events on psychic development and the impact of the inner world and unconscious fantasy life on human interaction. Speaking of "the" therapeutic action of psychoanalysis in the singular is surely misleading inasmuch as there are undoubtedly a multiplicity of ways in which psychoanalysis acts therapeutically. Understanding the therapeutic action of psychoanalysis is therefore one of the "big" topics, beyond the scope of any single article. Herein, I take up one of the most intriguing and consequential aspects of the problem, namely, how to construct a model that takes into account both intrapsychic and intersubjective dimensions of therapeutic action and the necessity of their mutual interaction in the development of reflexive self-awareness. I use the terms *intrapsychic* and *intersubjective* as Benjamin (1995) defined them, to refer to two types of relationships to the self and to the other, two complementary modes of experience, in which individuals relate both to the self and to the other as both subject and as object. This is their technical meaning within the broad framework of Benjamin's (1988, 1995, 1998, 1999a) version of intersubjectivity theory.

I propose that the ongoing (interpersonal) enactment of (intrapsychic) relational configurations leads to the potential for psychic change as patient and analyst reciprocally internalize and externalize, introject and project, passing back and forth between them a wide range of relational roles and representations, including images of each other as subjects and objects. I elaborate on a model of the reflexive self-function that is based on the capacity to hold in mind both the subjective and objective aspects of both self and object. The range of one's self-reflexivity is expanded, and its capacity is deepened as one learns to use the dialectics of self and mutual regulation (Beebe & Lachmann, 1998) as key dimensions of mentalization (Fonagy & Target, 1995, 1996, 1998; Target & Fonagy, 1996).

My technical use of the term *self-reflexivity*, or the reflexive function of mind, needs to be carefully distinguished from the more usual understanding of self-reflection. Self-reflection ordinarily connotes a cognitive process in which one thinks about oneself with some distance, as if from the outside, that is, as if examining oneself as an object of thought. The way I use self-reflexivity here, by way of contrast, includes the dialectical process of experiencing oneself as a subject as well as of reflecting on oneself as an object. It is not, therefore, exclusively an intellectual observational function, but an experiential and affective function as well, and my focus on the importance of maintaining the tension between subjective and objective self-awareness includes as one aspect of this conceptualization the ability to integrate observing and experiencing functions, to connect thought and affect, mind and body, the observational mode and the experiential mode. Furthermore, I argue that self-reflexivity develops within the relational matrix (Mitchell, 1988a) and is inherently an intersubjective process. Again, to restate an essential point, self-reflexivity is not the same as "introspection," which is based on the dubious assumption that the self has privileged access to its own internal states. It is for these reasons that I prefer to speak of the self-reflexive function rather than of the reflective function, which connotes a more intellectualized and distant activity.

My understanding of the reflexive function has been decisively shaped by the writings of Sheldon Bach (1985, 1994), although, in recent years, the topic of self-reflexivity has emerged at the cutting edge of psychoanalytic thought and has been taken up by numerous theorists from divergent points of view. Indeed, it is not my intention herein to propose a new model or explanation, but rather to pull together bits and pieces of theory that have emerged across a wide range of psychoanalytic discussions and points of view. I am particularly indebted to the work of John Auerbach and Sidney Blatt (Auerbach, 1993; Auerbach & Blatt, 1996), who, like me, were heavily influenced by the earlier work of Bach. I also believe, however, that there is a convergence of interest taking shape in this area, as seen in Peter Fonagy and Mary Target's (Fonagy & Target, 1995, 1996, 1998; Target & Fonagy, 1996) fascinating studies of reflective mental functioning, or what they call the person's capacity for "mentalization." These concepts are rooted in psychological research on attachment processes as well as on the related research area known as "theory of mind" and seem highly compatible with the approach that I develop here. Related areas of interest include much of what has been learned about the impact of trauma on thinking, states of consciousness, self-regulation, and dissociation (Bromberg, 1996; Davies, 1996; Krystol, 1988; Seligman, 1999a; van der Kolk, 1996); developments in the study of psychosomatics and alexithymia (Nemiah & Sifneos, 1970; G. J. Taylor, 1992a, 1992b); and recent understandings of the ways in which people benefit from psychoanalysis itself, especially in clarifying what is meant by "psychological mindedness" (McCallum & Piper, 1997). In an earlier effort (Aron, 1998b), I explored the relation between self-reflexivity and the mind-body problem, and this article is a further elaboration and refinement of that effort.

My understanding of intersubjectivity and its technical consequences, as I have elaborated extensively elsewhere (Aron, 1991, 1996a, 1996b), builds on the contributions of Jessica Benjamin (1988, 1995, 1998), whose work I return to below, and indeed I intend to develop some interesting connections between Benjamin's work on intersubjectivity and Sheldon Bach's writings on narcissism. A discussion of intersubjectivity, however, should commence with an elaboration of the meaning of the concept of subjectivity, and I begin with William James (as did Sheldon Bach).[1] In his classic *Principles of Psychology*, James (1890/1981) delineated four aspects of human subjectivity: (a) agency, (b) distinctiveness, (c) continuity, and (d) reflection (see Damon & Hart, 1988). From agency one derives one's sense of autonomy, will, the self as agent, author of one's experience. From distinctiveness one derives the sense of individuality, what Benjamin Wolstein (1974, 1983b) called "the psychic center of the interpersonal self" (p. 347). (Wolstein, too, traced his thinking back to James and considered James's pragmatist contributions to be at the heart of the American interpersonal tradition. I believe that one cannot understand what is uniquely American about American psychoanalysis without understanding the often invisible, but nevertheless dominant, influence of William James, whose person-centered, humanistic approach to psychology emphasized such central American values as tolerance, pragmatism, perspectivism, eclecticism, and a focus on immediate experience; see E. Taylor, 1992.) The third aspect, continuity, is the basis for stability and evokes what Winnicott (1963) famously called the experience of "going-on-being" (p. 86). Reflection, for James, refers to awareness of one's own awareness, and this "meta-cognitive awareness," to anticipate Mary Main's (1991) phrase or what Fonagy and Target (1998) referred to as representations of representations, is what makes for human self-consciousness and allows individuals to give meaning to life. These are four dimensions of subjectivity, and through their operation the self is viewed as initiating, organizing, and interpreting experience.

Psychoanalysts, of course, would want to include in any definition of subjectivity the notion that individuals are inevitably and continuously subject to unconscious forces and that people's inner subjective world cannot be understood without appreciating the influence of unconscious fantasies and meanings. I also add that James's use of the term subjectivity is closer in spirit to what is today called the self, as in our postmodern era *subjectivity* is a more general term, referring rather loosely to a person's experience of being in the world (Fairfield, in press). James's theory, with its own legitimizing and normativizing tendencies, constitutes more of a self-psychology, with his articulation of the self being a culturally saturated version of human subjectivity. However, James would go on in the years that followed the *Principles*, as he became increasingly dissatisfied with positivism, to increasingly emphasize exceptional mental states, multiple selves, and consciousness beyond the margins (see E. Taylor, 1996). Indeed, James's approach to the self is riddled with contradictions because he chose to stay with, rather than evade, the vital questions of psychology. His approach anticipates the postmodern appreciation of paradox and dialectic that has been articulated for psychoanalysis by Ghent (1992), Hoffman (1998), Ogden (1994a), Pizer (1998), and others. Indeed, Gordon Allport (1943) wrote a commemorative paper on James titled "The Productive Paradoxes of William James."

James's examination of subjectivity led him to distinguish between two perspectives on the self: the *I* and the *me*. James described the *me* aspects of self as the actual qualities that define the self-as-known. This includes, for James, material (body, possessions), social (roles and relations), and spiritual characteristics (consciousness and psychological mechanisms). The *me* in James' theory of the self refers to the person's self-concept, all that one could know about oneself through one's own observations or through feedback from others. In this sense, the *me* has been referred to as the more objective aspect of the self. Interestingly, just as Freud (1923/1961) wrote that "the ego is first and foremost a bodily ego" (p. 26), so too did James propose that the body and the "bodily me" provide the structural basis of the self. Indeed, for James, with the fall of waking awareness below the threshold of consciousness there is a descent of consciousness into the body.

For James, the *I* refers to the self-as-knower in that the essence of the *I* is its subjectivity. The *me* is often referred to as the objective self, and the *I* is referred to as the subjective self, but I think that this terminology is misleading because it is unclear in what respect one could think of the self-concept as objective. I suggest that it is much clearer and closer to James's meaning to refer to James's *me* as the sense of the self-as-object, and to the *I* as the self-as-subject. James's theory of the self, then, is a comprehensive theory that includes the sense of the self-as-subject, the *I*, as an integrated experience of agency, continuity, distinctness, and reflection constituting the self that initiates, organizes, and interprets experience, and to the self-as-object, the *me*, the self as observed by a subject, which forms the basis of the self-concept.

Bach (1985), following James, distinguished between *subjective awareness* and *objective self-awareness*. According to Bach, in certain states of consciousness, which he referred to as subjective awareness, individuals are totally immersed in their own thoughts and actions; in these states people are aware of themselves as agents or the subject of thought and action. In contrast, there are other states of consciousness, referred to as objective self-awareness, in which one takes oneself as the object of his or her thoughts or actions.

> Thus, one might say that the child is confronted with the double or complementary task of establishing a sense of self as a center for action and thought and of viewing this self in the context of other selves as a thing among other things. What is required is both a subjectification and an objectification, two different perspectives on the same self.
>
> (p. 53)

Bach (1985, 1994) suggested that a good deal of narcissistic and borderline pathology, including such structurally related conditions as perversions, addictions, eating disorders, and psychosomatic disorders, may be best understood in terms of the patient's inability to maintain appropriate tension between these two perspectives on the self. When immersed in a state of consciousness of subjective awareness, the self is experienced as the agent, in Kohut's (1977, p. 99) words, as "a center of initiative and a recipient of impressions"; at the extreme, this may lead the patient to experience grandiosity and entitlement and to be unable to experience the self as an object among other objects or a self among other selves. When immersed in the state of consciousness of objective self-awareness, the patient can only view him- or herself as an object among other objects and cannot experience the sense of agency or vitality that comes with being a subject, a distinct center of thoughts, feelings, and actions. Some patients (and certain forms of pathology) are more apt to maintain one side of this polarity over another. Nevertheless, according to Bach, the real problem with all of these pathologies is that both types have persistent difficulties moving back and forth between these two perspectives on the self and integrating them into their representational world.

Bach (1994) proposed that it is an important developmental achievement for the individual "to integrate his sense of wholeness and aliveness (subjective awareness) with his parents' and his own developing perspective on himself as one person among many others (objective self-awareness)" (p. 46). Accordingly, psychopathology is understood in terms of the person's inability to tolerate ambiguity and paradox, to deal with metaphor (which is inherently ambiguous and may simultaneously express contradictory points of view), or to maintain multiple points of view, especially about the self. Psychopathology involves the inability to "stand in the spaces" (Bromberg, 1998) or to "build bridges" (Pizer, 1998) between contradictory aspects of one's multiplicity. Instead, in psychopathology, there is polarization, splitting, either-or thinking, dissociation, manic and depressive mood swings, and sadomasochistic role reversals.

Auerbach and Blatt (Auerbach, 1993; Auerbach & Blatt, 1996), drawing on Bach's ideas, elaborated what they referred to as *self-reflexivity*. Reflexive self-awareness, or self-reflexivity, is the capacity to move smoothly between subjective and objective perspectives on the self; to put this in the terms that I prefer, self-reflexivity refers to the capacity to maintain the dynamic tension between experiencing oneself as a subject and as an object. Auerbach (1993), following Bach, goes on to elaborate narcissism as the attempt to escape the conflicts that result from self-reflexivity. "Kernberg's narcissists, in their shameless grandiosity and entitlement, overemphasize subjective self-awareness; Kohut's narcissists, in their shame ridden hypersensitivity, vulnerability, and submissiveness, overemphasize objective self-awareness" (p. 83). Once again, to put this into somewhat different terminology, those narcissists who overemphasize subjective awareness tend to view themselves only as a subject, and not as one object among other objects or one subject among other subjects—for to view oneself as a subject among other subjects is to objectify oneself. Because they do not see themselves as one among many, they come across as grandiose and entitled. Those narcissists who emphasize objective self-awareness tend to view themselves predominantly as one object among many, without experiencing themselves as a subject, agent, or center of initiative. Therefore, they come across as vulnerable, fragile, or depressed, with little sense of control over their lives, an incapacity to will.

In discussing the dialectics of meaning and mortality, Hoffman (1998) similarly pointed out that the relationship between our sense of being and our anticipation of nonbeing constitutes a tension between figure and ground that is incorporated into our sense of self. The dialectics of our sense of being and our sense of mortality is the foundation for our sense of meaning, and Hoffman links this to the related dialectic of subjectivity and objectivity. Self-reflexivity must include the ability to view oneself both as a subject, alive and vital, and as an object that like any other object exists only as a material entity in time.

Self-reflexive functioning encompasses the capacity to move back and forth smoothly, to hold the tension between these two forms of consciousness, and it is the basis on which participation in the psychoanalytic process rests for both the patient and the analyst.[2] Self-reflexive functioning is a critical psychological capacity that is impaired in different ways across the various psychopathological forms as a result of psychological conflict, deficit, and trauma. Much psychopathology seems to be mediated by an incapacity for reflexive self-functioning, and much of the impact of trauma, specifically, seems to take its toll by interfering with self-reflexive functioning, leaving the "body to keep the score," just to hint at the work of van der Kolk (1996) and other trauma researchers (see Seligman, 1999a, 1999b). All dissociation is rooted in the primal dissociation of body from mind, of subjective awareness from objective awareness, of *I* from *me*, and of thought from affect. My thesis is that psychoanalysis is the only treatment that operates directly to improve the capacity for self-reflexivity, a process that can only occur relationally because reflexive awareness is a developmental achievement that necessitates an interpersonal context.

One might think that I am claiming a reversal of the traditional view of the suitability criteria for psychoanalytic treatment. On the basis of my claim that psychoanalysis is uniquely suited to improve the capacity for self-reflexivity, one might think that I am claiming that psychoanalysis is the treatment of choice only for severely disturbed patients who lack a self-reflexive capacity.[3] Although I do believe that psychoanalysis is often the treatment of choice for severely disturbed patients, I also argue that healthier patients (those traditionally thought of as analyzable) benefit from psychoanalysis precisely because in the area permeated by their major conflicts they are not able to optimally utilize the self-reflexive function. For a similar analysis, see Seligman (1999b), who described failures in reflective thinking even in "higher functioning" personalities.

An excellent example of this, I think, is Freud's (1912/1957) description of psychical impotence as due to "the failure of the affectionate and the sensual currants in love to combine" (p. 184). In cases of psychical impotence, Freud's explanation that these two currents have failed to fuse and that to obtain a "normal attitude in love" one must integrate the sexual and the affectionate streams may be usefully considered in the terms that I have advanced herein. Namely, in cases of psychical impotence, which in Freud's broad usage referred to an almost universal phenomenon, the individual (man or woman) has not succeeded in, or has lost the ability to, integrate a view of him- or herself or the other as both a separate subject and an object. To love, one must be able to experience oneself and the other as separate yet related and similar subjects, whereas to lust, one must be able to experience the other as an object of one's desire and one must also be able to "let go" of one's own self-as-agent, in charge and in control. To integrate love and sexuality requires an integration of mind and body, thought and affect, subjective and objective awareness. One can see here a connection to the recent work of Benjamin (1999a), who described a central conflict in intersubjective life between Eros and narcissism, recognition and omnipotence, a tension within the individual between omnipotence, the illusion of control, and the wish for contact with the external other.

The concept of self-reflexivity and related ideas are more than just new terms for what have heretofore been called insight and expanded awareness; instead they represent an incremental advance in the precision by which the therapeutic action of psychoanalysis is understood. These new conceptualizations continue in the tradition of Freud, Ferenczi, and Sterba's descriptions of the split between an observing and experiencing ego, and they also maintain continuity with such traditional notions as Strachey's understanding of the therapeutic action of psychoanalysis as based on the patient's identification with the analyst's superego functioning. Current notions of self-reflexivity, however, include a "theory of mind" that builds on Hegel's discussion of mind becoming self-conscious only through intersubjective struggle, negation, and recognition: I learn to reflect on my mind because another person regards me as having a mind to reflect on, and my discovery of this is a discovery that that person has a mind too, and I only become conscious of myself because someone else takes me to be a self. This relational assumption includes a recursive looping that creates a triangular space emergent from within an interpersonal dyad. This revitalizes earlier and more static and linear notions, such as that of the observing ego as proposed by Sterba (1934).

A long-established principle of psychoanalysis is that the analyst needs to form an alliance with the patient's observing ego, which is split off from the patient's experiencing ego. This idea goes back at least as far as Sterba (1934) and is a commonly accepted aspect of classical psychoanalysis, as is the related distinction between experiential and observational aspects of the ego. What I have been developing herein, however, moves beyond these insights in a number of respects. Sterba's article was extremely valuable; as a matter of fact, I think that rereading it in light of contemporary psychoanalytic developments makes it all the more fascinating. Indeed, Sterba recommended the establishment of a therapeutic dissociation, and he was strikingly free in describing dissociative phenomena and double consciousness at a time in the history of psychoanalysis when these terms were rarely used. Furthermore, he quoted Freud in support of his position that dissociation can have healthy and not only pathological functions:

> We wish to make the ego the matter of our enquiry, our very own ego. But is that possible? After all, the ego is in its very essence a subject; how can it be made into an object? Well there is no doubt that it can be. The ego can take itself as an object, can treat itself like other objects, can observe itself, criticize itself, and do Heaven knows what with itself. In this, one part of the ego is setting itself over against the rest. So the ego can be split; it splits itself during a number of its functions—temporarily at least.
>
> (Freud, 1933/1964, p. 58)

Elsewhere (Aron & Harris, 1993), Adrienne Harris and I observed that as early as 1919, years prior to Sterba's paper, Sandor Ferenczi (1919), who was keenly observant of the wide range of states of consciousness in himself and his patients, described the need for the analyst to alternate between "the free play of association and phantasy" and "logical" and "critical scrutiny" (p. 189). The oscillation between experience and self-criticism that Ferenczi (1919) described in the analyst is strikingly similar to Sterba's (1934) description of the fate of the patient's ego in analytic therapy.

The capacity for self-observation, however, was taken for granted by classical analysts in that it was this very potential that was the determining criteria of analyzability (see Bromberg, 1996). For today's analysts, by way of contrast, the capacity for self-awareness may be considered more the goal of analysis than a prerequisite for it. Furthermore, contemporary analysts across a variety of schools and in accordance with postmodern trends have championed the conceptual power of multiplicity (Bromberg, 1998; Davies, 1996; Harris, 1996; Mitchell, 1991; Seligman & Shanok, 1995). To become self-aware, a person must break the identification with any one aspect of self and engage in the internal dialogue of the multiple voices of subjectivity. Self-reflection, from this point of view, is based on the capacity for internal division, healthy dissociation, "standing in the spaces" between realities (Bromberg, 1998), building bridges (Pizer, 1998), the transcendent, oscillating, or dialectical function. Ultimately, practice and experience with the oscillating function leads to a qualitative change in the structure of thinking such that thought takes into account the position of the Third (Aron & Benjamin, 1999b).

Benjamin and I have been collaborating for many years on developing this notion of the Third, and it is beyond the scope of this article to elucidate in any detail on our conceptualizations. Briefly, however, we propose the analogy (following Benjamin, 1999a) that the capacity to think requires mental space, and that space does not exist within a line connecting two points, but rather requires the inclusion of a third point to form triangular space. Similarly, one cannot learn to think about oneself unless the dyad formed between oneself and the other is qualitatively transformed into triangular space that allows for the inclusion of two different perspectives on the self and the other. It is the possibility of a Third perspective that allows the dyad to move to the level of metacommunication (Ringstrom, 1998). To create triangular space within the analytic dyad, one of the participants must begin by establishing a relationship to him- or herself in the presence of the other such that three subjectivities are brought into relation with each other. I draw on Bollas's (1989) elaboration of "the dialectics of difference," which entails the analyst's establishing him- or herself as a subject within the analytic process. This requires that the analyst allow—and even welcome—the patient to observe some of the relations among the analyst's multiple selves. In particular, in this article, I am emphasizing the relation between two central dimensions of the analyst's self, namely, subjective and objective self-awareness. In establishing a dialectics of difference by inviting the patient to observe the analyst's relation to him- or herself as both subject and object, a triangular space is opened up within the "analytic dyad." I soon return to this idea of the Third in examining how intersubjectivity plays a role in the therapeutic action of psychoanalysis.

One implication of this formulation is that at the end of an analysis it is not insight or other knowledge of psychic content that would best demonstrate the patient's growth or the success of the treatment, but rather it is the capacity for self-reflexivity. Analysts have always known this in the sense that they have regularly said that the goal of analysis is the capacity for self-analysis following termination. But they have never succeeded in being able to demonstrate this acquired skill, and furthermore, not all patients report that they engage in continued self-analysis. Although people may not deliberately engage in any kind of systematic self-analysis following termination, they may very well have improved self-reflexive functioning based on greater intercommunication among their own multiple selves as well as increased ability to maintain the tension in their relation to others as both subjects and objects. Empirical research with the Experiencing Scale (for a review, see Greenberg & Safran, 1987) suggests that conceptualizations such as these may in fact be measurable. The Experiencing Scale attempts to measure the process of focusing inward in order to solve problems, and the conceptualization of experiencing merges affective and cognitive processes into an integrated whole. Research with the Adult Attachment Interview, similarly, may allow for the measurement of processes related to those I describe herein, namely, the ability to maintain both subjective and objective self-awareness. (See Coates, 1998, for an elegant description of the implications of research with the Adult Attachment Interview [George, Kaplan, & Main, 1985] and its relationship to attachment processes and Fonagy's ideas about reflective functioning.) In time, the operationalization of these constructs could lead to empirical research to test these hypotheses, leading psychoanalysts to refute, modify, or confirm these theories and refine their understanding of therapeutic action.

The idea of self-reflexivity, however, more than the traditional notion of insight, focuses on affectivity as much as cognition; it emphasizes process rather than static knowledge, and it highlights the intersubjective rather than self-contained awareness. It is this recognition that self-reflexivity is an inherently intersubjective as well as intrapsychic process that advances these new concepts (self-reflexivity, mentalization, and meta-cognitive awareness) beyond the more traditional notions of insight and self-analysis.

What I suggest is that the term *insight* was used to connote an achievement within a one-person psychology in that it was often thought of as the awareness that one person gained about his or her own mind, even if this knowledge was often gained with the help of another, primarily through interpretation. The reflexive function and mentalization are concepts that lend themselves better to a two-person psychology in that self-reflexivity is more readily conceptualized as a process that inevitably goes on between people rather than only in one of them. As Fairfield (in press) astutely observed, however, contemporary formulations about multiplicity do not reflect a thoroughgoing postmodernism, although they have been influenced by postmodern trends. What I am proposing continues to rely on the notion of a developing self (whether viewed as singular or multiple) and maintains such essentialist and normativizing features as self-reflexive functioning that it becomes yet a new characteristic of what is considered natural and healthy.

I believe that the notion of the reflexive function, as I have developed it here, constitutes a necessary bridge between the study of the intrapsychic world and the realm of the intersubjective. Fonagy and Target (1998) suggested that most modern psychoanalytic theories assume that subjectivity develops through the perception of oneself in another person's mind. Attachment between infant and caregiver becomes the critical mediator in the development of mentalization. It is important to recognize, however, that this conceptualization implies not only a dyadic relationship of infant-mother, but an emerging triangular relation of self, other, and the other's view of the self. This intersubjective view of mentalization has clinical ramifications in that it implies that the intrapsychic cannot be explored in isolation from the interpersonal and intersubjective triangular space. Exploring the meaning of others' actions is crucially linked with the ability to find meaning in one's own psychic experiences. This provides additional theoretical justification for such clinical contributions as John Steiner's (1993) idea of "analyst-centered interpretations" as well as my own earlier contributions (Aron, 1991b) that emphasized the psychoanalytic exploration of "the patient's experience of the analyst's subjectivity" as one critical dimension of the analysis of the transference. Whether focusing on the perception of oneself as a subject and object or the perception of the analyst as a separate subject as well as the object of one's wishes, in both cases a triangle is created rather than a simple dyadic relation, thus allowing for the development of a richer and more complex experience of intersubjectivity.

Jessica Benjamin (1995) called for psychoanalysts to move beyond an object-relations to a subject-relations theory—"where objects were, subjects must be." Her particular version of intersubjectivity theory, with its recognition for both the intrapsychic and the intersubjective as important realms of psychoanalytic exploration, extends and deepens the work on reflexive self-awareness to include both internal negotiations and tension among multiple selves as well as external dialogue between oneself and another. Benjamin has highlighted both the child's and the patient's developmental need for both recognition and identification. Recognition is a dimension of relatedness that entails an emphasis on self and other as separate and independent subjects, whereas identification highlights a dimension of relatedness as like subjects. Mutuality implies subject-to-subject relatedness, whereas complementarity involves subject-object relatedness, and the intersubjective and the intrapsychic are both necessary because mutuality and complementarity are both always in operation. Clinical psychoanalysis therefore requires that patient and analyst be available to play both kinds of roles with each other, complementary roles along the lines of subject-object relatedness and roles that entail mutuality, with intersubjectivity being a developing capacity that entails the capacity to encompass both of these dimensions. In practice, this means that patient and analyst must come to see each other as separate and independent subjects as well as subjects who are alike and connected, in addition to seeing each other as the objects of their own wishes and needs. It is here that my collaboration with Benjamin extends our individual contributions. By elaborating on the analytic situation as triangular space constituted initially by the analyst's establishing a relation to him- or herself, a dialectics of difference in Bollas's (1989) terms, we are suggesting that the patient learns to establish a more complex self-relation by playing out an exchange of roles with the analyst, who is not locked into any single view of this exchange because he or she has a more complex and multiple relationship with him- or herself, thus permitting multiple views of the analytic exchange and the internalization of a multiplicity of perspectives.

It is in the play of roles, the interactional enactment of these mutual and complementary roles and relations, that individuals learn to expand the parts that they play and learn to think about their internal self-relations and participation with others. Conversely, it is when individuals get locked into narrowly defined roles with limited interactional options that they stop thinking in action. Mitchell (1988a) has consistently elaborated a relational approach to psychoanalysis that views the expanding of interactional roles, including enlarged possibilities for imagining oneself, as at the heart of psychoanalytic change. In Mitchell's relational approach, the analyst discovers him- or herself within the shifting configuration of the relational matrix thus enabling the analysand to broaden and expand that matrix. Among the many extraordinary accomplishments of Davies and Frawley's (1994) work is that they beautifully illustrated the application of this approach to adult survivors of sexual abuse, highlighting the way in which treatment progressed to the extent that patient and analyst could become free to enact emotionally powerful and rapidly shifting relational configurations. One can deconstruct the polarization of thought and action and see that it is in the very act of shifting relational roles and adopting expanded intersubjective possibilities that one may come to think-in-action, to think intersubjectively.

I am suggesting that the enactment of a variety of roles, relationships, ships, and me-you configurations between the patient and analyst constitutes a playing out, a trial action or experimentation with a variety of aspects of the self that have hitherto not had an opportunity for conversation and integration. The enactment of these multiple roles in analysis, including especially the enactment and subsequent bringing together of the subjective and objective aspects of the self, is made possible by and permits the further expansion of a triangular mental space in which self-reflexivity is possible. This process is made possible initially by the analyst's demonstrating some capacity to establish a relationship with himself in the presence of and with the participation of the patient. This further allows for the expansion of one's self-definition to encompass multiple selves. My description is necessarily too linear and does not capture that all of these processes are simultaneous and mutually reinforcing.

Charles Spezzano (1996) put forth what he referred to as a "two-person ontological proposition about mind" (p. 608) that significantly addresses this approach. For Spezzano, the presence of two minds is a necessary feature of consciousness. "Consciousness is both necessary and understandable only because there are other minds besides one's own" (p. 608). Consciousness aims at communication to others so that one's effects and representations can be mixed with those of others "to create something new and better." Compare this with Karen Maroda's (1995) description of people needing their affective communications to be received by the recipient and returned to them in some form. Maroda's approach views affect as an interpersonal activity that is not fully developed unless the communicated affect is returned to the subject so as "to complete the cycle of affective communication." From a relational perspective, a person can hold in mind the affects and representations of another and then return these contents to the other in modified form. But now these contents have been "objectified"; they come from the outside other and so can be reflected on as aspects of both subjectivity and objectivity. I want to allude here to the reverberations of Bion's (1967) theory of thinking, his "alphabetizing function," that occurs between mother and infant, analyst and analysand, and that is so much in the background of all attempts to develop an intersubjective theory of thinking.

Spezzano's (1996) relational model further suggests that self-reflexivity is only achievable interpersonally:

> From such an intersubjective perspective all of us have come to know our emotional lives only to the extent that our affects and our allusions to them were recognized by others who could tolerate in themselves whatever they felt in the face of our feelings, could think about what they felt, and could then communicate to us something psychologically usable by us.
>
> (p. 612)

I would point out here the indebtedness to both Sullivan (1953) and Fairbairn (1952), who were in strikingly similar ways (Mitchell, 1988a) among the first psychoanalysts to suggest that whatever in the child's thoughts and affects that was not tolerable to the parents is dissociated into the "not me" and is then not available for reflexive self-awareness.

For patients who have not achieved a capacity for symbolization, unformulated affective experiences can only be vicariously experienced by intersubjective communicating them to another, a process that some analysts describe by speaking of projective identification. Sands (1997) described that patients are motivated to communicate these unarticulated experiences to the analyst using projective identification, in order to "have one's communication viscerally received, contained, 'lived through,' symbolized, and given back in such a way that one knows that the other has 'gotten' it from the inside out" (p. 699). On the basis of his studies of dissociative phenomena, Philip Bromberg (1991) had earlier remarked that the patient's unarticulated longing is to have the analyst know the patient "from the inside out." Clearly, the analyst cannot accomplish this without considerable wear and tear on his or her own body and psyche.

Working from within this co-joint analytic skin ego (Anzieu, 1985) analysts use their capacity for self-reflexivity to process associations with patients. Where the patient is not capable of using symbolic or metaphoric thought, the analyst may only receive communications in nonverbal form, often in the form of bodily communications, a change in the climate, the air (mediated by the breath), a change in the feel of things (mediated by the skin). Ferenczi (1915/1980a) referred to aspects of this as "dialogues of the unconscious." Here, the analyst must be attuned to the nonverbal, the affective, the spirit (breath) of the session, the feel of the material, to his or her own bodily responses, and to his or her own enactive participation so that these may be gradually used to construct metaphors and symbols that may be verbally exchanged between the analytic pair, gradually permitting the differentiation of the more primitive shared skin ego and the construction of a more developed, articulated, and differentiated personal attachment. (This is an idea that Fran Anderson and I tried to highlight in our recent collection, *Relational Perspectives on the Body*, 1998.) Hence, explicit reflection, verbalization, and articulation lend organization to what had previously been "unformulated experience" (Stern, 1997).

Recent work in neuroscience suggests that emotion functions to coordinate the mind and the body, but according to Regina Pally (1998), who is working on bridging psychoanalysis and the neurosciences, "Emotion connects not only the mind and body of one individual but minds and bodies *between* individuals" (p. 349). The nonverbal communication of affect is fundamental to all forms of social interaction and serves to regulate the biological functioning of both people. Psychosomatic and traumatized patients, those who rely on dissociation and who have been described as alexithymia, are impaired not only in the verbal identification of emotion but in the nonverbal expression of emotion as well. This impairment in their ability to express emotion verbally or nonverbally interferes in others' abilities to provide feedback to them, to soothe them, or to aid them in self-soothing and self-regulation. It would seem that a great deal of the analytic work that needs to be done with patients in this state must involve the mutual, nonverbal transmission, containment, and processing of affect with the analyst carrying on much of the analytic processing internally and only gradually achieving increased reflexive self-awareness and completing the cycle of affective communication by gradually sharing this effort with the patient. Also developing and elaborating on new models of therapeutic action as an interactional, intersubjective process, Stern et al. (1998) described how patient and analyst gradually relate to one another in new and expanded ways, leading to changes in "implicit relational knowing," especially during "moments of meeting."

At moments when patients are unable to use reflexive awareness, the analyst must carry much of the analytic work, psychosomatically processing the patient's communications and use his or her own "transcendent function" (Jung, 1916/1969) to bring together conscious with unconscious; body with affect; unformulated experience with words and symbols; self-as-subject with self-as-object; and the verbal, iconic, and enactive realms—all of these as they are played out and put into words in the matrix of transference–countertransference. Both patient and analyst achieve and at moments lose the capacity to relate to each other as subjects and objects, moving back and forth between object relating and object usage, the realm of the intrapsychic and the intersubjective, the imaginative and the symbolic, relating to a self-object or connecting to an interpersonal other, oscillating between "I-it" and "I-thou" relatedness (Buber, 1923/1970), between the paranoid-schizoid and depressive positions, between collusion and intimacy (Frankel, 1993).

At moments, both patient and analyst lose this capacity, but in the crucible of transference and countertransference through ongoing oscillations, role-responsiveness (Sandler, 1976), enactments, role-reversals, projections, and introjections, they may mutually help each other to sustain, regain, and improve reflexive awareness. It is precisely in the analyst's loosing and regaining this ability that he or she engages in a relationship with him- or herself, self-reflexively, thus creating a triangular space within the analytic relationship in which thinking becomes possible (see Aron, 1995; Aron & Benjamin, 1999b; Benjamin, 1999a; Britton, 1989).

As patient and analyst move back and forth viewing each other as subject and object, they reciprocally pass between them affects, ideas, and representations. These may be experienced by each as subjective aspects of themselves or as objects from the outside, objects in the mind of another. Patient and analyst alternate viewing self as subject and self as object, viewing the other as subject and the other as object, these roles being passed back and forth until, gradually, they develop a greater capacity to experience themselves and the other as both subjects and objects. The analysand gets stuck for a moment, unable to use this reflexive process, and the analyst intervenes to get it going once again, and the analyst too loses the ability for reflexivity until something the patient says gets the process going once again.

Reflexive functioning is created between them as together they verbalize, imagine, embody, and enact representations of self and other as subject and object and learn to hold the tension among these representations.

To conclude, reflexive self-awareness is both an intellectual and emotional process; involves conscious and unconscious mentation; draws on symbolic, iconic, and enactive representations; involves the mediation of the self-as-subject with the self-as-object; the *I* and the *me*; the verbal and the bodily selves; the other-as-subject and the other-as-object. It is a conceptualization that necessarily draws together the intrapsychic and the intersubjective. It is not static, firmly acquired knowledge, but rather a process that occurs in internal conversation among multiple selves as well as in external dialogue with another, who must be viewed as both a subject and an object, thus creating a triangular mental space, a Third emerging from what on the surface appears to be a dyadic relation. Reflexive self-awareness is not the achievement of an isolated mind in private contemplation, as the traditional concepts of insight and self-analysis may have implied; rather, self-reflexivity always involves an affective engagement, a meeting of minds (Aron, 1996a).

Notes

1 I only mean to say that in clarifying the meaning of the term and concept *intersubjectivity*, it seems preferable to begin by defining subjectivity. I do not mean to say that individual subjectivity precedes intersubjectivity developmentally or that it is primary philosophically. For arguments about the relative philosophical priority of subjectivity and intersubjectivity, see Benjamin (1999b); Frie (1997); Reis (1999); and Stolorow, Orange, and Atwood (1999).
2 Wilner (1999), also inspired by William James, developed the idea of emergent or self-moving experience in which there is no self or subject acting on an object and no object on which a self can act. Although Wilner's formulation is different from mine, I appreciate his efforts to get at something similar in deconstructing the distinction between subjective and objective states of awareness.
3 I am indebted to Robert Michaels, who brought this to my attention in a discussion of a draft of this article.

Chapter 8

Clinical choices and the relational matrix (1999)

Introduction by Donnel B. Stern

"Clinical Choices and the Relational Matrix" was delivered as the sixth annual Bernard N. Kalinkowitz Memorial Lecture in 1998. When Kalinkowitz died in 1992, the Annual Lecture was established, and for the next number of years, it was the greatest honor that could be bestowed on an analyst associated with the NYU Postdoctoral Program. It was natural, of course, for Lew Aron to deliver one of these lectures. And deliver he did. This chapter puts on full display Lew's capacity for the quality of generative, synthetic thought that he shared with his great friend Steve Mitchell. Lew read widely and ecumenically. Study wasn't a purely intellectual pursuit for him, in psychoanalysis any more than in Judaism. He loved psychoanalysis. He loved psychoanalysis the way he loved guitar—which is to say, wholeheartedly, with the deepest kind of feeling. He loved all kinds of psychoanalysis. He was as comfortable as a Freud scholar (and he was one) as he was as a relational analyst, and he cared deeply about both—and about every other school of psychoanalysis, too. He had his commitments, of course; and this chapter is about precisely that—our intellectual and clinical commitments. But his commitments never stopped him from learning the psychoanalysis that existed outside the boundaries of his own, beloved relational psychoanalysis.

Lew offers a statement of his theme: "If, as I am suggesting, our identities as psychoanalysts are established through our relationships to psychoanalytic theory and to the psychoanalytic community—and to the values and ideals established by this society and embodied in its theories and practices—then psychoanalysis itself functions as the Third to analysts' one-on-one relationships with their patients."

Remember that the year is 1998. Lacan's conception of the Third is still commonly cited as the origin of the idea. (Lacan's idea still occupies that position, of course; but the idea of the Third has become so prominent in contemporary North American psychoanalysis that Lacan's version is cited less frequently than it once was.) Jessica Benjamin's landmark contributions to this area have yet to appear. But you can certainly see the continuity between Lew's work and Benjamin's; and that continuity is not just a matter of their participation in a common *Zeitgeist*. The two of them were close collaborators during this time, talking, thinking, and sometimes writing together (the one paper I know they wrote together has not been published). Lew published just one other paper centrally concerned with the Third (Aron, 2006), but he was deeply involved with the concept for many years.

Lew's understanding of the Third is different than Benjamin's. All concepts of the Third involve relationships made of three interacting points, of course; and two of these three points in all models are the subjectivities of the two people involved. But where Benjamin's understanding of the Third is a developmental model in which processes of intersubjectivity, especially recognition, depend on rhythmicity and differentiation, Lew emphasizes instead what we might call empathic, social processes such as our identifications with our own institutes, our theories, and our history and traditions: "What I want to emphasize about all of these uses of the Third is that in one way or another they point beyond the patient and the analyst as two individuals meeting in isolation, which might lead to an overly romanticized view of the psychoanalytic process as purely a personal encounter. Instead, these trends push us to consider the psychoanalytic relationship as always existing within the context of both the psychoanalytic community and the broader culture...."

I mentioned that Lew read ecumenically and found something to admire in all schools of psychoanalysis. But I also said that he loved relational psychoanalysis; and that deep involvement in relational thinking appears in this chapter. In the end, says Lew, the Third is a personal construction, reflecting our own subjectivities. Yes, it is about history and shared theory and values. But each of us selects which of these theories and values, and therefore which part of psychoanalytic history, we will embrace: "...[A] although all cultural contexts shape the values and ideals of its members, with analytic communities there is a further personal factor in that we are not born into analytic communities but rather we choose the communities with which we affiliate. In choosing which institute to attend, which society to join, which subgroup to identify with, we choose which set of values and ideals we wish to be shaped by. The Third is itself a personally infused or constructed force."

Lew loved good times, and he had plenty. The good-time guy in him often had an impish quality, and I see that quality in the "clinical" example he constructed for this chapter. I can just see him in the process of writing it. He's grinning. The example is a real clinical vignette, which Lew imagines the analyst presenting to three former (and imaginary) supervisors. Their orientations are not specified, but we see clearly enough that the first one is a fairly traditional Freudian of that day, the second one is someone whose theory of therapeutic action has more to do with the analyst's direct emotional impact on the patient, maybe a Franz Alexander-type practitioner of the corrective emotional experience, an object relations analyst of a certain kind, or a self-psychologist—and the third one is relational. Now, each of these supervisors has good points to make, and each presents a coherent point of view—which is to say, Lew's example is not tendentious. But which supervisor do you think pulls the whole thing together and leaves Lew with the wisdom he needs to write the rest of the chapter? I'll give you a hint: In introducing the illustration, Lew tells us that it is "modeled on the joke about the priest, the minister, and the rabbi."

You can see him grinning, can't you?

Aron, L. (1999). Clinical choices and the relational matrix.

Psychoanalytic Dialogues, 9(1), 1–29.

In recent years, we have witnessed wide-ranging public debate and intellectual commentary concerning multiculturalism and the seeming relativization of moral and ethical codes and standards associated with the increasing diversity of American culture. This controversy has been accompanied by heightened anxiety that there will be an erosion of standards as the very foundations of Western culture are shaken up. Within psychoanalysis, too, is growing concern about objective standards and normative procedures. As psychoanalysis has celebrated its new found diversification of schools and pluralism of perspectives, the very foundations of our discipline have come into question, and our once "mainstream" theory of technique has been challenged. Our increasing emphasis on the subjectivity and intersubjectivity of the psychoanalytic situation has led to some anxiety about standards of practice and how to avoid an "anything goes" approach to psychoanalytic treatment. As we learn to live with the pluralism of contemporary psychoanalysis, what is left of the foundations upon which we may build a theory of psychoanalytic technique?

For many decades, it was a widespread practice to teach courses in psychoanalytic institutes under the title "standard" or "basic model technique." The phrase, "basic model technique," was taken from Eissler's (1953) classic paper in which he defined parameters in terms of their deviations from this ideal, and, as Wallerstein (1995) points out, Eissler's basic model technique was widely accepted as "the definitive version of the classical psychoanalytic technique inherited from Freud" (p. 111). Analysts could take this prescriptive theory of technique and apply it to individual patients. Remember that Hartmann (1960) referred to clinical psychoanalysis as a "technology." Let me be clear that there is nothing intrinsically harsh or inhumane about viewing psychoanalysis as a technology. There is, after all, nothing in that approach that suggests that this theory must necessarily be applied rigidly or dogmatically. A sensitive and well-functioning psychoanalyst was expected to take the theory, which is after all intended as a general statement of principles, and apply it to the unique individual patient with whom that analyst is working at the moment. Hence, even the standard or basic model technique—when viewed as a technology—required sensitive, empathic, and individually tailored application. Nevertheless, it was generally accepted that a standard or a model did exist, and its application was viewed rather mechanistically.

The idea of a standard or model technique worked fairly well so long as there was some sense of unanimity to the way psychoanalysis was conceptualized, taught, and practiced. Remember that for many decades, almost all psychoanalytic institutes taught only one version or so-called school of psychoanalysis. Institutes, until recently, were either Freudian or Kleinian, interpersonal or self-psychological. Now, it is true that, even within the most mainstream institutes, there was some diversity. There had always been differences and disagreements regarding principles of psychoanalytic technique. One need look no further than Fenichel's (1941) authoritative monograph or to the classic collection of 1920s and 1930s papers on controversies in psychoanalytic technique collected by Bergmann and Hartman (1976) to get a glimpse of the rich diversity of opinion regarding psychoanalytic principles of praxis. Nevertheless, even with all of this diversity, there was a clear consensus, within any institute, as to the correct or true vision of psychoanalysis. Where variance remained, the belief was that one side was right and the other wrong, that one version of psychoanalysis would ultimately prevail as the standard technique and the other approaches would prove to be mere deviations or heresies.

Contrast this with psychoanalysis in this, our postmodern, constructivist age, in which the nature of the analyst's authority (and, of course, the teacher's and supervisor's authority) has become less clear. Mitchell (1993a) has referred to a crisis of confidence in what an analyst can know, a crisis of confidence in what our patients need from us, and a crisis of authority in our analytic self-image. How can we say to a trainee that this is what the psychoanalytic response should be in a given situation, that this is the proper psychoanalytic intervention, based on the standard or model psychoanalytic technique, when we and the student know that there are any number of other analysts and supervisors, often in the same institute, who would disagree and do things differently? At most, one can say only that this is what I would do, or this is what I think I would do with a patient like this. But, this brings into psychoanalysis what Freud tried so desperately to keep out, what he called, in a letter to Ferenczi, "the subjective factor," which he equated with arbitrariness and with the analyst's unresolved personal complexes (letter of January 4, 1928, cited in Grubrich-Simitis, 1986, p. 271). Nevertheless, in the context of reflecting on Ferenczi's clinical contributions, Freud (1937) wrote: "Among the factors which influence the prospects of analytic treatment and add to its difficulties in the same manner as the resistances, must be reckoned not only the nature of the patient's ego but the individuality of the analyst" (p. 247).

In reevaluating Hartmann's view of clinical psychoanalysis as a technology, Schafer (1997) suggested that one reason Hartmann chose what seems from today's vantage point to be such a "chilling" trope lies in his classicist mentality

> Classicism valorizes formalization, systematization, thoroughgoing rationalism, and rigorously enforced clarity and consistency. Ideally, classicistic work is so impersonal that contributions can be made with a minimum of individualistic coloring. The ideal does not tolerate self-expressiveness other than a minimum of personal style in the use of one's own reason.
>
> (p. 205)

Because of this mind-set, within the long-dominant, mainstream, analytic school, analysts were thought to be "relatively interchangeable" (Kantrowitz, 1997, p. 127). All of this was in line with Freud's wish that psychoanalysis be like any other empirical science in that it was to rely on a standard methodology that would yield replicable facts. It was in this spirit that Freud (1927) wrote, "Psychoanalysis is a method of research, an impartial instrument, rather like the infinitesimal calculus" (p. 36).

Today, by way of contrast, when someone suggests to me that analytic trainees must begin their education learning the basic model technique, I ask them to whose basic model technique they are referring. And yet, as someone who teaches and supervises psychoanalysts-in-training, I would forcefully argue that systematic and rigorous thinking about psychoanalytic technique remains essential and that it is in the very process of establishing a personal relationship to psychoanalytic theory and to the profession that one becomes a psychoanalyst.

If, as I am suggesting, our identities as psychoanalysts are established through our relationships to psychoanalytic theory and to the psychoanalytic community—and to the values and ideals established by this society and embodied in its theories and practices—then psychoanalysis itself functions as the Third to analysts' one-on-one relationships with their patients. The Lacanian concept of the Third, for example, points beyond the psychoanalytic dyad to the larger context, background, or container within which the dyad exists. Because the dyad is framed by the Third, the partners are able to relate without merging. For Muller (1996a), it is the semiotic code (the cultural limits and borders) that frames and holds the dyad. Although Muller emphasizes the rules or code of the society that exists in the symbolic register and that are shared by both patient and analyst, my own stress here is somewhat different, as I focus on the analyst's relation to theory and to the analytic community within which it is always embedded. Theory functions as an expression of the Third, as psychoanalytic theory exists as one aspect of our common cultural context, and this relation to the Third keeps the analytic situation from degenerating into nothing but a personal encounter, and a regressive one at that.

But Muller's Lacanian informed elaboration of the concept of the Third is only one of many similar ideas that refine our understanding of psychoanalysis as a multivariable psychology. (For an interesting comparison of Lacanian and relational views of the Third, see the exchange between Crastnopol, 1999 and Muller 1996 a. My own use of the term is closer to that of Crastnopol.) Among those who have influence my thinking about the importance of the analytic Third is Spezzano (1998), who has argued along lines, similar to those of Muller and Crastnopol, that the psychoanalytic community functions as a third element intersecting the analytic pair. For Spezzano, the analyst's relation to the patient is never purely dyadic but always forms a triangle with one vertex representing the analytic community (hence, the title of his 1998 paper, "The Triangle of Clinical Judgement"). Greenberg (1997) discusses similar issues pertaining to the authorizing impact and legitimizing influence of the wider analytic group culture on the analytic dyad. Greenberg suggests that membership in an analytic community commits one to that community's standards and thus provides a basis for both analytic authority and analytic restraint.

Perhaps the most influential development of the idea of an analytic Third has been in the work of Ogden (1994a), for whom the "analytic third" is neither subject nor object but is jointly created, intersubjectively, by the analytic pair: "The intersubjective and the individually subjective each create, negate, and preserve the other," and created out of the dialectical interplay of these forces is the "intersubjective analytic third" (p. 64). Although Ogden's ideas are fascinating and influential, they do not neatly fit with the way I am conceptualizing the Third in this chapter, and this difference needs to be kept in mind. Ogden uses the "analytic third" to refer to another subjectivity that emerges from the patient—analyst interaction, one that both patient and analyst participate in, shape, and are transformed by. My own emphasis in this chapter extends to the wider professional, social, and historical culture in which the dyad is embedded.

But speaking of the analytic situation in triangular terms is certainly not anything new within the analytic conversation. One of my most beloved supervisors, the late Donald Kaplan, used to teach that he always thought of "the clinical situation as an oedipal triangle—the patient, the analyst, and the profession to which the analyst is married, a marriage creating primal scene issues for the patient" (1988, personal communication). But, if there is something to the universality of this triangular relation, it is also true that each analyst carries on a unique and idiosyncratic marriage to the profession and that patients are often sensitive to the specific quality of their analyst's professional marriage. In this context, I am often reminded of one patient who would point to the picture of Freud on my wall and yell at me that I was doing or not doing something for him at that moment because, "You love him more than you love me!" Analysts working with a relational slant are not inclined to reduce this kind of situation to the patient's intrapsychic oedipal structure but are likely to emphasize specifically what the patient has observed or inferred about this particular analyst's idiosyncratic love relationship with Freud and the analytic profession.

Thinking of the analytic situation as a three-variable psychology does not necessarily entail imposing an oedipal triangular structure. The interpersonal tradition, and particularly the so-called cultural school, has long emphasized the importance of social, cultural, and historical contexts in understanding psychopathology. There is a trend among contemporary psychoanalysts to take increasing account of the context within which the analytic dyad operates—to think of the contextual Third in addition to the oedipal third. Altman (1995) and Cushman (1995) have each independently referred to a need to think in terms of a three-person psychology—by which they mean to refer to the larger social, cultural, and institutional contexts in which the dyadic interaction takes place.

What I want to emphasize about all of these uses of the Third is that in one way or another they point beyond the patient and the analyst as two individuals meeting in isolation, which might lead to an overly romanticized view of the psychoanalytic process as purely a personal encounter. Instead, these trends push us to consider the psychoanalytic relationship as always existing within the context of both the psychoanalytic community and the broader culture, and, therefore, although contemporary psychoanalysis emphasizes the subjective, the intersubjective, and the unique relational matrix rather than regard itself as a technology to be applied by an anonymous (and relatively interchangeable) analyst following a basic model technique, there are some (relatively objective) constraints placed on what we mean by psychoanalysis, and these restrictions are imposed not only by the individuals directly involved (subjectively) but by a wider set of forces, including not only contemporary influences but the voices of history and tradition as well.

To return now to the problem with which I began this essay—if there is no basic model or standard technique, if there are all sorts of ways of imagining and practicing psychoanalysis, if these are numerous in any single institute, then how is one to teach a student any principles that are to hold up? After all, it is not as if analysts have lots of common ground clinically and disagree only in their metapsychologies, as Wallerstein (1990) unsuccessfully tried to convince us. Quite to the contrary, my experience in teaching and supervising is that analysts really do see things quite differently. What one analyst sees as resistance, another views as a progressive cooperative step toward growth on the patient's part, perhaps an important exertion of will. Of course, it may be both, but we often approach these matters with dramatically different emphases.

On those rare occasions in our literature when someone publishes a full-length treatment of what he or she considers to be a well-analyzed, successful, psychoanalytic case, and when these cases are commented on by other psychoanalysts, there is typically substantial disagreement not only about the particulars of the analyst's approach, theory, or technique but even considerable disagreement as to whether the patient substantially improved. My point is that we disagree about far more than our metapsychologies and about far more than just our clinical approaches to patients. We disagree with one another to the core because psychoanalysis is so thoroughly value laden. We cannot agree on what a success is, on what our goals are, or on what constitutes a true psychoanalytic process because many of us (and the many different psychoanalytic communities and subgroups with which we are affiliated) maintain quite different sets of personal and professional values and ideals.

In what follows, I elaborate on the profound subjectivity of psychoanalytic technique and highlight how much of our psychoanalytic approach is embedded in our moral vision. The moral dimension seems to underlie our theoretical narratives and animate our technical approach. Nevertheless, I also argue that our technique is inevitably theoretically informed, that one cannot function as an analyst without an (at least) implicit theory of technique, and therefore it behooves us to be as explicit as we can as to what our underlying theory of technique is. I hope to demonstrate that idiosyncratic, personal, and subjective factors (the romantic vision psychoanlysis) must be continually counterbalanced by more general, objective, and impersonal considerations (a classicist vision) and that, among the analyst's many professional responsibilities, one is to manage the polar tension between these forces (see Hoffman, 1996a). The analyst's only hope in managing this tension comes from the very fact that he or she can rely on the Third, the sustaining background of professional allegiances to theory and community, values, and beliefs.

Throughout this chapter, I move back and forth between the dyadic considerations of the relational matrix (issues of mutual regulation) and the analyst's relation to the Third—psychoanalytic theory, the psychoanalytic community, and the wider culture within which these exist (all of which are used by the analyst to maintain self-regulation).[1] However, the way in which I have just put it, speaking of moving back and forth between dyadic considerations and the analytic Third, already simplifies a more complex dynamic in that it focuses on two seemingly separate dimensions of what is more accurately recognized as a dynamic, shifting triangle.

The notion of the Third as a point in a triangle, and not only as a container or frame, connotes a more actively triangulated dynamic among the patient, the analyst, and the analyst's professional community, theoretical positioning, and psychoanalytic affiliation. If there is a patient-analyst-Third triangle, then there are several charged, shifting vectors of relations among them. There are many complexities to the way these three points interact as a triangle and, as in any triangular relationship, shifts in what the dyads do for each other.

An obvious example of this concerns patients who are themselves in psychoanalytic training and who therefore have their own explicit relationship to the Third. However, even patients, who are not members of our profession, have complicated relationships to their images of psychoanalysis, as seen so often, for example, in their offhand remarks about Freud or the profession. Perhaps we are most dramatically made aware of the Third in a concrete form as patients are treated in psychoanalytic clinics where these triangular dynamics often take on central importance, however often this may be neglected in supervision and in training.

We also encounter these complicated dynamics now, as psychoanalysis has been besieged by managed care and health care reform, assailed by academics as a pseudoscience, and maligned by hostile media reports. Interestingly, for some patients, at some moments, all of these attacks are reason to join in with their analysts in a spirit of "us against them"; other patients are unsettled by this assault and position themselves more skeptically distant in relation to their analysts. Often these reactions are even more complicated and ambiguous, but all of these scenarios make the analyst aware of the convoluted tensions that take place in the triangle constructed among the patient, the analyst, and the psychoanalytic community and profession—as well as the culture in which these are embedded.

It is not only the patient, of course, who has transferences to the profession of psychoanalysis, to analytic theory, and to its critics. Analysts maintain complicated, transferential, and often highly charged relationships to their analytic institutions (as well as to those other psychoanalytic associations with which they are not affiliated), often affected by as well as expressed in their relationships to teachers, supervisors, colleagues, institutes, psychoanalytic organizations, and, most important, their analysts. Later, I have more to say about the relation between the analyst's subjectivity and his or her choice of theory and affiliation with a particular psychoanalytic community and the mutual impact of individual subjectivity and the analytic community, as well as the consequences of this mutual influence on theory construction and clinical practice. In this chapter, however, I can only begin to outline the enormous complexity of these shifting dynamic triangular relations. Although I recognize that there is some slipperiness in my presentation, I believe that to some extent this is inevitable because of the circularity created by the interpenetration of these forces on one another.

The following illustration is fictitious. I use it for teaching purposes. None of the characters depicted is meant to portray any real identifiable analyst or supervisor. The case material, though disguised, is real, and all aspects of the vignette are based on actual occurrences. It is modeled on the joke about the priest, the minister, and the rabbi:

> A male analyst's (A's) office was part of a suite with a shared waiting room. Magazines tended to accumulate quickly, and every so often A threw out all but the most recent of these magazines. On one or two occasions over the years, when a young woman patient (P) had come early to her analytic sessions, she had apparently seen A as he dumped magazines into the trash. One day, P began a session by mentioning that she had noticed that the magazines in the waiting room were accumulating. She wondered whether A would mind if she took some. She reminded A that she teaches disabled children, and one of the activities that she usually does with them is make collages out of various items, including pictures from magazines. She knew that A threw his magazines away as they accumulated, and, of course, she said that she would take only the older magazines and not the more recent ones. Is that all right? She asked A.

What follows is my attempt to imaginatively convey what went on in the mind of the analyst as he was thinking of what to say next. There was, of course, no way to stop time and think through all of the following considerations, but I think that this story conveys something about what the analyst struggled with for a moment before responding to P. A imagined that he had the opportunity to present this clinical situation to three of his previous supervisors, supervisors X, Y, and Z, who will remain genderless for the purposes of this illustration.

A imagined the following. He reported to supervisor X relevant information about the patient's background and presented detailed process notes of the sessions that led up to this request. The last session dealt at some length with P's childhood and family life. She was the only girl among five siblings. Growing up, it had seemed to P that her parents had an ideal marriage. Her father, a physician, clearly was committed to and loved all of his family. He was, however, distant and strict; he seemed rigid and ungiving, more concerned with rules, principles, and ideals than with what his daughter needed at any given moment. She envied and resented her brothers, to whom the father seemed more responsive. She longed for gifts from her father that would make her feel special and close to him, like one of the boys.

Supervisor X suggests that the patient is acting out in the transference, attempting to get A to enact an old childhood longing that the analyst/physician/father give her some special sign of his love, in the form of a concrete gift. She wants to be treated as special, to be gratified, and so the magazines represent oral as well as phallic-narcissistic supplies. He has so many magazines, whereas she and her handicapped students have so little. His magical gift should serve to undo her castration and make her potent like him, one of the boys; at the same time, it would be experienced as an expression of her analyst/father's love and hence be a phallic-oedipal gratification. As, in supervisor X's view, the patient is a high-functioning, analyzable patient with a good working alliance, X suggests that the analyst not accede to the request, at least not immediately, but rather engage P in an investigation of what the magazines and the request mean to her at this moment in the analysis. What feelings are evoked in P as she requested the magazines, and what feelings would be elicited if the analyst acceded to or denied her request?

In his imagination, analyst A next consulted supervisor Y, who, as you must certainly expect, had different advice for A. Y pointed out that P's father was experienced by her as a caring but rigid man who went by the rules rather than treating situations as they arose. Y suggested that P's experience of A was structured along lines very much as she described her own father. From Y's point of view, P experienced her analyst as caring and concerned, but rather distant and professional. Like her father, she imagined that he had a perfect marriage to his profession and to Freud. Y thought that P was now testing her analyst. She wanted to know how much the analyst was really like her father. How giving or withholding was he? Would he stick to his rules and principles in a rigid way, or could he be flexible? Would he care more about his marriage to his profession, his commitment to Freud, or his love for her? Hence, for supervisor Y as well as X, there were important oedipal as well as preoedipal issues being enacted in P's request. Y thought that all of this needed to be explored but suggested that it could be best explored after agreeing to her request. Y was less concerned than X was about gratifying her wishes. He was more interested in disconfirming her rigid interpersonal expectations and thereby modifying the structure of her object relations. Y thought that approaching her request with flexibility and a willingness to gratify her would disconfirm P's expectation that A is precisely like her father and provide her with a different and more flexible experience, one oriented to her individual needs. Y argued that what was important was not frustrating her libidinal needs, as X had suggested, but gratifying her need for a therapeutic object relation. Y, like X, wanted to know what it was like for P to make her request, and Y, too, was curious about what she would feel if A agreed to give her the magazines or declined, but Y thought that exploring this at this point might prove counterproductive, and so Y suggested holding off on this exploration for later.

From supervisor X's perspective, if A follows Y's advice, he will deprive the patient of the opportunity to reexperience her childhood trauma in the here-and-now of the analytic process. It is not only that giving her the magazines will be overly gratifying and thus derail the full emergence of her transference longings, but, more important, it represents a refusal on A's part to accept his transferential role as the traumatogenic object. Now, without really knowing more about supervisors X and Y, I cannot be sure, of course, but my guess is that supervisor X would probably believe that, with almost all analytic patients (assuming that by his criteria they are analyzable), it would be better to remain abstinent, not to grant their special requests for anything outside of the analytic frame. Although X may make a good case for not giving the magazines to P in light of her history, it is likely, I think, that this would be X's typical advice for all patients in analysis.

And, although I can be no more sure of Y's general behavior, my guess would be that Y is typically less concerned with the principle of abstinence and more concerned with providing the patient with a therapeutic object relation, otherwise known as a corrective emotional experience. So, although Y may make a good case for the advisability of giving P the magazines in this case, this recommendation is consistent with Y's general approach to all other patients as well. Both X and Y have considered the patient's individual needs. Neither is simply following rigid rules in a cold or unempathic manner. They both believe that their theory of technique is in line with their assumptions about how the mind works, how people develop emotional and interpersonal problems, and how they are best helped to change and grow.

Being faced with such strikingly different opinions, analyst A was quite confused and decided to get yet another imaginary consultation. (This may be a manifestation of the repetition compulsion.) Now, in real life, unlike in academic exercises, no two supervisors get to hear the same data any more than any two analysts hear the same material from patients. For one thing, supervisees, like patients, present differently to different supervisors. Different supervisors, like different analysts, elicit different information, and, furthermore, their own personality styles tend to evoke different aspects of their supervisee's characters. So, it is possible, or even inevitable, that the patient that X heard about is not exactly the same patient that Y heard about.

Enter supervisor Z. After listening to A's presentation, Z had many questions. Z said that, aside from getting to know patient P, it was also important for Z to have a better acquaintance with analyst A. As A and Z got to know each other, many questions were raised. What is the history of P and A's relationship in regard to negotiating other requests and exchanges? What is it like for A to give and receive gifts in general? How does A generally feel about saying no to people when asked for something by them? What would it be like for A to say no to P in this instance? What does A imagine or fantasize would happen next if he gave P the magazines? How hard would it be for A to have P be mad at him over this? When A thinks of saying no to P, how does he imagine saying no? Would he give some explanation? How would he do it? What would it feel like? Would he feel self-righteous, virtuous, resolute, and ornery? How conflicted did A feel about giving the magazines to begin with? If he weren't in supervision, would this even be an issue for him? What was his first temptation upon hearing the request? What did A's analyst do in this kind of situation? Or, is A the kind of fellow who never asked his own analyst for anything? What would it have been like for him to have asked such a thing of his analyst? As A's wife is also in the field and shares the office space, how would she feel about A's giving away the magazines? Does A's wife ever give her patients gifts? Did she have an analyst who gave her gifts? How has A felt about this? How does A generally feel about following rules and about being "correct"? How committed is A to a particular version of psychoanalytic technique? What kind of marriage does he have to his profession? Perhaps most critical, Z wanted to know more about the specifics of this particular analytic relationship and how A experienced himself in relation to P. How is it, for example, that at this point he felt hesitant about giving her the magazines—so much so that he got involved in such a lengthy obsessional daydream as a result of her request—when he ordinarily experiences himself as being more spontaneous and less bound by conservative principles of analytic restraint? Conversely, how is it that, though generally more cautious about violations of a secure frame, still just now, in relation to P, his first impulse was to think it would be a good idea?

In short, analyst A seems to be of more than one mind about this decision. At times he can be giving, at other times withholding; at times radical, at other times conservative; at times reserved, at times freewheeling. Which analyst A is being elicited by P just now in this analysis? It is not simply a question of A's character or identity but of who he has become in relation to P and, for that matter, who he has become when sitting with X, Y, and Z. Z was very thoughtful and explored many of the possible meanings of the magazines for both P and A, but he never did get around to saying what A should do or, for that matter, what he himself might have done in this situation.

What was Z's theory? Did Z have a theory of technique at all? Was Z a radical deconstructionist or a postmodernist? Is that a theory or a nontheory? Was Z a radical interpersonalist who believes only in the power of a detailed inquiry but refuses to embrace any metapsychology? Can we really consider either Z's questions or A's answers to these personal questions independently from our consideration of theory?

Certainly there are other questions that Z did not think to ask. This reminds me of Levenson's (1988) quip that countertransference is what the analyst does not think to ask. What I am suggesting here is that what we think to ask or do not think to ask is influenced by personal, subjective factors as well as by those theoretical commitments that steer us in one direction or another. The very questions that Z asked were to some degree influenced by Z's theoretical commitments, whether these are consciously articulated by Z or not. Similarly, to consider A's responses as simply personal is to exercise an approach of naive realism, one that elevates what the analyst feels to a special epistemological status independent of the influence of theory. After all, what A is able to become aware of feeling in regard to wanting to give P the magazines may itself be shaped and structured by theoretical commitments as much as by personal idiosyncrasies. Furthermore, Z's reaction to A's revelations will be similarly influenced by theoretical presuppositions, whether or not these underlying assumptions are explicitly articulated. The subjective and the intersubjective inevitably interact with theoretical and metapsychological variables.

Let us now look at one commonality between supervisors X and Y. Both X and Y were attempting to apply, to an actual case, a general psychoanalytic theory. By a general theory, I really mean a complex, hierarchically structured system of theories that includes a theory of psychopathology, a theory of mind, a theory of development and a theory of psychoanalytic technique. Both supervisors, X and Y, applied these consistently layered theories to the specific individual case of P. But, they both assumed that this comprehensive theoretical system could be applied by a competent analyst to the individual needs of a patient, without any need, at least in theory, to take into account the individuality of the psychoanalyst, who was, after all, going to apply the intervention. Furthermore, they did not take into account what Greenberg's (1995) has called the "interactive matrix," the unique makeup of a particular analytic dyad. According to Greenberg, the interactive matrix includes "the beliefs, values, commitments, hopes, needs, fears, wishes, and so on that both analyst and patient bring to any particular moment in the treatment" (p. 11).

Greenberg's contribution is quite radical, not because he advocates any wild or unconventional behavior on the analyst's part. Quite to the contrary, Greenberg's technique is conservative, disciplined, cautious, and highly self-reflective. It is radical, however, in that it shakes up our basic assumptions about the relation between the theory of technique and its application. Greenberg's conceptualization of the interactive matrix, or the relational matrix (Mitchell, 1988a), not only makes some room within our methodology for the "subjective factor," the analyst's individuality, but, even more, it places this unique singularity of the analytic dyad at the very center of our concerns.

Greenberg's clinical illustration is of an analyst who chooses to apologize to a patient regarding a mistake made in a previous session. Greenberg notes a variety of rationales in favor of apologizing in the service of good analytic technique; he also provides a good rationale for not apologizing. Ultimately, he demonstrates that this dilemma cannot possibly be resolved without taking into account the analyst's (not to mention the patient's) individual attitudes and feelings regarding apologies. How does this particular analyst feel about apologizing in general, in his daily life, not only in his work? How does this analyst feel when someone else who has wronged him apologizes to him? Do these very personal individual differences matter in determining the optimal analytic technique for a given analyst? Will the course of the analysis depend on the congruence and incongruence of the analyst's and patient's personalities regarding the many variables that arise in the course of the analysis?

Here I think of Atwood, Stolorow, and Trop's (1989) notion that the continual interplay between the patient's and analyst's psychological worlds leads to two basic situations—intersubjective conjunctions and intersubjective disjunctions. Greenberg (1995) similarly places great emphasis on whether the analytic dyad is "concordant" or "discordant"—that is, whether analyst and patient share roughly the same or discrepant sensibilities. Another interesting dimension of Greenberg's theorizing is his idea that analytic inquiry and interpretation are more likely to occur when the dyad is discordantly related. The person of the analyst is thus a critical factor that determines what can be known about the patient. In the example presented here, we need to broaden our focus to consider the intersubjective conjunctions or disjunctions among patient, analyst, and supervisor. Furthermore, I think that we need to consider the conjunction or disjunction of the analyst and his or her theory along with the complex interactions among the theory (or theories), the analyst, the patient, and the supervisor. (For a discussion of supervision and contemporary psychoanalytic theories, see the papers collected by Rock, 1997.)

Supervisors X and Y, although coming from quite different theoretical bases of operation, have a great deal in common. Both were operating out of what Schon (1983) has termed technical rationality, the idea that practice follows directly from theory—a model that derives from and imitates the natural sciences. It is the model that Hartmann (1960) had in mind when he described psychoanalysis as a technology. Schon studied the way managers, architects, therapists, and other professionals go about problem solving in their daily work. What he found did not match the image of the professional as beginning with a systematized knowledge base resting on fundamental scientific laws of behavior, which is then applied to the individual case in practice. Rather, Schon found that practitioners function in complex, uncertain, unstable, and unique situations in which value conflicts abound and that they rely on trial and error and "reflection in action"—reflection that is often prompted by unexpected events that occur in the course of practice and that allows the practitioners to keep alive, in the midst of an action, a multiplicity of views of the situation.

What supervisors X and Y have in common, in spite of their alternative rationales for treatment, is that their theories minimize the individuality of the analyst's character and the way in which this individuality is an essential aspect of each understanding reached and each intervention made. The supervisors also do not consider who the analyst has become with this particular patient—not in terms of the patient's transference, but rather in the sense that the highly specific situational factors of who the patient is with this analyst influence who the analyst is with this patient.

Traditional psychoanalytic theories, except for those of the interpersonal school, did not highlight the individuality of the analyst or the uniqueness of the interactive matrix. In practice, of course, analysts have always known that the personality of the analyst mattered. Analysts have always considered this factor, for example, in making referrals. But, although this was implicitly acknowledged in practice, it was acknowledged, at most, on the margins of the theory.

Contemporary psychoanalysis is beginning to put the interactive matrix at the center of its theoretical and methodological agenda, but note that putting the relational matrix at the center does not mean abandoning theoretical and professional considerations, and it does not imply that the analyst operates purely in reaction to momentary, idiosyncratic considerations. The analyst is inevitably subject to the pushes and pulls of the immediate, interpersonal analytic moment, to mutual regulation, and yet the analyst also must continually maintain the asymmetric, professional, and ethical responsibilities of conducting a psychoanalysis.

The dilemma facing contemporary psychoanalysts is the question with which I began this essay: After we recognize the overriding importance of the relational matrix, acknowledge the irreducible subjectivity of the analytic situation (Renik, 1993), and disclaim the standard or basic model approach, with its technical rationality, what is left that we may consider fundamental? Is any foundation left upon which we may build a theory of psychoanalytic technique?

The dilemma revolves around the following dichotomization. Those who have emphasized a theory of technique have the advantage of clear guidelines and some basis for deciding what is and is not a psychoanalytically productive process. The downside of their approach is that, as there will always be some discrepancies between the practical implications of the theory and the practitioner's personal proclivities, it is likely that practitioners will either follow the theory at the expense of their own subjectivities or, more likely, operate from a secret or private theory that better suits them as individuals but that is dissociated privately and disclaimed publicly. Hence, Sandler (1992) has distinguished between the "public face" of psychoanalytic practice and our largely unconscious use of a private hodgepodge of technical formulations. Although Sandler seemed to suggest that this state of affairs permits analysts to work productively, Mayer (1996) has challengingly suggested that this discontinuity between our private and public theories is destructive to our profession, as many analysts, not practicing as their explicit theory suggests they should, begin to feel that they are not doing "real" psychoanalysis. In my illustration, analyst A might decide, for example, to give P the magazines but think to himself that, at least for the moment, what he was doing was not "real" psychoanalysis. Not only would this be detrimental to A's professional self-image, but, more important, it would have clinical implications in that he might well feel guilty that he had betrayed his "marriage" to psychoanalysis and sided with the patient in a dyadic love affair that excludes the Third—the theoretical, professional, communal side of the triangle.

On the other hand, those who have been critical of fundamentalist assumptions have been left with nothing but an appeal to the analyst's authenticity, spontaneity, moral scrupulousness, and ongoing self-reflection. It is not that I wish to depreciate these criteria, far from it. However, the downside of this approach is that, at the extreme, it may lead to an anything-goes strategy in which there is no basis for determining when an intervention is or is not within a psychoanalytic framework—that is, whether it leads to a deepening of the psychoanalytic process. To return to our vignette, without any fundamental theoretical assumptions, analyst A might be led to simply grant or deny the patient's wish based primarily on how he is feeling at the moment with her, without any clear psychoanalytic rationale to guide his behavior. This would collapse what in my view should be the analytic Triad into a simpler two-person dyad.

However, one formulates an analytic goal, purpose, or aim, some of the analyst's clinical actions are more cogent and useful, and some are less so, in achieving the aim; some seem to make the work progress, and some seem to inhibit it. Keep in mind, however, that the actions seem to make the work progress or seem to inhibit it only from a particular perspective, a perspective determined by theoretical and personal factors. What the analyst thinks at a given moment about what seems to deepen the work may be strikingly different from what he or she thinks moments or sessions or years later. This may differ strikingly from how it seems to the patient; and all of this may differ yet again from how it seems to the patient's spouse or to the analyst's supervisor.

What I am suggesting is that the best way to think of the theory of psychoanalytic technique is not as a system of rules and regulations but rather as an interlocking network of clinical concepts and dimensions that the analyst can use as a framework within which to evaluate the potential benefits and drawbacks of any form of behavior within the individually unique interactive matrix. Berman (1996) has recently argued, along quite similar lines, that the idea of a standard technique has become obsolete. Instead, he proposes, "What needs to be learned is not any list of steadfast rules but an introspective and empathic sensitivity to the actual sources and actual impact of our actions and inactions" (p. 166). My proposal is also in line with Bromberg's (1994) invaluable formulation that the analyst's choices derive their meaning not on the basis of their status as technique but rather from the ongoing context of the relationship in which they take place. "Any attempt," he writes, "to turn a therapeutic discovery that emerges from a relational context into a technique that can be 'applied' to other patients is an illustration of what I believe to be the single most ubiquitous failing in all analytic schools of thought as methods of therapy" (p. 541).

Consider one well-known area in which prominent analysts have advocated contradictory rules of analytic understanding and technique. Kohut (1971, 1977) recognized that a common countertransferential response to work with narcissistic patients is to become uncomfortable with being idealized. Analysts would then intervene in such a way as to derail the patient's idealization. Kernberg (1975), on the other hand, suggests that these idealizations serve defensive purposes and that the underlying hostility will ultimately destroy treatment if not addressed. He urges analysts to confront these defensive idealizations. Hence, two schools of psychoanalytic thought, two understandings of clinical phenomena, two rules of technique. Josephs (1995) has elegantly critiqued this polarization of psychoanalytic theory and technique in which Kernberg's analysis of primitive defenses is matched against Kohut's empathy for archaic self-object needs. Josephs's strategy is to resolve the contradiction between the approaches by suggesting that we need both but in a certain order. Empathy for archaic self-object needs must precede yet be counterbalanced by the interpretation of the defensive function of archaic self-object transferences. Neither Kernberg's approach nor Kohut's technical recommendations take the analyst's personality traits directly into account.

Josephs's approach is balanced, synthetic, and clinically sophisticated; here too, though, his recommended technical approach does not sufficiently consider the individuality of the analyst or the interactional matrix. Josephs may concede that, for at least some patients, what looks (to an outside observer) like an empathic approach might be more threatening than the more "distant" approach reflected in defense analysis. He does not attend, however, to individual differences among psychoanalysts. My concern is that Josephs's proposals may lead to a new set of technical rules—to a new, perhaps more sophisticated rulebook with precise guidelines for the optimal sequence of analytic work—but that, like the old rules, they too would underemphasize the clinical significance of the idiosyncratic features of the analyst's character or how the analyst has become a certain character with this individual patient.

Let's look at the problem from a different angle. Does the best technical approach in the face of a patient's idealization depend at least somewhat on how comfortable the individual analyst is with being idealized? Does it not also depend a great deal on how comfortable an analyst feels being confrontational? Some of us love being idealized and work well in mutually admiring relationships. Some of us become uncomfortable being idealized and avoid these situations. Some of us are quite confrontational in our daily lives, whereas some of us go to great lengths to avoid confrontation. (And, I should quickly add, just as those who are confrontational assume that those who avoid confrontation need more analysis, so too do those who avoid dispute assume that those who are drawn to it need more analysis.) Now you might at first think that those analysts who enjoy being idealized should become self-psychologists and that those who do not like it should become Kernbergians. But it is not so simple. Some analysts who are uncomfortable being idealized may be drawn to become self-psychologists precisely because the approach would help them regulate their discomfort, just as some analysts who are comfortable with idealization may find themselves tending to work in a more Kernbergian manner because his approach helps them regulate their desire to be admired. Similarly, analysts who tend to be confrontational in their nonprofessional lives might be inclined to adopt a Kernbergian technical approach because it suits their personal style, whereas analysts who avoid confrontation in their nonprofessional lives might be drawn to a Kernbergian technical approach precisely because it would help them to use confrontation within the framework of their professional work. As most of us tend to have some trouble with both idealization and confrontation, we are lucky in this age of psychoanalytic pluralism in that we can draw on both theories to help us regulate our participation.

In other words, I am suggesting that a theory may fit a particular analyst because it is concordant with who the analyst is or because it compliments who the analyst is—two different ways in which theory functions as a form of self-regulation. This way of thinking invalidates any simple rule, such as, "Allow the patient's idealization to unfold, systematically confront it, or do one and then the other." This way of thinking implies, then, that the question of what really or truly constitutes the psychoanalytic process is poorly framed; there may be many different analytic processes used by different analytic dyads.

So, if we cannot teach a set of rules, what can we teach? Consider the issue of idealization: rather than teach our supervisees to confront idealizations or to allow idealizations to flourish, I think we need to teach them to recognize the likely consequences of either tactic and encourage them to experiment with these options as they work with different patients and learn how each way of thinking and intervening matches or compliments their own personal style, idiom, and character.

The some holds for self-disclosure (for a more comprehensive discussion of self-disclosure, see Aron, 1996b). Analysts with a propensity for exhibitionism may choose a theory that encourages self-disclosure because it matches their own personal proclivities; other analysts with the very same exhibitionistic tendencies may choose a more conservative theory of technique precisely in an effort to modulate these tendencies. What is important didactically is to help student-analysts examine the impact of whatever choices they make on their analytic work so as to enable them to become increasingly self-reflective about their analytic participation. In this way, students learn to use theory as the Third to help them manage and regulate their capacity for self-reflection or reflection in action. (Of course, theory may also act as a Third in the sense of an intruder or barrier between patient and analyst, as when the analyst uses theory defensively rather than as an aid in self-reflection.)

As I see it, our technical maxims operate much like common clichés of everyday life. They all contain an element of wisdom, and yet they may be contradictory. It is wise to remember to look before you leap, but it is equally sagacious to keep in mind that she who hesitates is lost. It may well be that the road to hell is paved with good intentions, but sometimes one ought to take the thought for the deed. Out of sight, out of mind, but absence makes the heart grow fonder. Similarly, interpret from the surface to the depths but always interpret at the point of maximal urgency or deepest anxiety. We need to be empathic, to mirror and affirm our patients' subjective reality, and yet we need to confront their evasions and illusions. We need to intervene with careful tact, timing, and dosage, and yet we need to respond authentically, spontaneously, and without guile. Listen with evenly suspended attention but listen for hidden allusions to the transference. These maxims are contradictory not just because they derive from conflicting theoretical systems but also because analysis, like life, is complicated.

We need to teach and remember both sides of these contradictory pieces of advice. Ultimately, no standard formula can direct us as to when to rely on one or another of these principles. You cannot look before you leap and act without hesitation. Sometimes, one may empathize first and then confront; other times, one may be better off confronting first and then empathizing. And it does not depend just on the variability of the patient; it also depends on the character of the analyst and on the nature and quality of the unique analytic interactive moment in which the patient and analyst have come to be as they are for each other. (As an aside, I would add that what at one moment you think is empathetic may not be so from the patient's perspective or from your own at another moment: in fact, the very dichotomy of confrontation and empathy is untenable, as a good confrontation may well be experienced as deeply empathic. To further complicate matters, the very same intervention may be read as empathic when viewed under the influence of one theory and as unempathic from the perspective of another theory. It is theory that determines how we view what is too often mistakenly taken to be simple clinical observation.)

The story of analyst A and his three imaginary supervisors may have mistakenly given the impression that I believe that, given enough time to think through all of the dynamic and technical issues, an analyst could decide on a technically correct course of intervention. Actually, even if one could stop the clock and think through all of the relevant considerations, the analyst would still have to wait for the patient's response in order to sort out the various meanings and effects of any intervention. There is an inherent ambiguity and indeterminacy to any intervention that precludes a linear predictability of the impact of the analyst's behaviors. Nevertheless, in spite of this very indeterminacy, the analyst must continually make disciplined and responsible clinical choices. Mitchell (1997) concludes his latest book on just this note, writing, "Good analytic technique concerns not correct actions but hard thinking, in a continual process of reflection and reconsideration. There are no singularly correct clinical actions (although there are certainly some singularly incorrect ones)" (p. 268). The example of analyst A and his fantastic supervisions is meant to illustrate this peculiarly psychoanalytic form of hard and rigorous thinking.

The abandonment of metapsychological Truths and the questioning and destabilization of theoretical foundations do not necessitate the surrender of ethical standards, professional responsibility, or clinical judgment. Quite the contrary, the affirmative postmodern sensibility that has so shaped contemporary relational and intersubjective psychoanalysis leads to the recognition that analysts must accept responsibility for the fact that it is their own personality, their own subjectivity, that underlies their values and beliefs, infuses their theoretical convictions, and forms the basis for their technical interventions and clinical judgments. There can be no technical choice or clinical decision that is not imbued with the analyst's subjectivity (see, in Aron, 1996a, my discussion of the application of the principle of dialectical objectivity to psychoanalysis). Hoffman (1995) forcefully states that, instead of regarding the countertransference as one factor among many to be considered by the analyst in making any intervention, we must recognize the "analyst's subjective, personal, countertransferential experience as the superordinate context in which everything else, including theory, is embedded" (p. 108). Therefore, rather than disclaim personal responsibility and attribute their understandings to an abstract metapsychology or universal theory, analysts must accept personal responsibility for their interpretive understandings and clinical interventions. Our understanding is always value laden, and, in turn, our values are always personal. Still, I emphasize that our values are not only personal—they are also shaped by our analytic education, training, and experience, and they are embedded within the norms of our particular analytic communities. They reflect aspects of the analyst's subjectivity, and yet they also partake of the Third—the analyst's profession, the norms and values of the local analytic community—and it is these qualities of the Third that allow subjectivity to be subordinated to professionalism, even if in a personal integration by each individual analyst.

Here I must return to the slipperiness and circularity that I began to articulate earlier, for there is in reality less of a clear division between the analyst's subjectivity and the Third, as reflected in the analyst's community, theory, and institutional affiliations. The Third is shaped by the forces of loyalty and challenge among its members and by the new ideas and extensions of theory and practice that, when introduced, push against its boundaries and self-definitions. So, although the community shapes the analyst, there is a continual reciprocity of influence in this dyad too, with the individual analyst influencing the community in turn. Remember too that, although all cultural contexts shape the values and ideals of its members, with analytic communities there is a further personal factor in that we are not born into analytic communities but rather we choose the communities with which we affiliate. In choosing which institute to attend, which society to join, which subgroup to identify with, we choose which set of values and ideals we wish to be shaped by. The Third is itself a personally infused or constructed force.

Lesser (1996) provides a particularly engaging illustration of the role of the analyst's values. Lesser describes an elderly woman who was asked what her sex life had been like during her long marriage.

The woman said that sex had always been for her husband and not for herself. She felt no regret about this, as she believed that this was simply the way women are—asexual. Lesser quite forthrightly acknowledges that, if this woman were in analysis with her, the chances are good that, by the time she terminated the analysis, this woman would have experienced anger or regret about her sexual life. Lesser asks, "Would it be right for me to think that this was because she was always angry and rueful, and was just not aware of it before?" Lesser suggests that a better interpretation is that, as the analyst, she would have provided the analysand with a new way to understand her experience, and together they would co-construct a new narrative that would create sadness and anger by establishing the possibility that women can indeed be sexual and have the right to sexual pleasure. Lesser wrote, "What we are used to calling 'narratives' are really sets of beliefs that are profoundly imbricated with morality, power, and politics."

In Lesser's illustration, is the anger that would be expressed by the elderly woman analysand to be understood as discovered or constructed? Was it inside of her, repressed, dissociated, or unformulated and waiting to be uncovered or formulated in words? Or is it a new creation of the analytic situation and process? We can only answer, "Both/and." Human experience is both discovered and constructed in psychoanalysis (see also Gabbard, 1997)—a recognition that led Hoffman (1996a) recently to change the name of his psychoanalytic approach from social-constructivism or critical-constructivism to dialectical-constructivism.

As analysts, we long for indubitable, foundational knowledge. We want a solid and reliable theory to guide us and relieve our anxieties, to aid us in our self-regulation. But we, like our patients, must struggle without easy solutions. We can and we must continue to make technical choices, to practice at any given moment in one way rather than in another, to create certain ground rules for ourselves and our patients, to believe in some things and not in others. But we must also accept that these choices reflect our own subjectivities; they are personal, reflective of moral values and commitments, and are not only technical or theoretical choices. We must choose, but we cannot disclaim our choices as inevitable outcomes of abstract and universal principles. Neither can we claim, however, to be operating simply on the basis of our immediate personal experience, as we are always influenced by some community of psychoanalysts, by some institutional affiliations, and by some theoretical assumptions that play some role in constructing our subjective experience. The acceptance of the interpenetration of the personal and the theoretical—the recognition that we are involved not only in a dyadic relationship with our patient but in a triadic relation with the patient and the analytic Third—potentially leads to more checks and balances in making clinical choices. We may compare and contrast our immediate subjective experience, our affective responses, our intuitive tendencies to respond to patients in particular ways with our knowledge of theory, with the norms and expectations of our community, and with the values and ideals of our institutions.

However, one advantage of our current plurality of psychoanalytic perspectives is that, although operating from one theoretical framework, we may take advantage of another theoretical framework as a tool to help us reflect on the actions we take on the basis of the first theory. For example, when reflecting on my participation with a patient at a moment when I am operating using a self-psychological framework, it may be useful to question myself by asking how a Freudian or interpersonalist might view my participation. It is sort of like going to supervisors X, Y, and Z. In the context of our contemporary pluralism, one may objectify oneself and one's participation by adopting the standpoint of an outside critic. What I am advocating is that the analyst adopts a maximally self-reflexive strategy—a goal similar to the goal that we set for our patients. Nevertheless, I also recognize that even this kind of broad recommendation has prescriptive features that may not be suitable to all analysts. Some analysts, for example, may find it more natural than others to move back and forth among different theories. Other analysts may find themselves working better when they stick to viewing their clinical work within the framework of a single theory. Thus, I recognize that any recommendation that I make needs to leave room for the fact that analysts with unlike personalities may have to proceed quite differently. Clearly, the position that I am advocating has significant ramifications for psychoanalytic education and clinical training. Following the American pragmatist tradition, I am putting an emphasis on perspectivism, pluralism, practice, practical consequences, and personal experience.

So, when supervisees ask questions about technique, issues of timing, the depth to which the analyst should allow immersion in self-experience, when to validate a patient's experience, when to empathize and when to analyze, when to contain and when to interpret, when to remain ambiguous and when to self-disclose, I do not believe that we serve them best by answering with the rules of analytic technique, the basic or standard model. Rather, I think we serve them best when we help them to keep in mind the most salient clinical issues and to search with their patients for what seems to work for themselves, even as we acknowledge the radical ambiguity in determining what constitutes evidence that an intervention has indeed "worked." We learn with every patient through trial and error, even as we hope to be able to carry some general principles with us from one case to another and even as we expect to pass on some words of wisdom, contradictory as these words may be, to our students and supervisees.

Throughout the history of the development of the theory of psychoanalytic technique has been an attempt to construct and revise a standard, fundamental model—a linear and hierarchically organized system of recommendations and guidelines, if not rules and procedures. Although I am not opposed to sketching out the advantages of certain analytic strategies over others, the purpose of this chapter has been to stake out room in our theory for due consideration of the analyst's individuality and of the impact of the uniqueness of the analytic dyad while attempting not to lose sight of the critical role of theory, belief, and analytic community. We need to maintain some tension between the advantages of general rules, principles, and guidelines and the personal, subjective, and idiosyncratic features of the clinical situation. In fact, there has been an ongoing tension between these two pulls throughout the history of psychoanalysis. Bergmann (1997) has explored the debate between Reich, whose character analysis aimed at a systematic approach to psychoanalytic technique that would have minimized the reliance on the analyst's intuition and subjectivity, and Reik, who emphasized that genuine psychoanalytic insight occurs as a surprise to both patient and analyst. According to Bergmann, various forms of this debate have persisted throughout the history of psychoanalysis: "Some analysts seek ways of standardizing psychoanalytic technique, while others stress that the *individuality of the analysand* makes every analysis a unique and unrepeatable event" (p. 80, italics added). What I wish to add to Bergmann's remark is that, in my view, the individuality of the analyst as well as the particularity of the analysand makes every analysis a unique and unrepeatable event.

Ferenczi wrote in 1931 that "analytical technique has never been, nor is it now, something finally settled" (p. 235). I am pleased to say that it is no more settled now than it was then. Remember that, on a number of occasions, Freud himself said that his technique "has proved to be the only method suited to my individuality; I do not venture to deny that a physician quite differently constituted might feel impelled to adopt a different attitude to his patients and to the task before him" (1912a, p. 111). As I have argued elsewhere (Aron, 1996b), ironically, by taking Freud as a model of a clinician who was insistent upon working in a way that was personally satisfying, some of us may find ourselves working in ways very different from Freud's, using clinical techniques and principles that are perhaps better adapted to our own characters. Furthermore, as we each may be quite different characters with different patients at different moments in the process, we each may inevitably need to be different analysts with different patients at varying moments.

The theoretical and the technical form a complex system of mutual influence with the personal, the subjective, and the intersubjective, and, in the teaching and practice of psychoanalysis, these factors need to be considered together as functioning in complex and often elusive ways.

Note

1 I have elsewhere discussed how theory serves as an aid in the analyst's self-regulation (Aron, 1998). My ideas about self-regulation and mutual regulation are loosely based on Lachmann and Beebe (1996).

Chapter 9

"With you I'm born again": themes and fantasies of birth and the family circumstances surrounding birth as these are mutually evoked in patient and analyst (2014)

Introduction by Merav Roth

At the end of this unique article Aron shares with us the following: "After checking with Al [the patient discussed in the article] by phone, I sent a draft of this article to him for his review and comments. As I wrote the letter accompanying the article, I realized to my complete astonishment that it was the day before Al's birthday and that the paper would be delivered to him on his birthday. Was this a birthday present? And was it one that I was giving to Al, or with his permission to 'present' this material, was he giving a present to me? He was grateful that I had shared the paper with him and wished me good luck in presenting it, but also asked if he could have a series of sessions to discuss the strong feelings that it had stirred up in him" (pp. 354–355).

Following the above, I feel deep gratitude for the present handed to me by Galit Atlas, embedded in the opportunity to reflect on the prominent contribution of this article, and "discuss the strong feelings that it had stirred up" in me as well. For many years, I knew Lew Aron only through his writings. Reading Lew's intriguing ideas has been always confusing to me because they felt so closely related to my Kleinian psychoanalytic upbringing, although at the same time they differed from it and challenged it. After many years of reading Lew,

I was lucky to meet him in Israel, a place that he considered a second home and where he was (and shall remain) a beloved leading figure in the psychoanalytic community. A warm friendship soon developed, and in our meetings of minds and hearts, I realized that Lew was indeed an extraordinarily knowledgeable person and scholar in general, and in classical psychoanalysis in particular. I believe that this is part of the reason—alongside his great wisdom and creativity—why his writings are so influential and transformative to psychoanalysts from each realm of thought.

"With You I'm Born Again" presents the general idea that every analytic encounter involves fantasies of birth—both by the patient regarding his personal history, and by the analyst, regarding his personal history, fantasies about the patient's rebirth in analysis as well as the analyst's rebirth in analysis, all interwoven in meaningful ways that are worthy of noticing and exploring internally and with our patients.

Aron presents the case of Al, and four significant contributions from four supervisions he took as a young psychoanalyst during the years of this analysis—with Christopher Bollas, Joyce McDougall, Andre Green, and Benjamin Wolstein. From each supervisor Aron stressed a particular contribution.

Although Aron writes how each of his supervisors influenced him, it is evident that Wolstein, who challenged Aron's countertransference wishes and fantasies, paved the way to his fascinating and illuminating reflection on his own birth fantasies and the way that they entangled with Al's. Maybe it is not a coincidence that he named his patient Al, the initials to Lewis Aron.

I want to stress one insight made by Aron following his free associations regarding his own birth myth: "My own fantasies were both concordant and complementary to Al's. Which one of us was the mother, who the newborn? Which one of us was struggling to be born and to survive?" (p. 354). From a Kleinian perspective, this is a profoundly important reminder of the fact that in terms of projective identification, it is often the case that as analysts we tend to focus on complementary projections (us in the role of the object), whereas in fact it is on many occasions the concordant ones (us in the role of the subject) that tell us a great deal about the patient's deepest phantasies and experiences. It is eye-opening to read how, for instance, when Aron thinks of himself as the infant striving to be penetrated by a strong father and liberated from a suffocating mother in this analysis, that he gains sight into the deep and most crucial aspects in his patient's mind, and they are both freed from their "transference-countertransference interlock" (using Wolstein's terminology).

Finally, I want to add, in the light of this article's theme, that Lew Aron is not only responsible to the birth of many psychoanalytic illuminating terms, ideas, and lines of thought. He was also inspiring in the way that he allowed *himself* to be reborn, time and again, through intellectual conceptions that for him were never detached from their human roots and from the potential presents they offer to patients, supervisees, and readers. This article is a very moving example of such a fertile conception.

Aron, L. (2014). "With You I'm Born Again": Themes and fantasies of birth and the family circumstances surrounding birth as these are mutually evoked in patient and analyst.

Psychoanalytic Dialogues, 24(3), 341–357.

Themes of birth and rebirth, being born and born-again, are readily observed in clinical psychotherapy and psychoanalysis even as they remain undertheorized. Freud, Klein, and Bion each considered birth to be among those "preconceptions" of which we have inherent knowledge; primal fantasies known all along from inherited knowledge (Spillius, 2007). There is a dearth of literature on the birth fantasy in psychoanalysis. The psychoanalytic symbolization of birth was aborted early in our professional history, a casualty of the "heresy" of Otto Rank and the controversies waged over his dissent. Rank (1924), drawing on Freud's own idea, first thought of birth trauma along quite literal lines, only gradually coming to think of it as metaphorically expressing aspects of separation-individuation from the preoedipal mother (Lieberman, 1985). The heated controversy within the "secret committee" surrounding Freud revolved around Rank's championing of the birth trauma as the paradigmatic key to understanding neurosis (Obaid, 2012).[1]

For Freud and his followers, the emphasis on birth trauma detracted from the centrality of the Oedipus complex, repression, and castration as the nuclear core of neurosis. Ferenczi (1925/1952b), after initially defending Rank, later articulated the mainstream Freudian response to Rank, arguing that birth fantasies "represent a regression in phantasy from the Oedipus-conflict to the birth-experience" (p. 296). Nevertheless, Ferenczi also maintained that a mother's conscious and unconscious aversions to her future child, before and during pregnancy, could influence the child's psychological and physical development.[2] Obaid (2012) suggested that the controversy with Rank was responsible for Freud's reformulation of his theory of anxiety and for his understanding of the role of signal anxiety. In addition, I am suggesting that the controversy may well have inhibited analysts from attending to clinical manifestations of birth imagery and symbolism, to fantasies of birth, rebirth, and related themes.

Yet within psychoanalysis there has always been a tradition, perhaps a romantic tradition (Strenger, 1989), which did highlight the theme of birth. Eshel (2004) provided a clinical approach based on visions of psychoanalytic change that incorporate the striving for a "new beginning," "new opportunity for development," and rebirth. She drew especially on the two terms "a new beginning" (Balint) and "a new opportunity/chance for development" (Winnicott) that are interwoven in Balint's (channeling Ferenczi) and Winnicott's notions of therapeutic regression.[3]

Birth myths, narratives, and related fantasies of origin include primal scene fantasies related to children's efforts to understand how they were conceived and how their very existence owes itself to their parents' relationship (Aron, 1995). Family romance fantasies elucidate the child's place or lack of place in the family. This group of fantasies might well include ideas about the embryonic experience in the mother's womb or fantasies about delivery or adoption.

My focus includes these themes but is directed to understanding the child's entry into the family, the family circumstances surrounding a child's entry into the family as these are elaborated in the child's fantasies, and the related familial issues of attachment and relatedness, as well as to separation and individuation, autonomy and independence (see Aron, 1996c). I assume that many birth-related fantasies are connected to the parents' desires and beliefs about their offspring: For example, was the child wanted or unwanted, planned or accidental? Did the parent want a child of a different sex or one with different physical or psychological characteristics? Are a child's characteristics associated with the traits of the parent, grandparents, or ancestors? Many fantasies reflect the individual's ideas about how his or her birth affected the family system within which he or she arrived. These fantasies range from conscious daydream-like narratives to unconscious or fleetingly conscious fragments and are layered and recursively embedded in the clinical material (Arlow, 1991). Nevertheless, in a comprehensive review of psychoanalytic ideas about fantasy, Person (1995) does not mention anything at all about birth fantasy and, even in discussing fantasies of having a baby, does not connect these fantasies with the individual's own birth fantasies, which I suggest are typically evoked in parenthood.

I want to draw attention to a loose grouping of fantasies that share some relation to the individual's thoughts, beliefs, and feelings about his or her own origins and birth and to the family circumstances surrounding the child's entry into the family. When studied psychoanalytically, birth fantasies and related myths and narratives of origin reflect significant aspects of individual and family development, character, and psychopathology. My focus here is on fantasies that relate to a person's entry into the world, especially into the world of one's immediate family environment. I do not think of these fantasies as distortions or misunderstandings of reality but rather as the best efforts to comprehend one's origins and to come to grips with one's birth into a particular family made up of significant others with very specific physical and psychological characteristics.

It should be clear that by birth fantasy I am not necessarily referring to a graphic depiction of the birth process but rather to a wide range of ideas, feelings, and images connected to one's entry into the family and the world of relations as well as to one's "psychological birth." In my view, fantasy is best conceptualized and understood clinically as a means of understanding, sorting out, elaborating on, and coping with individual, developmental, interpersonal, and especially familial, and often enigmatic experience. My approach is quite consistent with Litowitz's (2007) conclusion that "unconscious fantasies represent children's theories about their reality: experiences with significant persons, routine and critical events and activities" (p. 220). It may be that what I am calling fantasy others might prefer to think of as "organizing principles" (Stolorow & Atwood, 1989) and, in some ways, personal origination and birth fantasies or narratives may be akin to cognitive schemata, screen memories (Freud, 1899), "personal myths" (Kris, 1956), or "global fantasies" (Shane & Shane, 1990) that "are seen to define, and perhaps even determine, the life course of a given patient" (p. 75). They may even be well conceptualized or categorized as "model scenes" (Lachmann & Lichtenberg, 1992). Nor is it always easy or even possible to distinguish precisely what aspects of the material relate to conscious, preconscious, or unconscious fantasy (see Busch, 2006). I use the term fantasy (or systems of fantasy) because the term maintains diachronic continuity with the psychoanalytic past and provides synchronic connection across many traditions of psychoanalysis. To me, the term fantasy seems closer to the clinical data while remaining most evocative of the fundamental imaginative aspects of psychic life. But what in analysis may be verbalized or constructed as fantasy may be better understood as having been previously "unthought known" (Bollas, 1987), implicit procedural knowledge (Lyons-Ruth, 1999), "procedural memories" (Schacter, 1992), and "unformulated experience" (Stern, 1997). Indeed, much of what the Kleinians think of as unconscious *phantasy* may be better conceptualized as having existed only in the form of implicit procedural rules until words were used to construct these *phantasies* in analysis. In other words, I believe that much of what we call unconscious fantasy is a psychoanalytic construction, a co-construction or emergent property of the dyad, "the analytic third" (Ogden, 1994b). Thus, fantasy mediates not only desire and defense, the intrapsychic and the interpersonal, internal and external relations, but also the personal and the social, the individual, and the family. Birth fantasy, as I use the term here, includes such ideas as: How does a person think about one's parents as they were at the time of one's birth? Who were they? How did they relate to each other? What were their internal and external circumstances? Did they love each other? Did they love me? What was their relation to their own families of origin? Or if born to or adopted by a single mother or same-sex parents, what was their mental and social status at the time of their arrival? How did their arrival affect that relationship? How did it affect their parents' social or financial status or their relations to other family members or community?

Corbett's (2001) creative clinical study of children in nontraditional families demonstrated the importance of primal scene and family romance stories in children with lesbian and gay families, multiparent families, and single-parent families, as well as in families utilizing modern reproductive technologies. Corbett emphasized that fantasies often have their genesis in stories repeatedly told between parents and children as part of family bonding. "Children frequently request that stories of conception and birth be repeatedly told, as they strive to comprehend reproduction, parental sexuality, and family formation. Heroic and miraculous accounts of birth, for example, are often given a special place in family stories" (p. 601).[4]

What does one imagine about one's parents' wishes, hopes, fantasies, and conflicts before one's birth? For Lacan,

> even before a child is born he or she is already assigned a place in the world of language in the sense that he or she is expected by the parents and thus already symbolized in their minds. He may already have a name; she may already be the bearer of many of her parents' expectations. In that sense the parents' unconscious and conscious signifiers will be projected onto this imaginary child and will continue to surround the baby after its birth.
> (Gurewich, Tort, & Fairfield, 1998, p. 9)

One psychoanalyst who took the birth experience very seriously was Donald Winnicott. In a fascinating discussion of the impact of birth on the individual, Winnicott (1988) suggested that many people believe that at birth the newborn is not yet a person, not yet a human being, and so from this point of view there can be no effect of birth on a person. Winnicott argued against this view, suggesting instead that at full term there is already a human being in the womb, one capable of having experiences and registering body memories. In short, for Winnicott, there is, in normality, always already a self at birth. To be a self is to be an active agent, and so Winnicott views this newborn self as possessing agency. Winnicott theorizes birth, or should I say that he imagines or fantasizes birth, as directed by the newborn.

...it is possible to conceive of a birth in which, from the infant's point of view, the change from the unborn to the born state is brought about *by the infant*, who is biologically ready for the changes and who would be adversely affected by their delay. By this I mean that the infant has a series of impulses and that the progression towards being born comes within the infant's capacity to feel responsible. We know of course that the birth was brought about by the uterine contractions. It was the infant's impulse *from the infant's point of view* that produced the changes and the physical progression usually head first, towards an unknown and new position.

(1988, p. 144)

One should keep in mind in reading this account of the birth process that Winnicott, as a pediatrician, was exceptional, and pointed out that what most psychoanalysts know about birth and infancy is largely derived from the psychoanalysis of adult patients. Even with his extensive pediatric experience, his "conception" of birth is fantastic, but even as playful metaphor it has implications for how we think of the origins of the self. In his paper "Birth memories, birth trauma, and anxiety," Winnicott (1949/1957) described a traumatic birth as the basic matrix of experience for later life, as prenatal and birth memories remain in the body. He wrote, "The feeling one gets is, however, that the child's body knows about being born" (p. 180), and "I do find in my analytic and other work that there is evidence that the personal birth experience is significant, and is held as memory material" (p. 177).

In his new book, *The Birth of Experience*, Eigen (2014) writes, "Dreams have long been associated with the birth of experience, as if we dream life into being, dream ourselves into being." A schizophrenic patient reported to Wilfred Bion that he had a dream in which he "was walking along the river bank with my children, when they fell into the river, and they were carried by the very strong current toward the weir, the waterfall which is in the river." The patient then "jumped in to rescue the children, and was at once carried with them toward the weir, toward the sluice, this channel which disappeared underground" (Aguayo & Malin, 2013, p. 56). In trying to explain how certain patients have experiences which are unformulated, that they cannot express in words, which they express through reminiscences of early and primitive sensual experiences, Bion explains that this dream depicts the patient's fear of emerging from his fetal state of mind. To use words and language is a form of psychological birth, emerging from one state of mind into another and it is to risk being swept away.

As psychoanalysts we should not avoid Freud's (1910a) great insight that meanings are often represented by their opposites. Speaking of birth should lead us to also consider the significance of death. Beginnings may allude to endings, and being to non-being. In his existential examination of the terror of death, Yalom (2008) summarized Epicurus's argument that the state of non-being after death is the same state we were in before our birth. He quoted from Vladimir Nabokov, who in his autobiography wrote,

> The cradle rocks above an abyss, and common sense tells us that our existence is but a brief crack of light between two eternities of darkness. Although the two are identical twins, man, as a rule, views the prenatal abyss with more calm than the one he is heading for (at some forty-five hundred heartbeats an hour).
>
> (p. 81)

Indeed, one of Ferenczi's (1929) great insights is that an unwanted child, one whose parents wish that he or she had never been born, often develops a psychophysiological disorder, severe self-destructiveness, and suicidal tendencies. "Slipping back into this non-being might therefore come much more easily to children" (p. 128). Slipping back into this non-being, pre-birth, is the legacy of those who feel they were not meant to be born, that their birth was not desired, what Ferenczi called "unwelcome guests of the family" (p. 126). So as we examine birth narratives and themes, we should listen for echoes of darker undertones.

In regard to Ferenczi, we should also recall his description of the fantasy or dream of the "Wise Baby" (Ferenczi, 1923/1980b), the precocious infant who speaks at birth and related themes of the infant as prophet, whom Ferenczi regarded as having to raise him or herself, to become his own parent. In his review of narcissistic fantasies, Bach (1985) highlighted the wise baby as an example of fantasies that are primarily about the self and self-regulation, rather than object relations, and in this context, he discussed other fantasies of birth and their countless religious and mythological manifestations.

Themes of conception and birth fill world literature and mythology. Think of the Biblical genealogies and infancy narratives of Jesus. The Gospel of Matthew compares the life of Jesus with the narrative traditions of Moses's early life. In both cases, the babies are saved so that each can later become the savior of the people. The circumstances of their conceptions, their births, their genealogies, even their naming, became the basis for a great deal of rich literature precisely because birth themes are understood to anticipate the meaning of a person's life. In his discussion of Moses, Freud (1939) draws on Rank's earlier work on mythology to make the point that the history of the birth of the hero "came to be especially invested in phantastic features" (p. 10), and Freud relates these myths of birth to the family romance. In her study of miraculous conceptions and births in Mediterranean antiquity, Talbert (2006) examined the scene in Plutarch's "Romulus" when Numitor first sees Remus. He is amazed at the youth's great strength and vitality of spirit and asks who he is and "what were the circumstances of his birth?" Talbert concluded that in this literature, "Birth explains later deeds and character!" (p. 84).

Freud (1933, p. 95) famously said that our metapsychology was our mythology. Following him, analysts have understood our theory, more generally, to be our collective professional fantasy (Arlow, 1991; Grossman, 1982; Roustang, 1976). An understanding of fantasy as the individual's best efforts to understand his or her world is analogous with a conception of theory as the psychoanalytic community's best effort to comprehend and depict the life of the mind. Thus, we need to examine not only the patient's fantasy systems but also the analyst's fantasies, and the profession's collective fantasies, otherwise known as psychoanalytic theory. Likewise, my emphasis on birth fantasies and myths of origin also points to the significance of the historiography of psychoanalysis, especially our profession's understanding of our own historical origins, early development, and the many myths surrounding the birth of psychoanalysis. Perhaps it is worth recalling here how Freud (1900) recorded that throughout his childhood, a story was repeatedly told that at his own birth an old peasant woman prophesized to his mother that she had given the world a great man. This is the kind of birth-related theme that is elaborated in the individual's fantasy system and that often provides data critical to understanding the individual's place within their family system and narrative.

"It's my birthday"

Al began his analysis with me soon after I completed my formal analytic training almost 30 years ago. After my training cases, he was my first private analytic patient. I tell you this history because it is significant that his case presentation is so intricately tied to my own birth as an analyst. Because of his special place in my professional development, I kept detailed process notes on most sessions and also presented this case to supervisors and consultants throughout the many years of his treatment. In this chapter, I will draw on my experiences presenting to Christopher Bollas throughout a daylong clinical case seminar as well as in private consultations, and to Joyce McDougall, Andre Green, and Benjamin Wolstein, who were seen in small group supervision.

My group mates when presenting to McDougall and Green included Jessica Benjamin, Adrienne Harris, and Jay Frankel. It was an intensely stimulating group experience, and I am indebted to each of them. I am in agreement with Wolstein (1984), who articulated a persuasive argument for expanding our supervisory model to include small group supervision, which at times facilitates study of unconscious aspects of the therapeutic relationship.

Among the first things that Al told me of his developmental history was that he was his mother's firstborn and had a traumatic arrival. He was born late and, as a result of a difficult, forceps-assisted delivery, suffered a broken collarbone.[5] He understands that he came home wearing a cast and cried all the time for at least several weeks. Al grew up in an upper-class New England home and had moved to New York following graduation from an Ivy League college to work in the financial district. He began his treatment following a painful separation and divorce from a brief and tumultuous marriage. He was in his late 20s and suffered from numerous physical complaints, including allergies, skin sensitivities, painful stomach ulcers that had gone undiagnosed for many years, a long-standing eating disorder probably related to the stomach pain, sleep difficulties, troubling obsessions, and anxiety.

I presented the first months of this treatment to Christopher Bollas,[6] who was, to my mind, a psychoanalytic celebrity. I found consultations with him inspiring and affirming. We discussed Al's birth trauma and, as one might expect from a leading Winnicottian thinker, Bollas emphasized the need for the analysis to be a good-enough holding environment for Al. I had told Bollas Al's very first words to me, "Is this room soundproof?" Even before introducing himself, or perhaps, in his signature manner of introducing himself, Al drew attention to the adequacy or not of the holding environment.

> I'm tired, today's my birthday—I got smashed last night and was hung over. I just took the subway and someone had taken a shit in the car and I sort of rode it up in the stink. The car adjacent to mine was packed—didn't want to fight people. At 86th Street I'm accosted by homeless people asking for money—a real New York experience—depressing. I didn't give money to them, there's too many of them. I can't give money to everyone, have to pick and choose, the situation is out of hand. I guess, I do feel guilty—frustration with them—obnoxious—yelling obscenities—always on the edge that it's going to happen—shit spread around—really disgusting. I just can't understand where their families are. I can't imagine that a cousin or a brother of mine would be on the street and no one would help them. It's depressing! Where are the mothers, brothers, sisters, cousins? I feel that must sound naïve. My father surprised me for my birthday.

The themes and images captured here were repeated again and again, highlighted in this instance by being positioned between two references to birthdays. But the reader should magnify the impact of allusions to intrauterine life and the birth process as they are evoked in this very brief snippet of narrative. In the early years of the treatment, Al questioned and tested every aspect of the clinical environment. The room was not warm enough or too warm. Al heard sounds from the waiting room and from the room next door. The window was opened too little or too much. The couch was too firm and the headboard too high. The air blew too strongly or not enough. Changes in appointment times were inconvenient, quickly forgotten, or simply missed.

In Al's associations quoted here, one may easily perceive birth imagery, dangerous, shitty, messy imaginings associated with feelings of utter helpless vulnerability, and out-of-control aggression and violence. Among the advice that Bollas gave me—and I trace the theme of this chapter to his proposal—was that I ask Al what he knew about his parents' family circumstances at the time of his birth. I was looking for suitable opportunities to investigate this theme with Al because of the traumatic nature of his birth, and also because of other traumatic aspects of his holding environment. Early on in the analysis he described his mother as unable to comfort him from the start, instead going into rages while blaming him for crying. From what he has been told by both his parents, as well as by older cousins with whom he is close, his mother could neither pick him up nor put him down without his crying. Al went on to tell me that while pregnant with him, his mother had found out that his father was having an affair. He had been told this a few years earlier, when his mother warned him about her suspicions that his wife was cheating on him. He went on to describe numerous incidents where he had felt humiliated by his mother and by other women in the family.

With Bollas, I had developed an initial formulation that Al's early holding environment had been seriously defective. He lived with the belief that his mother had not been able to pick him up or put him down without either hurting or abandoning him. Bollas and I expected it to be likely that Al and I would play out this dynamic, with Al feeling that the clinical environment could never be right, and with my having to sustain an adequate analytic hold while withstanding the bombardments of his aggression—all this without my retaliating by humiliating, hurting, or withdrawing from him and thus reenacting the abandonment.

Bollas viewed Al as a variant of a "normotic" illness (see Bollas, 2011, p. 22), in presenting himself as abnormally normal. The distinctive identifying feature of normotic illness is the individual's disinclination to entertain the subjective elements in life. Certain psychosomatic disorders and eating disorders (Al had both) may be forms of normotic breakdown in which psychological pain is expressed concretely rather than symbolically. Bollas himself relates normotic illness to Joyce McDougall's idea of the "anti-analysand," which we discuss shortly. Bollas warned me to not get overly invested in or overly interested in Al's concrete symptoms as he believed that if I did Al could become my very own "Wolfman," who would produce increasing spirals of dramatic symptoms to keep my interest. Fascinatingly, Bollas (2011) described that the normotic person seems to be "unborn." "It is as if the final stage of psychological birth were not achieved" (p. 26). What is lacking is the development of subjectivity and an interest in subjective states, in Bion's terms there is a deficiency of Alpha function. "The attack on alpha function means that the person never really comes alive, and is therefore only partially born" (p. 27).

In consultation with Bollas's close friend and colleague, Andre Green,[7] I learned to think about the structural basis for many of Al's symptoms as being rooted in his unconscious fantasy of his mother's unconscious conflicts toward him. A year had gone by, and it was his next birthday:

> Let's see. J [an old colleague/friend] called me to wish me a happy birthday. I had been mad at her for not calling but she told me she had a bad month. I thought here I was mad at her and I didn't think about what was going on in her life. I again was more relaxed and didn't tie myself into knots. I feel I have more faith, like it's not going to be such a disaster. But still my obsession is worse when I'm here. Blowing my nose, if I don't, I won't be able to breathe and snot will show. [I commented on his need to be spic and span clean with me.] My mother would clean my ears hard and hurt me. My breathing is confined, trapped. When I cry and let out emotion I blow my nose and clean out my system. My mother had lots of allergies and asthma since she was a child. I need to get this emotional stuff out, lots of emotional stuff, painful memories. I'm really controlling things, a taskmaster, if not, things will get out of control.

This is of course a tiny fragment of material, but on the basis of associations like these, Green proposed a different perspective. Situating conflict more centrally in understanding Al's symptoms, Green speculated that Al fantasized that his mother had been conflicted about him from the start. Perhaps he imagined that he arrived late because his mother couldn't decide whether to hold on to him or to expel him. Was she holding on to him to control and crush him, to squeeze the life out of him, to not let him be born at all, or was she trying to push him out and get rid of him? Any of these fantasies of his mother's unconscious conflict might explain why he was born late and injured.

Here, a second internationally famous analyst/consultant was placing a birth-related fantasy at the center of dynamic understanding. Both sets of fantasies related to the mother and to the holding environment. As Bollas understood Al's unconscious beliefs, whatever the mother had done was wrong, should she pick him up or put him down? Either way he cried, or she hurt or abandoned her infant. I could relate to that very easily. Anything I did was wrong. I, too, couldn't please Al. It was easy enough to feel incompetent, rejected, and retaliatory. And Al never complained in a hostile or aggressive manner so that it would be simple for me to blame him. Instead, he was extremely proper, respectful, and delicate in asking me to change some aspect of the clinical environment. So I could only feel angry with myself, not with him, if I couldn't get it just so, and everything had to be just so. But with Green's focus on conflict, things took a slightly different slant. Now the question was about Al's mother's intentions and motivations, and hence transferentially my own desires. Did I want to hold on to Al too tightly, control him too much, and in doing so injure him? Or was I eager to get rid of him, to push him out? Would my very conflict about controlling him and holding on to him cause him to break? What kind of birth, what quality of delivery, would Al experience in this analysis?

The primal moment of one's history

By his next birthday, I was working with Joyce McDougall,[8] who encouraged me to fantasize and theorize about Al's primal scene fantasies. Less concerned about the systematic analysis of defenses before content, McDougall seemed much less obsessional than I. Strongly believing that Al's psychosomatic symptoms resulted from his inability to symbolize and fantasize, she encouraged me to get him to elaborate fantasy consistently and to use my own imagination more freely to enter Al's inner world. McDougall (1989) was just at this time writing her book on a psychoanalytic approach to psychosomatic illness. She knew that many analysts of the era were reluctant to treat psychosomatic patients because they were considered too concrete, did not have availability of affect, lacked imaginative capacity, and had difficulty expressing themselves in words. It was also feared that the analytic process would exacerbate their illness. McDougall's clinical experience (and her extremely hopeful and caring personality traits) led her to encourage analysts to try by systematically elaborating fantasy, particularly imaginings of childhood.

Al associated to trying to go to sleep at night and being terrified listening to his parents fighting. Recall his first question to me upon initially entering the consultation room: "Is this room soundproof?" Al grew up listening to sounds, messages, and communications that were deeply disturbing. Al's primal scene is one of sadistic battling, war zones, imagery of stinking shitty trenches, and streams of waste. The primal scene merges with fantasies of intrauterine life where he is drowning in excrement, struck by other bodies (dead babies inside his mother?), and only saved this time in a dream image by a helpful, but black, and in his prejudiced view, untrustworthy, policeman. Al's father was weak and ineffectual at home and could never take a stand with his wife, although in various ways he did make some effort to be of help to Al outside of the mother's sphere. One of the central problems for the child in the primal scene is the conflict over which parent to identify with and which to desire. Themes of sexual and gender fluidity reverberate around this fantasy (see Aron, 1995). In his associations and dreams, heterosexual and homosexual fantasies are complexly layered, defending against each other dialectically. Competitive themes of masculinity and male aggression alternate with Al's fantasy of female masochism and castration anxiety, all reasonably understood as referring to his family history as well as to the transference.

Meanings and interpretations were fluid and constantly shifting; this was especially marked around themes of gender and sexuality. For a period of about a year, he so took for granted that I was homosexual that he told his friends he had a gay analyst. Following from the dialectic implicit in the primal scene fantasy, my perceived homosexuality both devalued me in his view, thereby keeping me relatively harmless, and expressed disavowed sexual wishes. Did Al's competitiveness with me, or his aggressive attacks, cover his dependence, longing, and loving feelings? Or were his expressions of closeness and sexual fantasies toward me attempts to cover his aggression and submit to me sexually before I attacked him? Al knew that his mother had discovered other women in his father's life, but he wondered if there might also have been men. (I will take up my own feelings and conflicts soon. I have birthdays too!)

Al believed that his conception and birth broke his parents' marriage as well as his very body. As I mentioned previously, it was while pregnant with him that his mother discovered his father's philandering. Perhaps if he were a girl his mother would have loved him or at least might not have been repulsed by his very body. He would lie in bed at night and fall asleep to sounds of shouting, accusation, humiliation, pain, and sex. Whatever significance the primal scene has regarding sexual life, whether involving perceptions of parental sexuality and aggression, or regulating sexual stimulation, it seems to me that primal fantasies are also a means of imagining the significance of one's origins, the primal moment of one's history, of one's entry point into the world (compare to Laplanche & Pontalis, 1973).

It's my birthday too

I move on to one last consultation and set of fantasies. I brought the case to Ben Wolstein,[9] who was at the time known as one of the leading interpersonal analysts in New York. I told him about the various fantasy systems that I had been exploring and especially about my own efforts to provide Al with a good-enough holding environment. Ben confronted me, as was his style, by challenging my own countertransference wishes and fantasies. He wanted to know why it was so important for me that I be so good, that I do it just right. After all, he pointed out, here I am running around to all of these international experts trying to find the right way to analyze Al; to do it just so. What was my need to be so good all about? What was *my* fantasy here? Wolstein did not have to push very hard to come across what he had described as early as 1959 as a transference-countertransference "interlock" (Wolstein, 1959, pp. 133–134; see also Bonovitz, 2009).

Weren't my obsessional, anal fantasies of being good, staying clean, and doing it right a symmetrical match to Al's obsessional symptoms? Wolstein's intervention had a powerful effect over time in gradually helping to free me from my own perfectionist efforts to be nice, good, and helpful. As a result, Al's analysis shifted over the next several years into a deeper exploration of sadomasochistic themes emerging directly between us. As I had less need to be the "good object"; "good mother"; the perfect, clean container; the solid and steady frame, I could be more free to intervene less cautiously, and Al could in turn both express more direct aggression, but also could then allow himself to be the good one in our relationship. Roles oscillated and gradually, very gradually, Al moved from the paranoid-schizoid to a depressive position, by which I mean simply that black-and-white thinking (recall the black policeman) splitting, polarized thinking, and two-dimensional portrayals of himself and of the significant figures in his life became richer, more complex, and less polarized.

I can of course only give the briefest of hints here as to some of my own dynamics in regard to birth fantasy, but here is some background just to suggest the ways in which intersubjective dynamics mutually construct a relational unconscious. (It always seems odd to me that analysts talk about the emergence of a "two-person psychology" and yet case presentations often consist of the presentation of the dynamics of only one person.) My own birth was a long-awaited event, as it had taken my parents many years to conceive and I was thus repeatedly told stories of my mother's pregnancy and my delivery. As an only child, I lived not only with my parents' child-focused attention but also with my maternal grandfather, and me, the only grandchild living nearby. My father was older, having spent many years in the military fighting the Second World War, and he had long wanted to become a father. My mother's own mother had become very ill when my mother was a little girl and died when she was 12. She always had a depressive and anxious tendency with attachment and separation as central concerns. I thus was surrounded by constant parental and grandfatherly love and attention with all of the advantages and disadvantages that such love and specialness bring. I was never left alone. When my parents went out, they left me with my grandfather, and on those very rare occasions when they all had to leave, I was left with close family friends, never a baby-sitter, as far as I can recall. Separations were carefully avoided until I was a late adolescent, and that soon precipitated entering my own personal analysis. Among the costs of such attention was my perceived need to take care of my mother by being her good boy, reinforced by my father's tendency to masochistically submit to her demands out of his own need to protect and appease her. Being a good boy meant doing things right, just so, justifying my mother's belief that I was special, and thus that she was special. The most often repeated story I heard about my own birth was that I was born during Christmas week (yes, undoubtedly a Messiah fantasy). That weekend I was the only boy baby in the maternity ward, and so the nurses placed me in a center crib surrounded by the girl babies. My own analyst had interpreted that my fantasy of being encircled, being the center of the group, represented being enfolded by my mother. Is it any accident that I spend my life teaching and working with study groups and psychoanalytic institutions largely composed of women and thus surrounded by them? Or that I was a devoted and loyal student/son to a series of analyst/supervisor/fathers whom I regarded as solid and powerful and willing to share their strength with me in my psychoanalytic family romance?

While this is a very brief sketch, it is my hope that it is sufficient for us to consider this analysis from the perspective of a two-person rather than a one-person psychology, and so here I want to tie my own personal "birth fantasies" to my professional birth, my unique way of being born as a psychoanalyst. Al was my first "analytic" case following training, and I wanted to give birth to a son who was just so, so as to give birth to myself as just so. But these efforts to be so good also concealed (among other things) the anger and rage that I repressed or split off, arising from the need to be so compliant. My own exaggerated efforts to provide a supportive holding environment and to create a solid and secure psychoanalytic frame may ironically have contributed to Al's expressing so much of the aggression and sadism in the early years of the analysis in that I split these feelings off while identifying with these characteristics in him. One might not recognize from hearing this early material just how kind, warm, generous, and caretaking Al could be in his life. If Al had been in pain and in danger during his birth and early years, so too was his mother, and Al had strong leanings to protect her and make reparation for the damage to her for which he felt responsible. As the years went by, Al could hold in mind and own more of these formerly opposed split-off aspects of himself and of his view of significant others.

Al's conviction that I was gay was an important aspect of our relationship and one that I believed I should not refute, especially since he never asked for my input.[10] After all, we are not talking about a simple conscious social identity but about unconscious fantasy, internal identifications, and so the question of sexual identity is always ambiguous. Maybe Al knew something that I was disavowing in a public marriage and lifestyle. I had, as part of my own analysis, examined my homoerotic fantasy life and wondered about my own analyst's sexuality. I very much admired my analyst's nondisclosure of his personal and social reality, as his firm anonymity signified for me, at that time, a testimony to his phallic masculinity and heterosexuality. The only time that my analyst's heterosexual bias may have been inferred was once when I wondered if he had interpersonal leanings and he interpreted that I was accusing him of having homosexual tendencies! I consider that the classic negative oedipal complex in men is among the most neglected aspect of all analyses (see Aron, 2013). The longing for homosexual penetration by a strong man is a powerful wish serving multiple functions in all men and is among the most denied and disavowed of all wishes, as Freud (1937) made clear in his description of the repudiation of femininity (pp. 250–251). For me, it served both as a wish for my father's strength, for his helping me to separate from my mother, and to have his child and so free him as well as myself from my mother, while also disguising positive oedipal longings for my mother and pre-oedipal wishes and fears of merging with her. My wish to be my analyst's perfect patient repeated and reenacted all of these wishes and was enacted inversely with Al, and in different ways yet again with these various supervisors. I viewed it as a sign of strength and masculinity that I could tolerate my patient's conviction without becoming unnecessarily defensive. In doing so, I was also identifying with my own analyst/father and thus enacting yet another Oedipal dynamic. Al and I shared congruent fantasies in which we imagined ourselves as a perfect parent-child couple united against an outside third whom we villainized, as well as complementary fantasies in which we alternated roles of controlling and dominating each other or abandoning each other. All of this repeated not only our own family histories and personal birth myths but also my experiences with my personal analyst (personal analytic myths). Hence shared fantasy, congruent, and complementary is one important basis for the intergenerational transmission of psychological themes and dynamics in both families and psychoanalytic lineage (Person, 1995). The above excursion into my own dynamics is not at all meant to be definitive or exhaustive, but simply to point toward the inevitability of the intersubjective third, of co-created relational unconscious dynamics and mutual coconstructed fantasy.

In the transference, I had to play many roles: perhaps the most difficult was playing the obstetrician who, in trying to help Al separate from his mother, ended up breaking his bones and nearly killing him. Indeed, as Stepansky (1999) highlighted, whereas Freud modeled the psychoanalyst on the surgeon, Ferenczi described the analyst as an obstetrician and analysis as a psychological form of childbirth, with the analyst passive but with forceps in hand (Ferenczi, 1919/1952a). In Al's case, the obstetric process was especially laden with risk. Here, and perhaps in all analyses, it was not only the patient who was being born through the analysis, but also analyst. By needing to have my first analytic child come out just right would I break him, squeeze the life out of him, push too hard, and pull on the reins too tightly? I wonder to what extent I was creating a new family for Al, while reenacting his old family by gathering together psychoanalytic grandparents, who again and yet differently, would know better than his parents just how to raise him. As I have said, this also enacted my own birth into a fantasized family romance of superior, even noble, analyst and supervisor parents and grandparents.

Roustang (1976) views transference as constituted by the interplay of reciprocal fantasies and desires between patient and analyst. "Every psychoanalyst unavoidably works upon his own fantasies on the basis of those he hears from his patients, and works upon their fantasies on the basis of his own" (p. 93). Later, Baranger, Baranger, and Mom (1983) famously described the crystallization of the field around a "shared fantasy" (p. 2). In these early years of the analysis, my own fantasy life had been overly restricted and confined. In an effort to be an ideal analytic instrument, a clean container, I had inhibited my own fantasy life and did not allow myself or Al enough access to my unconscious process. In my effort to be pure and spotless, so that he wouldn't treat me as the unwanted, repulsive baby, I risked becoming sterile and barren, and in my attempt to remain rational and mature I maintained Al in the position of the disturbed one. My own fantasies were both concordant and complementary to Al's. Which one of us was the mother, who the newborn? Which one of us was struggling to be born and to survive? In searching out analytic parents and grandparents, manifestly in the service of helping Al, I created an imaginary psychoanalytic family of my own, giving myself a lineage and family tradition. Now, fathers and mothers, grandfathers and grandmothers, with all the complexities that go with family entanglements, were there to assist me as I simultaneously delivered Al and was myself delivered. Still I had my own doubts about whether and what I could deliver through my work with him, and Al had to survive those doubts, anxieties, and conflicts.

I gained a great deal from all of these supervisory consultations. I took from each consultant what I needed at the time. Of the many penetrating insights and recommendations that each supervisor made, I recall only those few that I selected for whatever were my own reasons. This hardly does justice to the intuition, teaching, and wisdom conveyed by each of them. There may also be a natural progression from holding to greater differentiation, and it may be interesting to speculate about how things would have gone differently if I had consulted these supervisors in a different chronological order or at different moments in my own development (Slochower, 1996). If I had been with Wolstein earlier on, isn't it possible that he too would have helped me create an empathic frame? If I had gone to Bollas later in the analysis, isn't it altogether possible that he would have been less focused on the establishment of a secure hold?

"Paper delivery"

Al terminated his analysis and has gone on to seemingly do well in his life, remarried, established in his career, and he remained in contact with me for some years with occasional consultations. After checking with Al by phone, I sent a draft of this article to him for his review and comments. As I wrote the letter accompanying the article, I realized to my complete astonishment that it was the day before Al's birthday and that the chapter would be delivered to him on his birthday. Was this a birthday present? And was it one that I was giving to Al, or with his permission to "present" this material, was he giving a present to me? He was grateful that I had shared the chapter with him and wished me good luck in presenting it, but also asked if he could have a series of sessions to discuss the strong feelings that it had stirred up in him. What did it mean to him to learn just how significant a patient and person he had been to me? It is probably inevitable that in the process of obtaining informed consent some key treatment issues and dynamics will once again be reenacted. Obtaining a patient's permission to publish case material is ethically essential but raises many complicated issues that are well beyond the scope of this chapter.

Attending to the fantasies, beliefs, stories, and family mythology surrounding the patient's birth and entry into the family has proven to be useful in understanding my own life and in my clinical work. Family legend concerning births carry emotional significance and transmit family hopes, dreads, and values. While I encourage analysts to ask about these themes at opportune moments, I think what is most important is to listen for them as one organizing psychoanalytic story line. I hope to have illustrated the centrality of birth fantasy and imagery and the utility of speculating about phantasmagoric scenes as a means of locating patterns and thematic structures that deepen the surface narratives. I hope that I have suggested some ways in which fantasy systems are layered and complexly embedded within each other, yet also always expressing unconscious conflict of one kind or another. In examining our patients' fantasies, we must also make room for recognizing and exploring our own, as well as the various conflicts which they express as they emerge in relation to our patients. Our own fantasies and shared fantasies, conceived in our interactions with patients, are formed in the context of our extended psychoanalytic families and are gradually transformed into the theories that embody our familial and community myths. All analysts have fantasy-imbued narratives of their own psychological birth as analysts in relation to a family romance of analytic parents, grandparents, and extended professional families. The manifest content of these fantasies are often represented by our theories and psychoanalytic associations. These fantasies inevitably conjoin with our patients' fantasies as patient and analyst struggle with a relational unconscious constituted by shared fantasies of being born and reborn anew.

Acknowledgments

I would like to thank Galit Atlas, Tony Bass, Neil Grill, Steven Kuchuck, Stephen Seligman, Karen Starr, Meridee Stein, and to the members of my study groups for their helpful suggestions, and specially thank my disguised patient for all he taught me and for permission to use his clinical material.

Notes

1 Nevertheless, Rank's focus was not on childbirth from the point of view of the new mother, from the perspective of women, but rather maintains a patriarchic viewpoint. For a discussion of childbirth from the point of view of the woman with a focus on women's bodies, see Balsam (2013).
2 See Blazy (2012) for a review of psychoanalytic ideas concerning the influence and impact of prenatal life on ego-formation.
3 The theme of birth enters the consulting room in a more direct and concrete way when the therapist or patient is pregnant, circumstances that have been explored in numerous psychoanalytic articles and books; see, for example, Suchet (2004) and Atlas-Koch (2008).
4 Butler (2004b), influenced by Corbett's work, wrote, "What is the fantasy of homosexual love that the child unconsciously adopts in gay families? How do children who are displaced from original families or born through implantation or donor insemination understand their origins? What cultural narratives are at their disposal, and what particular interpretations do they give to these conditions?" What are the fantasies of the children and of parents who adopt, have egg and sperm donors, utilize frozen eggs or alternative reproductive technologies? As Ehrensaft (2007) suggested, we need to rewrite the traditional birth stories for young children in the 21st century to include "birth others." Nor should we only be considering fantasies surrounding literal birth but also—and especially—symbolic birth. For example, Sharabany and Israeli (2008) usefully examined how immigration from one's motherland to a new country, adopting one's new country, may be experienced and symbolized as a re-birth.
5 While I cannot be sure that it was an identical trauma, the article by Morningstar (2012) on "Shoulder Dystocia: How the Body Holds the

Experience and How the Psyche Resolves It" seems closely related to the case presented here.

6 A leading figure in contemporary psychoanalysis, Christopher Bollas (born 1943 in Washington, DC), a professor of English who trained at the Institute of Psychoanalysis in London, is one of the most widely read authors in the field and an influential cultural critic. Some of his best known concepts have become staples of clinical psychoanalytic thought. These include "the unthought known," "the transformational object," "violent innocence," "extractive introjection," "psychic genera," "human idiom," and many others. My purpose in this paper is to stay close to my own clinical experience with the patient and in the supervisory consultations, and I am therefore not making any effort to systematically examine Bollas's writings on these themes but only what I recall of the consultations. This will be the case for all four of the consultants that I describe. Their written work is well worth systematic review and scholarship, but that is beyond the scope of this article.

7 Born in Cairo, Egypt to a Sephardic Jewish family, André Green (1927–2012), was an internationally renowned independent psychoanalyst who became president of the Paris Psychoanalytic Society and Vice President of the International Psychoanalytic Association. He was among the most significant innovators of our psychoanalytic era and masterfully drew on classically Freudian, French Lacanian, and British, especially Winnicottian and Bionian, theories. Green had a particular interest in the psychology of pregnancy and maternity, which he wrote should "take on a miraculous dimension for the mother." Elaborating on Winnicott, Green (1972) referred to "normal maternal madness" (p. 245). Always attuned to conflict and contradiction, Green observed that the mother must paradoxically foster the birth of the child's instinctual life, but also must make it tolerable.

8 Joyce McDougall (1920–2011) was born in New Zealand and trained in London with Anna Freud and D. W. Winnicott before moving to Paris. She made significant contributions to the understanding of perversions, psychosomatic symptoms, female sexuality, creativity, and addictions. Joyce McDougall was a beautiful and brilliant, elegant and charming, inspiring and personally generous teacher, mentor, and friend, and I cherish her memory.

9 Benjamin Wolstein (1922–1998) came to psychoanalysis with doctorates in both philosophy and psychology and a special interest in the contributions of William James. He had pursued rabbinical studies early in his career, and described himself as possessing "a Western psychoanalyzed mind, an Eastern Yogic body, and a Hassidic Jewish soul" (Hirsch, 2000, p. 193). He was one of the pillars of contemporary interpersonal psychoanalysis, and having been analyzed by Clara Thompson, he had a particular interest in rediscovering the clinical contributions of her

analyst, Sándor Ferenczi. Following our clinical experience together, I had the great fortune of becoming friends with Ben before his untimely death as we worked together processing the implications Ferenczi's *Clinical Diary*.

10 Interestingly, when I told Joyce McDougall about my patient's fortuitously seeing me with my wife, she suggested that I tell the patient something along the following lines: "Oh, I would just say, forget that you saw me with her, how unfortunate that reality has entered the picture, go right back to believing that I am homosexual and forget what you saw. All we care about is your fantasy world, not about reality!" This was quite typical of McDougall in being creative, dramatic, playful, and focusing exclusively on psychic reality over material reality.

Part III

The ethics of clinical practice

Chapter 10

Mutual vulnerability: an ethic of clinical practice (2016)

Introduction by Jessica Benjamin

It seems impossible to begin a commentary on this wonderful chapter without first expressing my continual amazement at the capaciousness of Lew's mind. While unmistakably infused with Lew's unique interests and perspectives, it also is a testimony to his ability to recognize and acknowledge the most important and diverse contributions of others—indeed, his recognition of the other.

The title of the chapter is overly modest, belying its scope. The chapter speaks not only to a clinical ethic, a position that grounds our practice, but also to a pragmatic that grounds all our work in this field by embracing the vital standpoint of accepting our vulnerability. And as essential as that acceptance of vulnerability is for our clinical work, Lew shows us how that embrace is essential to our broadest moral, social, philosophical, and human concerns. Furthermore, by identifying the tragic consequences within the organizing principles of classical analysis, which required the analyst's dissociative off-loading of vulnerability, this perspective also provides a trenchant critique of objectivism. The essay therefore also expresses an epistemological position, the need to ground psychoanalysis not in the subject-object knowledge of Western tradition but an intersubjective view that includes a critical understanding of the binary oppositions that led to impasses within that tradition. And that critique, in turn, is interwoven with the understanding of the historical and social conditions of patriarchy, anti-Semitism, homophobia, racism, and colonialism that gave rise to the repudiation of vulnerability. All of these intersecting points—the ethical, the clinical-pragmatic, the epistemological, and the social—are represented in the overarching synthesis Lew develops here. A tour de force.

Lew begins by proposing a deep psychoanalytic explanation for Freud's tragic flaw: the effects of patriarchy and anti-Semitism on his mind. Taking up Gilman's analysis of how anti-Semitic tropes of feminizing Jews constructs an atmosphere of racialized, sexualized humiliation refracted in Freud's own awareness of such issues as bisexuality, the Oedipus, and the ultimate bedrock of repudiating femininity. That is, he contends that psychoanalysis was founded in the midst of collective trauma that shaped both an acute awareness of vulnerability to suffering and also a disposition to dissociate and project that vulnerability.

Lew braids together the repudiation of femininity, linked to the idea of masculine objectivity, with the devaluing of dependency and relationality associated with "contaminating effeminate and primitive" characteristics. These projected aspects, he argued, had to be purged from psychoanalysis as a science, which would then be preserved as a powerful tool and legitimate instrument of the master. Pursuing the consequences of this move toward control, Lew shows how in America this masculinist position employed the rhetorical strategy of opposing psychoanalysis to a devalued opposite: psychotherapy, in which by contrast to the analyst a clinician is neither neutral nor disengaged.

Thus Lew builds on his earlier critique of analytic neutrality and defense of mutuality in *A Meeting of Minds*, where he integrated feminism with the clinical project of relational analysis, embracing the analyst's subjectivity. He thus added the clinical dimension to my analysis of how the splitting of gender and the denial of the mother's subjectivity bar the way to intersubjective recognition.

In this piece, Lew explicates further why gender splitting cannot simply be transcended by a simple reversal in favor of revaluing dependency and relationality, vulnerability and empathy with suffering. To avoid falling back into the binary, it is also necessary to maintain the value of differentiation, individuation, and separation altogether. In a particularly elegant movement, Lew offers as an example of how tension can be maintained Bion's idea of the caesura, employing but also transcending the revaluing stance toward the maternal. Bion's development of Freud's idea that the caesura of birth contains a primal continuity with prenatal life turns on the proposal that we are linked and separated in the same place. Union and differentiation are not opposed.

However, that metaphor itself does not answer or seamlessly tie up our questions, especially about the clinical dimension. In his earlier work, Lew famously and crucially cautioned that mutuality does not cancel out the analyst's asymmetrical responsibility. Thinking this through again, Lew seeks to show the re-owning of vulnerability, re-valuing and redeeming all that was consigned to the primitive and feminine, would collapse without some effort to attain a third position and hold the tension of opposites.

The direction he takes here pushes more deeply into the implications of using the idea of the Third. The necessity of this Third, an idea which Lew and I worked on together (see Aron, 2006; Benjamin, 2004), is fleshed out in terms of Lew's spiritual beliefs and influences, culminating with his image of tearful God who suffers for us. He returns again to the inspiration behind the Third, its religious aspects in the mystical traditions that unite Christianity and Judaism.

In his discussion of the Third, Lew brings together the moving parts of relational analysis as developed by a whole cohort of thinkers, acknowledging the whole orchestra. He reviews how the moral Third is established as the analyst works through rupture and repair, acknowledges without submitting, surrenders, and so creates mental space for recognizing the different voices within. Multiple self-states emerge from the trap of doer and done to. The analyst shows him- or herself to be permeable, penetrable, reachable—again refiguring the association of femininity with vulnerability in the Freudian psychosexual lexicon. In this way, Lew recursively ties all his themes.

Finally, then, Lew brings back Ferenczi, communing and mingling his tears with his patient, moved by empathy and knowledge of his own suffering. Without giving up our separate responsibility, he declares us capable of holding this mutuality. The power of his faith in mutual recognition, that we can always work toward re-establishing connection and lawfulness after breakdowns, is affirmed, and we are left inspired and a little breathless at how far we have come in such a short time. I wish Lew had tarried much longer with us, but his vision of our journey will remain with us and in that way he is still by our side—both sides.

**Aron, L. (2016). Mutual vulnerability:
An ethic of clinical practice.
In D. M. Goodman & E. R. Severson (Eds.),**

**The Ethical Turn (pp. 19–40).
London: Routledge**

In our book, *A Psychotherapy for the People* (Aron & Starr, 2012), Karen Starr and I trace a genealogy, an architecture, a deep binary structure embedded in the history of psychoanalysis along the fault lines of the split between psychoanalysis and psychotherapy, especially psychoanalytic psychotherapy. We trace this history to a two-stage, *nachträglich* development of psychoanalysis, first in Europe and then in post-Second World War America, by founding analysts who were on the margins of their society, at most second generation immigrants, Jews repeatedly fleeing persecution, poverty, prejudice, and anti-Semitism; people who were traumatized and vulnerable. To summarize, we argue that psychoanalysis repeatedly arose out of traumatic circumstances. The discipline of psychoanalysis therefore suffers from a traumatic history that accounts for its lack of history, its disrupted narrative, its tendency toward splitting and fragmentation, and its structure of reversal and manic defense in which all vulnerability is projected, displaced, denied, and dissociated.

My earlier study of "the third," developed with Jessica Benjamin (Aron, 2006; Aron & Benjamin, 1999b) led me to focus on impasses and stalemates in analytic therapy by recognizing the ways in which patient and analyst became polarized around certain issues and for one reason or another could not negotiate those polarities. Hence Benjamin's (1999a) brilliant explication of, "doer-done to," "push me-pull you," "see-saw" or "one up/one down," "my way or the highway," sadomasochistic relations. My examination of these dynamics led to the recognition that not only did analysts get caught up in these clinical interactions with patients, but that there was something about psychoanalysis itself, its history, its institutionalization, and its social and economic structure that actually contributed to enacting these configurations socially and professionally. Psychoanalysis had defined itself in opposition to, and hierarchically elevated above, suggestion and psychotherapy along the lines of a set of binaries in which psychoanalysis was always on top. Furthermore, the very structuring of the analytic process lent itself to the analyst and the analytic functions being viewed as hierarchically elevated relative to the patient. Hence only a search for some form of "the third" could free us from the various clinical and cultural impasses in which psychoanalysis has been trapped.

According to Derrida (1976), Western thought, especially metaphysics, is based on dualistic oppositions that are often value-laden and ethnocentric, and that create a hierarchy that inevitably privileges one term of each pole. Derrida's (1976) deconstructive strategy does not rest with reversing dichotomies, but rather aims to undermine the dichotomies themselves, and to show that there are "undecidables" items that do not belong on either side of a dichotomy. These "undecidables" are "third" terms. Deconstruction contends that in any text, there are inevitably points of" undecidability" that betray any stable meaning an author might seek to impose upon his or her text. According to Derrida (1976), the dominance of reason, the logos, is allied with the archetypically male will to dominate society, which he described as "phallogocentrism." One can easily see how feminists such as Derrida's close friend and colleague Helene Cixous (2004) could utilize Derrida's concepts to develop a deconstructive approach to the usual binaries by which men and women, as well as stereotypical male and female characteristics, were polarized. The male term, as Derrida suspected, is almost always hierarchically superior to the female term, dominating it and reinforcing a male domination of women. Cixous (2004) argues that masculine sexuality and masculine language are phallocentric and logocentric, fixing meaning through such binary oppositions as father/mother, intelligible/sensitive, logos/pathos, which rely for their meaning on the primary binary opposition between male and female, phallic/castrated, all reproducing patriarchy and the subordination of women. Benjamin (1988) demonstrated that gender was socially constructed by repudiating and splitting off all that was weak and dependent to create femininity. Applying deconstructive principles to relational psychoanalysis, Muriel Dimen (2003) writes,

> Dualism's separate-but-equal masks a hierarchy: the one behind the two is always on top. In the table of opposites that have been

around since the pre-Socratics—for example, male-female, light-dark, reason-emotion, mind-body, nature-culture—one term is always implicitly better or higher than the other. Hence the usual deconstructive reading: a binary always conceals a hierarchy.

(p. 7)

Let me add here a "link" to the work of Bion (1977) and to more contemporary post-Bionian psychoanalytic thought (Levine & Brown, 2013). Freud (1926) had indicated that there was much greater continuity between intrauterine life and earliest infancy than "the impressive caesura of the act of birth would have us believe" (p. 138). Building on Freud's remark, Bion (1977) used the term "caesura" to signify that which both unites and separates simultaneously, difference and continuity, presence and absence, the proto-mental and the mental, non-symbolic and symbolic, life and death. The caesura is, for Bion, a link between what seem to be independent categories but which are in fact connected with the caesura being the indicator and regulator of their connection. Trachtenberg (2013) spells out that the caesura signifies the undecidability of categories and that each "link" is a point in which one cannot decide what belongs to one category or the other, subject or object, mother or baby, analyst or patient. In short, Bion's link, the caesura, serves the same function in Bionian theory that the undecidable serves for Derrida's deconstruction. From this perspective, Bionian theory stresses process and paradox. Trachtenberg (2013) notes how, "Bion says that, when he talks of hate, he is referring to a pole of love, since there cannot be shadow without the presence of light" (p. 235). Bionian theory, from this vertex, is radically dialectical, and his link or caesura serves the function of "the undecidable" or thirdness (Benjamin, 2004), that space that regulates the tension between opposites and permits us to move beyond binary dualities and complementarity.

An understanding of these dichotomies and how they have structured psychoanalysis is a radically liberating insight. Once we see how these dualities undergird psychoanalytic thought, we are in a much better position to recognize and correct trouble spots in the theory and practice of psychoanalysis. The process involves finding "undecidables" or "thirds" and using them to break down polarized thinking. One must be careful to clearly keep in mind that deconstructing a polarity does not mean eliminating difference. As you think through my deconstruction of the psychotherapy/psychoanalysis binary, keep in mind that the point is to critique the polarization and hierarchization, rather than to eliminate all difference. For example, I am not contending that seeing a patient once a week or four times a week are equivalent. Rather, the issue is whether to think of psychotherapy and psychoanalysis as dichotomous and hierarchical, and much of the literature in our field has worked with that fundamental assumption, much to our detriment.

The argument I am making is that psychoanalysis has always defined itself in opposition to something else. At first, in Freud's work, that something else was suggestion. Later, in America, it was psychotherapy. From its inception, psychoanalysis identified itself and the analyst with what was masculine, autonomous, rational, scientific, and objective, as opposed to what it viewed as feminine, relational, irrational, unscientific, and subjective—all characteristics that were later attributed to psychotherapy, which was then devalued. In Freud's age, a viciously anti-Semitic era in which Jewish men were "othered," debased as effeminate, immoral, and concrete, Freud projected these debased characteristics onto the other "other," women (Boyarin, 1997; Gilman, 1993). For example, where Jewish men had been regarded as of low moral character and possessing poor abstract abilities, Freud would view women as having weaker superegos and as more concrete. Likewise, in America in the 1950s, psychoanalysis projected the devalued qualities of dependency and relationality onto psychotherapy, keeping itself at a distance from these contaminating effeminate and primitive qualities. Most psychoanalytic institutes would not even teach psychotherapy, as it might contaminate the purity of analytic training.

Genius that Freud was, he was nevertheless caught in a matrix of binaries that permeated his culture and his very existence. As a Jewish man in Austria, he was regarded by his anti-Semitic countrymen as circumcised and thus as effeminate, perverse, and homosexual. In this virulently anti-Semitic milieu, Jews were viewed as immoral, degenerate, and perverse, tied to the concrete and the body, and incapable of rationality and science. Like all colonized and oppressed people, Freud, to some degree, internalized these attributes (Boyarin, 1997; Gilman, 1993). Freud and his creation, like all Jews and their productions, were freakish, monstrous, and perverse. Larry Friedman (2006) celebrates psychoanalysis as being freakish, weird, bizarre, and unnatural—a monster. The salient characteristic of a monster is precisely that it does not fit neatly into natural categories. As a monster, psychoanalysis is neither art nor science; not quite a method of research nor a medical treatment. To insist that psychoanalysis is one thing or another is to tame the beast. Similarly, ghosts are not quite alive but not thoroughly dead. Psychoanalysis is haunted—*heimlich* and *unheimlich*—and, as Freud proclaimed, could only have been invented by "a Godless Jew" (as cited in Gay, 1987, p. vii); that is, by a monster, someone who never fit neatly into standard categories, always already "Other," as Derrida, also a "Godless Jew," wrote: "the undecidables." The development of psychoanalysis required the subjective position of one who was "optimally marginal," neither this nor that, in or out. Optimal marginality creates the necessary conditions for optimally observing-participation, or thirdness.

According to Philip Reiff (1966), "a tolerance of ambiguity is the key to what Freud considered the most difficult of all personal accomplishments" (p. 57). Fortunately for psychoanalysis, Freud's thinking was always more complex and nuanced than the binaries in which he was culturally caught. Freud's very place on the boundaries, as both insider and outsider, and as neither insider nor outsider, is precisely what allowed him to appreciate ambiguities. Freud was neither Austrian nor German nor Jewish. Neither was he white or Black, as Jews were regarded as mulattos. He was a doctor, but not a real university doctor, as Jews could not obtain those positions. While in some ways conventionally straight and even patriarchal, Freud was not a phallic man from the point of view of his anti-Semitic surround, since he was circumcised and therefore castrated and effeminate. Nor was he a woman, onto whom he would project all dependency, shame, and inferiority. Rather, according to the anti-Semitic trope, Freud, like all Jewish men, was in some ways effeminate and perverse; Jewish men were a third-sex. Boyarin (1997) writes, "Gilman has provided a vitally important piece of information by observing how thoroughly Jewishness was constructed as queer in *fin de siècle* Europe" (p. 214). He continues, "the Jew was queer and hysterical—and therefore, not a man" (p. 215). Freud had been in love with a male friend, Fliess, with whom he championed bisexuality, had regular "congresses," and compared menstrual cycles. In short, Freud was a monster: a ghost, queer, undecidable, mulatto, circumcised, *unheimlich*, a third. Who else could discover such a monster as psychoanalysis? Janus-like in its doublenesses (Boyarin, 1997, p. 244), always on the boundary's edge, Freud's writing can serve as a basis for drawing diametrically opposed conclusions. His work is the basis for both conservative and radical projects. Freud longed to be culturally German, civilized, cultured, but was always vulnerable to prejudice, to castration.

Before moving on I'd like to add a word to clarify that as Starr and I explain in our book, we are not reducing patriarchy and misogyny to anti-Semitism, but rather we are exploring the intersection of misogyny, racism, anti-Semitism, and homophobia. Feminism has exposed the inherent relationship between patriarchy and misogyny, and postcolonial studies have investigated the interrelations between racism, misogyny, and homophobia. A psychoanalytic study of the intersection of anti-Semitism, racism, homophobia, and misogyny enriches and usefully complicates the findings of feminism. I want to add that our focus on anti-Semitism in understanding Freud's disavowal, displacement, projection, or dissociation of his vulnerability is also not meant to ignore or displace personal biographical understandings. Hence, it seems clear that Freud's aversion to helplessness, to childishness, and to human vulnerability was rooted in his personal childhood, familial experiences as the eldest son of a narcissistic mother, his later disillusionment with his father, as well as family tragedies like the loss of his brother. All of these personal factors of his biography would shape his personal reactions to anti-Semitism.

Here I will argue that a central binary underlying the dichotomizatin of psychoanalysis and psychotherapy is vulnerability and invulnerability. In its "halcyon days" psychoanalysis viewed the analyst as well enough analyzed so as not to be vulnerable to the patient's efforts to dislodge the analyst's neutrality and equanimity. In the classic debates about psychotherapy and psychoanalysis of the 1950s, Leo Rangell (1954) said that in psychoanalysis the analyst sits at the margins like a referee in a tennis match, while in psychotherapy the therapist is on the court interacting with the patient. Similarly, Fenichel (1941) had written that the principle goal in the management of transference is "not joining the game" (p. 73). Well, if you are off the field, not playing the game, then you can't get scored on. You aren't likely to get hurt, and if you call the ball out, then it's out; you are invulnerable.

There is a significant trend among philosophers to ground the philosophy of ethics in the experience of vulnerability. In my view, the ethics and practice of psychoanalysis also need to be grounded in the experience of vulnerability. I am suggesting that the ethos of psychoanalysis be rooted not in neutrality and objectivity, but rather in our acceptance and acknowledgement of mutual vulnerability. In *Precarious Life* (2004a), Judith Butler builds on Freud's discussion of mourning to argue that mourning entails an acceptance that one is changed by the loss, that mourning depends on our acceptance of or submission to being transformed by the loss, a transformation that we cannot fully control, predict, or determine. The language of the law and legal rights are argued in terms of bounded individuals and groups, delineated subjects before the law. But Butler (2004a) suggests that while this language establishes our legitimacy within a legal framework, "it does not do justice to passion, grief, and rage, that tear us from ourselves, bind us to others, transport us, undo us, implicate us in lives that are not our own, irreversibly, if not fatally" (p. 25). In other words, we are joined in the game, not off the field in the margins, and ethics is grounded in our shared human vulnerability.

Donna Orange (2011) articulated a hermeneutic, intersubjective approach to psychoanalysis which devotes exquisite attention to our receptivity to human suffering. For Orange, following Gadamer, understanding is constituted by receptivity and suffering. Elaborating on Gadamer, Orange (2011) writes,

> Not only are we required to witness and to participate emotionally in the suffering of our patients, but, in addition, the process of understanding itself means that we place ourselves at risk and allow the other to make an impact on us, to teach us, to challenge our preconceptions and habitual ways of being, to change us for their sake, even to disappoint and reject us.
>
> (p. 23)

In Orange's (2011) psychoanalytic application of Gadamerian hermeneutics, analytic listening means listening in a truly open way, "holding oneself open, vulnerable, to the conversation" (p. 64). Employing the contributions of Emmanuel Levinas, Orange goes even further in placing vulnerability at the center of psychoanalysis.

Levinas's philosophy emerged from his experiences in the Holocaust and was rooted in the study of trauma, persecution, and suffering. Orange cites Michael Kugel, an authority on Levinas, who argues that "This reevaluation of vulnerability is the basic task of Levinas's thinking ... a phenomenology grounded in an optical situation established in Auschwitz, established not by Levinas but by Hitler" (as cited in Orange, 2011, p. 60). For Levinas, the suffering of the face of the other places you in contact with the infinite, the sacred or the holy. With this view of listening to the suffering stranger the psychoanalytic vocation itself becomes something of a sacred calling. Levinas claims that the Western proclivity to conceive the subject in terms of freedom and rationality mistakenly obscures and distorts our humanity by hiding the significance of human vulnerability and dependence, or what Freud called helplessness. As Hilary Putnam (2008) put it, "In Levinas's image of man, the *vulnerability* of the other is what is stressed, in contrast to what Levinas sees as the Enlightenment's radiant image of the human essence" (p. 83). The Jewish view of ethics that Levinas paradoxically champions and universalizes is based not on reason and rationality but on human vulnerability seen face-to-face.

Drawing on Levinas, Katz (2012) argues that the rabbinic commentary on the Hebrew Bible, the *midrash*, fills in the gaps in the text and hence focuses on alterity. *Midrash* thus gives voice to those whose voices were left out of the text and thus opens us to the presence of the Other. What is most uniquely original and of value in Levinas is his call for an ethics free of narcissism and egocentrism. A non-egocentric ethics must recognize and engage the other as other, not as a like-subject but as Other. My ethical obligation must not depend on my recognition of similarity or even on comprehension of the other, nor on abstract, rational, and universal principles, nor on an expectation of reciprocity. Rather my obligation is grounded on the direct perception of the other person as other. To respond to the other only as a like-subject similar to you and therefore arousing of sympathy is to be trapped in one's own egocentricity. That many believe Levinas carried this ethical asymmetry too far is irrelevant for our purposes today. Even while Levinas's contribution may be criticized, it can be appreciated for his dramatic and powerful charge to respond to the suffering of the other as other.

Freud and psychoanalysts following him have long differentiated the primitive from the civilized, primitive versus mature defenses or psychic mechanisms, primitive populations versus those that are better structured, higher in the development of sophisticated mental operations. Celia Brickman (2003) has suggested that what analysts mean by "primitivity" is essentially "vulnerability." For Freud, this was thematically expressed throughout his work in terms of penetrating and being penetrated. To penetrate was to be phallic, whole, and firm, whereas to be penetrated was to be castrated, permeable, and vulnerable.

Drawing on the French tradition of interest in the monstrous, Julia Kristeva (1982) developed the idea of the abject as that which is rejected by and disturbs social reason. Abjection is done to the part of ourselves that we exclude: the mother. We must abject the maternal, the object which has created us, in order to construct an identity—that is our identity requires boundaries in place of fluidity. The corpse, as well as bodily fluids, exemplifies Kristeva's concept since it literalizes the breakdown of the distinction between subject and object that is crucial for the establishment of identity. Lucy Irigaray (1985) also describes the privileging of solid over fluid mechanics, which she attributes to the association of fluidity with femininity. Whereas men have sex organs that protrude and become rigid, women have openings that leak menstrual blood and vaginal fluids. Although men too emit fluids, this aspect of their sexuality is deemphasized. It is the rigidity of the male organ that counts, not its fluid flow which is devalued. Martha Nussbaum (2010) demonstrates in *From Disgust to Humanity* that misogyny is rooted in "projective disgust" (p. 15). Males distance themselves from bodily, animal vulnerability by associating women with bodily fluids, and dissociating themselves from their own corporeality. Homophobia is structured along the same lines as misogyny. Nussbaum (2010) writes:

> What inspires disgust is typically the male thought of the male homosexual, imagined as anally penetrable. The idea of semen and feces mixing together inside the body of a male is one of the most disgusting ideas imaginable—to males, for whom the idea of nonpenetrability is a sacred boundary against stickiness, ooze, and death.
>
> (p. 18)

Jonathan Schofer (2010), in *Confronting Vulnerability*, argues that it is vulnerability which is the bedrock of classic Jewish, that is, Rabbinic, ethics. It is striking that Freud (1950/1895) too attributed ethics to the condition of human vulnerability. He wrote, "the initial helplessness of human beings is the primal source of all moral motives" (p. 318). Schofer (2010) provides a series of studies of how vulnerability organized the structure of rabbinic law. He begins with a symbol quite similar to Nussbaum's imagery of bodily fluids. Quoting an ethical maxim from Mishna Avot, "Know from where you come ... from a putrid secretion" (Schofer, 2010, p. 2). The image of humans emerging from semen is humbling and captures precisely the bodily fluidity that Nussbaum highlights. "Ethics cannot presume a continually healthy, strong, independent agent who encounters weak, needy others" (Schofer, 2010, p. 3). The rabbis, according to Schofer, emphasize a variety of forms of vulnerability, old age, persecution, drought, poverty, widowhood, orphan hood, being a stranger, and especially death, precisely because we have a tendency to deny our vulnerability. Schofer (2010) explains, "Confronting vulnerability becomes central to ethical cultivation" (p. 4). While of course the analyst's personal analysis should help the analyst be in touch with vulnerability, too often it is used as a rationalization to deny vulnerability and thus to project all vulnerability into the patient.

As a nineteenth-century European man, Freud believed the height of civilization was the achievement of individual autonomy, later theorized as "ego autonomy." Having clear and firm boundaries meant that you were independent and whole, phallic and impenetrable. To be merged with another, to experience the "oceanic feeling," fluidity, was to be penetrable, vulnerable to the influence of the other, susceptible to infection. This was primitivity (Brickman, 2003), and as Nussbaum (2010) argues, it signified vulnerability and mortality. It was the primitive who was suggestible—the hysteric, the woman, the African, Asian, or Jew, the poor and uneducated. For the Western Jew, it was the Eastern Jew. Primitivity was vulnerability to penetration, contamination, and death. Gilman noted that non-Jewish men were viewed as phallic while the clitoris was referred to as the Jew and female masturbation as "playing with the Jew" (Gilman, 1993, p. 39). Boyarin (1997) points out that where non-Jews referred to Jews as both the pinky and the clitoris, Jews returned the favor by referring to the non-Jews as the thumb (p. 4). Here we see so clearly the interdigitation of racism, anti-Semitism, homophobia and misogyny as the clitoris, the circumcised penis, and the Jew are regarded as primitives. In Freud's day, Jews were regarded as smelly, contaminated, and contagious. This ideology culminated with Hitler, for whom Jews were "maggots inside a rotting body" (as cited by Nussbaum, 2010, p. 23). As circumcision was the embodied mark of the Jew as feminine and castrated, castration anxiety took on a central role in Freudian clinical theory and practice. This explains why Freud (1937) believed that the bedrock of psychoanalysis was "the repudiation of femininity" (p. 403). This was not just a slip or passing sentiment—it was at the core of his values. The repudiation of femininity, that is castration anxiety, was essential to patriarchy. Phallic/castrated and masculine/feminine were binaries running in parallel with Aryan/Jew, White/Black, heterosexual/homosexual, civilized/primitive, health/illness, and life/death. Carol Gilligan (2011) defines patriarchy as constituted by those attitudes and values, moral codes and institutions that create separations between the men from the boys as well as between men and women, and divide women into the good and the bad. Gilligan (2011) links patriarchy with trauma and psychic fragmentation, writing, "As long as human qualities are divided into masculine and feminine, we will be alienated from one another and from ourselves" (p. 178). Gilligan's (2011) call is for the recognition that "Vulnerability, once associated with women, is a characteristic of humans" (p. 43). I would add that it is a characteristic of analysts as well as patients, and characteristic of senior analysts as well as of our students, and that compassion, being with suffering, with our patients, co-participants, requires the acceptance and acknowledgement of our own vulnerability.

From the classical perspective, to help a patient get better by utilizing suggestion could only reinforce the patient's primitivity, even if it helped them in other ways (so-called transference cures), or was necessary due to practical circumstances, such as limited resources. Psychoanalysis proper had to eliminate suggestion; porousness was to be replaced by firm ego boundaries. Certainly it did not eliminate all "influence," for how else could you help someone? Freud (1921) distinguished between two types of influence. He objected to the kind of influence based on interpersonal effect—the force of one's personality or subjectivity. Rather, as an enlightenment science, analysis influenced the patient through rational means. To be influenced by accepting a rational argument means you have used your own reason to evaluate the influence, and so you remain independent and autonomous—that is why in its later formulation, psychoanalysis was supposed to work by interpretation alone (Gill, 1954, p. 775). In contrast, in hypnotic influence, you are subject to the direct interpersonal influence of the other person. Hypnotic suggestion relies on dependence and merging with the will of the other—penetration and passivity—homosexual submission to the father, and hence is thought to reinforce dependence and "primitive" lack of differentiation.

Celia Brickman, in her brilliant 2003 book, *Aboriginal Populations in the Mind*, demonstrates that the origins of psychoanalysis coincided with European colonialism. She makes use of postcolonial studies to show the influence of evolutionary anthropology on Freud's thinking. The racialized "primitive, savage, and barbarian," together with the religious "heathen, infidel, pagan" (Brickman, 2003, p. 19), were the outsiders, the "not-us." Much to Freud's credit, he demonstrated that primitivity is universal: each of us has a "primitive" part of our minds. That was quite an achievement at a time when those around him saw themselves as civilized. Freud showed that we each have an ego and an id, an ego and a "Yid," a German and a Jew. The id, the unconscious, is primitive, unstructured, timeless, unbound, incapable of reason or delay, dark and feminine. This is consistent with Freud's championing of bisexuality—we each have male and female characteristics. We all have unconscious perverse and homosexual inclinations. This was a revolutionary idea. However, by arguing that we all have a "primitive" mind, with "primitive" drives, Freud reinforced the duality of civilized/primitive. While that duality might now be understood to be universal, it remains a duality and a hierarchy.

In the Middle Ages religion was dominant, and the duality was Christian/heathen. With the advent of the Enlightenment, the human mind "matured" into "rationality" and there was a "simple reversal," by which in "civilized" circles, to be religious was to be primitive, superstitious, or magical. In the operation of any binary, one can flip the power relations but maintain and even reinforce the binary structure. Hence while Christian/heathen was originally lined up with right/wrong, Heaven/Hell, mature/immature, the hierarchy was then reversed, such that the binary became secular/Christian, lined up with rational/irrational, mature/immature. With increasing industrialization, the value of delayed gratification, considered by evolutionary theorists to be the mark of the civilized man, became more prominent. To be "civilized" and adult was to be disciplined, while "primitives" were thought to be impulsive, seeking immediate gratification. Adult/child lined up with civilized/primitive, conscious/unconscious, White/Black, responsible/irresponsible, and culture/nature. To be civilized was to have a history, to live in time. To be primitive was to be pre-historical, out of time. The unconscious, being primitive, does not know time.

All these polarities were mapped onto male/female. Men were considered civilized and adult, while women were regarded as more like children—irrational, concrete, immoral, and impulsive. What Freud (1937, p. 252) called the "bedrock" answer for both sexes was to "repudiate femininity"; for men, the fear of castration, and for women "penis envy." Freud noted that in his culture masculinity was active, while femininity was passive. To be a woman (or male homosexual) is to be passively penetrated. The feminine-masochistic wish is to be penetrated, just as it is the wish of the "primitive" to be dominated. To be phallic is to be the active one who does the penetrating/dominating. To be phallic and not penetrable is to be solid, bounded, invulnerable, and autonomous. To be female is to be penetrated, porous, vulnerable, submissive, masochistic, dependent, embodied, oozing bodily fluids and therefore porous, contaminating, and associated with death. Ultimately, to be primitive is to be subject to domination and penetration—to actually long to be dominated to give up autonomy. In analysis, this dichotomy positions the patient as primitive and the analyst as civilized. The analyst, of course, was to be "opaque," impenetrable, and courageous, even heroic. The patient is childish, pathological, out of time and history. The dark, feminine, oozing unconscious is penetrated by the analyst's interpretations—the firm analytic instrument." (While this phrase is strongly associated with Otto Isakower (1963), he based it directly on Freud (1912a, p. 116).)

Let's now return to contemporary relational theory, which is an attempt to move beyond binary oppositions by emphasizing "both/and" rather than "either/or" conceptualizations, culminating in the conceptualization of the intersubjective third. Benjamin (2011) has described the "moral third" by referring to the sense of lawfulness and trust in reestablishing connection after disruption. Patient and therapist (like mother and infant) establish a rhythm, some ongoing regulation that facilitates predictability and that allows each of them to feel sensed and known by the other and thus come to know the other and to know themselves (Beebe et al., 2012; Lachmann & Beebe, 1996). At some point this rhythm inevitably breaks down, and the difference between the two is highlighted. Then comes repair and reestablishment of connection. This is "the law" of intersubjective life; it is about the co-creation and breakdown of patterns of mutual regulation and mutual recognition. This is not paternal Oedipal law, but rather as Benjamin quips, it is more like the law of gravity, just the way things work. We move between collisions and acknowledgment. Analysis is a study of these configurations as they are relived, reenacted, and reworked while being examined and articulated. Benjamin credits Tronick as well as Beebe and Lachmann, who following Kohut described this cycle of rupture and repair. We have traced the origins of this approach back to Ferenczi. Ferenczi (1932) was explicit in arguing that the analyst would inevitably repeat (we would say "enact") with the patient the traumatic experiences of childhood, but unlike the earlier objects who denied their participation in the crime, analysts had to take responsibility and acknowledge their participation and guilt.

The analyst acknowledges the rupture, and through this nondefensive validation reestablishes the ongoing regulation, leaving the patient with a feeling of having been recognized, a moment of meeting, a meeting of minds and hearts. The analyst's acknowledgement shows that the injury is perceived as a violation of an expectable pattern, "the law," and thus it relieves the felt emotional abandonment. Both patient and therapist "surrender" to the trust that exists between them, trust in the process, trust in love, in faith, some call it God, in something beyond them, to which they both surrender. Thus they are not submitting to the other so much as surrendering to thirdness, to a moral law, to lawfulness itself—the law that all relationships are inevitably constituted by rupture and repair, and can then go on being or be resurrected into new life.

The surrender being described here must be differentiated from submission. If the analyst too quickly takes all the responsibility, takes all the "bad object" (Davies, 2004b) experience onto him or herself, or simply apologizes to the patient for the disruption of attunement and failure of mutual regulation, then this hardly lends itself to the creation of thirdness. That would more precisely be an enactment of a simple reversal in which the "hot potato" has been thrown from one person to another, in other words, the good and bad objects have simply been reversed rather than transformed. Self-disclosure of the analyst's bad object feelings and the confessional "mea culpa" prayer, "through my fault, through my fault, through my most grievous fault," can be too easily mistaken for an intersubjective psychoanalytic process that only slowly and step by step leads beyond cycles of mutual blame, accusation, confession, and forgiveness which can perpetuate complementarity good/bad, God/sinner, or victim/victimizer relations. The analyst's acknowledgement of participation in collisions must include an analytic process that allows such acknowledgement to take place in a space that transcends these binary good/bad splits, and this can only happen intersubjectively between patient and analyst as they work together to find a way to a third position, beyond kill or be killed, doer done-to polarities. If done explicitly self-disclosures are not technical maneuvers or confessions, but are rather undertaken as part of a disciplined relational process of exchanging relevant, mutually generated clinical data in the service of opening up space for both greater "relational freedom" (Stern, 2013) and intersubjective reflection which together reestablish thirdness—that is they move us beyond binary dualities.

If this sounds suspiciously religious, it is. Benjamin (1988, 2004, 2011) absorbed German idealism, particularly Hegel. It reverberates with Christian theology, the trinity, the one in the third and the three in the one. As Marie Hoffman (2011) has so persuasively elaborated, think here of incarnation, crucifixion, and resurrection. Yet the idea can also be traced very clearly to prominent themes in the Hebrew Bible. God recognizes and loves "his" people, Israel. The people sin and lust after foreign Gods and are punished; Israel returns and is forgiven. Think ongoing regulation, heightened affect moments, disruption and repair—it's the main theme throughout the biblical narrative.

Undoubtedly most of us can associate the theme of thirdness with the many centuries of Christian theological controversy concerning the Trinitarian Creed, especially the first four hundred years from the

Apostles to the Church Fathers, culminating by the end of the fourth century in the doctrine of the Trinity. God exists as three *persons*, or *hypostases*, but is one being having a single divine nature: one in the third and the third in the one. But many of us are less familiar with this theme in Jewish scholarship. Consider one example from medieval Jewish theology that illustrates how closely Benjamin's ideas are to traditional themes in the Jewish tradition. The pre-rabbinic schools or houses of Hillel and Shamai were known for their heated disputes regarding the law, and though they disagreed and at times argued for diametrically opposite conclusions, nevertheless Jewish tradition has it that a voice from Heaven proclaims "these and these are the words of the Living God." How can opposites both be true? Rabbi Judah Loew, widely known as the Maharal of Prague, was an important sixteenth-century Talmudic scholar, Jewish mystic, writer, and philosopher. In his work, *Tif'ereth Yisrael* ("The Glory of Israel"), he describes the mystical power of the number three. Drawing on Loew, Kolbrener (2011) writes, "In three, two separate lines are transformed into 'one' through a third line that joins them. Through the Maharal's geometry, three is at the same time *less* and *greater* than two" (p. 77); three represents the paradox of both unity and division.

When patient and therapist are in an enactment or impasse, it often takes the form of a clash, a tug of war, a push me-pull you, doer-done to, or sadomasochistic enactment. This is precisely where Benjamin (1988) began in *The Bonds of Love*, looking at gender relations in terms of sadomasochism. When in these states we are often dealing with binaries. Either I am guilty or I am a victim, either you started it or I did, either it's your fault or mine, either you really are withholding from me or I am too demanding, either you really let me down or I expect too much, either you are the best therapist in the world or you suck, either you are crazy or I am. Each of these is a binary, and we are talking about splitting, or more specifically two people who both get caught in splitting. This is why it is called complementarity—it is complementary splitting or enactment resulting from mutual defensiveness and dissociation.

Following collisions, the therapist needs to acknowledge, implicitly if not always explicitly, the way in which he or she has hurt the patient, broken the trust or the rhythm, recognize how they were unattuned. We are predominantly focusing on analysts acknowledging to themselves their own participation in enactments, and also their validating the patient's sense of having been injured by them. Previously I suggested (Aron, 2006) that the therapist needs to open space within herself to reflect on how she is conflicted or torn, how she can think or feel more than one way about something, and how she can open up to differences within herself; "stand in the spaces" (Bromberg, 1996,) or "build bridges" (Pizer, 1998) to her own multiple self-states. For example, the therapist may be both angry with the patient and also blaming himself for something. In creating some room for difference within the self, a "dialectics of difference" as Bollas (1989, pp. 64–67) called it, one creates triangular space or thirdness, perhaps something like what Bion (1962a) meant by "binocular vision" (p. 86). Rather than being stuck in a polarization, there is some room within which to think/feel.

What I am adding today is the simple clarification (simple to say, not so easy to do) that a psychoanalytic ethic of mutual vulnerability facilitates the creation of such triangular space and helps free us from such blaming and self-blaming polarizations. The mistaken and inhuman ideal of being so thoroughly analyzed that one is impervious to the patient's transference, capable of not being caught up in the game, was and remains a great impediment to acknowledgment (even to oneself) of analytic ruptures, of splits in the analyst's self, of shared anxieties, defenses, and conflicts, of mutual resistances and regressions. In sum, what Benjamin and I are each calling for in conceptualizing the third is a change in analytic sensibility from analytic opaqueness and impenetrability toward greater inter-penetrability and mutual recognition of shared vulnerability. Stated in the more contemporary language that has become associated with relational psychoanalysis and especially with the contributions of Jody Davies, Philip Bromberg, and Donnel Stern, the analyst's acknowledgement of her participation in enactments involves a form of mentalization or self-reflective awareness that creates room for multiplicity and dialog among multiple self-states, within the analyst, the patient, and intersubjectively, in co-created shared space between patient and analyst. This is an analytic ethos rooted in the assumption of mutual vulnerability.

It should not be surprising that psychotherapy and psychoanalysis, contemporary secularized derivatives of religious guidance and moral wisdom traditions, incorporate and recirculate these principles. As we increasingly recognize the influence of our own subjectivity on our theories and practice, our religious and spiritual subjectivity is inevitably relevant. As an illustration of this inspiration, I (2004) have previously highlighted the connection between my psychoanalytic vision and my religious ethos. Mutual vulnerability is a concept at the heart of the particular Jewish philosophy that inspired me. Abraham Joshua Heschel in his classic 1962 study of *The Prophets* suggested that we have to understand the prophetic God as a God of pathos, a feelingful God who cares about the world and about people. This led his student, and my teacher, Neil Gillman to articulate a vulnerable God whose vulnerability is in our hands. The mutual vulnerability between God and humanity becomes the cornerstone of Gillman's theology. Gillman (2013) frequently illustrates God's vulnerability with the *midrash*, classic rabbinic story, that when the Temple was destroyed and Jerusalem burned, God sat and wept over the fate of the people. The angels insisted that God not cry. "You must not cry, you are God!" After several pleas God replied to the angels, "If you don't let me cry, I'm going to go into my private bedroom, close the door, lock it, and cry by myself" (Gillman, 2013, p. 33). This particular word picture of a tearful God is only one of many diverse metaphors, but I am suggesting that to the degree that our religious values affect our interpersonal relationships, this model offers a useful ideal for the humanity and vulnerability of the analyst.

And while crediting teachers who have influenced me, I want to add here that I believe many of us learned this clinical approach directly from Stephen Mitchell. In my view, this was at the heart of Mitchell's clinical approach, and it is characteristic of Mitchell's methodology both to clinical practice and to comparative psychoanalysis. I can only hint at this fascinating argument here and perhaps develop it in our later discussions.

Mitchell (1988a), who had learned a good deal of this approach from Edgar Levenson's (1983) formulation of "resisting transformation," repeatedly emphasized that patient and analyst had to get caught up in impasse and that therapeutic action consisted in working our way out of such gridlocks (295). He wrote about one case in 1991: "We seemed trapped in the closed world of these two relational configurations in which he was either cruelly deprived or lovingly crippled.

This was, in my view, precisely the sort of trap in which we needed to be caught...." (p. 168). Notice here that Mitchell was describing precisely what Benjamin (2004) calls "push me-pull you" or "doer-done to" configurations. He continues,

> Perhaps there was a way for us to acknowledge both and thereby work our way out of the trap we had created. The collaborative, interpretive delineation of the impasse itself began to provide a way out, an alternative way for us to engage each other which broadened the constrictive grasp of the old relational configurations.
>
> (p. 169)

I am suggesting that deconstructing binaries, finding thirds, opening up triangular space, was characteristic of Mitchell's methodology whether he was solving theoretical or clinical dilemmas. (For a more detailed exegesis of this aspect of Mitchell's clinical and theoretical methodology, see Aron, 2003.)

The dialectics of difference requires permeability; the therapist implicitly or explicitly reveals something about being moved by the patient. The therapist is not masochistic or without boundaries but is penetrable, movable, reachable. As Adrienne Harris has emphasized, analytic vulnerability needs to be accompanied by self-care, including bodily self-care, as well as by analytic responsibility (Harris & Sinsheimer, 2008). Neither patient nor therapist need be phallic or castrated, civilized, or primitive. Meanings and interpretations are not given and received as much as negotiated and co-created. Empathy and even acknowledgment are not given by the therapist but are mutual and bi-directional, even if the therapist tries to lead in some areas of conflict. Thirdness means moving beyond binary oppositions and the inevitable hierarchy that accompanies splitting, thus opening up space to think/feel.

It has been said that there are two types of people—those who divide the world into two categories and those who do not. The very opposition of binary thinking versus moving beyond binaries is itself a binary; contrasting split complementarity with the third may be read as yet another binary even when it is intended to be dialectical. If it seems that while deconstructing various binaries that I have myself become stuck in binary thinking or created new oppositions, that is inevitable. It is the law, the law of rupture and repair, of deconstruction as an ongoing and always unstable activity, of the third not as some final resolution but as a fleeting moment in an ongoing process. Binaries (and the associated splitting) do have their usefulness, providing stability and structure until such time as integrations of greater complexity can be achieved.

In *A Meeting of Minds* (1996c), I presented relational psychoanalysis as characterized by a variety of forms of mutuality including mutual influence, mutual recognition, mutual resistances, mutual empathy, the mutual generation of data, many other dimensions of mutuality, as well as by some aspects of asymmetry in role, function, and responsibility. Here, I want to add an explicit emphasis on mutual vulnerability but again want to be clear that mutuality does not mean equality nor does it imply symmetry. Patient and analyst are mutually vulnerable, but the analyst has a different role and distinct responsibilities, and in some respects the therapist holds power over the patient often leaving the patient with greater exposure and less protection. In acknowledging one's own permeability and vulnerability, however—one's embodiment, mortality, and humanity—one does not need to project all of the conflict, splitting, shame, disgust, animalistic embodiment, penetrability, and vulnerability onto the patient. By owning one's own vulnerability the analyst reduces the patient's shame and thus allows the patient to face vulnerability with less pain and dread. In his *Clinical Diary* Ferenczi (1932) wrote:

> Should it ever occur, as it does occasionally to me, that experiencing another's and my own suffering brings a tear to my eye (and one should not conceal this emotion from the patient), then the tears of doctor and patient mingle in a sublimated communion, which perhaps finds its analogy only in the mother-child relationship. And this is the healing agent, which like a kind of glue, binds together permanently the intellectually assembled fragments, surrounding even the personality thus repaired with a new aura of vitality and optimism.
>
> (p. 65)

This is the image of mutual vulnerability and bodily fluidity (that is, as we have seen, so often associated with feared, devalued, and contagious femininity) that leads not to disgust and shame but is rather transformed, sublimated, and spiritualized into healing.

The Yom Kippur, "*Selichot*," penitential liturgy, includes the prayer "*Mol Levavenu*," "Circumcise our hearts," based on the biblical phrase "And the LORD your God will circumcise your heart, and the heart of your offspring, to love the LORD thy God with all your heart, and with all your soul, that you may live" (Deut. 30:6). The prayer includes the commentary, "Circumcision creates a wound, and the one who is wounded is vulnerable" (Teutsch, 1999). Here we see that in Jewish tradition, not only is circumcision viewed positively, as a symbol of the desired covenant with God, but also that vulnerability is acknowledged, even valued, as a necessary prerequisite for relationship and connection. Intersubjective methodology might help analysts not only with clinical impasses and stalemates, but with professional, theoretical, sexual, cultural, and historical deadlocks as well. Not only in the clinical interaction, but as a profession and discipline, by owning our vulnerability, attachment, and dependency, by not refuting femininity, psychoanalysis need not split itself off from psychotherapy as its inferior, shameful other. The discipline of psychoanalysis and the psychoanalytic practitioner, in touch with vulnerability and not needing to split off and project it onto others, is capable of mutual recognition, empathy, and moral responsibility.

No longer invulnerable, we cannot remain safely behind the couch in our private practices. We must become socially, politically, and environmentally active and bring complexity, depth, dialectics, and dynamic understanding to problems in our communities and in the wider world, as legitimate psychoanalytic praxis. We would invoke Levinas's Biblical call to serve the poor, the orphaned, and the widowed, and apply it to Freud's vision of making psychoanalysis "a psychotherapy for the people" (p. 168). No longer dissociating our vulnerability, and without disclaiming our agency, we will move toward a progressive psychoanalysis.

Chapter 11

Beyond tolerance in psychoanalytic communities: reflexive skepticism and critical pluralism (2017)

Introduction by Joyce Slochower

Lew, Sue Grand, and I were in the midst of co-editing *Deidealizing Relational Theory* and *Decentering Relational Theory*, in which this essay of Lew's appeared, when his cancer overtook him. And so the celebratory book party we had planned was shadowed by our anticipatory grief.

That's the least of it, of course. We have lost a psychoanalytic great. Like so many others, I remain haunted by his loss and the pain of his final weeks. It's an extraordinary honor to write an introduction to one of his last contributions to the field.

Lew had a gift for encouraging dialogue and facilitating discussions that moved beyond binaries and polarizations. He loved theoretical disputes. They excited him and, to my knowledge, never caused him to lose his cool. Lew didn't get defensive; his openness to critique softened polarizing arguments; and he knew how to argue without attacking or alienating the other position. I saw this when he presented on cross-theoretical panels and when he ran meetings at NYU Postdoc, a training program that aims to facilitate candidates' exposure to theoretical multiplicity. During his time as Director, NYU Postdoc itself became far less theoretically fractious; under Lew's guidance, Freudian, relational, interpersonal, and independent faculty were increasingly able to straddle divides without divisiveness.

Lew's love of argument underlies his essay on reflexive skepticism and critical pluralism. His text embraces theoretical multiplicity and intellectual engagement. As Lew notes, some view such pluralism as creating a destructive splintering that engenders clinical/theoretical wars. They believe that we must work to find a common theoretical ground.

But Lew saw things differently. He firmly believed that such warring could be resolved only if we embrace our theoretical and clinical pluralism and engage across that which divides us. He passionately believed in the value of argument. He was convinced that, provided such arguments are lodged and embedded in a position of respect and recognition, we can move past polarization and toward intersubjective dialogue. Lew wanted us to develop knowledge "not by accumulating supporting evidence but by subjecting our beliefs to the staunchest criticism we can gather" (p. 202). He was convinced that such self-examination and self-criticism are the royal road to deeper understanding.

Written first for *Psychoanalytic Perspectives*, Lew's essay represents the central position paper around which he, Sue, and I organized our two edited volumes. In *Deidealizing Relational Theory*, we invited prominent relational authors to engage in theoretical and clinical self-critique while being careful to avoid self-denigration or the temptation to polarize opposing positions.

But self-critique is not enough. We also need critique from without, uncomfortable though that may feel. Lew notes that such critique invites us to "ambivalate" our own belief system—to destabilize the assumptions on which we've unthinkingly relied. This was the aim of *Decentering Relational Theory*; Lew's essay is the last in our second volume. Here he unpacks the dynamic sources of our resistance to critique and suggests that this resistance originates mainly in our narcissistic vulnerabilities. Only when the other's critique can be assimilated within a system that is sufficiently like our own can we make use of it without excessive feelings of threat—feelings that otherwise foreclose open engagement with alternative ideas.

Lew, Sue, and I hoped that the position we took in *Deidealizing* and *Decentering* would represent an invitation to other psychoanalytic schools of thought to engage in precisely this kind of reflective self-examination and self-critique. We're still hopeful.

I'd like to add an additional thought to Lew's argument. Although there's much to be gained from the dialogic position he advocates, there's also a potential risk inherent in it.

Pluralism invites us to embrace both/and positions that are inclusive and integrative. We complicate our own theoretical perspective by addressing both internal and external critique; we move toward "a dialectic rather than a binary" (p. 210). Might there be loss here too—loss of the potential value of that binary?

When we move away from binaries, we lose the satisfaction inherent in feeling that we've got the "best" theory and/or clinical method. We certainly lose our sense of certainty. We're likely to encounter self-doubt, perhaps even a weakened connection to our own professional position and to those who share it. After all, if your position is as valuable as mine, what's the point of remaining loyal—theoretically, clinically, or personally—to what was "ours"? Might we run the risk of diluting our sense of connection to the perspective we most strongly identify as our own?

I suspect it's the fear of losing all of this that makes some of us cling too tightly to that which is familiar and known. Such certainly reflects anxiety and resistance to change, but I also suspect there's a real loss to contend with here. There's value, after all, in group cohesion, in knowing that our beliefs are shared by a cohesive community distinct from other communities. That we can deepen and support our psychoanalytic vision from within. That our defensive loyalty isn't merely lodged in our narcissistic vulnerabilities; that it has inherent value.

I'm not suggesting we circle the wagons. On the contrary. I wholeheartedly embrace Lew's position and the value of dialogic theoretical exchange. But I think it's important that we simultaneously recognize, rather than negate or denigrate, the value of group cohesion and theoretical connection. Here's yet another dialectic that we can, perhaps, encompass rather than split.

I'm sure Lew would agree.

Aron, L. (2017). Beyond tolerance in psychoanalytic communities: reflexive skepticism and critical pluralism.

Psychoanalytic Perspectives, 14(3-), 217–282.

Psychoanalysis is widely known for its long history of splits and schisms among schools of thought. It has for this reason often been compared to religion where schisms frequently involve mutual accusations of heresy. In the United States, for many decades, psychoanalysis was largely under the hegemony of American Ego Psychology, which dominated the psychoanalytic mainstream. The fall of this largely monistic psychoanalytic consensus coincided with the decades of the decline of the prestige of psychoanalysis as a male medical specialty, with the increasing feminization of the field; challenges from psychopharmacology; the health-care industry; managed care; alternative therapies; the demand for empirically supported and evidence-based medicine; the Freud Wars and the new Freud Studies; a growing self-help movement; the critiques from feminists; gay, lesbian, and queer studies; and the loss of the status and institutional bases of psychoanalysis in psychiatry and clinical psychology. (This history is reviewed in *A Psychotherapy for the People*; Aron & Starr, 2012).

With this loss of status and prestige has come a newly found and hard-won plurality of perspectives. Psychoanalysis is no longer psychoanalysis but rather many psychoanalyses. Multiplicity and pluralism is the state of the discipline today around the world. Many psychoanalytic institutes now teach multiple points of view and have various diverse tracks and orientations; each school tends to support its own journals, assign different core texts, maintain separate canons of literature, and speak its own idiom; and each school has its founding heroes or patron saints as well as its denigrated enemies.

For some observers and commentators, our present state of multiplicity is a sign of the demise of psychoanalysis. Stepansky (2009) told the story of a once cohesive discipline that has splintered into rivalrous "part-fields" and now struggles to survive under siege. He viewed our multiplicity as a fragmentation, the result of the inevitable marginalization of any profession that resists integration into the scientific mainstream of its time and place. Other scholars, notably Wallerstein (1990), called for reestablishing common ground rooted in our shared clinical experience in consulting rooms where therapists relate comparably to the immediacy of the transference and countertransference interplay with their patients. Many other psychoanalytic leaders applaud and celebrate our multiplicity, not as a sign of disintegration and demise but to the contrary as the mark of creativity, intellectual excitement, and generativity. Mitchell (1993b), for example, described pluralism in psychoanalytic thought as essential and nourishing of growth. Cooper (2008), although welcoming this "pluralism," made the point that it is unfortunately a multiplicity of authoritarian orthodoxies, multiple monistic views, each derived from a thinker and tradition. Cooper holds out the hope that empirical research might solve the problem. Some analysts, such as Govrin (2016), have even called for a future of psychoanalysis in which dogma and pluralism can coexist in what he refers to as "fascinated" and "disenchanted" communities.

In this chapter, I argue that our multiplicity is not inherently good or bad, but what will determine its value is what we do with that diversity, how we view each other and make use of the range and variety of approaches now available. Until the 1970s there was hardly any discussion of "comparative psychoanalysis," a term associated with Schafer, who first used it in 1979 (Schafer, 1979). How could there have been a discipline of comparative psychoanalysis when analysts were convinced that any disagreement with the dominant view was heresy? In our own era, there have been passionate calls for a comparative and integrative approach (Willock, 2011). I argue here that we need to move beyond "comparative psychoanalysis," and even beyond theoretical integration. In my view, informed by recent developments in the philosophy of science, the multiplicity and diversity of psychoanalysis, the many diverging psychoanalyses, may be best utilized when we focus in a balanced way on both common ground and difference, not for comparison and contrast alone, or to achieve integration, but to learn from each other's opposing views. We can gain the most, I believe, by moving beyond mutual respect and tolerance toward a genuine appreciation of the other, for what they can offer to us and what we can offer to them. The other, the other school, viewpoint, or orientation, can provide a function that we cannot do for ourselves nor they for themselves. In this view, the criticism of the other can become a unique gift, mutually exchanged among schools.

Critical pluralism

The ideas that I develop in what follows are derived from the work of the Israeli historian and philosopher of science, Menachem Fisch.[1] Trained in physics, philosophy, and the history and philosophy of science, Fisch has argued for a contemporary philosophy of science that steers a course between the Scylla of uncritical dogmatism and the Charybdis of radical relativism. His approach is influenced by

Karl Popper's "critical rationalism," the contention that scientific knowledge grows not by accumulating supporting evidence but by subjecting our beliefs to the staunchest criticism we can gather. Although Popper himself dismissed psychoanalysis as a "pseudoscience" because he believed its propositions could not be "falsified," that is empirically tested and challenged, I argue that, ironically, the post-Popperian approach articulated and applied by Fisch befits the current challenges of psychoanalysis. Although it is beyond the scope of this essay to present in any detail, it is of interest that Fisch utilizes his philosophy of science not just to understand developments in the world of natural science but to facilitate interreligious dialogue and critique. That his approach lends itself to the study of religion as well as science may point to its relevance and suitability to psychoanalysis, which has affinities with both realms of discourse.

As a philosopher and historian of science, Fisch studies how one scientist gets another scientist to change his or her mind about a theory. It seems to me that this question should be of much interest to psychotherapists who are always trying to get patients (as well as colleagues) to change their ways of thinking.

Fisch's "reflexive skepticism" suggests that self-doubt and self-criticism is our best attitude toward our own convictions because to assume that we are imperfect, limited, or just plain wrong is the attitude that will most likely lead us to ongoing problem solving and improvement. If we allow ourselves to expose our vulnerabilities and our shortcomings and remain open to criticism, then we are in the best position to continually problem solve and improve. This is not a call for self-effacement or masochism, as Popper's theory was among the most optimistic and constructive of scientific philosophies; it is rather an appeal to the value of ongoing improvement and refinement that is gained by continuing dialogue and unending critique.

In today's psychoanalysis, we have improved our attitudes toward one another's communities greatly. In some societies and institutes today there is respectful dialogue across perspectives and the various schools of thought have more often found ways to coexist. Our reading lists now refer to theories beyond our own schools and journals. But getting along and mutual respect, peaceful coexistence, is not sufficient. Fisch's reading of the history and philosophy of science calls on us to go beyond liberal tolerance. Tolerance is essentially the granting of the right for the other to be mistaken, but not in any way a recognition of their viewpoint being of value. In Fisch's model, the other is not seen as a threat but comes to be regarded as an asset, providing an essential benefit. Others challenge our assumptions, raise questions that we might not think to ask, upset our complacency.

The underlying assumption is that self-critique is always somewhat limited, or perhaps another way of stating it is that we are not as good at self-observation and self-criticism as we often like to imagine. Our beliefs, assumptions, and convictions are often egocentric, and we are so invested in these norms and suppositions that we take them for granted. As fish, we may not notice the water we swim in. It is only when our breathing is disturbed that we pay attention to the air. By focusing on our weaknesses and limitations, and by exposing these to analysis by those who have somewhat different beliefs, we gain a unique opportunity to improve.

Recent developments in psychoanalysis have, I believe, been overly influenced by an overly simplistic utilization of the excesses of postmodernism and associated trends in philosophy of science. Ludwig Fleck (1981) articulation of the idea of "Thought Communities," Thomas Kuhn's (1970) model of "Paradigm Shifts," and perhaps especially Rorty's (1979) "pragmatism" have been used to argue for the "incommensurability" of theories. Whether an intrinsic problem of Kuhn's or a result of a faulty misapplication, this has led to a form of radical relativism where it is argued that scientific developments do not proceed rationally but are more like changes in taste or aesthetics. The problem, as I understand it, is this: If we believe with full conviction that our own views are correct or the most highly developed, the best, or absolutely true, then why would we bother talking to those with other, more "primitive" views? But if we cannot systematically compare our theories and argue rationally for the advantages of one or the other, then why should we bother talking to each other? We might agree to live together, respectfully, with liberal tolerance, but if our theories are incommensurable, if we cannot agree on any shared norms, then on what basis could I expect that you could ever convince me of the rightness or wrongness of your views? Whether monists or relativists, absolutists or pragmatists, there is no need to talk with or learn from those others who have different beliefs. We might liberally tolerate them, but we have no need for them in their very otherness.

For reflexive skeptics, the other is not merely tolerated but is regarded as essential in and for their very otherness.

The framework problem

Now we must ask: How could the other ever convince us that we are wrong? If they persuade us that we are incorrect on one level, isn't it because they have appealed to our norms, to our framework of understanding, on a higher level? If they persuade me that my theory of mind does not capture the complexity that another theory reveals, it is because they can appeal to my wider frame of belief regarding the psychical. If not, then on what basis could I conclude that I had been mistaken? But then how can they convince me that these background assumptions are themselves limited? Only by appealing to a yet higher level of assumptions. But this model would lead to an infinite regress in which there would always be a need for yet some higher level of norms and assumptions that would serve as the basis for challenging one's beliefs and convictions. In philosophy of science this is called "the framework problem."

Fisch and his colleagues have proposed a solution to the framework problem along the following lines. Essentially Fisch argued that although we cannot be convinced by others, because of the framework problem, we can be "ambivalated" by critics. By ambivalated he means that our convictions may become destabilized, some hesitation or unease is introduced, and then we can promulgate these doubts within our own communities. To become so ambivalated, however, we must have sufficient "trust" in these outside critics. Often this comes in the trading zones of ideas outside our immediate scientific communities, in teaching to nonspecialized audiences or at conferences where we meet people in related disciplines or associated schools of thought. In the process of this trading and conversing outside of our immediate like-thinking colleagues, we may be open enough to destabilizing and ambivalating forces of external criticism.

Why do we need criticism from the other? Why isn't self-criticism sufficient? We are simply too close to our own ideas, and even if we can challenge our own ideas, it is even harder to challenge the norms and values upon which these ideas rest. And even if we can challenge those values, it is even harder yet to challenge the underlying norms upon which those values themselves rest, and on and on. The respectful challenges, criticisms, and questions of the other are essential in our efforts to improve.

The chimera and like-enough subjects

It is here that I think psychoanalysis itself may make a small contribution to Fisch's thought. I would suggest that Bach's (2016) symbol of the chimera is a useful metaphor for understanding Fisch's solution to the framework problem. Here is how I understand it. We are all egocentric, especially about newly acquired ideas and theories, but also about all our beliefs and convictions. Decentering is always a challenge. In Bach's terms, we tend toward a narcissistic state of consciousness, a state of being, heavily leaning toward subjective self-awareness. In this state of being, the other is perceived as a threat to our very existence. Why would we risk trusting our own mind to that of a stranger? Our narcissistic defenses are designed to deal with the other's strangeness and to gradually allow the other to be recognized, affirmed, and slowly metabolized. The immune system classifies a foreign body as distinct from the self, and therefore as dangerous, but this must change to take in a foreign body. The other must become the self, or like enough to the self to pass. It is this process that Bach calls chimerization.

This process is also reminiscent of the affect regulation literature when developmentalists like Gergeley and Watson (1996) showed how mothers teach infants to define and evaluate their feelings by "marked" matching responses. Human caregivers provide "marked" affective mirroring signals, expressions that are altered displays of the responses that the caregiver would normally use to express affect states. In other words, the parental mirroring is not like a real mirror, but rather it mirrors with a difference. It is close to the child's affective experience but not the same, and it is precisely in its commonality and yet difference that it is taken in as a marked response.

I translate the preceding to mean that to take in the other, we must generally make them "like-enough subjects," to paraphrase and condense Winnicott (1965) and Benjamin (1995), or transform them into chimeras, with mixed or shared DNA, such that we take them in as parts of ourselves. Their criticisms of our theories, of our assumptions, norms, and values, must share enough commonality so that we are fooled into thinking that they are us. We can then take in their criticism as if it were our own without our antibodies attacking their criticism. In short, we identify with their criticism, which is what allows their ideas to penetrate our defensive narcissistic barriers and destabilize us, "ambivalate" us from the inside-out. Relational theory adds to Fisch's model that mutuality facilitates change. We would be much more likely to open ourselves up to becoming "ambivalated," if we saw that our other was influenced by our criticisms of them. Benjamin (2018) suggests that if we embrace the centrality of learning from rupture and repair, of acknowledging our vulnerability and imperfection, then the other's protest can be turned into an asset and advantage. This approach to protest and criticism strengthen Fisch's model and is valuable in interschool psychoanalytic dialogue and debate.

The question for psychoanalytic communities is the following: Do we want only to sustain, protect, and perpetuate our schools, our approaches? Or do we want to continually test them, challenge, and improve them? Is preservation alone a recipe for stagnation? Are we best off maintaining that our own school of thought (Contemporary Freudian, Kleinian, Kohutian, Relational, Lacanian, or whatever) is the most advanced, deepest, most sophisticated, most comprehensive, answering all the problems with which we deal? Or are we better off assuming our theories and approaches are limited, problematic, incomplete, and in need of constant improvement to be brought about only by being challenged and criticized? Reflexive skepticism is the neo-Popperian attitude that respects the other precisely for the challenge that they provide, stimulating our own questioning and self-examination.

Freud as reflexive-skeptic

In this regard, I want to argue for a view of Freud's achievement somewhat different from the way he is often imagined and presented. Especially with the rise of the New Freud Studies, Freud's embattlement, and his excommunication of dissenters, has been highlighted. It is thought that Freud had little use for anyone who disagreed with the shibboleths that he enumerated (the unique importance of sex, Oedipus, dreams, and the unconscious). But I want to suggest that although Freud politically may have exiled his dissenters, nevertheless he took their criticism seriously and often in fact made their criticisms his own—even while he disavowed such influence. An example of this is his paper "On Narcissism" (Freud, 1914). The paper is unfortunately read as part of teaching Freud's work, without reading the works of Adler and Jung that had led up to it. It is essential in my view that one reads these works, and especially Jung (1972), who also criticized Adler for his overemphasis on the psychology of the self, and criticized Freud for not having a self-psychology. When one reads "On Narcissism" in this context, not only does one understand Freud's paper differently, that is, as a response to and attempt to integrate the criticisms of Adler and Jung, but one sees that Freud spent years struggling with his critic's arguments. It is not simply that Freud was trying to persuade his followers that his views were superior to Adler's and Jung's—that is not the only or superordinate concern. Freud may have denigrated their theories and contributions, he may have split them off politically and socially from the psychoanalytic profession, but he took their criticism seriously and spent years struggling with their perspectives, even if he often took their arguments and ideas and made them his own. I am not suggesting that this is proper personal conduct or good ethics but rather that Freud did use others' criticism to bolster his own theory. In his *Interpretation of Dreams*, he had written that "My emotional life has always insisted that I should have an intimate friend and a hated enemy" (Freud, 1900, p. 483), and Freud made excellent use of these many enemies to criticize, challenge, and improve his own theories.

One can readily see that despite his polemic writing style, that often made him seem so certain about his contributions, that there is another Freud, perhaps an altered and dissociated self-state, a second state of consciousness, a Freud who was very much a reflexive skeptic! To add one illustration, consider how Freud made use of the challenges of critics to reconsider his wish fulfillment theory of dreaming when confronted with traumatic dreams. Even concerning such a favored and hypervalued contribution as his own theory of dreams, Freud in fact maintained a reflexive skepticism that allowed him to revise his theories. I understand that this may be considered a very generous reading of Freud, and I acknowledge that it is not the only Freud we are familiar with, but it is one of his multiple selves.

Freud seems to have used the criticism of others (external criticism) to facilitate his self-criticism (internal criticism). Self-criticism and self-examination are essential, but when used alone they are weak tools. Whereas Mitchell (1993b) described self-reflection as the distinguishing characteristic of the analytic function, it should not be forgotten that this analytic self-reflection takes place in the relationship with another, that is, with the patient, who as Bion (1980) described is the analyst's "best colleague." Try as hard as we may, as sincerely as we might, we are egocentric beings who take many of our assumptions for granted, and it is hard for the eye to see itself (Stern, 2004). Stern argued that the eye can see itself, that we can begin to self-observe using our multiplicity. But that multiplicity is itself discovered through enactments with others who hold and embody other versions of ourselves. I would suggest that what Stern called "snags" and "chafing" (p. 208), which he described as some tension, a sense of something wrong, contradictory, or uncomfortable, is quite like what Fisch described as becoming "ambivalated." Self-criticism and self-examination need to be supplemented and amplified by criticism from significant and like-enough others so that we can take in their criticism in the form of chimeras, we can identify with their criticisms, and make them our own.

The relational tradition: internal and external criticism

Relational Psychoanalysis was arguably the first American school of psychoanalysis to emerge following the decline of the dominance of Ego Psychology and the resulting proliferation of multiple schools of psychoanalytic thought (Aron, 1996c). Its initial formulation was the result of a comparative psychoanalytic project (Greenberg & Mitchell, 1983). Mitchell once spoke to me of relational psychoanalysis as a form of "critical eclecticism."[2] Certainly, it became a big tent, an overarching perspective, which is why Mitchell and I (1999) referred to our first collection of relational articles as "the emergence of a tradition" rather than a school. It was also, undoubtedly, offered as a corrective to what were perceived to be excesses in what had previously been viewed as the "mainstream." Important as well, its rise coincided with the development of the Division of Psychoanalysis (39) of the American Psychological Association and therefore offered a new perspective to a national audience of psychologist-psychoanalysts, many of whom had been excluded for decades from the mainstream. It was a broad and unifying theoretical framework that was fresh, contemporary, post-women's movement, postclassical, post-gay rights, and perhaps most important uniquely its own and not that of the heretofore medical association.[3] This is not to reduce important theoretical developments to politics and professional factors alone, but rather to emphasize that there was a sociopolitical context within which the relational tradition could burgeon.

That efflorescence of the relational tradition occurred in the 1980s and it has now been almost 30 years since its institutionalization. It went from being an intimate and local movement in New York City to quickly become a national movement and eventually an international force in psychoanalysis.

It is typical among psychoanalytic schools to argue for the advantages of one school over another, for leaders to point to the deficiencies of other schools and to champion their own. This can be part of a healthy development. The competitiveness of the schools for students and adherents can be constructive and may stir a sharpening of conceptualization and formulation. As I have argued throughout this chapter, external critique, when respectful and based on sufficient common ground and shared values, can be useful and even essential to growth.

It is required for generativity that each school be receptive to learning from these critiques and not just defending against them. Why do we not have a tradition for schools of psychoanalysis to openly and publicly engage in self-critique (critique by insiders)? In retrospect, this is surprising. After all, doesn't every doctoral dissertation and published research always include a section on the study's limitations and inadequacies? Why wouldn't we expect that psychoanalytic texts would also be willing to expose their limits, restrictions, and biases? As I argued earlier in the chapter, this is not a call for masochistic submission to the other, nor does it require us to be overly hesitant or modest in our formulations. We can and should argue for and persuade others of our convictions as much as any school of thought.

We can speak and write strongly and yet remain open, vulnerable, responsive to criticism and to corrective feedback. This is a strength and not a weakness.

Relational psychoanalysis was based on conceptualizing the nature of transference and countertransference not as distortion, displacement, and false connection but as a personal idiosyncratic but plausible construction. This shift in our understanding of transference phenomena led the relational clinician to respond to so-called negative transference as based on plausible perceptions of the analyst's participation with the patient, rather than dismissing the observations as distortions and displacements from past objects.

Why would relational writers reject theoretical criticism as based on misunderstanding, misreadings, distortions of relational theory, when these same analysts listen to criticism from patients and strive to understand the plausibility of the criticism? We no more believe that our patient is always "right" than we assume that our critics are always right. What we do believe is that when external criticism seems to be accompanied by good will and an effort to understand and respect our point of view, it may offer us valuable insight that we would and could not achieve as readily on our own. Internal and external criticism dialectically inform each other. Criticism that may have been rejected when it came from outsiders may have nevertheless been sufficiently internalized such that it led to some "destabilization," and this slight shaking up of perspective may then spread among insiders.

When we acknowledge the contributions of others, this in turn may make them more likely to accept our own reciprocal feedback about their approach. Psychoanalysts have increasingly been promoting an ethos of "mutual vulnerability" (Aron, 2016). Such an attitude among the "schools" might prove valuable as well. As in any transitional phenomena (Winnicott, 1953), it may become impossible to say whether the criticism came from inside or outside. This is the chimera (Bach, 2016), with its mixed DNA, a self-object that allows us to internalize otherness, without fearing for our lives because we have metabolized the other's feedback, and the other has become us. This chimera may then save our lives.

For our approaches to grow, thrive, remain alive and vibrant, we need the dialectic of internal and external criticism and we need to allow ourselves ongoing ambivalating. To facilitate its occurrence, psychoanalytic educators need to make space for students and practitioners to "practice ambivalating," that is, to practice being responsive to the snags and chafing that inform us of limits and contradictions and allow us to awake from our dissociations.

The seemingly dualistic opposition of "internal" and "external" critique fails to capture the richness of the critical process, and instead I suggest that we view internal and external critique as a dialectic rather than a binary (see Aron & Starr, 2012). The point is that the very distinction between internal and external critique is simplistic precisely because of the arguments made in this chapter. Internal critique would be weak indeed without the benefit of a viewpoint outside of one's own perspective. We need more than one vertex to decenter. Luckily, we each have multiple self-states, and we have identifications in multiple directions that allow us to feel some snags and chafing such that the eye can come to see itself (Stern, 2004). Internal and external create, sustain, and define each other dialectically.

Perhaps you will disagree with these arguments. You may point out the limitations of my thesis and contradictions in my propositions. As a reflexive skeptic, I hope to have argued strongly and stated my proposal with conviction. I do, after all, wish to persuade and convince and promote my own ideas as much as monists and relativists do. If you have reasoned objections and can prove me wrong, well then—that would certainly make my point, wouldn't it?

Notes

1 Menachem Fisch is a prolific author, and a good select bibliography of his work may be found in Tirosh-Samuelson and Hughes (2016), which also includes several representative articles, an editorial overview, and an intellectual overview. I am not a historian or philosopher of science and have no expert competence in evaluating Fisch's professional contributions. I have been influenced by his work, but the responsibility for any misuse or misunderstanding of his theory is mine alone. Other books of his that I have studied are included in the reference section (Fisch, 1997; Fisch & Benbaji, 2011). Special thanks to Daniel Marom for introducing me to the philosophical writings of M. Fisch. Marom is responsible for curricular and pedagogical development at the Mandel School for Educational Leadership in Jerusalem, where we have been collaborating in an ongoing study of psychoanalytic education.

2 Unfortunately, I have not been able to find a published reference to his using this phrase to describe his own form of theorizing, but there are several times when he did speak against "uncritical eclecticism" or "muddled eclecticism," and this usage does support my memory that he considered his own approach a form of "critical eclecticism."
3 It is significant that Greenberg and Mitchell's (1983) book coincided with the first annual meetings of Division 39, and that the establishment of the Relational Orientation at NYU's Postdoctoral Program in Psychotherapy and Psychoanalysis in 1988, and the establishment of *Psychoanalytic Dialogues* in 1990, immediately followed the lawsuit against the American and International Psychoanalytic Associations, which was settled in November 1988 with the institutes promising not to discriminate against psychologists or other "nonmedical candidates" (see Wallerstein, 2013).

Chapter 12

Ethical considerations in psychoanalytic writing revisited (2016)

Introduction by Jay Greenberg

Few problems are as challenging to our efforts to develop psychoanalysis as an intellectual discipline as the problem of patient confidentiality. On the one hand, it is hard to imagine inviting patients to share what they hate or fear most about themselves without promising that we will do everything we can to preserve their privacy. On the other hand, for psychoanalysis to work either as a method for exploring human experience or as a therapy, we must be able to fully communicate to our colleagues about what happens—what *really* happens—in our consulting rooms.

As Lew notes in this chapter, the problem has been with us from the beginning. Freud was aware that the very possibility of treatment depended on patients' trust of their doctors. Although he formulated the source of that trust in the tormented concept of an "unobjectionable" part of the transference (Freud, 1912b), he was clear that outcome also depends on the behavior of the analyst and that discretion is a crucial element of that behavior. But of course Freud's ambition was not simply to cure those who came to him but to convince the world that he had created a science that could change our understanding of what it is to be human, and that this goal required showing the world what he had done and how he had done it.

In the century since Freud first grappled with the problem, and especially in the last 20 years, the challenge has only grown worse. With the burgeoning of the internet, most analysts assume that our patients routinely Google us before making their first phone call, and that some continue to do so regularly during the course of treatment or at least when something has happened that stirs their curiosity. It is, accordingly, foolhardy to assume that anything we have written will not be discovered, although of course there are also many patients who steadfastly avoid learning anything at all about us.

That means that "disguise"—however we understand or implement it—must not only prevent the patients' acquaintances from figuring out who they are, it must also keep the patients from finding themselves in our reports. This makes crafting our case reports more difficult, and it also raises the stakes. Contemporary clinical vignettes include a great deal of discussion of the analyst's inner experience, including countertransference experience that we may believe is best kept from our patients. Patients who are still in treatment, and even those who no longer are, can easily be injured by what they learn, even if the analyst correctly believes that his or her awareness of the countertransference was a crucial aspect of the eventual success of the treatment.

Lew's approach in this chapter is wide ranging; in a way that is typical of him, as he openly explores as much of what has been written and said as he possibly can. His primary focus, though, is on the problem—I use the word advisedly, although many analysts present it as the solution—of "informed consent." Informed consent, required by the ethical guidelines of many although not all professional organizations, should (and sometimes is) challenged by the psychoanalytic assumptions of transference and the unconscious. What does it mean for patients—current and even past—to be "informed"? Lew's long experience as the director of a psychoanalytic training program reminds him constantly that the problem of confidentiality has legal as well as ethical and technical ramifications. Accordingly, in both this chapter and its 2000 predecessor, he concludes that asking for permission is necessary at least in most cases, even as we remind ourselves never to assume that we adequately understand either the dynamics or the effects of doing so.

In fact, he raises the question of whether even asking for permission is ethical. This strikes me as a very interesting although rarely addressed aspect of the problem. Most of us would agree that asking a patient *for* anything—from something relatively benign like a restaurant recommendation to something much more volatile like a stock tip—is questionable technique. And although we don't talk about it much, technical lapses can blend, sometimes imperceptibly, with ethical lapses; consider, as a simple example, flirting with patients.

A good example of the problems—technical and ethical—that can come up when analysts ask for something is bringing up the possibility that patients donate to the analyst's institute or professional association. These requests are widely considered unethical, despite their long history. And, like asking for permission to publish, they are designed to benefit the profession at large, although of course it also benefits the analyst personally.

It is with this in mind that Lew arrives at one of his important conclusions in this chapter. In one of those comments that leave the reader thinking "Why has that never occurred to me?" he writes: "It is probably wise to think that all presentations and publications of clinical material represent some form of enactment ... enactments, after all, are often played out through ... management of the therapeutic frame" (p. 289). He advises seeking consultation whenever we are considering writing or presenting our work with a particular patient.

But solutions, however prudent and however wise, are not Lew's main interest. His quest, growing out of an impressively solid grounding in all that has been written and fueled by a restless curiosity about what it all means, is a model for exploring difficult issues without demanding closure. Toward the end of the chapter, he writes a sentence that should be in the minds of all psychoanalysts regardless of whether they write and regardless of how theoretically inclined they are: "That we do not have consistent answers does not justify the neglect of addressing the dilemma" (p. 288). This is the spirit that pervades not only this chapter, but Lew's project throughout his life.

Aron, L. (2016). Ethical considerations in psychoanalytic writing revisited.

Psychoanalytic Perspectives, 13(3), 267–290.

Until fairly recently, clinical material used in professional writing was considered to be "owned" by the psychoanalyst. Disguising a patient's identity from friends and family was the unofficial professional standard for publication. Two factors have dramatically changed this position. The first is the evolution of psychoanalytic theory from a one-person to a two-person model. That is, psychoanalytic process and content are increasingly viewed as co-created by analyst and patient. It is therefore less reasonable for the analyst to make unilateral decisions regarding the use of clinical material. In a related vein, medical patients and all consumers in society now expect a higher level of collaboration than they did years ago. Second, the Internet has greatly transformed accessibility to published material. Twenty years ago it would have been unlikely that patients, not themselves professionals, would come across their analysts' writings. Now one can simply Google one's therapist and potentially recognize oneself in the text of any publication (Kolod, 2010).

These factors have made it increasingly necessary for clinicians to ask their patients for consent before publishing case histories, even when the clinician has carefully disguised identifying information. However, involving the patient in the process of writing and publication of a case history may complicate the treatment in ways that are both for the better and for the worse. Many clinicians who might otherwise present or publish case histories are made anxious or are intimidated by these complications and therefore do not write about their patients.

Bridges (2007) described her experience in asking for patients' permission to use their case stories before publishing a book. She pointed out that society's emphasis on patients' rights and consumer-oriented attitudes lend themselves to obtaining consent, and she noted that journal editorial boards are increasingly suggesting or insisting that patients be asked to provide consent to publication. Seeking patients' consent to publish case histories is attractive from a patients' rights point of view. It eliminates the possibility of patients discovering "disguised" material and unexpectedly recognizing themselves in print; after all, who decides what is an adequate "disguise" if the patient has not reviewed the material? Involving the patient in the clinician's writing process inevitably complicates the treatment in unpredictable ways. Worst-case scenarios include the patient experiencing the therapist's writing as a malignant reenactment or a betrayal that may even result in unfortunate termination of the treatment (Bridges, 2007).

With the dominance of "evidence-based medicine" and reliance on quantifiable, data-driven, and standardized procedures has come a decline and even devaluation of the case history. Fewer case histories are now published in medical journals, and the case history plays less of a role in medical education generally (Montross, 2015). These trends are reinforced by the alarm felt by clinical writers who fear that they will be accused of ethically violating their patients' privacy. This decline in the prominence of the case history is particularly problematic for psychiatry and the mental health disciplines. Psychoanalysis, in particular, has historically relied on rich, detailed, and nuanced case histories for education, communication among colleagues, and its empirical foundations.

In 1998, I presented a review essay on "Ethical Considerations in the Writing of Psychoanalytic Case Histories" at the Division (39) of Psychoanalysis Annual Spring Meetings, later published in *Psychoanalytic Dialogues* (Aron, 2000). To my astonishment, over the next decade I received repeated requests for consultation by people who identified themselves to me as having been written about by their therapists, without their consent having been solicited. Several of these people had been deeply wounded by what they experienced as a betrayal by a trusted figure, and not surprisingly this violation resonated with previous infidelities in their lives. I worked in short- and long-term therapy and analysis with several of the former patients and consulted with others. I do not describe these treatments or provide details about these patients because, often, our agreement from the start was that I would not use material from their treatments for teaching or writing. I also do not generalize about these people's dynamics or pathology because, although it is easy to demonstrate that they "masochistically" or "narcissistically" participated in a reenactment of some previous betrayal, to jump to such generalizations would be to abuse them yet again in the form of blaming the victim after the crime. Later, as I increasingly spoke at professional meetings about ethics related to case writing, I was also consulted by numerous colleagues who were thinking about publishing case material but were at a loss as to how to proceed ethically, legally, and clinically. In the two decades since the initial paper was written, a good deal has changed in regard to professional standards of confidentiality. The Internet has become ubiquitous such that it is much easier and more likely for patients to come into contact with their therapists' writings. This chapter therefore updates my earlier survey and makes use of the consulting experience I have gained in the ensuing years.

I will say at the start that my personal experience as a consultant, and as the director of a large training program in psychotherapy and psychoanalysis, has been that this topic makes people anxious! Both students and faculty are unsure about what is clinically, ethically, morally, professionally, and legally the most responsible way to proceed. My observation is that they unfortunately avoid the topic by not discussing their cases, not writing about them for publication, or presenting clinical cases in various settings without carefully thinking through how they are handling the relevant privacy issues. As one important example, I have spoken with faculty members who teach clinical case seminars where students routinely present clinical cases. Some of the faculty indicated that they do not examine with their students how the question of patients' informed consent is handled. I have been told by more than one instructor that they fear highlighting this question out of concern that it will inhibit the already limited willingness of students to present cases in depth. An important educational opportunity is then bypassed, repressed, or dissociated.

In 2000 I argued that an essential principle of psychoanalytic practice is the maintenance of strict confidentiality, and yet the presentation and publication of psychoanalytic case histories necessitate considerable public disclosure of the lives of our patients (Aron, 2000). Inasmuch as psychoanalysis is an especially frequent, intensive, and lengthy process, a report of the unfolding of an analysis necessarily entails a marked degree of revelation concerning patients, their inner worlds, and their life circumstances. This use of confidential material raises innumerable ethical concerns, and psychoanalysis, with its unique emphasis on unconscious mental processes, also adds to the complexity of ethical considerations by demanding that unconscious factors be taken into account. When speaking, for example, of "informed consent" as an ethical principle, psychoanalytic clinicians must grapple with the problem of whether to take a patient's manifest acquiescence at face value. It is ironic that psychoanalysts who think clinically of patients as having "multiple self-states" and being "divided selves" will assume that patients give consent as if they are unified coherent agents, transparent to themselves (Saketopoulou, 2015).[1]

Anecdotes from years past

The following stories have influenced my thinking about these issues. Some are derived from the history of psychotherapy and psychoanalysis, and some are more personal experiences, selected illustrations of dilemmas that have come to my attention regarding the presentation and publication of case histories. I tell many of these stories colloquially so as to preserve some of my feelings and experiences when I first encountered these incidents.

Mediating for New York University

Some years ago in the month of August, when analysts tend to be taking it easy, I received a call from a dean at New York University (NYU) in my role as the director of the Postdoctoral Program in Psychotherapy & Psychoanalysis, a free-standing program in the Graduate School of Arts and Science that provides advanced education, beyond the doctoral level, to licensed mental health professionals. Now, typically, the deans do not contact me very often, and it is almost always by e-mail, so a midsummer phone call was unusual and raised my alarms. Sure enough, the dean was anxious and told me that a university lawyer had contacted him due to a threat of a lawsuit by a patient who claimed that one of our faculty had written about her in a professional journal. I knew nothing about this, and so told the dean I would get right back to him after looking into the matter. I called the director of our clinic, but he too had heard nothing at all. As it turned out, an analyst on our faculty did write about a patient, but it was a patient seen in the analyst's private practice, not in any way connected to the university. The analyst had then published an article in an edited book, and the chapter appeared on his course syllabus, which was available to the public on the NYU Postdoc website. Several years after ending treatment, the patient searched for her former therapist on Google and found the article, leading her to contact the university. When the university administration realized that the patient was not directly connected to NYU, they asked me, via the patient's legal counsel, to mediate between the patient and the therapist. With the patient's consent, I agreed to do so.

It emerged that the patient readily admitted to having given consent. The patient also acknowledged that she had been disguised and was not worried about being identifiable. Well then, what was the problem? The patient explained to me that when her therapist had asked for consent to publish a report of their work together, she had told him that she was not ready to read the draft because she felt it would be too upsetting. Nevertheless, the patient had acquiesced and notified her therapist that he may submit the report for publication. The patient had not given consent in writing but did not deny authorizing the submission. The patient believed that she had agreed to be included as data in a therapist's research article. In other words, if she were being treated for an anxiety disorder, then she thought the therapist would be using her as one subject in a study of anxiety-disordered patients. But when the patient looked up the published article years later, she was astounded at what she found. The article included verbatim accounts of her dreams with deeply personal imagery. Now, she readily acknowledged that no one would recognize this personal material other than herself. However, the patient was shocked and appalled that her personal material was laid out for all the world to see, even if they did not know it was hers.

The patient forwarded to me copies of rulings from judges in New York State, obtained from her lawyer, indicating that informed consent by a psychotherapy patient must be in writing and declares that the patient read what was published. After all, if the patient does not know what is being published, then in what sense can one claim that she or he is informed?

It should be obvious that the patient had sought out the therapist due to unresolved feelings about the treatment and that numerous psychological dynamics were being played out. But it is also obvious that a therapist had his own feelings and unconscious dynamics operative when he chose to publish an article including much personal detail, when the patient had made clear that it would be too upsetting to read the draft.

I was able to negotiate to a point approaching a settlement, but in the middle of my work I never heard back from the patient and do not know the final result. I do know that the therapist was required to provide and was agreeable to a monetary settlement, promising to take all references to the chapter off his reading lists and to remove the chapter from any future reprints of the book. The university was simply happy that none of the proceedings included them. I learned quite a lot from this incident about the legal rights of the patient to know what being written once is asked for informed consent, but also about how quickly this can become an institutional concern, and especially about the problems of a too quick acceptance of "consent."

Unintended publicity: a series of vignettes

A highly regarded analyst from London was visiting San Francisco and presented a "disguised" case history for which she had not received patient consent. The analyst believed that the institute was quite small and far from home and so chances were remote that anyone could recognize the patient. The presentation was well received. After the conclusion of the talk, a faculty member of the institute asked to include the case in an upcoming issue of the institute's local newsletter. The analyst agreed to the request. Sometime later, the same faculty member contacted the London analyst, asking to include the case history in an edited book being prepared by members of the institute. The London analyst hesitated, explaining that because she had never obtained informed consent she could not agree to have the case in a published book. The faculty editor responded, "But it is already on the Internet." "How could that be?" asked the analyst. In the intervening years, the local newsletter had grown into a small journal and was now on the Psychoanalytic Electronic Publishing (PEP-web) Internet database, which had retroactively published all of the issues of the newsletter. Now the analyst, in somewhat of a panic, contacted her former patient, explained apologetically what she had done, and was met by a stormy reaction. The analyst feared that she would hear from a lawyer, but instead some months later the patient, who appreciated the analyst's belated straightforwardness, called asking to come back into treatment.

Reversing directions: A well-known New York analyst presented a case history to a London audience, also believing that the case would not be recognized across the Atlantic. The analyst was prepared to present the case orally at a meeting but had not obtained permission for publication. The conference organizers later published an edited book that included the case material. The analyst insisted that he had not authorized the dissemination of his work and initiated a lawsuit against the editors and publisher. As a result, the books were pulled from the shelves and needed to be republished without the case material. The brouhaha severed several collegial relationships and almost resulted in a split in the professional association involved. One therapist spent several years preparing and revising a detailed case history about a woman patient. After the therapist submitted the draft to a publisher, the journal's editorial board insisted that the author obtain written consent from the disguised patient. However, the therapist/author had never thought to do so, nor had she been trained in the process of obtaining consent. Feeling under pressure with the journal ready to publish her work, the therapist asked the patient for permission, only to have the patient react with great upset and conflict. The patient remarked, "But I want to tell my own story." The patient had, in fact, been writing her own short story about her life and therapy (of which the therapist was aware) and the week before the therapist had brought up the question of consent, the patient's own article had been accepted by a magazine for publication (she had not yet told her therapist). One aspect of the patient's childhood narrative was that her mother had been very competitive with her. The patient had a specific childhood memory of writing a story, showing it to her mother, and the mother writing her own stories in response. In this case, the patient did not want to read what her therapist had written and deliberated about whether she would be willing to consent to her therapist's publication in a journal. The therapist wisely, although with great disappointment, decided not to publish the article. Nonetheless, the patient was so angry that she opted to discontinue the treatment.

A therapist was working with a young woman who consented to publication of an article that detailed aspects of her personal life—in particular, sexual fantasies about her female analyst. The analyst was careful about having her read it and work through its meanings before deciding to publish the article. Some years later, the patient, after having benefited from the analysis, decided to change careers and go back to graduate school to become a psychologist. Guess which article was one day assigned for her class to read? Yes, the former patient sat through an entire class discussing her own analyst's article about her. Although she was not recognizable in the article, this incident brought her to seek further treatment, as it stirred up powerful old feelings and conflicts about her analyst, as well as about her sexuality, all of which had fresh meaning to her in the context of her new professional context.[2]

Some time ago, I received an e-mail from an individual whom I did not know. She addressed the e-mail to me and to two other senior analysts known for their writings about boundary violations, ethics, and issues related to writing about patients. She attached to the e-mail notes between her analyst and herself and claimed to have 500 pages of documentation about her analysis. The former patient was writing to lodge a complaint against her analyst, who had published her case history in a way that she described as inaccurate and self-serving.

I quickly received an apologetic e-mail from the analyst, who was rather contrite and quite embarrassed about the incident. She wrote, "Sorry that you have been subject to what is to me a quite embarrassing report of my work. Sorry for me even more, I suppose. Some of the distortions in my article reflected a lame effort at disguise. However, my work with this patient definitely did not reflect my finest hour, though I did try to be candid about this in my writing. She is not in our field, I did not ask her for permission to write about our work and I naively assumed that she would never come across my writing. This latter point, indeed is a lesson to me. I'm not sure what else to say or do" (Anonymous, personal communication, January 18, 2015).

I wrote the following to my colleague in response: "This is indeed everyone's nightmare. Our practices, policies, procedures, and ethics in regard to writing about patients are changing rapidly, especially because of the Internet and Google searches. Frankly, I don't know any good way to resolve all of the problems that emerge and my best guess is that we are all going to become increasingly cautious, if not altogether paranoid and inhibited. Let's hope she leaves it as is at this point." The other expert clinicians quickly e-mailed their agreement. Based on my lawyer's advice, I did not respond to the patient. The clear message from my attorney was that having no contact at all was the best way to protect my own legal and professional interests and to avoid any legal complications. I mention this here, but later in the chapter I come back to the general legal counsel that I have received on these matters.

Jungians

In my earlier paper (Aron, 2000), I reviewed some of what Freud had to say, as well as some of his practices, regarding the writing of case accounts. Rather than repeat the material here, I describe an important, but troubling, narrative from the Jungian tradition.

To the American psychoanalytic audience, the name of Michael Fordham is unfortunately not as familiar as it should be. He is widely regarded as the founder of the London Jungian approach, often called the developmental approach—a method that integrated Jungian with Kleinian and object-relational theory and technique. In 1933, Fordham had a seven-month analysis with Peter Baynes—a friend of Fordham's father, the leader of the British Jungians, and a patient, friend, and translator of Jung. In 1934, Fordham traveled to Zurich, where Baynes had sent him in order to be analyzed by Jung. However, at that time, foreigners were ineligible for work permits in Switzerland, and Fordham was unable to afford the analysis. Fordham returned to London and was further analyzed by Baynes between 1935 and 1936. Baynes also began to groom Fordham as his successor. Later, after consulting with Jung, Fordham switched analysts and worked with Hilde Kirsch, who had never before practiced. Fordham was her first patient (and so, in recommending her, Jung legitimated her as an analyst). When Fordham began to develop an intense erotic transference to Hilde, she dealt with the difficulty by inviting Fordham to dinner with her husband, the prominent Jungian analyst James Kirsch. Jung analyzed both James and Hilde in the 1930s. At the time that Fordham called on Kirsch, she was pregnant with Thomas Kirsch, who would later grow to become a leading Jungian theorist and historian of Jungian analysis, and it is from Kirsch (2000) that we know much of this story.

Now, returning to the initial analysis with Baynes, at one point while Fordham was in a trancelike state, Baynes encouraged him to paint his dream images. Fordham produced many artistic drawings and worked in analysis using imaginary dialogues with figures that emerged. As Fordham could not afford to pay Baynes's fee, he offered to treat Fordham in exchange for the use of the drawings. In his 1940 book, *Mythology of the Soul*, where Baynes features two cases, one patient was evidently Fordham, whose identity was disguised only minimally. Baynes included the narrative of the analysis, as well as Fordham's drawings, and erroneously diagnosed him as schizophrenic. When Fordham traveled to see C. G. Jung, whom he could not afford, he was significantly distressed following the treatment episode with Baynes.

The betrayal of his confidence became a lifelong albatross around Fordham, which was then used against him by his critics.

In Fordham's biography, written upon the suggestion of his later analyst/supervisor Donald Meltzer, Fordham cited his trauma as one reason that he included almost no clinical case reports of adult patients in the book. He did write about children, who he believed were harder to identify. The silver lining of Fordham's painful experiences with his two classical Jungian analysts was that it led to his most important innovations. Fordham was the key figure to integrate psychoanalytic ideas about transference and childhood into Jungian theory and technique, thus shaping much of contemporary Jungian practice. He ran a study group that regularly included such psychoanalysts as Bion and Winnicott. For our purposes, let us assume that Fordham's analyst obtained his consent to publish case material by agreeing to charge him less for sessions. Is that ethically responsible? Does an analyst do something similar when she or he tells clinic patients that they can receive psychoanalysis at a low fee with an analyst in training, understanding that the student will be discussing the patient with supervisors and colleagues in classes and colloquia? Of course, there are also a range of situations, for example, a graduate school clinic may have different expectations than a postgraduate clinic where the therapists are already licensed professionals. A hospital setting may be different from a university setting. But the questions being raised here need to be considered whatever the professional context may be. Unfortunately, many graduate students have told me that supervisors have never even brought up with them the question of the ethics or clinical concerns involved in presenting work with their patients in classes and case seminars.

Among the earliest advocates for obtaining patients' consent before writing about them was Robert Stoller (1988). The following two quotations convey his strong and very early opinions about the matter. "We would do better ethically and scientifically if throughout the process of writing and publication, we let our patients review our reports of them" (p. 371). Stoller concluded simply and directly: "We should not write about our patients without their permission to do so and without their view of the matters about which we write" (p. 391).

We have to be constantly alert to the effects of countertransference on what our patients are telling us in confidence. To report a case can be a powerful stimulus for countertransference enactment. And to report a case verbally can be more dangerous than to report it in writing. In addition to the betrayal of trust is the possibility of acting out sadistic, masochistic, exhibitionistic, aggressive, or narcissistic needs.

The benefits of writing about and with patients

It is important to take note that some clinical writers have told stories that convey the benefits of having written about patients on the clinical work itself. Stuart Pizer (2000), for example, reported his reactions to one patient upon her learning of his writing about her.

To my surprise, she responded with enthusiasm. She told me that it felt easy for her to give her consent because she felt reassured by my writing, presenting, and publishing. She said that, in the face of the personal risks she experienced in her analysis, she felt that much safer knowing that our work was linked to a professional community and to my own serious commitment to contributing to my field. For her, the writing added to a sane context for her terrifying analytic journey (p. 258).

> Similarly, Gerson (200) wrote the following:
> I believe that the wish to discuss one's work, in publication or verbally, is essential to one's function as a therapist ... First, there is the need to hold the patient's experience in one's own mind in a manner whereby it can be an object of reflection for both patient and analyst. Second, and a requisite for the accomplishment of the first need, is the need to have a relationship to an "other" that extends beyond the intimacy of the immediate experience with the patient. These two needs of the analyst are not in opposition to the patient's needs.
> (p. 263)

However, nothing in the previous two opinions suggests that the therapist should write without the patient's informed consent.

The letter

A few years ago, the NYU Postdoctoral Program sponsored a conference featuring a clinical case discussion. Before the presentation was composed, I encouraged the speaker to ask the patient for consent. The analyst received the following letter from her patient, and the case was later published (Oram, 2013). In this case, asking for permission seemed to be a turning point in unblocking a certain treatment stalemate. The patient went from feeling that she could only take from the therapist to feeling that she could also contribute. The therapist had not been aware of this dynamic until after she obtained the patient's permission to present the case report.

> Dear Kate, Would I mind if you referred to our work together at a Postdoctoral Program presentation at the Institute of NYU? Of course I wouldn't!! For someone like me who never met a boundary in a relationship that she didn't try to cross, this is a dream come true!!! I don't even have to do anything; you are doing all the work. You don't have to worry about disguising my identity … I'm sitting here imagining Margot [her friend who had helped her find her the therapist who had been so helpful and who had died a number of years ago] in the discussion group … howling out loud, "I know her"! Oh, that she was here; she would love this. Please know that I don't want to know any of the details unless I ask about it in a session with you. If it gets me little nuts, I want to be in a position to deal with it with you in the confines of your office. Besides, one of us has to keep up some semblance of a normal doctor-patient relationship here. [She puts in a smiley face at this point.] … Finally, it is an understatement, but thank you for making and keeping me a part of your work. Have happy holidays.
> Peace,
> Rosalie (Oram, 2013, pp. 596–597)

A risk that paid off

In *The Enigma of Desire*, Galit Atlas (2015) presented the case history of Leo, a Latin American man in his late 20s. Leo had previously worked with only male analysts until seeking out Atlas, a female analyst. Leo warned Atlas from the start that she would never be able to love him; that she would reject him, and be repulsed by him. Atlas quickly became afraid of Leo, his aggressiveness, intrusiveness, and his violent sexuality. She vividly describes Leo's intense need to control the sessions, even to the point of not letting her breathe freely. Leo narrated rape fantasies in minute and sadistic detail. Quickly, Atlas imagined ridding herself of Leo. However, she skillfully utilized her own emotional reactions of shame, fear, and vulnerability to open up analytic space for exploration and connection.

Atlas's remarkable description of Leo is graphic, is animated, and incorporates her own personal, emotional reactions to him as a patient. In spite of her powerful articulation of internal fear, Atlas took a risk in asking Leo to read her account and give informed consent to publish the case vignette. Her courageous act could not have been easy. Atlas could not possibly have been certain of Leo's reaction to the request to do something for her, or to the way in which she described him and her own impressions of him. Nor could there be any definitive way to predict the impact on the unfolding treatment. Atlas was relieved that Leo reacted appreciatively. Leo felt honored that he was respectfully asked to participate in a collegial role. He sensed that the ability to give to his therapist helped even out the power imbalance in the relationship. We have now seen in several stories how patients often feel that they are not giving enough back to the therapist, presumably even if they are paying a regular fee, or they may go along with giving consent in exchange for a lower fee. Issues of power, control, influence, and exchange may then be bypassed, avoided in the treatment as they are enacted in the frame of treatment.

Reading Atlas's case narrative was the first time that Leo recognized how aggressive and frightening he could be, this in spite of the fact that Atlas had shared her reactions with him throughout the treatment in the form of therapeutic interventions and interpretations. Prior to reading Atlas's draft, Leo had ended a relationship with a romantic partner. Leo's girlfriend had also told him about his aggressiveness, but he minimized her comments and trivialized the feedback. Seeing the depth of his internal dynamics spelled out in writing penetrated him in a more powerful way. Undoubtedly, Leo also recognized that in the act of sharing her report with him and asking for his permission to publish, his analyst was strong enough to tolerate his response and could stand up to his aggression with confidence and faith in their relationship.

Recent professional developments
Psychoanalytic journal editorial policies and the ICMJE

A number of professional developments that require consideration and reflection have occurred since my chapter was published in 2000. In 1995, the International Committee of Medical Journal Editors (ICMJE) established a new international standard of editorial policy, requiring written informed consent by the subject for every case report published in a medical journal. This policy has had a direct effect on psychiatry and, therefore, on many psychoanalysts and psychotherapists.

Within psychoanalytic organizations the adoption of transparent ethical codes has been slow, and there is no consensus. Tuckett (2000, p. 1066) has deleted the clause specifying that confidentiality be maintained "within the contours of applicable legal and professional standards" from the ethics section of its procedural code. Consequently, the parameters remain deliberately vague.

David Tuckett (2000), as editor of the *International Journal of Psychoanalysis*, expressed the view that the ICMJE (1995) requirements for all disclosed clinical records to be undisguised, and for the informed consent of the patient to be obtained prior to inclusion in any study, are in conflict with the very nature of psychoanalytic work. Tuckett acknowledges that his is a plea for psychoanalysis to adopt a *less rigorous* standard than that required by other medical professions. He acknowledged,

> If arguments to privilege psychoanalysis are taken too far, they may be viewed as a statement made by a profession that is not capable of regulating itself in a manner that is consistent either with Human Rights legislation, which is becoming more radical, or with ordinary standards of transparency and accountability.
> (p. 1067)

Nevertheless, he rejected the guidelines presented by the ICMJE that one should both ask permission and not anonymize data by disguising the facts, as these procedures are not desirable for psychoanalysis. The nature of informed consent in clinical psychoanalysis is too complex given the centrality of transference and the unconscious. Tuckett concluded by endorsing Glen Gabbard's (2000) recommendations, published alongside Tuckett's editorial in the same issue. The editorial board of the *International Journal of Psychoanalysis* requires that confidentiality be preserved, but rules of how to protect confidentiality are thought to be best left undefined.

In his paper, Gabbard (2000) dealt with possibilities for resolving the conflict that arises between the protection of the patient's privacy and the educational and scientific needs of analysis when clinical material is presented for publication. He offered five strategies by which this dilemma can be resolved, as well as guidelines to assist analysts wishing to present their clinical cases. Gabbard's approach is a complex one, not an either/or solution. The five strategies—thick disguise, patient consent, the process approach, the use of composites, and the use of a colleague as author—are presented with some detail. They are rooted in the author's experience and in statements appearing in recent years in clinical literature, as well as those issued by various organizations, dealing with the ethical issues surrounding patients' confidentiality.

The editors of the *Journal of Clinical Psychoanalysis* (*JCP*) cite the Hippocratic oath *primum non nocere* (above all do no harm) as the bedrock of their patient privacy policies. For the *JCP* editors, confidentiality applies equally to the patient and to the analytic process. Nothing should be done directly "by violating privacy" or indirectly by "vitiating the process." The editors wrote that there are patients for whom contraindications to publication are present, such as mental health professionals, and well-known personalities. They consider disguise a better option than consent. Levine and Stagno (2001), commenting on *JCP*'s editorial policy, observed that, although seeming to be ethically appealing, the request for informed consent may, under some circumstances, itself be unethical, potentially harm patients, and erode the use of case reports as a valuable teaching method in psychiatry and psychotherapy.

According to Alfonso (2002), dynamic psychiatrists and psychoanalysts may continue to affirm their medical identity without having to accept the restrictive, albeit well-intentioned, ICMJE publication guidelines. Psychoanalytic writers may choose from a variety of options to report cases ethically and judiciously. They may obtain informed consent, avoid identifying details, disguise without distorting the essence of what is being reported, create case composites, and/or present excerpts of verbatim process. Alfonso argued that clinician writers should make use of all of these tools freely and creatively.

Individual theoretical positions

Judy Kantrowitz's (2006) comprehensive text, *Writing about Patients*, is the culmination of an extremely impressive research project. Inspired by Glen Gabbard's (2000) seminal article discussed earlier, Kantrowitz had the excellent idea to systematically survey the attitudes of analysts toward vexing questions of principle and practicality faced by anyone wishing to do clinical writing. Kantrowitz's study was comprehensive and extended, and I am highlighting only a few sample findings here and refer the reader to her work for much greater study.

Her data set comprised responses from 141 analysts who had published clinical material in the *Journal of the American Psychoanalytic Association (JAPA)*; the *International Journal of Psychoanalysis*; analytic journals in Canada, Argentina, and Brazil; and *Psychoanalytic Dialogues*. Authors in *JAPA* who had published between 1977 and 1981 and between 1995 and 2000 were interviewed, as were international analysts who had published between 1977 and 1981 and between 1995 and 2001. Utilizing a split-sample design enabled Kantrowitz to monitor shifts in attitudes over two decades in the two samples. Authors in *Psychoanalytic Dialogues*, a journal of relational perspectives founded in 1990, were not available from years 1977–1981.

Kantrowitz found that *JAPA* authors were divided between using disguise only and additionally asking for patient consent. The more international group publishing in *International Journal of Psychoanalysis* tended slightly to prefer disguise of patient details alone. Viewing the data longitudinally, Kantrowitz found an increasing trend of analysts varying "their approach depending upon the patient and/or the analytic situation" and to ask patient permission before publishing (p. 62).

Most of the analysts in the sample identifying as relational, ostensibly seeing themselves as co-creators with their patients of the analytic process, routinely requested consent, believing the request to promote a collaborative atmosphere. Some analysts also indicated that the request for consent, and patients' subsequent reading of written material about themselves, brought focus to central issues related to patients' conflicts and character. In their view, seeking consent promotes the analytic process.

Kantrowitz's very carefully researched findings yield a collection of opinions, tentative conclusions, conflicting results, and unresolved questions. Analysts, once convinced of collaborating with a patient in presenting a case, sometimes demonstrated a change of heart. Others, who were equally sure that one should never tell a patient about either a proposal or a finished product, were later transformed into partners in writing with their patients. Many of the analysts interviewed by Kantrowitz, irrespective of theoretical view, were equally convinced of the correctness of their position. Among the most radical critics of a conventional approach to patient confidentiality is Peter Rudnytzky (2007), as he brought to light the uncomfortable irony of the psychoanalytic writer. Traditionally, analysts were free to decide whether to ask a patient's consent before using clinical material in a suitably disguised form, or whether disguise alone constituted an adequate safeguard of the patient's welfare. Whereas psychoanalysts have traditionally prided themselves on respect for the dignity of the individual, by making informed consent optional rather than mandatory analysts arguably show less respect for patients and their rights than is the norm for all other health-care professionals and medical researchers.

Rudnytzky (2007) suggested that clinicians are not likely to notify patients before initiating treatment, that they may write about the patient without the patient's knowledge or consent. He argued that the decision not to ask permission is made not for the patient's benefit but rather to keep power and control in the hands of the clinician. Rudnytzky addressed Kantrowitz's (2006) concern that limiting the publication of case studies to those authorized by patients will skew the data forming the body of psychoanalytic knowledge. This is a legitimate concern, he acknowledged, but it assumes that the current practice does not produce any distortions, and he is not so certain that the consequences will be as disastrous as Kantrowitz believes. On the other side, he argued, if we do require informed consent, then readers may "be confident that our literature will exemplify the respect for otherness and intersubjective attunement that are the hallmarks of the best analytic work" (pp. 1410–1411).

Psychotherapy roundtable

In 2012, the journal *Psychotherapy* published a special section dedicated to ethical issues in clinical writing. The collection features a lead article by Barbara Sieck (2012) that examined the issue, along with several discussants and commentators. Important to note, the journal is broadly intended for a general psychotherapy audience, not just for analysts. In striking contrast to Rudnytzky, Sieck's conclusions are conservative: She emphasizes the dangers of asking for permission over the advantages. I examine her overview and the commentators' responses, emphasizing reasons for the lack of consensus.

Sieck (2012) argued that if a clinician believes that a client will react poorly to the request for informed consent, or if the clinician does not have enough evidence to reasonably predict the client's response, he or she should consider an alternative to clinical writing. One might wonder, however, in considering this argument, whether we ever have enough evidence to predict the patient's response to such a request. Sieck noted that case studies can take many forms, including a presentation at a conference, a textbook chapter, or an anecdote in a popular magazine article. Clinicians should consider whether a patient's discovering the therapist's writing is likely, or whether it exists on a more theoretical level. How probable is it that a client will come across his or her own case study and recognize him- or herself in the process? If such a scenario is unlikely, then it may be more dangerous to engage in obtaining informed consent because of the negative impact such a request can have on the therapeutic alliance. The clinician should also take into account whether the written piece is in-depth (such as a comprehensive case study that goes into session-by-session detail) or a briefer client description.

I find myself uncomfortable with Sieck's conclusions. If one is trying to predict whether the patient is likely to come across a publication, does that not lend itself to the sense that the therapist is doing something sneaky? Behind the patient's back, so to speak? Are not psychotherapy and psychoanalysis based on greater principles of honesty and transparency?

Blechner (2012) took the most radical stand among Sieck's discussants. As former editor-in-chief of the journal *Contemporary Psychoanalysis*, he has a wealth of experience in negotiating patient confidentiality issues with prospective authors. Along with Richard Gottlieb (from the *Journal of the American Psychoanalytic Association*), he has also led a discussion group at the annual meeting of the American Psychoanalytic Association entitled, "Writing for Psychoanalytic Journals." Blechner, consistent with the 1995 policy of the ICMJE, is strongly against disguising client material by changing facts. In his view, the alteration of details in a clinical paper is equivalent to a scientific researcher publishing false data. The basic principle, according to Blechner, is that it is far better to omit than to falsify a detail. "The bottom line is this: If you want to disguise a patient, do so by eliminating identifying information, but not by putting in false details. Even if you think these false details do not change the basic thrust of the case, you cannot know that" (p. 17).

Per Blechner, patients should be asked in all instances for permission to have their clinical material published. Even if no one could recognize the patient as described, there is the basic question of who owns the rights to the patient's story. In Blechner's view, the story is the property of the patient. Blechner acknowledged that his is a minority position, but he is firmly against disguise and composites or any change in the facts of the case. Blechner (2012) offered the following commonsense guideline:

> If you want to publish clinical material, get your patient's consent. If the patient wants to read it, let him or her. If you think it will be damaging to the patient, or if you do not feel comfortable with asking for consent and letting your patient read your clinical description, do not publish it.
>
> (p. 17)

Constance Fischer (2012), in her discussion of Sieck, made the point that the term "clinical writing" and all of these considerations also apply to non-written presentations. These can include material shared at conferences, in workshops, classrooms, grand rounds, and professional consultations. She also raised the question of charging a patient for time spent discussing the presentation of their case.

It should be noted that in sharp contrast to Blechner's position—that no details of the case should be misrepresented—is the sharp alternative of writing fictional cases. Some therapists, made anxious by the thought of asking patients for consent, or simply concerned about the complexities of confidentiality, may choose to write what amounts to clinically inspired fiction. They may take as inspiration something that happened with a patient, or with several patients, and write a fictional case that they believe is "true" to the spirit of their clinical experience. The line between writing a "composite" and writing "fiction" can be a thin one. Of course, as I previously discussed (Aron, 2000), this practice makes it very difficult to claim that our case history literature is to be considered as "scientific data."

Other extreme positions

I have described positions such as Rudnytzky's and Blechner's as "radical" in strongly moving away from the old, accepted consensus that the analyst had the authority to publish case material, autonomously deciding what constituted adequate disguise, without asking for permission. Whatever the differences among the radical critics, they all emphasize patients' rights and patients' ownership of their case narrative. Contrast these radical positions with the following opinions, which I describe as "conservative," "ultraconservative," or "reactionary."

Ronald Pies (2007) argued that the physician's narrative—whether a case study, an essay, or a poem—is the intellectual or artistic work product of the physician. In his view, so long as adequate measures are taken to disguise the identity of the patient, the physician has no obligation to obtain the patient's permission to publish case material. Indeed, any putative "right" of the patient to approve or edit such material creates potential barriers to the unfettered transmission of medical knowledge. Pies, relying on other psychiatric authorities, opined that it may actually be unethical to ask patients for permission to publish, especially if they are still in treatment, and even for many who have already terminated. His rationale is that it crosses a professional boundary by inserting the doctor's professional agenda into the treatment and may disturb or destabilize some patients.

Another conservative voice is that of Levin (2003), who referred to obtaining informed consent as an ethical-bureaucratic device. He argued that analysts have a conflict of interest between their own desire to present and publish and the obligation to protect the treatment. Why does the patient think that the analyst is asking for permission? To protect himself, or because he feels guilty or afraid of the patient? How long does one analyze before making the decision to publish? And who pays for this time? Does the analyst give the patient the right to censor or change the presentation? Is there bargaining involved? If the patient refuses, does the patient feel guilty, and to what degree can the analyst analyze this guilt when he or she may be resentful about the patient's refusal? Levin saw advantages in obtaining general permission before the analysis begins. I consider: Would not the analyst still have to show a draft to the patient before presenting or publishing the case? Would a blanket consent actually solve the problem of eventually having the patient read what is being presented or published? Perhaps it lays some groundwork and makes the later and more detailed request a more reasonable or foreseen possibility. Levin cautioned that we need to be careful not to involve the patient in the process of deciding what should be reported. Levin thinks that some analysts can ask for informed consent because they are remarkably open and self-confident or because their style is to maintain a very high degree of emotional interactive enmeshment with the patient.

Levin believes that writing case histories is a legitimate professional use of experience and that professionals are too guilty about the slightest break, betrayal, or violation, resulting in a demonization of case writing. Levin distinguished writing for members of the profession versus literary self-promotion for the public, but what does the distinction mean in the current technological climate? Levin suggested that patients must look hard to find themselves in the analyst's publications. But how hard is it to seek out one's therapist with search engines like Google? Levin viewed the underlying issue of patient confidentiality in terms of the analyst having a separate life and existence apart from the patient. He concluded that anonymous disclosures of clinical material in supervision, teaching, or scientific presentations are not breaches of confidentiality at all.

Finally, also along conservative lines, in a plea for the continued usefulness of clinical case narratives in psychiatry, Montross (2015) argued,

> There are those who would argue that any physician who writes about a patient encounter violates the patient's privacy, even when identifying details are obfuscated or eliminated. Those who hold this perspective often insist that the case history belongs to the patient and hence may only be told by her or his own choosing.
>
> (p. 5)

But Montross argued that "asking 'whose story is it?' creates a false dichotomy—medical narrative can include both the first-person story of a person's illness and the story observed by the person who tries to cure it or alleviate the suffering it causes" (p. 9). An unthinking involvement in the consumer rights movement, evidence-based medicine, and standardized quantifiable medical procedures have led to the unfortunate decline of case history writing, and Montross passionately pleads for clinicians to continue the tradition of clinical writing. Of course, Montross did not take up the possibility that one might be able to both maintain clinical case writing and seek patients' informed consent.

Toward a conclusion

I hope that my very selective review of the literature, especially the various opinions expressed in the past two decades, demonstrates that our field has not reached a consensus as to the ethics of obtaining informed consent from patients when one writes about them, either while they are still in treatment or after they finish. There are opinions on all sides of this issue, from the most conservative or reactionary—we own our stories and we are the experts who have an obligation to publish with appropriate disguise—to the most radical—the patient owns his or her story, patients should read what the therapist is saying or publishing and give explicit written permission before the therapist proceeds, and no facts should be changed because that would constitute scientific fraud. Frankly, I cannot think of any professional issue in our field that is as split and contentious as this controversy.

The management of confidentiality and informed consent and the handling of our patients' personal information are of particular, perhaps unique, importance because it is relevant to all case presentations, oral and written, public and professional, scholarly and educational. Thus, ethical dilemmas and how to deal with them affect everyone from a new student or candidate presenting a case to a supervisor, class, or small supervision group, to the most senior analyst's presentation at a national conference or publication in a professional journal. Although different considerations apply in each case, in all of these situations the presenter/therapist has a responsibility to think through the most ethical and clinically responsible way to proceed.

Editorial guidelines

As editors of the *International Journal of Psychoanalysis*, Glen Gabbard and David Tuckett attempted to establish recommendations that address both the ethical need to protect patients and with the scientific need to maintain the integrity of clinical reporting (Gabbard, 2000; Tuckett, 2000). They are to be credited with encouraging the field of psychoanalysis to move in the direction of a more systematic and thoughtful consideration of this publishing dilemma. Their guidelines include a sizable range of factors to keep in mind when making decisions about writing. They manage to avoid the extreme positions taken by others and articulate a balanced view, at some cost to clarity and certainty.

I am in complete agreement with their proposal that decisions should be individually crafted by the writer based on the unique clinical considerations of the particular patient being discussed. Nevertheless, in the more than 15 years since their recommendations were made there have been several changes, including easier and more available access to professional publications. Psychoanalysts and their patients can now log on to the worldwide range of psychoanalytic journals and even local newsletters that were once hard to find. In the past 15 years the Internet has developed significantly, and it is now routine and expectable that patients, and their friends and families, can easily Google a therapist's name to find out about his or her recent presentations anywhere in the world, let alone publications.

The content of such clinical presentations may end up online even if only summarized in the form of a blog. Indeed, not only professional communication but also our very notion of privacy has been altered in the last 15 years. In conjunction with these changes, the past decades have also been a time when consumer and patients' rights have become more vigorously protected, and patients are much less willing than previously to hand over to their doctors the authority to make independent decisions about their medical records. Not only throughout medicine, but also in other related disciplines such as education, psychology, and law, clients have become accustomed to a much greater sense of collaboration and participation in decision-making. It behooves us as professionals to revisit our guidelines in light of these ongoing changes in the culture.

The guidelines not only need to be considered for publication in print journals but also should be held in mind when preparing presentations for live workshops, colloquia, conferences, and even class use or presentation to small supervision groups. Patients can be, and indeed have been, recognized and exposed in all of these forums. Certainly it matters if one is presenting to a small private group versus to a large audience, and it does seem to matter whether presenting to licensed mental health professionals who understand the sensitive nature of confidentiality as opposed to writing for or presenting to the public. Nevertheless, licensed mental health professionals are not bound to maintain privacy over material that has been presented in a public forum, and it also seems unreasonable to assume that a large auditorium of mental health providers can be told about an identifiable patient and hold it within their professional confidence.

It appears reasonable to weigh into one's decision-making the purposes of the presentation or publication. The use of patient material in a magazine article written for the public for the purposes of education may be different from the criteria used when the purpose is for entertainment. Discussing a patient's progress for the purposes of supervision or consultation may push for a different guideline of stringency than sharing a case presentation with a class for educational purposes, and that may yet be different than using the material to illustrate a particular methodology to a large audience. There are no clear criteria or guidelines available for these situations, but these factors should be weighed in making a decision.

Training and education

What is to be made of the polar division in professional guidelines regarding the practical and important matter of writing about patients? My conclusion is that this "split" in the field is due to rapid changes in the profession and in society at large. Psychoanalysis has lost much of its revered status, and the demographics of the profession have changed over several decades, notably with a dramatic shift in the profession from medical to nonmedical and from male to female analysts. External and internal pressures have encouraged the shift from a very personal, ideographic, case-by-case model to one that insists on quantifiable, empirically supported, evidence-based, and standardized procedures. Society has been changed by the consumer and patients' rights movement, and the Internet has radically redefined the nature of what is private and what is public. It seems to me that the splitting among experts results from our being caught in changes that we have not yet been able to catch up with, process, or metabolize.

Under these circumstances I do not advocate siding with either extreme position. Indeed, the radical critics make the valuable points that we cannot disregard patients' rights to their life stories and that asking for consent may sometimes be extremely valuable to the treatment. The conservative position makes the point that one may not be able to predict when asking for permission will be useful or disruptive. Indeed, in reading the accounts of the radical position, I found myself wondering if these therapists ever had a very bad reaction from a patient and how that affected their thinking. But in reading the conservative writers, I found myself wondering if they were oblivious to how frequently patients do in fact read what their therapist is publishing, or if they had personally struggled with the pained and even traumatized reactions of some of these patients.

My main conclusion, therefore, is not to adopt one side or other, but rather that the ethical dilemma of writing about patients, and all of its considerations, should be discussed from the very beginning of professional education and throughout. We do not yet have stable and consistent answers to give our students—and perhaps that is one of the main reasons we avoid the topic! But if students don't discuss, consent, and how to manage these tensions from the beginning of their training, then they will not know how to handle them clinically or ethically when they are later out practicing, presenting, and writing. Clinical instructors and institutes should be discussing questions of ethics, and clinical concerns related to the use of clinical material, when students present cases from the start in classes, at colloquia, clinical seminars, and so forth. Discussion among colleagues and with students will immediately bring to light the wide swath of variations and relevant considerations. What is the nature of the media—oral or written? To whom is it being presented? A public or professional audience? How large a group? For what purpose? Is it a comprehensive and detailed case history or a brief vignette? That we do not have consistent answers does not justify the neglect of addressing the dilemma. Students will learn about relevant dimensions and make the most thoughtful and ethical decisions that they can under the circumstances.

Legal considerations

I would strongly suggest that presenters of case material know the laws governing privacy and confidentiality in their state or location. I have checked with a variety of mental health legal experts in New York State, including lawyers representing insurance companies and lawyers who have sat in on ethics hearings within the state. The lawyers have each indicated that the law is unclear, and they largely formulate their opinions based on their relevant experience. I have been told that they have never seen cases in New York where anyone has been held responsible for violating confidentiality if the patient was disguised sufficiently such that only the patient could recognize him- or herself. In other words, one is not at risk utilizing clinical material even if the patient can recognize him- or herself so long as no one else can recognize them. I add that this is not a foolproof guideline. After all, what if a patient had published a memoir in which they revealed their dreams and the analyst then used these dreams in their own case history thus giving away the identity of the patient? Stranger things have indeed happened. What if the patient had told friends that he or she was in analysis with this analyst, thus making it much easier for acquaintances to identify them in the clinician's material? There simply are no answers that solve all of the difficulties. Nevertheless, it should be stated that the legal experts with whom I have consulted advised me to not involve the patient in my professional life, to not get involved in a complicated dual relationship, but rather to disguise the material carefully and keep the patient at a distance from my professional use of the clinical material. I have to admit that although my own leanings are somewhat to the more radical side of these debates (that is, I lean toward always obtaining informed consent), hearing these cautions from my lawyers has kept me more restrained and conservative than I would otherwise be. This is a case where ethics and legal wisdom may conflict, apart from the clinical interests of the patient. Still, all of this could change with the next lawsuit!

Conclusion

I have raised questions that cross over among ethical, legal, clinical, professional, and educational concerns. It is readily apparent that at this stage of our profession's history we do not have a single unified position or anything like a consensus, and expert opinions range from ultraconservative to radical. Furthermore, each situation, and each patient-therapist dyad, is unique, requiring the application of general principles to distinctive situations. The purpose of this chapter is not to provide an answer or even to give my own opinion so much as to call for ongoing discussion, debate, and thoughtful deliberation both among colleagues, and especially with our students, where it is too often avoided altogether. It is probably wise to think that all presentations and publications of clinical material represent some form of enactment of unconscious dynamics; enactments, after all, are often played out through our technical interventions and through management of the therapeutic frame, and therefore it is advisable to give careful thought and to seek consultation on all cases one considers presenting, both at early and later stages of the writing and publications process. Most important, I am calling for these issues, positions, and debates to be made part of our curriculum and clinical education throughout all phases of psychoanalytic education.

Acknowledgments

I thank Benjamin A. Rubin, PsyD, for his skillful help in editing and revising this chapter

Notes

1 The reader should consult my earlier article (Aron, 2000) for an examination of these fundamental questions.
2 This is an excellent illustration of Freud's early concept of *nachträglichkeit*, often translated as "afterwardness" or "deferred action," where earlier memories are reworked in accordance with later experiences and circumstances. See Laplanche and Pontalis (1973).

References

Aguayo, J., & Malin, B. (2013). *Wilfred Bion: Los Angeles seminars and supervision*. London: Karnac.

Alexander, F., & French, T. M. (1946). *Psychoanalytic therapy, principles and application*. New York: Ronald Press.

Alfonso, C. A. (2002). Frontline: Writing psychoanalytic case reports: Safeguarding privacy while preserving integrity. *Journal of the American Academy of Psychoanalysis, 30*(2), 165–171.

Allport, G. W. (1943). The productive paradoxes of William James. *Psychological Review, 50*, 95–120.

Altman, N. (1995). *The analyst in the inner city: Race, class, and culture through a psychoanalytic lens*. Hillsdale, NJ: The Analytic Press.

Anzieu, D. (1985). *The skin ego*. New Haven, CT: Yale University Press.

Arlow, J. A. (1980). The genesis of interpretation. In H. P. Blum (Ed.), *Psychoanalytic explorations of technique: Discourse on the theory of therapy* (pp. 193–206). New York: International Universities Press.

Arlow, J. A. (1986). Discussion of transference and countertransference with the difficult patient. In H. C. Myers (Ed.), *Between analyst and patient: New dimensions in countertransference and transference* (pp. 75–86). Hillsdale, NJ: The Analytic Press.

Arlow, J. A. (1987). The dynamics of interpretation. *The Psychoanalytic Quarterly, 56*, 68–87.

Arlow, J. A. (1991). *Psychoanalysis: Clinical theory and practice*. Madison, CT: International Universities Press.

Arlow, J. A., & Brenner, C. (1964). *Psychoanalytic concepts and the structural theory*. New York: International Universities Press.

Aron, L. (1989). Dreams, narrative and the psychoanalytic method. *Contemporary Psychoanalysis, 25*, 108–126.

Aron, L. (1990a). One-person and two-person psychologies and the method of psychoanalysis. *Psychoanalytic Psychology, 7*, 475–485.

Aron, L. (1990b). Free association and changing models of mind. *Journal of the American Academy of Psychoanalysis, 18*, 439–459.

Aron, L. (1991a). Working through the past—Working toward the future. *Contemporary Psychoanalysis, 27*, 81–109.

Aron, L. (1991b). The patient's experience of the analyst's subjectivity. *Psychoanalytic Dialogues, 1*, 29–51.

Aron, L. (1992a). From Ferenczi to Searles and contemporary relational approaches. *Psychoanalytic Dialogues, 2*, 181–190.

Aron, L. (1992b). Interpretation as expression of the analyst's subjectivity. *Psychoanalytic Dialogues, 2*, 475–507.

Aron, L. (1993). Working toward operational thought: Piagetian theory and psychoanalytic method. *Contemporary Psychoanalysis, 29*, 289–313.

Aron, L. (1995). The internalized primal scene. *Psychoanalytic Dialogues, 5*, 195–237.

Aron, L. (1996a). From hypnotic suggestion to free association: Freud as a psychotherapist, circa 1892–1893. *Contemporary Psychoanalysis, 32*, 99.

Aron, L. (1996b). Symposium on the meaning and practice of intersubjectivity in psychoanalysis: Introduction. *Psychoanalytic Dialogues, 6*, 591–597.

Aron, L. (1996c). *A meeting of minds: Mutuality in psychoanalysis*. Hillsdale, NJ: The Analytic Press.

Aron, L. (1998a). Clinical choices and the theory of psychoanalytic technique: Commentary on papers by Mitchell and by Davies. *Psychoanalytic Dialogues, 8*, 207–216.

Aron, L. (1998b). The clinical body and the reflexive mind. In L. Aron & F. S. Anderson (Eds.), *Relational perspectives on the body* (pp. 3–38). Hillsdale, NJ: The Analytic Press.

Aron, L. (2000). Ethical considerations in the writing of psychoanalytic case histories. *Psychoanalytic Dialogues, 10*, 231–245.

Aron, L. (2003). Clinical outbursts and theoretical breakthroughs: A unifying theme in the work of Stephen A. Mitchell. *Psychoanalytic Dialogues, 13*(2), 259–273.

Aron, L. (2004). God's influence on my psychoanalytic vision and values. *Psychoanalytic Psychology, 21*, 442–451.

Aron, L. (2006). Analytic impasse and the third: Clinical implications of intersubjectivity theory. *International Journal of Psychoanalysis, 87*, 349–368.

Aron, L. (2013). The transference is indeed a cross: Commentary on paper by Sue Grand. *Psychoanalytic Dialogues, 23*, 464–474.

Aron, L. (2016). Mutual vulnerability: An ethic of clinical practice. In D. M. Goodman & E. R. Severson (Eds.), *The ethical turn* (pp. 19–40). London: Routledge.

Aron, L. (2017). Beyond tolerance in psychoanalytic communities: Reflective skepticism and clinical pluralism. *Psychoanalytic Perspectives, 14*(3), 271–282.

Aron, L., & Anderson, F. S. (1998). *Relational perspectives on the body.* Hillsdale, NJ: The Analytic Press.

Aron, L., & Benjamin, J. (1999a). The development of intersubjectivity and the struggle to think. Paper presented at the spring meeting of Division 39 (Psychoanalysis) of the American Psychological Association, New York, NY.

Aron, L., & Benjamin, J. (1999b). Intersubjective processes (recognition and identification) in the therapeutic action of psychoanalysis. Paper presented at the Spring Meeting of Division 39 of the American Psychological Association, New York, NY.

Aron, L., & Harris, A. (1993). *The legacy of Sandor Ferenczi.* Hillsdale, NJ: The Analytic Press.

Aron, L., & Starr, K. (2012). *A psychotherapy for the people: Toward a progressive psychoanalysis.* New York: Routledge.

Atlas, G. (2015). *The enigma of desire.* London: Routledge.

Atlas-Koch, G. (2008). Three pregnancies and psychoanalysis. *Psychoanalytic Review, 95*, 259–283.

Atwood, G. E., Stolorow, R. D., & Trop, J. L. (1989). Impasses in psychoanalytic therapy: A royal road. *Contemporary Psychoanalysis, 25*, 554–573.

Auerbach, J. S. (1993). The origins of narcissism and narcissistic personality disorder: A theoretical and empirical reformulation. In J. M. Masling & R. F. Bernstein (Eds.), *Empirical studies of psychoanalytic theories: Psychoanalytic perspectives on psychopathology* (Vol. 4, pp. 43–108). Washington, DC: American Psychological Association.

Auerbach, J. S., & Blatt, S. J. (1996). Self-representation in severe psychopathology. *Psychoanalytic Psychology, 13*, 297–341.

Bach, S. (1985). *Narcissistic states and the therapeutic process.* New York: Jason Aronson.

Bach, S. (1994). *The language of perversion and the language of love.* Northvale, NJ: Jason Aronson.

Bach, S. (2016). *Chimeras and other writings.* Astoria, NY: International Psychoanalytic Books.

Bakan, D. (1958). *Sigmund Freud and the Jewish mystical tradition.* Princeton, NJ: Van Nostrand.

Balbus, I. D. (1982). *Marxism and domination: A neo-Hegelian, feminist, psychoanalytic theory of sexual, political, and technological liberation.* Princeton, NJ: Princeton University Press.

Balint, M. (1968). *The basic fault.* London: Tavistock.

Balsam, R. H. (2013). (Re)membering the female body in psychoanalysis: Childbirth. *Journal of the American Psychoanalytic Association, 61,* 447–470.

Baranger, M., & Baranger, W. (1966). Insight in the analytic situation. In R. E. Litman (Ed.), *Psychoanalysis in the Americas* (pp. 56–72). New York: International Universities Press.

Baranger, M., Baranger, W., & Mom, J. (1983). Process and non-process in analytic work. *International Journal of Psychoanalysis, 64,* 1–15.

Basescu, S. (1987). Behind the "seens": The inner experience of at least one psychoanalyst. *Psychoanalytic Psychology, 4,* 255–265.

Bearison, D. J. (1974). The construct of regression: A Piagetian approach. *The Merrill-Palmer Quarterly, 20,* 221–229.

Beebe, B., & Lachmann, F. M. (1988a). The contribution of mother-infant mutual influence to the origins of self- and object representations. *Psychoanalytic Psychology, 5,* 305–337.

Beebe, B., & Lachmann, F. M. (1988b). Mother-infant mutual influence and precursors of psychic structure. In A. Goldberg (Ed.), *Frontiers in self-psychology: Progress in self-psychology* (Vol. 3, pp. 3–25). Hillsdale, NJ: The Analytic Press.

Beebe, B., & Lachmann, F. M. (1998). Co-constructing inner and relational processes. *Psychoanalytic Psychology, 15,* 480–516.

Beebe, B., & Lachmann, F. M. (2002). *Infant research and adult treatment.* Hillsdale, NJ: The Analytic Press.

Beebe, B., Lachmann, F. M., Markese, S., Buck, K. A., Bahrick, L. E., Chen, H., Cohen, P., Andrews, H., Feldstein, S., & Jaffe, J. (2012). On the origins of disorganized attachment and internal working models: paper II. An empirical microanalysis of 4-month mother-infant interaction. *Psychoanalytic Dialogues, 22,* 352–374.

Bem, S. L. (1993). *The lenses of gender.* New Haven, CT: Yale University Press.

Benjamin, J. (1988). *The bonds of love: Psychoanalysis, feminism, and the problem of domination.* New York: Pantheon Books.

Benjamin, J. (1991). Father and daughter: Identification with difference—A contribution to gender heterodoxy. *Psychoanalytic Dialogues, 1,* 277–301.

Benjamin, J. (1992). Discussion of Judith V. Jordan's "The relational self: A new perspective for understanding women's development." *Contemporary Psychotherapy Review, 7,* 82–96.

Benjamin, J. (1995). *Like subjects, love objects.* New Haven, CT: Yale University Press.

Benjamin, J. (1995). Sameness and difference: Toward an "overinclusive" model of gender development. *Psychoanalytic Inquiry, 15*(1), 125–142.
Benjamin, J. (1998). *Shadow of the other.* New York: Routledge.
Benjamin, J. (1999a). A note on the dialectic. *Psychoanalytic Dialogues, 9,* 395–399.
Benjamin, J. (1999b). Afterword. In S. Mitchell & L. Aron (Eds.), *Relational psychoanalysis* (pp. 201–210). Hillsdale, NJ: The Analytic Press.
Benjamin, J. (2004). Beyond doer and done-to. *Psychoanalytic Quarterly, 73*(1), 5–46.
Benjamin, J. (2011). Beyond doer and done to: An intersubjective view of thirdness, with afterword. In L. Aron & A. Harris (Eds.), *Relational psychoanalysis* (Vol. 4, pp. 91–130). New York: Routledge.
Benjamin, J. (2018). *Beyond Doer and Done To.* London, UK & New York, NY: Routledge.
Bergmann, M. S. (1997). The historical roots of psychoanalytic orthodoxy. *International Journal of Psychoanalysis, 78,* 69–86.
Bergmann, M. S., & Hartman, F. R. (Eds.) (1976). *The evolution of psychoanalytic technique.* New York: Basic Books.
Berman, E. (1996). Psychoanalytic supervision as the crossroads of a relational matrix. In M. H. Rock (Ed.), *Psychodynamic supervision* (pp. 159–186). Northvale, NJ: Jason Aronson.
Bion, M. (1980). *Bion in New York and São Paulo.* Perthshire, Scotland: Clunie Press.
Bion, W. R. (1962a). *Learning from experience.* London: Tavistock.
Bion, W. R. (1962b). A theory of thinking. *International Journal of Psychoanalysis, 43,* 306–310.
Bion, W. R. (1967). *Second thoughts.* London: Heinemann.
Bion, W. R. (1970). *Attention and interpretation.* London: Heinemann.
Bion, W. R. (1977). Caesura. In F. Bion & M. Patterson (Eds.), *Two papers: "The grid" and "Caesura"* (pp. 35–59). London: Karnac, 1989.
Bird, B. (1972). Notes on transference: Universal phenomena and the hardest part of analysis. *Journal of the American Psychoanalytic Association, 20,* 267–301.
Blazy, H. (2012). Thinking the unthought. *Journal of Prenatal and Perinatal Psychology and Health, 26,* 249–258.
Blechner, M. J. (2012). Commentary. Confidentiality: Against disguise, for consent. *Psychotherapy, 49,* 16–18.
Bloom, H. (1987). *Kafka, Freud, Scholem: Three essays.* Boston: Beacon Press.
Blum, H. P. (1979). On the concept and consequences of the primal scene. *Psychoanalytic Quarterly, 48,* 27–47.

Bollas, C. (1987). *The shadow of the object: Psychoanalysis of the unthought known*. London: Free Association Books.

Bollas, C. (1989). *Forces of destiny: Psychoanalysis and human idiom*. London: Free Association Books.

Bollas, C. (2011). *The Christopher Bollas reader*. London: Routledge.

Bonime, W. (1962). *The clinical use of dreams*. New York: Basic Books.

Bonovitz, C. (2009). Looking back, looking forward: A reexamination of Benjamin Wolstein's interlock and the emergence of intersubjectivity. *International Journal of Psychoanalysis, 90*, 463–485.

Boyarin, D. (1997). *Unheroic conduct: The rise of heterosexuality and the invention of the Jewish man*. Berkeley: University of California Press.

Brenman Pick, I. (1985). Working through in the counter-transference. *International Journal of Psychoanalysis, 66*, 157–166.

Brenneis, C. B. (1975). Theoretical notes on the manifest dream. *International Journal of Psychoanalysis, 56*, 97–206.

Brenner, C. (1976). *Psychoanalytic technique and psychic conflict*. New York: International Universities Press.

Brickman, C. (2003). *Aboriginal populations in the mind*. New York, NY: Columbia University Press.

Bridges, N. A. (2007). Clinical writing about patients: Negotiating the impact on patients and their treatment. *Psychoanalytic Social Work, 14*, 23–41.

Britton, R. (1989). The missing link: Parental sexuality in the Oedipus complex. In J. Steiner (Ed.), *The Oedipus complex today: Clinical implications* (pp. 83–102). London: Karnac.

Bromberg, P. M. (1985). The politics of analytic treatment. *Contemporary Psychoanalysis, 30*, 893–894.

Bromberg, P. M. (1989). Interpersonal psychoanalysis and self-psychology: A clinical comparison. In D. W. Detrick & S. P. Detrick (Eds.), *Self psychology: Comparisons and contrasts* (pp. 275–291). Hillsdale, NJ: The Analytic Press.

Bromberg, P. M. (1991). On knowing one's patient inside out: The aesthetics of unconscious communication. *Psychoanalytic Dialogues, 1*, 399–422.

Bromberg, P. M. (1994). "Speak! That I may see you": Some reflections on dissociation, reality, and psychoanalytic listening. *Psychoanalytic Dialogues, 4*, 517–547.

Bromberg, P. M. (1996). Standing in the spaces: The multiplicity of self and the psychoanalytic relationship. *Contemporary Psychoanalysis, 32*, 509–535.

Bromberg, P. M. (1998). *Standing in the spaces*. Hillsdale, NJ: The Analytic Press.

Bruner, J. (1986). *Actual minds, Possible worlds*. Cambridge, MA: Harvard University Press.

Buber, M. (1957). *Eclipse of God: Studies in the relation between religion and philosophy.* New York: Harper Books.
Buber, M. (1970). *I and thou* (W. Kaufman, Trans.). New York: Charles Scribner's Sons (Original work published 1923).
Burke, W. F. (1992). Countertransference disclosure and the asymmetry/mutuality dilemma. *Psychoanalytic Dialogues, 2,* 241–271.
Busch, F. (2006). A shadow concept. *International Journal of Psychoanalysis, 87,* 1471–1485.
Butler, J. (1990). *Gender trouble.* New York: Routledge.
Butler, J. (2004a). *Precarious life.* London: Verso.
Butler, J. (2004b). *Undoing gender.* New York: Routledge.
Casement, P. J. (1982). Some pressures on the analyst for physical contact during the re-living of an early trauma. *International Review of Psychoanalysis, 9,* 279–286.
Chasseguet-Smirgel, J. (1984). The femininity of the psychoanalyst in professional practice. *International Journal of Psychoanalysis, 65,* 169–178.
Chasseguet-Smirgel, J. (1991). Book review: The Oedipus complex today: Clinical implications. *International Journal of Psychoanalysis, 72,* 727–730.
Chodorow, N. J. (1978). *The reproduction of mothering: Psychoanalysis and the sociology of gender.* Berkeley: University of California Press.
Chodorow, N. J. (1989). *Feminism and psychoanalytic theory.* New Haven, CT: Yale University Press.
Chrzanowski, G. (1980). Collaborative inquiry, affirmation and neutrality in the psychoanalytic situation. *Contemporary Psychoanalysis, 16,* 348–366.
Cixous, H. (2004). *Portrait of Jacques Derrida as a young Jewish saint.* New York: Columbia University Press.
Coates, S. W. (1998). Having a mind of one's own and holding the other in mind: Commentary on paper by Peter Fonagy and Mary Target. *Psychoanalytic Dialogues, 8,* 115–148.
Cooper, A. M. (2008). American psychoanalysis today: A plurality of orthodoxies. *The Journal of the American Academy of Psychoanalysis and Dynamic Psychiatry, 36,* 235–253.
Corbett, K. (2001). Nontraditional family romance. *Psychoanalytic Quarterly, 70,* 599–624.
Crastnopol, M. (1999). The analyst's professional self as a "third" influence on the dyad: When the analyst writes about the treatment. *Psychoanalytic Dialogues, 9,* 445–470.
Cushman, P. (1995). *Constructing the self, constructing America.* Reading, MA: Addison-Wesley.
Damon, W., & Hart, D. (1988). *Self-understanding in childhood and adolescence.* Cambridge, England: Cambridge University Press.

Davies, J. M. (1996). Linking the "pre-analytic" with the postclassical: Integration, dissociation, and the multiplicity of unconscious process. *Contemporary Psychoanalysis, 32*, 553–576.

Davies, J. M. (2010). Transformations of desire and despair. In J. Salberg (Ed.), *Good enough endings* (pp. 83–106). New York: Routledge.

Davies, J. M., & Frawley, M. G. (1994). *Treating adult survivors of childhood sexual abuse.* New York: Basic Books.

Davies, J. M. (2004b). Whose Bad Objects Are We Anyway?. *Psychoanalytic. Dialogue.*, 14(6):711–732

Derrida, J. (1976). *Of grammatology* (G. C. Spivak, Trans.). Baltimore: John Hopkins University Press.

Dimen, M. (1991). Deconstructing difference: Gender, splitting, and transitional space. *Psychoanalytic Dialogues, 1*, 335–352.

Dimen, M. (2003). *Sexuality, intimacy, power.* Hillsdale, NJ: The Analytic Press.

Dinnerstein, D. (1976). *The Mermaid and the Minotaur: Sexual arrangements and human malaise.* New York: Harper & Row.

Dupont, J. (Ed.) (1988). *The clinical diary of Sandor Ferenczi.* Cambridge, MA: Harvard University Press.

Ehrenberg, D. B. (1984). Psychoanalytic engagement, II: Affective considerations. *Contemporary Psychoanalysis, 20*, 560–599.

Ehrensaft, D. (2007). *Mommies, daddies, donors, surrogates.* New York: Guilford.

Eigen, M. (1993). *The electrified tightrope.* Northvale, NJ: Jason Aronson.

Eigen, M. (1998). *The psychoanalytic mystic.* Binghamton, NY: ESF Publishers.

Eigen, M. (2014). *The birth of experience.* London: Karnac.

Eissler, K. R. (1953). The effect of the structure of the ego on psychoanalytic technique. *Journal of the American Psychoanalytic Association, 1*, 101–143.

Elkind, D. (1974). *Children and adolescents: Interpretive essays on Jean Piaget.* New York: Oxford University Press.

Erikson, E. (1954). The dream specimen of psychoanalysis. *Journal of the American Psychoanalytic Association, 2*, 5–56.

Eshel, O. (2004). From the "Green Woman" to "Scheherazade." *Contemporary Psychoanalysis, 40*, 527–556.

Esman, A. H. (1973). The primal scene: A review and a reconsideration. *Psychoanalytic Study of the Child, 28*, 49–82.

Etchegoyen, R. H. (1991). *The fundamentals of psychoanalytic technique.* London: Karnac.

Fairbairn, W. R. D. (1952). *An object-relations theory of the personality.* New York: Basic Books.

Fairfield, S. (2008). Analyzing multiplicity: A postmodern perspective on some current psychoanalytic theories of subjectivity. *Psychoanalytic Dialogues, 11*, 221–251.
Fast, I. (1984). *Gender identity*. Hillsdale, NJ: The Analytic Press.
Fast, I. (1990). Aspects of early gender development: Toward a reformulation. *Psychoanalytic Psychology, 7*, 105–117.
Fast, I. (1992). The embodied mind: Toward a relational perspective. *Psychoanalytic Dialogues, 2*, 389–409.
Feffer, M. H. (1967). Symptom expression as a form of primitive decentering. *Psychological Review, 74*, 16–28.
Feffer, M. H. (1970). Developmental analysis of interpersonal behavior. *Psychological Review, 77*, 197–214.
Feldman, M. (1989). The Oedipus complex: Manifestations in the inner world and the therapeutic situation. In J. Steiner (Ed.), *The Oedipus complex today*. London: Karnac.
Fenichel, O. (1941). *Problems of psychoanalytic technique*. Albany, NY: Psychoanalytic Quarterly.
Fenichel, O. (1945). *The psychoanalytic theory of neurosis*. New York: Norton.
Ferenczi, S. (1919). On the tecnique of psychoanalysis. In J. Richman (Ed.) and J. Suttie (Trans.), *Further contributions to the theory and technique of psychoanalysis* (pp. 177–197). London: Karnac Books.
Ferenczi, S. (1929). The unwelcome child and his death-instinct. *International Journal of Psychoanalysis, 10*, 125–129.
Ferenczi, S. (1931), Notes and fragments. In M. Balint (Ed.), *Final contributions to the problems and methods of psychoanalysis* (pp. 216–279). London: Hogarth Press, 1955.
Ferenczi, S. (1932). *The clinical diary of Sándor Ferenczi* (J. Dupont, Ed., M. Balint, & N. Jackson, Trans.). Cambridge, MA: Harvard University Press, 1988.
Ferenczi, S. (1933). Confusion of tongues between adults and the child. In M. Balint (Ed.), *Final contributions to the problems and methods of psychoanalysis* (pp. 156–167). New York: Brunner/Mazel.
Ferenczi, S. (1952a). On the technique of psychoanalysis. In J. Rickman (Ed.), *Further contributions to the theory and technique of psycho-analysis* (pp. 177–189). New York, NY: Basic Books (Original work published 1919).
Ferenczi, S. (1952b). Psychoanalysis of sexual habits. In J. Rickman (Ed.), *Further contributions to the theory and technique of psycho-analysis* (pp. 259–296). New York, NY: Basic Books (Original work published 1925).
Ferenczi, S. (1980a). Psychogenic anomalies of voice production. In J. Rickman (Ed.), *Further contributions to the theory and technique of psycho-analysis* (pp. 140–145). New York: Brunner/Mazel (Original work published 1915).

Ferenczi, S. (1980b). The dream of the clever [wise] baby. In J. Rickman (Ed.), *Further contributions to psycho-analysis* (pp. 349–350). London, UK: Karnac (Original work published 1923).

Fisch, M. (1997). *Rational rabbis: Science and Talmudic culture*. Bloomington, IN: Indiana University Press.

Fisch, M., & Benbaji, Y. (2011). *The view from within: Normativity and the limits of self-criticism*. South Bend, IN: University of Notre Dame Press.

Fischer, C. T. (2012). Commentary. Comments on protecting clients about whom we write (and speak). *Psychotherapy*, *49*, 19–21.

Flavell, J. H. (1963). *The developmental psychology of Jean Piaget*. Princeton, NJ: Van Nostrand.

Flavell, J. H., & Wohlwill, J. (1969). Formal and functional aspects of cognitive development. In D. Elkind & J. Flavell (Eds.), *Studies in cognitive development: Essays in honor of Jean Piaget*. New York: Oxford University Press, 1969.

Flax, J. (1990). *Thinking fragments*. Berkeley: University of California Press.

Fleck, L. (1981). *The genesis and development of a scientific fact* (T. J. Trenn & R. K. Merton, Eds.). Chicago, IL: University of Chicago Press.

Fonagy, P., & Target, M. (1995). Understanding the violent patient: The use of the body and the role of the father. *International Journal of Psychoanalysis*, *76*, 487–501.

Fonagy, P., & Target, M. (1996). Playing with Reality: I. Theory of mind and the normal development of psychic reality. *International Journal of Psychoanalysis*, *77*, 217–233.

Fonagy, P., & Target, M. (1998). Mentalization and the changing aims of child psychoanalysis. *Psychoanalytic Dialogues*, *8*, 87–114.

Fosshage, J. L. (1987). A revised psychoanalytic approach. In J. L. Fosshage & C. A. Loew (Eds.), *Dream interpretation: A comparative study*. New York: P. M. A. Publishing.

Foulkes, D. (1982). *Children's dreams: Longitudinal studies*. New York: John Wiley and Sons.

Foulkes, D. (1985). *Dreaming: A cognitive-psychological analysis*. Mahwah, NJ: Lawrence Erlbaum Associates.

Fox, R. P. (1984). The principle of abstinence reconsidered. *International Review of Psychoanalysis*, *11*, 227–236.

Frankel, J. B. (1993). Collusion and intimacy in the analytic relationship. In L. Aron & A. Harris (Eds.), *The legacy of Sandor Ferenczi* (pp. 227–248). Hillsdale, NJ: The Analytic Press.

Freud, S. (1894). The neuro-psychoses of defense. In J. Strachey (Ed. & Trans.), *The standard edition of the complete psychological works of Sigmund Freud* (Vol. 3, pp. 43–61). London: Hogarth Press.

Freud, S. (1895). Project for a scientific psychology. In J. Strachey (Ed. & Trans.), *The standard edition of the complete psychological works of Sigmund Freud* (Vol. 1, pp. 281–391). London: Hogarth Press.

Freud, S. (1899). Screen memories. In J. Strachey (Ed. & Trans.), *The standard edition of the complete psychological works of Sigmund Freud* (Vol. 3, pp. 301–322). London: Hogarth Press.

Freud, S. (1900). The interpretation of dreams. In J. Strachey (Ed. & Trans.), *The standard edition of the complete psychological works of Sigmund Freud* (Vols. 4–5). London: Hogarth Press.

Freud, S. (1905). On the sexual theories of children. In J. Strachey (Ed. & Trans.), *The standard edition of the complete psychological works of Sigmund Freud* (Vol. 9, pp. 205–226). London: Hogarth Press.

Freud, S. (1910a). The future prospects of psycho-analytic therapy. In J. Strachey (Ed. & Trans.), *The standard edition of the complete psychological works of Sigmund Freud* (Vol. 11, pp. 141–151). London: Hogarth Press.

Freud, S. (1910b). The antithetical sense of primal words. In J. Strachey (Ed. & Trans.), *The standard edition of the complete psychological works of Sigmund Freud* (Vol. 11, pp. 153–161). London: Hogarth Press.

Freud, S. (1912a). Recommendations to physicians practicing psycho-analysis. In J. Strachey (Ed. & Trans.), *The standard edition of the complete psychological works of Sigmund Freud* (Vol. 12, pp. 109–120). London: Hogarth Press.

Freud, S. (1912b). The dynamics of transference. In J. Strachey (Ed. & Trans.), *The standard edition of the complete psychological works of Sigmund Freud* (Vol. 12, pp. 97–107). London: Hogarth Press.

Freud, S. (1914). On narcissism. In J. Strachey (Ed. & Trans.), *The standard edition of the complete psychological works of Sigmund Freud* (Vol. 14, pp. 67–102). London: Hogarth Press.

Freud, S. (1918). From the history of an infantile neurosis. In J. Strachey (Ed. & Trans.), *The standard edition of the complete psychological works of Sigmund Freud* (Vol. 17, pp. 3–123). London: Hogarth Press.

Freud, S. (1920). Beyond the pleasure principle. In J. Strachey (Ed. & Trans.), *The standard edition of the complete psychological works of Sigmund Freud* (Vol. 18, pp. 7–64). London: Hogarth Press.

Freud, S. (1921). Group psychology and the analysis of the ego. In J. Strachey (Ed. & Trans.), *The standard edition of the complete psychological works of Sigmund Freud* (Vol. 18, pp. 65–144). London: Hogarth Press.

Freud, S. (1923). Remarks on the theory and practice of dream interpretation. In J. Strachey (Ed. & Trans.), *The standard edition of the complete psychological works of Sigmund Freud* (Vol. 19, pp. 109–121). London: Hogarth Press.

Freud, S. (1926). Inhibitions, symptoms and anxiety. In J. Strachey (Ed. & Trans.), *The standard edition of the complete psychological works of Sigmund Freud* (Vol. 20, pp. 75–176). London: Hogarth Press.

Freud, S. (1927). The future of an illusion. *Standard Edition*, 21:3–145, 1961.

Freud, S. (1931). Female sexuality. In J. Strachey (Ed. & Trans.), *The standard edition of the complete psychological works of Sigmund Freud* (Vol. 21, pp. 223–246). London: Hogarth Press.

Freud, S. (1933). New introductory lectures on psycho-analysis. In J. Strachey (Ed. & Trans.), *The standard edition of the complete psychological works of Sigmund Freud* (Vol. 22, pp. 3–182). London: Hogarth Press.

Freud, S. (1937). Analysis terminable and interminable. In J. Strachey (Ed. & Trans.), *The standard edition of the complete psychological works of Sigmund Freud* (Vol. 23, pp. 209–254). London: Hogarth Press.

Freud, S. (1939). Moses and monotheism. In J. Strachey (Ed. & Trans.), *The standard edition of the complete psychological works of Sigmund Freud* (Vol. 23, pp. 3–137). London: Hogarth Press.

Freud, S. (1940). An outline of psychoanalysis. In J. Strachey (Ed. & Trans.), *The standard edition of the complete psychological works of Sigmund Freud* (Vol. 23, pp. 139–207). London: Hogarth Press.

Freud, S. (1957). On the tendency to debasement in the sphere of love. In J. Strachey (Ed. & Trans.), *The standard edition of the complete psychological works of Sigmund Freud* (Vol. 11, pp. 177–190). London: Hogarth Press.

Freud, S. (1961a). The ego and the id. In J. Strachey (Ed. & Trans.), *The standard edition of the complete psychological works of Sigmund Freud* (Vol. 19, pp. 3–68). London: Hogarth Press.

Freud, S. (1961b). The future of an illusion. In J. Strachey (Ed. & Trans.), *The standard edition of the complete psychological works of Sigmund Freud* (Vol. 21, pp. 1–56). London: Hogarth Press.

Freud, S. (1964). New introductory lectures on psychoanalysis. In J. Strachey (Ed. & Trans.), *The standard edition of the complete psychological works of Sigmund Freud* (Vol. 22, pp. 5–182). London: Hogarth Press.

Frie, R. (1997). *Subjectivity and intersubjectivity in modern philosophy and psychoanalysis*. Lanham, MD: Rowman & Littlefield.

Friedlander, D. J. (1997). The confluence of psychoanalysis and religion: A personal view. In C. Spezzano & G. J. Gargiulo (Eds.), *Soul on the couch* (pp. 147–162). Hillsdale, NJ: The Analytic Press.

Friedman, L. J. (1988). *The anatomy of psychotherapy*. Hillsdale, N.: The Analytic Press.

Friedman, L. J. (2006). What is psychoanalysis? *Psychoanalytic Quarterly, 75*, 671–689.

Fromm, E. (1980). *Greatness and limitations of Freud's thought*. New York: Harper and Row.

Gabbard, G. O. (1997). A reconsideration of objectivity in the analyst. *International Journal of Psychoanalysis, 78*, 15–26.

Gabbard, G. O. (2000). Disguise or consent: Problems and recommendations concerning the publication and presentation of clinical material. *International Journal of Psychoanalysis, 81*, 1071–1086.

Gabbard, G. O., & Williams, P. (2001). Preserving confidentiality in the writing of case reports. *International Journal of Psychoanalysis, 82*, 1067–1068.

Gay, P. (1989). *A Godless Jew: Freud, atheism, and the making of psychoanalysis*. New Haven, CT: Yale University Press.

George, C., Kaplan, N., & Main, M. (1985). The Berkeley Adult Attachment Interview. Unpublished manuscript, Department of Psychology, University of California, Berkeley.

Gergely, G., & Watson, J. S. (1996). The social biofeedback theory of parental affect-mirroring: The development of emotional self-awareness and self-control in infancy. *International Journal of Psychoanalysis, 77*, 1181–1212.

Gerson, S. (2000). The therapeutic action of writing about patients. *Psychoanalytic Dialogues, 10*, 261–266.

Ghent, E. (1989). Credo: The dialectics of one-person and two-person psychologies. *Contemporary Psychoanalysis, 25*, 169–211.

Ghent, E. (1992). Paradox and process. *Psychoanalytic Dialogues, 2*, 135–160.

Ghent, E. (2002). Wish, need, drive: Motive in the light of dynamic systems theory and Edelman's selectionist theory. *Psychoanalytic Dialogues, 12*, 763–808.

Gill, M. M. (1954). Psychoanalysis and exploratory psychotherapy. *Journal of the American Psychoanalytic Association, 2*, 771–797.

Gill, M. M. (1983). The interpersonal paradigm and the degree of the therapist's involvement. *Contemporary Psychoanalysis, 19*, 200–237.

Gill, M. M. (1982). *Analysis of transference, Vol. I: Theory and technique*. New York: International Universities Press.

Gill, M. M. (1987). The analyst as participant. *Psychoanalytic Inquiry, 7*, 249–259.

Gilligan, C. (1982). *In a different voice*. Cambridge, MA: Harvard University Press.

Gilligan, C. (2011). *Joining the resistance*. Cambridge, UK: Polity Press.

Gillman, N. (1992). *Sacred fragments*. Philadelphia: Jewish Publication Society.

Gillman, N. (2000). Contemporary Jewish theology. In J. Neusner & A. J. Avery-Peck (Eds.), *The Blackwell companion to Judaism* (pp. 441–460). Malden, MA: Blackwell Publishing.

Gillman, N. (2013). *Believing and its tensions*. New York: Jewish Lights Publishing.

Gilman, S. L. (1993). *Freud, race and gender.* Princeton, NJ: Princeton University Press.

Goldner, V. (1991). Toward a critical relational theory of gender. *Psychoanalytic Dialogues, 1,* 249–272.

Govrin, A. (2016). *Conservative and radical perspectives on psychoanalytic knowledge.* London: Routledge.

Gray, P. (1973). Psychoanalytic technique and the ego's capacity for viewing intrapsychic activity. *Journal of the American Psychoanalytic Association, 21,* 474–494.

Green, A. (1972). *On private madness.* New York: International Universities Press.

Greenberg, J. R. (1981). Prescription or description: Therapeutic action of psychoanalysis. *Contemporary Psychoanalysis, 17,* 239–257.

Greenberg, J. R. (1995). Psychoanalytic technique and the interactive matrix. *Psychoanalytic Quarterly, 64,* 1–22.

Greenberg, J. R. (1997). Analytic authority and analytic restraint. Presented at meeting of the Division of Psychoanalysis, 39. Denver, CO: American Psychological Association.

Greenberg, J. R. (1991). *Oedipus and beyond: A clinical theory.* Cambridge, MA: Harvard University Press.

Greenberg, J. R., & Mitchell, S. A. (1983). *Object relations in psychoanalytic theory.* Cambridge, MA: Harvard University Press.

Greenberg, L. S., & Safran, J. D. (1987). *Emotion in psychotherapy.* New York: Guilford Press.

Greenspan, S. I. (1979). *Intelligence and adaptation: An integration of psychoanalytic and Piagetian developmental psychology.* New York: International Universities Press.

Grolnick, S. (1990). *The work and play of Winnicott.* Northvale, NJ: Jason Aronson.

Grossman, W. I. (1982). The self as fantasy: Fantasy as theory. *Journal of the American Psychoanalytic Association, 30,* 919–938.

Grubrich-Simitis, I. (1986). Six letters of Sigmund Freud and Sandor Ferenczi on the interrelationship of psychoanalytic theory and technique. *International Review of Psychoanalysis, 13,* 259–277.

Guntrip, H. (1969). *Schizoid phenomena, object-relations and the self.* New York: International Universities Press.

Guralnik, O. (2019). A state of mind: Dissociation in service of the collective. Paper presented as the SICP lecture, Institute for Contemporary Psychoanalysis, New York, NY, February 8.

Gurewich, J. F., Tort, M., & Fairfield, S. (1998). *The subject and the self: Lacan and American psychoanalysis.* London: Aronson.

Hare-Mustin, R. T. (1986). The problem of gender in family therapy. *Family Process, 26*, 15–27.

Harris, A. E. (1991). Gender as contradiction. *Psychoanalytic Dialogues, 1*, 197–224.

Harris, A. E. (1996). The conceptual power of multiplicity. *Contemporary Psychoanalysis, 32*, 537–552.

Harris, A. E., & Sinsheimer, K. (2008). The analyst's vulnerability. In F. S. Anderson (Ed.), *Bodies in treatment* (pp. 255–274). New York: The Analytic Press.

Hartman, S. (2020). On the social primal scene. *Psychoanalytic Dialogues* [in review].

Hartmann, H. (1960). *Psychoanalysis and moral values*. New York: International Universities Press.

Heschel, A. J. (1959). *Between God and man*. New York: Free Press.

Heschel, A. J. (1962). *The prophets*. New York: Harper & Row.

Heschel, A. J. (1976). *God in search of man*. New York: Farrar, Straus & Giroux.

Hilda (H.D.) Doolittl (1933). Diary entry for 9 March. In *Tribute to Freud*. Manchester: Carcanet Press, 1985.

Hinshelwood, R. D. (1989). *A dictionary of Kleinian thought*. London: Free Association Books.

Hirsch, I. (1987). Varying modes of analytic participation. *Journal of the American Academy of Psychoanalysis, 15*, 205–222.

Hirsch, I. (2000). Interview with Benjamin Wolstein. *Contemporary Psychoanalysis, 36*, 187–232.

Hirsch, I., & Aron, L. (1991). Participant-observation, perspectivism and countertransference. In H. Siegel, L. Barbanel, I. Hirsch, J. Lasky, H. Silverman, & S. Warshaw (Eds.), *Psychoanalytic reflections on current issues* (pp. 78–95). New York: NYU Press.

Hoffman, I. Z. (1983). The patient as interpreter of the analyst's experience. *Contemporary Psychoanalysis, 19*, 389–422.

Hoffman, I. Z. (1991). Toward a social-constructivist view of the psychoanalytic situation. *Psychoanalytic Dialogues, 1*, 74–105.

Hoffman, I. Z. (1992). Some practical consequences of a social-constructivist view of the psychoanalytic situation. *Psychoanalytic Dialogues, 2*, 287–304.

Hoffman, I. Z. (1995). Oedipus and beyond: A clinical theory by Jay Greenberg. *Psychoanalytic Dialogues, 5*, 93–112.

Hoffman, I. Z. (1996a). The intimate and ironic authority of the psychoanalyst's presence. *Psychoanalytic Quarterly, 65*, 102–136.

Hoffman, I. Z. (1996b). Constructing "constructivism" for psychoanalysis. Presented at meeting of the Division of Psychoanalysis, 39. New York: American Psychological Association.

Hoffman, I. Z. (1998). *Ritual and spontaneity in the psychoanalytic process.* Hillsdale, NJ: The Analytic Press.

Hoffman, M. (2011). *Toward mutual recognition: Relational psychoanalysis and the Christian narrative.* New York: Routledge.

Ikonen, P., & Rechardt, E. (1984). On the universal nature of primal scene fantasies. *International Journal of Psychoanalysis, 65,* 63–72.

International Committee of Medical Journal Editors. (1995). Protection of patients' rights to privacy. *British Journal of Medical Psychology, 311,* 1272.

Irigaray, L. (1985). *This sex which is not one.* Ithaca, NY: Cornell University Press.

Isakower, O. (1963). Minutes of the faculty meeting of the New York Psychoanalytic Institute, November 20.

Jacobs, T. J. (1986). On countertransference enactments. *Journal of the American Psychoanalytic Association, 34,* 289–307.

James, W. (1981). *The principles of psychology.* Cambridge, MA: Harvard University Press (Original work published 1890).

Josephs, L. (1995). *Balancing empathy and interpretation.* Northvale, NJ: Jason Aronson.

Jung, C. G. (1916). *General aspects of dream psychology* (Collected Works of C. G. Jung, Book 8). New York: Pantheon, 1960.

Jung, C. G. (1953). Anima and animus. In *Two essays in analytical psychology* (pp. 198–223). New York: Merian.

Jung, C. G. (1969). The structure and dynamics of the psyche. In G. Adler & R. F. Hall (Eds. & Trans.), *Collected works* (Vol. 8). Princeton, NJ: Princeton University Press.

Jung, C. G. (1972). *C. G. Jung's two essays on analytical psychology* (Collected Works of C. G. Jung, Book 7). Princeton, NJ: Princeton University Press.

Kantrowitz, J. L. (1997). A different perspective on the therapeutic process: The impact of the patient on the analyst. *Journal of the American Psychoanalytic Association, 45,* 127–153.

Kantrowitz, J. L. (2006). *Writing about patients.* New York: Other Press.

Kaplan, D. (1988). Personal Communication.

Kaplan, L. J. (1991). *Female perversions.* New York: Doubleday.

Katz, C. E. (2012). *Levinas and the crisis of humanism.* Bloomington, IN: Indiana University Press.

Kernberg, O. F. (1965). Notes on countertransference. *Journal of the American Psychoanalytic Association, 13,* 38–56.

Kernberg, O. F. (1975). *Borderline conditions and pathological narcissism.* New York: Jason Aronson.

Kernberg, O. F. (1980). *Internal world, external reality.* New York: Jason Aronson.

Kernberg, O. F. (1987). Projection and projective identification: Developmental and clinical aspects. In J. Sandler (Ed.), *Projection, identification, projective identification* (pp. 93–115). Madison, CT: International Universities Press.

Kernberg, P. F., Ritvo, R., Keable, H., & The American Academy of Child and Adolescent Psychiatry Committee on Quality Issues (2012). Practice parameter for psychodynamic psychotherapy with children. *Journal of the American Academy of Child & Adolescent Psychiatry, 51*(5), 541–557.

Kirsch, T. B. (2000). *Jungians: A comparative and historical perspective*. London: Routledge.

Kolod, S. (2010). Every patient has a story. *Contemporary Psychoanalysis, 46*, 469–474.

Klauber, J. (1981). *Difficulties in the analytic encounter*. London: Free Association Books.

Klein, D. B. (1985). *Jewish origins of the psychoanalytic movement*. Chicago: University of Chicago Press.

Klein, M. (1927). Criminal tendencies in normal children. In *Love, guilt and reparation and other works* (pp. 70–185). New York: Delacorte Press/Seymour Lawrence.

Klein, M. (1928). Early stages of the Oedipus conflict. In *Love, guilt and reparation and other works* (pp. 186–198). New York: Delacorte Press/Seymour Lawrence.

Klein, M. (1929). Infantile anxiety situations reflected in a work of art and in the creative impulse. In *Love, guilt and reparation and other works* (pp. 210–218). New York: Delacorte Press/Seymour Lawrence.

Klein, M. (1930). The importance of symbol-formation in the development of the ego. In *Love, guilt and reparation and other works* (pp. 219–232). New York: Delacorte Press/Seymour Lawrence.

Klein, M. (1932). *The psycho-analysis of children*. New York: Delacorte Press/Seymour Lawrence.

Klein, M. (1945). The Oedipus complex in the light of early anxieties. *International Journal of Psychoanalysis, 26*, 11–33.

Klein, M. (1952a). Some theoretical conclusions regarding the emotional life of the infant. In *Envy and gratitude and other works* (pp. 61–93). New York: Delacorte Press/Seymour Lawrence.

Klein, M. (1952b). The origins of transference. In *Envy and gratitude and other works* (pp. 48–56). New York: Delacorte Press/Seymour Lawrence.

Klein, M. (1957). Envy and gratitude. In *Envy and gratitude and other works* (pp. 176–235). New York: Delacorte Press/Seymour Lawrence.

Kohut, H. (1971). *The analysis of the self*. New York: International Universities Press.

Kohut, H. (1977). *The restoration of the self.* New York: International Universities Press.
Kohut, H. (1984). *How does analysis cure?* (A. Goldberg & P. Stepansky, Eds.). Chicago: University of Chicago Press.
Kolbrener, W. (2011). *Open minded Torah.* London: Continuum.
Kris, E. (1956). The personal myth: A problem in psychoanalytic technique. *Journal of the American Psychoanalytic Association, 4,* 653–681.
Kristeva, J. (1982). *Powers of horror: An essay on abjection.* New York: Columbia University Press.
Krueger, D. W. (1986). *The last taboo.* New York: Brunner/Mazel Publishers.
Krystal, H. (1988). *Integration and self-healing.* Hillsdale, NJ: The Analytic Press.
Kubie, L. S. (1974). The drive to become both sexes. *Psychoanalytic Quarterly, 43,* 349–426.
Kuhn, T. S. (1970). *The structure of scientific revolutions* Chicago, IL: University of Chicago Press.
Lachmann, F. M., & Beebe, B. A. (1996). Three principles of salience in the organization of the patient-analyst interaction. *Psychoanalytic Psychology, 13,* 1–22.
Lachmann, F. M., & Lichtenberg, J. (1992). Model scenes: Implications for psychoanalytic treatment. *Journal of the American Psychoanalytic Association, 40,* 117–137.
Laing, R. D. (1972). *The politics of the family.* New York: Vintage Books.
Langs, R. (1982). *Psychotherapy: A basic text.* New York: Jason Aronson.
Laplanche, J. (1997). The theory of seduction and the problem of the other. *International Journal of Psychoanalysis, 78,* 653–666.
Laplanche, J., & Pontalis, J.-B. (1973). *The language of psycho-analysis* (D. Nicholson-Smith, Trans.). New York: Norton.
Lesser, R. C. (1996). "All that's solid melts into air": Deconstructing some psychoanalytic facts—"How women are." *Contemporary Psychoanalysis, 32,* 5.
Levenson, E. A. (1972). *The fallacy of understanding.* New York: Basic Books.
Levenson, E. A. (1983). *The ambiguity of change.* New York: Basic Books.
Levenson, E. A. (1985). The interpersonal (Sullivanian) model. In A. Rothstein (Ed.), *Models of the mind: Their relationship to clinical work.* New York: International Universities Press.
Levenson, E. A. (1988). The pursuit of the particular. *Contemporary Psychoanalysis, 24,* 1–16.
Levenson, E. A. (1989). Whatever happened to the cat? Interpersonal perspectives on the self. *Contemporary Psychoanalysis, 25,* 537–553.
Levin, C. (2003). Civic confidentiality and psychoanalytic confidentiality. In C. Levin, A. Furlong, & M. K. O'Neil (Eds.), *Confidentiality: Ethical perspectives and clinical dilemmas* (pp. 51–78). Hillsdale, NJ: The Analytic Press.

Levine, H. B., & Brown, L. J. (2013). *Growth and turbulence in the container/contained: Bion's continuing legacy.* New York: Routledge.

Levine, S. B., & Stagno, S. J. (2001). Informed consent for case reports: The ethical dilemma of right to privacy versus pedagogical freedom. *Journal of Psychotherapy Practice Research, 10*(3), 193–201.

Lewin, B. D. (1955). Dream psychology and the analytic situation. *Psychoanalytic Quarterly, 24,* 169–199.

Lichtenberg, J. D. (1983). *Psychoanalysis and infant research.* Hillsdale, NJ: The Analytic Press.

Lichtenberg, J. D., & Galler, F. B. (1987). The fundamental rule: A study of current usage. *Journal of the American Psychoanalytic Association, 35,* 47–76.

Lieberman, E. J. (1985). *Acts of will: The life and work of Otto Rank.* Amherst, MA: University of Massachusetts.

Limentani, A. (1989). *Between Freud and Klein: The psychoanalytic quest for knowledge and truth.* London: Free Association Books.

Lipton, E. L. (1991). The analyst's use of clinical data, and other issues of confidentiality. *Journal of the American Psychoanalytic Association, 39,* 967–985.

Lipton, S. D. (1977). Clinical observations on resistance to the transference. *International Journal of Psychoanalysis, 58,* 463–472.

Litowitz, B. E. (2007). Unconscious fantasy: A once and future concept. *Journal of the American Psychoanalytic Association, 55,* 199–228.

Little, M. (1951). Counter-transference and the patient's response to it. *International Journal of Psychoanalysis, 33,* 32–40.

Loewald, H. W. (1960). On the therapeutic action of psychoanalysis. *International Journal of Psychoanalysis, 41,* 16–33.

Loewald, H. W. (1979). The waning of the Oedipus complex. In *Papers on Psychoanalysis.* New Haven, CT: Yale University Press, 1980.

Loewald, H. W. (1986). Transference-countertransference. *Journal of the American Psychoanalytic Association, 34,* 275–287.

Lomas, P. (1987). *The limits of Interpretation.* Northvale, NJ: Jason Aronson, 1990.

Lowenstein, R. M. (1951), The problem of interpretation. *Psychoanalytic Quarterly, 20,* 1–14.

Lyons-Ruth, K. (1999). The two-person unconscious: Intersubjective dialogue, enactive relational representation, and the emergence of new forms of relational organization. *Psychoanalytic Inquiry, 19,* 576–617.

Main, M. (1991). Metacognitive knowledge, metacognitive monitoring and singular (coherent) vs. multiple (incoherent) model of attachment: Findings and directions for future research. In C. Parkes, J. Stevenson-Hinde, and P. Marris (Eds.), *Attunement across the life cycle* (pp. 127–160). London: Routledge.

Main, M., Kaplan, N., & Cassidy, J. (1985). Security in infancy, childhood and adulthood: A move to the level of representation. In I. Bretherton & E. Waters (Eds.), *Growing points in attachment: Theory and research* (pp. 66–104). Chicago: University of Chicago Press.

Maroda, K. (1995). Show some emotion: Completing the cycle of affective communication. Paper presented at the Meeting of Division 39 of the American Psychological Association, Santa Monica, CA.

Mayer, E. L. (1996). Changes in science and changing ideas about knowledge and authority in psychoanalysis. *Psychoanalytic Quarterly, 65*, 158–200.

McCallum, M., & Piper, W. E. (Eds.) (1997). *Psychological mindedness.* Mahwah, NJ: Lawrence Erlbaum Associates.

McDougall, J. (1980). *Plea for a measure of abnormality.* New York: International Universities Press.

McDougall, J. (1989). *Theaters of the body.* New York: Norton.

McLaughlin, J. T. (1981). Transference, psychic reality, and countertransference. *Psychoanalytic Quarterly, 50*, 639–664.

McLaughlin, J. T. (1987). The play of transference: Some reflections on enactment in the psychoanalytic situation. *Journal of the American Psychoanalytic Association, 35*, 557–582.

Mead, M. (1928). *Coming of age in Samoa.* New York: Dell.

Meltzer, D. (1973). *Sexual states of mind.* Perthshire, Scotland: Clunie.

Miller, J. B. (1987). What do we mean by relationships? In *Works in progress.* Wellesley, MA: The Stone Center.

Miller, J-A. (Ed.) (1988). *The seminar of Jacques Lacan, book I: Freud's papers on technique 1953–1954 (J. Forrester, Trans.).* New York & London: W. W. Norton.

Mitchell, S. A. (1988a). *Relational concepts in psychoanalysis.* Cambridge, MA: Harvard University Press.

Mitchell, S. A. (1988b). Changing concepts of the analytic process: A method in search of new meanings. Presented at the Relational Colloquium of the New York University Postdoctoral Program in Psychoanalysis.

Mitchell, S. A. (1991). Contemporary perspectives on self: Toward an integration. *Psychoanalytic Dialogues, 1*, 121–147.

Mitchell, S. A. (1993a). *Hope and dread in psychoanalysis.* New York: Basic Books.

Mitchell, S. A. (1993b). Reply to Bachant and Richards. *Psychoanalytic Dialogues, 3*(3), 461–480.

Mitchell, S. A. (1997). *Influence and autonomy in psychoanalysis.* Hillsdale, NJ: The Analytic Press.

Mitchell, S., & Aron, L. (Eds.) (1999). *Relational psychoanalysis: The emergence of a tradition.* Hillsdale, NJ: The Analytic Press.

Montross, C. (2015, October 16). In defense of case histories: Illness is our human story. The Chronicle of Higher Education. Retrieved from http://chronicle.com/article/In-Defense-of-Case-Histories/233674.

Morningstar, S. (2012). Shoulder dystocia: How the body holds the experience and how the psyche resolves it. *Journal of Prenatal and Perinatal Psychology and Health, 26,* 259–266.

Muller, J. P. (1996a). *Beyond the psychoanalytic dyad.* New York: Routledge.

Muller, J. P. (1999b). Toward a triadic relational theory. *Psychoanalytic Dialogues.* 9:4, 441–443.

Muller, J. P. (1999c). Commentary on paper by M. Crastnopol. *Psychoanalytic Dialogues.* 9:4, 471–480.

Nemiah, J., & Sifneos, P. (1970). Affect and fantasy in patients with psychosomatic disorders. In O. W. Hill (Ed.), *Modern trends in psychosomatic medicine* (Vol. 2, pp. 22–34). London: Butterworth.

Nunberg, H. (1931). The synthetic function of the ego. *International Journal of Psychoanalysis, 12,* 123–140.

Nussbaum, M. C. (2010). *From disgust to humanity.* Oxford: Oxford University Press.

Obaid, F. P. (2012). Sigmund Freud and Otto Rank: Debates and confrontations about anxiety and birth. *International Journal of Psychoanalysis, 93,* 449–471.

Ogden, T. H. (1986). *The matrix of the mind: Object relations and the psychoanalytic dialogue.* Northvale, NJ: Jason Aronson.

Ogden, T. H. (1989). *The primitive edge of experience.* Northvale, NJ: Jason Aronson.

Ogden, T. H. (1991). Analyzing the matrix of transference. *International Journal of Psychoanalysis, 72,* 593–605.

Ogden, T. H. (1994a). *Subjects of analysis.* Northvale, NJ: Jason Aronson.

Ogden, T. H. (1994b). The analytic third: Working with intersubjective clinical facts. *International Journal of Psychoanalysis, 75,* 3–19.

Ogden, T. H. (1995). Analyzing forms of aliveness and deadness of the transference-countertransference. *International Journal of Psychoanalysis, 76,* 695–709.

Olinick, S. L. (1969). On empathy and regression in service of the other. *British Journal of Medical Psychology, 42,* 41–49.

Oram, K. (2013). Poison cookies. *Psychoanalytic Dialogues, 23,* 589–598.

Orange, D. M. (2011). *The suffering stranger.* New York: Routledge.

O'Shaughnessy, E. (1989). The invisible Oedipus complex. In J. Steiner (Ed.), *The Oedipus complex today* (pp. 129–150). London: Karnac.

Pally, R. (1998). Emotional processing: The mind-body connection. *International Journal of Psychoanalysis, 79,* 349–362.

Palombo, S. R. (1978). *Dreaming and memory: A new information-processing model*. New York: Basic Books.

Palombo, S. R. (1984). Deconstructing the manifest dream. *Journal of the American Medical Association, 32*, 405–420.

Panel (1984). The clinical use of the manifest dream (O. Renik, Reporter). *Journal of the American Psychoanalytic Association, 32*, 157–162.

Pardes, I. (1992). *Countertraditions in the Bible: A feminist approach*. Cambridge, MA: Harvard University Press.

Pearce, J. (1950). *Sullivan's approach in therapy with his comments on particular patients*. Unpublished manuscript, May 19, 1950.

Person, E. S. (1995). *By force of fantasy*. New York: Basic Books.

Philips, A. (1988). *Winnicott*. Cambridge, MA: Harvard University Press.

Piaget, J., & Inhelder, B. (1969). *The psychology of the child* (H. Weaver, Trans.). New York: Basic Books (Originally published 1966).

Pies, R. (2007, December 2). Writing about patients: The perennial dilemma. *Psychiatric Times*. Retrieved from http://www.psychiatrictimes.com/bipolar-disorder/writing-about-patients-perennial-dilemma.

Pizer, S. A. (1998). *Building bridges*. Hillsdale, NJ: The Analytic Press.

Pizer, S. A. (2000). A gift in return. *Psychoanalytic Dialogues, 10*, 247–259.

Pulver, S. E. (1987). The manifest dream in psychoanalysis: A clarification. *Journal of the American Psychoanalytic Association, 35*, 99–118.

Putnam, H. (2008). *Jewish philosophy as a guide to life: Rosenzweig, Buber, Levinas, Wittgenstein*. Bloomington, IN: Indiana University Press.

Racker, H. (1968). *Transference and countertransference*. New York: International Universities Press.

Ragen, T., & Aron, L. (2013). Abandoned workings: Ferenczi's mutual analysis. In L. Aron & A. Harris (Eds.), *The legacy of Sandor Ferenczi* (pp. 217–226). Hillsdale, NJ: The Analytic Press.

Rangell, L. (1954). Similarities and differences between psychoanalysis and dynamic psychotherapy. *Journal of the American Psychoanalytic Association, 2*, 734–744.

Rank, O. (1924). The trauma of birth and its importance for psychoanalytic therapy. *Psychoanalytic Review, 11*, 241–245.

Rank, O. (1926). The genesis of the object relations. In P. Rudnytsky (Ed.), *The psychoanalytic vocation* (pp. 171–179). New Haven: CT: Yale University Press.

Reiff, P. (1966). *The triumph of the therapeutic*. New York: Harper and Row.

Reis, B. E. (1999). Thomas Ogden's phenomenological turn. *Psychoanalytic Dialogues, 9*, 371–393.

Renik, O. (1993). Analytic interaction: Conceptualizing technique in light of the analyst's irreducible subjectivity. *Psychoanalytic Quarterly, 62*, 553–571.

Ringstrom, P. A. (1998). Therapeutic impasses in contemporary psychoanalytic treatment: Revisiting the double bind hypothesis. *Psychoanalytic Dialogues, 8,* 297–315.

Rivera, M. (1989). Linking the psychological and the social: Feminism, poststructuralism, and multiple personality. *Dissociation, 2,* 24–31.

Rizzuto, A.-M. (1979). *The birth of the living God.* Chicago: University of Chicago Press.

Rock, M. H. (Ed.) (1997). *Psychodynamic supervision.* Northvale, NJ: Jason Aronson.

Rorty, R. (1979). *Philosophy and the mirror of nature.* Princeton, NJ: Princeton University Press.

Rosen, H. (1985). *Piagetian dimensions of clinical relevance.* New York: Columbia University Press.

Rosenau, P. M. (1992). *Post-modernism and the social sciences.* Princeton, NJ: Princeton University Press.

Rosenfeld, H. (1986). Transference-countertransference distortions and other problems in the analysis of traumatized patients. Presented to the Kleinian analysts of the British Psycho-Analytical Society, April 30, 1986.

Rothenberg, D. J. (1997). Formulation, psychic space, and time: New dimensions in psychoanalysis and Jewish spirituality. In C. Spezzano & G. J. Gargiulo (Eds.), *Soul on the couch* (pp. 57–78). Hillsdale, NJ: The Analytic Press.

Roustang, F. (1976). *Dire mastery* (N. Lukacher, Trans.). Baltimore, MD: Johns Hopkins University Press.

Rubin, G. (1975). The traffic in women: Notes on the "political economy" of sex. In R. Reiter (Ed.), *Toward an anthropology of women* (pp. 157–211). New York: Monthly Review Press.

Rudnytsky, P. L. (2007). Writing about patients: Responsibilities, risks, and ramifications. By Judy Leopold Kantrowitz. New York: Other Press, 2006, 335 pp. *Journal of the American Psychoanalytic Association, 55,* 1406–1411.

Rycroft, C. (1979). *The innocence of dreams.* New York: Pantheon Books.

Sandler, J. (1976). Countertransference and role-responsiveness. *International Review of Psychoanalysis, 3,* 43–47.

Sandler, J. (1992). Reflections on developments in the theory of psychoanalytic technique. *International Journal of Psychoanalysis, 73,* 189–198.

Sands, S. H. (1997). Protein or foreign body? Reply to commentaries. *Psychoanalytic Dialogues, 7,* 691–706.

Saketopoulou, A. (2015). Psychoanalysis: Between consenting adults. Paper presented at the Institute for Contemporary Psychotherapy, New York.

Sayers, J. (1989). Melanie Klein and mothering: A feminist perspective. *International Review of Psychoanalysis, 16,* 363–376.

Sayers, J. (1991). *Mothers of psychoanalysis*. New York: Norton.
Schacter, D. L. (1996). *Searching for memory*. New York: Basic Books.
Schafer, R. (1979). On becoming a psychoanalyst of one persuasion or another. *Contemporary Psychoanalysis, 15*, 345–360.
Schafer, R. (1983). *The analytic attitude*. New York: Basic Books.
Schafer, R. (1992). *Retelling a life*. New York: Basic Books.
Schafer, R. (1997). *Tradition and change in psychoanalysis*. Madison, CT: International Universities Press.
Schofer, J. W. (2010). *Confronting vulnerability: The body and the divine in rabbinic ethics*. Chicago, IL: University of Chicago Press.
Schon, D. (1983). *The reflexive practitioner*. New York: Basic Books.
Searles, H. (1959). Integration and differentiation in schizophrenia. In *Collected papers on schizophrenia and related subjects* (pp. 304–316). New York: International Universities Press.
Searles, H. F. (1966–1967). Concerning the development of an identity. In *Countertransference and related subjects*. New York: International Universities Press.
Searles, H. (1975). The patient as therapist to his analyst. In P. Giovacchini (Ed.), *Tactics and techniques in psychoanalytic theory* (pp. 95–151). New York: Jason Aronson.
Segal, H. (1957). Notes on symbol formation. *International Journal of Psychoanalysis, 38*, 391–397.
Segal, H. (1964). *Introduction to the work of Melanie Klein*. New York: Basic Books.
Segal, H. (1989). Introduction to the Oedipus complex today. In J. Steiner (Ed.), *The Oedipus complex today* (pp. 1–10). London: Karnac.
Seligman, S. (1999a). Integrating Kleinian theory and intersubjective infant research. *Psychoanalytic Dialogues, 9*, 129–159.
Seligman, S. (1999b, April). Thinking in relationships: A contemporary perspective. Presented at the Spring Meeting of Division 39 of the American Psychological Association.
Seligman, S., & Shanok, R. S. (1995). Subjectivity, complexity and the social world: Erikson's identity concept and contemporary relational theories. *Psychoanalytic Dialogues, 5*, 537–565.
Shane, M., & Shane, E. (1990). Unconscious fantasy: Developmental and self-psychological considerations. *Journal of the American Psychoanalytic Association, 38*, 75–92.
Sharabany, R., & Israeli, E. (2008). The dual process of adolescent immigration and relocation. *Psychoanalytic Study of the Child, 63*, 137–162.
Sieck, B. C. (2012). Obtaining clinical writing informed consent versus using client disguise and recommendations for practice. *Psychotherapy, 49*, 3–11.

Siegel, H. B., Barbanel, L., Hirsch, I., Lasky, J., Silverman, H., & Warshaw, S. (Eds.) (1991). *Psychoanalytic reflections on current issues* (pp. 78–95). New York: New York University Press.

Singer, E. (1977). The fiction of analytic anonymity. In K. Frank (Ed.), *The human dimension in psychoanalytic practice* (pp. 181–192). New York: Grune & Stratton.

Singer, I. (1968). The reluctance to interpret. In E. F. Hammer (Ed.), *The use of interpretation in treatment* (pp. 364–371). New York: Grune & Stratton.

Slap, J. W., & Trunnell, E. E. (1987). Reflections on the self state dream. *The Psychoanalytic Quarterly, 56,* 251–262.

Slochower, J. A. (1996). *Holding and psychoanalysis.* Hillsdale, NJ: The Analytic Press.

Smith, B. L. (1990). The origins of interpretation in the countertransference. *Psychoanalytic Psychology, 7,* 89–104.

Soloveitchik, J. B. (1984). *Halakhic man.* Philadelphia: Jewish Publication Society.

Soloveitchik, J. B. (1992). *The lonely man of faith.* New York: Doubleday.

Soloveitchik, J. B. (2002). *Worship of the heart.* New York: Ktav Publishing.

Soloveitchik, J. B. (2003). *Out of the whirlwind.* New York: Ktav Publishing.

Spence, D. P. (1982). *Narrative truth and historical truth.* New York: W. W. Norton & Co.

Spezzano, C. (1996). Toward an intrapsychic-intersubjective dialectic: Reply to commentary. *Psychoanalytic Dialogues, 5,* 675–688.

Spezzano, C. (1998). The triangle of clinical judgment. *Journal of the American Psychoanalytic Association, 46,* 365–388.

Spezzano, C., & Gargiulo, G. J. (Eds.) (1997). *Soul on the couch.* Hillsdale, NJ: The Analytic Press.

Spillius, E. (2007). *Encounters with Melanie Klein.* London: Routledge.

Steiner, J. (1993). *Psychic retreats.* London: Routledge.

Stepansky, P. E. (1999). *Freud, surgery, and the surgeons.* Hillsdale, NJ: The Analytic Press.

Stepansky, P. E. (2009). *Psychoanalysis at the margins.* New York: Other Press.

Sterba, R. (1934). The fate of the ego in analytic therapy. *International Journal of Psychoanalysis, 15,* 117–126.

Stern, D. B. (1989). The analyst's unformulated experience of the patient. *Contemporary Psychoanalysis, 25,* 1–33.

Stern, D. B. (1990). Courting surprise. *Contemporary Psychoanalysis, 26,* 452–478.

Stern, D. B. (1997). *Unformulated experience.* Hillsdale, NJ: The Analytic Press.

Stern, D. B. (2004). The eye sees itself. *Contemporary Psychoanalysis, 40*(2), 197–237.

Stern, D. B. (2013). Relational freedom and therapeutic action. *Journal of American Psychoanalytic Association, 61*(2), 227–256.

Stern, D. N. (1985). *The interpersonal world of the infant.* New York: Basic Books.

Stern, D. N. (1989). The representation of relational patterns: Developmental considerations. In A. J. Sameroff & R. N. Emde (Eds.), *Relationship disturbances in early childhood: A developmental approach* (pp. 52–69). New York: Basic Books.

Stern, D. N., Sander, L. W., Nahum, J. P., Harrison, A. M., Lyons-Ruth, K., Morgan, A. C., Bruschweilerstern, N., & Tronick, E. Z. (1998). Non-interpretive mechanisms in psychoanalytic therapy: The "something more" than interpretation. *International Journal of Psychoanalysis, 79,* 903–921.

Stoller, R. J. (1988). Patients' responses to their own case reports. *Journal of the American Psychoanalytic Association, 36,* 371–391.

Stolorow, R. D. (1978). Themes in dreams: A brief contribution to therapeutic technique. *International Journal of Psychoanalysis, 59,* 473–476.

Stolorow, R. D., & Atwood, G. E. (1989). The unconscious and unconscious fantasy: An intersubjective-developmental perspective. *Psychoanalytic Inquiry, 9,* 364–374.

Stolorow, R. D., Brandchaft, B., & Atwood, G. E. (1987). *Psychoanalytic treatment: An intersubjective approach.* Hillsdale, NJ: The Analytic Press.

Stolorow, R. D., Orange, D. M., & Atwood, G. E. (1999). Toward post-Cartesian psychoanalytic theory. *Psychoanalytic Dialogues, 9,* 401–406.

Strachey, J. (1934). The nature of the therapeutic action of psychoanalysis. *International Journal of Psychoanalysis, 15,* 127–159.

Strenger, C. (1989). The classic and the romantic vision in psychoanalysis. *International Journal of Psychoanalysis, 70,* 693–710.

Suchet, M. (2004). Whose mind is it anyway? *Studies in Gender and Sexuality, 5,* 259–287.

Sullivan, H. S. (1953). *The interpersonal theory of psychiatry.* New York: W. W. Norton & Co.

Sullivan, H. S. (1954). *The psychiatric interview.* New York: W. W. Norton & Co.

Sutherland, J. D. (1963). Object-relations theory and the conceptual model of psychoanalysis. *British Journal of Medical Psychology, 36,* 109–124.

Symington, N. (1983). The analyst's act of freedom as agent of therapeutic change. *International Review of Psychoanalysis, 10,* 783–792.

Talbert, C. H. (2006). Miraculous conceptions and births in Mediterranean antiquities. In A.-J. Levine, D. C. Allison, Jr., & J. D. Crossan (Eds.), *The historical Jesus in context* (pp. 79–86). Princeton, NJ: Princeton University Press.

Target, M., & Fonagy, P. (1996). Playing with reality: II. The development of psychic reality from a theoretical perspective. *International Journal of Psychoanalysis, 77*, 459–479.

Taubert, E. (1954). Exploring the therapeutic use of countertransference data. *Psychiatry, 17*, 331–336.

Taylor, E. (1992). The case for a uniquely American Jamesian tradition in psychology. In M. Donnelly (Ed.), *Reinterpreting the legacy of William James* (pp. 3–28) Washington, DC: American Psychological Association.

Taylor, E. (1996). *William James on consciousness beyond the margin.* Princeton, NJ: Princeton University Press.

Taylor, G. J. (1992a). Psychoanalysis and psychosomatics: A new synthesis. *Journal of the American Academy of Psychoanalysis, 20*, 251–275.

Taylor, G. J. (1992b). Psychosomatics and self-regulation. In J. W. Barron, M. N. Eagle, & D. S. Wolitzky (Eds.), *Interface of psychoanalysis and psychology* (pp. 464–488). Washington, DC: American Psychological Association.

Tenzer, A. (1983). Piaget and psychoanalysis: Some reflections on insight. *Contemporary Psychoanalysis, 19*, 319–339.

Tenzer, A. (1984). Piaget and psychoanalysis, II: The problem of working through. *Contemporary Psychoanalysis, 20*, 421–438.

Teutsch, D. A. (Ed.) (1999). *Kol Haneshana: Prayerbook for the days of awe.* Wyncote, PA: Reconstructionist Press.

Tirosh-Samuelson, H., & Hughes, A. W. (2016). *Menachem Fisch: The rationality of religious dispute.* Boston: Brill.

Trachtenberg, R. (2013). Caesura, denial, and envy. In H. B. Levine & L. J. Brown (Eds.), *Growth and turbulence in the container/contained: Bion's continuing legacy* (pp. 231–242). London: Routledge.

Tuckett, D. (2000). Reporting clinical events in the journal. *International Journal of Psychoanalysis, 81*, 1065–1069.

van der Kolk, B. A. (1996). The body keeps the score: Approaches to the psychobiology of posttraumatic stress disorder. In B. A. van der Kolk, A. C. McFarlane, & L. Weisaeth (Eds.), *Traumatic stress* (pp. 214–241). New York: Guilford.

Wachtel, P. (1986). On the limits of therapeutic neutrality. *Contemporary Psychoanalysis, 22*, 60–70.

Wallerstein, R. S. (1990). Psychoanalysis: The common ground. *International Journal of Psychoanalysis, 71*, 3–20.

Wallerstein, R. S. (1992). *The common ground of psychoanalysis.* New York, NY: Aronson.

Wallerstein, R. S. (1995). *The talking cures.* New Haven, CT: Yale University Press.

Wallerstein, R. S. (2013). *Lay analysis: Life inside the controversy.* London: Routledge.

Werner, H. (1957). The concept of development from a comparative and organismic point of view. In D. B. Harris (Ed.), *The concept of development* (pp. 125–148). Minneapolis, MN: University of Minnesota Press.

Willock, B. (2011). *Comparative-integrative psychoanalysis: A relational perspective for the discipline's second century.* New York: Routledge.

Wilner, W. (1999). The un-consciousing of awareness in psychoanalytic therapy. *Contemporary Psychoanalysis, 35,* 617–628.

Winnicott, D. W. (1941). The observation of infants in a set situation. In *Collected papers: Through paediatrics to psychoanalysis* (pp. 52–69). New York: Basic Books.

Winnicott, D. W. (1951). Transitional objects and transitional phenomena. In *Collected papers: Through paediatrics to psychoanalysis* (pp. 229–242). New York: Basic Books.

Winnicott, D. W. (1953). Transitional objects and transitional phenomena—A study of the first notme possession. *International Journal of Psycho-Analysis, 34,* 89–97.

Winnicott, D. W. (1954–1955). The depressive position in normal development. In *Through pediatrics to psychoanalysis* (pp. 262–276). New York: Basic Books.

Winnicott, D. W. (1957). Birth trauma, birth memories and anxiety. In *Through paediatrics to psycho-analysis: Collected papers* (pp. 174–193). New York: Basic Books.

Winnicott, D. W. (1960). Ego distortion in terms of true and false self. In *Maturational process and the facilitating environment* (pp. 140–152). New York: International Universities Press.

Winnicott, D. W. (1963). From dependence towards independence in the development of the individual. In D. W. Winnicott (Ed.), *The maturational process and the facilitating environment* (pp. 83–92). New York: International Universities Press.

Winnicott, D. W. (1965). The maturational processes and the facilitating environment. *International Psychoanalytic Library, 64,* 1.

Winnicott, D. W. (1969). The use of an object. *International Journal of Psychoanalysis, 50,* 711–716.

Winnicott, D. W. (1971a). *Playing and reality.* Middlesex, England: Penguin.

Winnicott, D. W. (1971b). *Therapeutic consultations in child psychiatry.* New York: Basic Books.

Winnicott, D. W. (1986). *Holding and interpretation: Fragments of an analysis.* London: Hogarth Press.

Winnicott, D. W. (1988). *Human nature.* New York: Schocken.

Wolstein, B. (1959). *Countertransference*. New York: Grune & Stratton.

Wolstein, B. (1974). "I" processes and "me" patterns: Two aspects of the psychic self in transference and countertransference. *Contemporary Psychoanalysis, 10*, 347–357.

Wolstein, B. (1981). The psychic realism of psychoanalytic inquiry. *Contemporary Psychoanalysis, 17*, 399–412.

Wolstein, B. (1983a). The pluralism of perspectives on countertransference. *Contemporary Psychoanalysis, 19*, 506–521.

Wolstein, B. (1983b). The first person in interpersonal relations. *Contemporary Psychoanalysis, 19*, 522–535.

Wolstein, B. (1984). A proposal to enlarge the individual model of psychoanalytic supervision. *Contemporary Psychoanalysis, 20*, 131–144.

Wolstein, B. (1988). Introduction. In *Essential papers on countertransference* (pp. 1–15). New York: New York University Press.

Yalom, I. (2008). *Staring at the sun*. San Francisco, CA: Jossey-Bass.

Zucker, H. (1967). *Problems of psychotherapy*. New York: Free Press.

Index

Note: Page numbers followed by "n" indicate notes.

abandonment of metapsychological truths 211
aboriginal populations 259
abortions 4
abstinence 121, 130–131, 199
Adult Attachment Interview 177–178
alexithymia 168, 183
Alfonso, C. A. 302
Allport, Gordon 170
alternative therapies 272
Altman, N. 193
American Ego Psychology 272
American Psychological Association 281
anal-rapprochement subphase 72
analysand's capacity 38
analysts: centered interpretations 179; interpretations 137; patient pair 117; professional community 195; self-expression 124–128; self-regulation 216n1; self-revelations 158; subjectivity 162–163; transferences 147; *see also* specific entries
analytic instrument 146
analytic situation 162
analyzing instrument 160

anonymity 114, 121
anti-Semitic tropes 246
anti-Semitism 245, 248, 253, 258
anxiety 38–40, 62
Arlow, J. A. 11, 34, 48
Aron, Lewis 4, 23–24, 48, 103, 107, 143, 218, 271; interpretation as expression of analyst's subjectivity 134–138; relational-perspectivist analysis 108
asexuality 212
assertiveness 83
Atheism 101
Atlas, Galit 217, 299–300
Atlas-Koch, G. 240n3
Atwood, G. E. 145, 185n1, 203
Auerbach, John 168
awareness 33–34, 38, 45–46, 54, 65, 169, 173; *see also* self-awareness

Bach, Sheldon 25, 165–166, 168–169, 172, 277
Balint, M. 120
Baranger, M. 128
Baranger, W. 111, 128
Basescu, S. 19
Baynes, Peter 296
Beebe, B. 90

Benjamin, Jessica 52, 54, 58, 86, 144, 165, 167, 169, 179, 185n1, 187, 227, 248–249, 262, 266, 277
Bergmann, M. S. 190, 215
Bion, Wilfred 63, 67, 165, 224, 280; birth and rebirth 219; ideas of alpha work 24
Bionian theory 250
bipersonal communication 109
Bird, B. 147
birth: conception and 226; fantasies 219–221, 235; myths 220; and rebirth 219
birth and family circumstances surrounding birth 217–227; birthday 227–231, 233–238; fantasies of birth 218; paper delivery 238–240; primal moment of one's history 231–233
Birth of Experience, The (Eigen) 224
bisexuality 51, 60, 84, 246, 259; completeness 54, 56; dispositions, feminine and masculine 55; Freud's concept of 56; phantasy 56
black-and-white thinking 234
blaming polarizations 264
blank screen approach 121
Blatt, Sidney 165, 168
Blazy, H. 240n2
Blechner, M. J. 306
Blum, H. P. 59
Bollas, Christopher 79, 117–118, 121, 123, 128–129, 145, 156, 177, 180, 218, 227–228, 241n6
Bonds of Love, The (Benjamin) 263
born-again 219
Boyarin, D. 252
Brandchaft, B. 145
Brenner, C. 11–12
Brickman, Celia 256, 259
Bridges, N. A. 288
British independent group 120
Britton, R. 44, 70, 82, 165

Bromberg, Philip 3, 161, 182, 206, 264
Buber, Martin 90, 101
Buddhism 103
Burke, W. F. 114–116, 126, 128
Butler, Judith 51, 54, 240n4, 254

Caligor, Lee 3
Casement, P. J. 130–131
centrality of sexuality 60
centration/focus 24
Charybdis of radical relativism 273
Chasseguet-Smirgel, J. 86
childbirth 240n1
childhood: phantasy of the primal scene 63; sexuality 53; system of thought 31; trauma 130
chimera and like-enough subjects 277–278
Chodorow, N. J. 86
Christianity 246
Christian theology 262
Cixous, Helene 249
classicism 191
clinical choices and relational matrix 186–216
Clinical Diary (Ferenczi) 112, 267
Coates, Susan 23
cognition 12
cohesion 26
collaborative inquiry 125
colonialism 245
combined parent figure 62–68
comparative psychoanalysis 273
competence 38–40
complex relational events 125
conception and birth 226
conceptualization 31
confidentiality 113
conflict 129
Confronting Vulnerability (Schofer) 257
consciousness 181
constructivism 140n3

contemporary psychoanalysis 204
contempt of other 80
Cooper, A. M. 272–273
co-participants 125
Corbett, K. 223
corrective emotional experience 127
countertransference 116, 146–148, 218, 297; expressive uses of 121–123; *see also* transference-countertransference
Crastnopol, M. 192
creativity 67
crisis of authority 190
critical-constructivism 213
critical pluralism 273–276
critical rationalism 274
cultural school 193
Cushman, P. 193

Damon, W. 165
Davies, Jody 165, 180, 264
decalage 39
Decentering Relational Theory (Lew, Sue Grand) 269–270
Deidealizing Relational Theory (Lew, Sue Grand) 269–270
denigration 80
depression 52
Derrida, J. 249
deuteronomy 103
devaluation 80
developmental program 160
dialectical-constructivism 213
dialectics of difference 122
dichotomies 86
differentiation 246
Dimen, Muriel 57, 86, 249
Dinnerstein, D. 144
disillusionment 141
disintegration 27
Division of Psychoanalysis 281
dominance 83

dreamers, integrity of self 7
dreams/dreaming 4–6; analysis 5, 9; constituents 5–6; dream interpretation 14; elements 17; false polarization 10; imagery 16; images 21; interpretation 19; meaning 7; mode of pursuit 9; parts 9–10; quality and composition 5, 11–12; self-state 6–7; significance for 5, 7; specimen 5; structural-conflict 6; structure 6; thematic aspects 6; topographic theory 8; transitional phenomena 21
drive-discharge model 53
dual-instinct theory of 88n6

egocentrism 24, 28–29, 31, 33–38, 54
ego-formation 240n2
Ehrenberg, D. B. 128
Ehrensaft, D. 240n4
Eigen, Michael 104
Eissler, K. R. 189
embodiment 267
emotional responsiveness 120
Enigma of Desire, The (Atlas) 299
Erikson, E. 6
Eshel, O. 220
Esman, A. H. 59–60
essentialist notions 53
Etchegoyen, R. H. 110, 117, 128, 132–134
ethical considerations in psychoanalytic writing 285–290; anecdotes 290–291; conclusion 309–310; editorial guidelines 310–311; extreme positions 307–309; individual theoretical positions 303–305; Jungians 295–298; legal considerations 313–314; letter 298–299; mediating for New York University 291–293; psychoanalytic journal editorial policies and the ICMJE 301–303;

psychotherapy roundtable 305–307; risk 299–300; training and education 312–313; unintended publicity 293–295; writing about and with patients 298
evidence-based medicine 288
exhibitionism 158

Fairbairn, W. R. D. 69
Fairfield, S. 178
family formation 223
Fast, Irene 47n1, 54, 56
father transference 76
feeding-breast analyst 80–81
Feffer, Melvin 23, 47n1, 47n5
Feldman, M. 82
female analyst 294
femaleness 83
feminism 54, 78, 81, 246, 253, 256, 268, 272
feminist 143; psychoanalytic criticism 144; psychology 86
Fenichel, O. 90, 190, 253
Ferenczi, Sándor 23, 83, 111, 128, 136, 142, 162, 182, 215, 220, 225; mutual analysis 113
Finkelstein, Rabbi Louis 90, 97
Fisch, Menachem 273–276, 283n1
Fischer, C. T. 306
Fisch's model 274–275, 278
Fitzgerald, F. Scott 26
Flavell, J. H. 31, 47n3
Fleck, Ludwig 275
fluidity 256
Fonagy, Peter 165, 168, 169, 178
Fordham, Michael 296
Fosshage, J. L. 12–13, 21
Foulkes, D. 1
Fox, R. P. 130
framework problem 276–277
Frankel, Jay 227
Frawley, M. G. 180
free association method 34
free-floating responsiveness 41

French psychoanalysis 43
Freud, Sigmund 5, 15, 20, 59, 76, 84, 88n5, 90, 107, 142, 162, 165, 189, 225–226, 235, 251, 256–258; attitude toward spiritual experience 89; on birth and rebirth 219; conscious and unconscious, conception of 109; embattlement 278; Freudian technique 6; as reflexive-skeptic 278–280; Studies 272; theory of gender development 53
Freudian dream theory 13; archaeological metaphor 15; dreaming in topographic theory 8; dream interpretation 14; dreams analysis 5–6; dream-thoughts 8; employing interpretation 10; investigation of his own dreams 8, 13; narrative quality of dreams 8–9; quality and composition of dreams 5; theoretical model 7–8; traumatic dreams 22n1
Freud Wars 272
Frie, R. 185n1
Friedman, Larry 251
Fromm, E. 14
frustration 52
fusion, splitting, and integration of gender 74–83

Gabbard, Glen 302–303, 310
gay families 240n4
gender: complexity 23; fluidity 49; identity 54, 57; indiscrimination 54; multiplicity 48–49; polarization 87
Gender as Soft Assembly (Harris) 23
genital sexuality 62, 67
Gerson, S. 298
Ghent, E. 52, 170
Ghent, Mannie 90, 103
Gill, M. M. 113, 126, 137, 148, 152
Gilligan, C. 84

Gillman, Neil 97, 265
Gillman, Rabbi Neil 98
Gilman, S. L. 252
Gilman's analysis 246
global fantasies 222
God: dreams for humanity 99; and Jewish people 100; proclamation 100; of the Rambam 98; of relationship 89–90
Godlike omnipotence 64
Goldner, Virginia 54, 57, 86, 88n5
grandiosity 52
Green, Andre 218, 227, 230, 241n7
Greenberg, J. R. 192, 203, 284n3
Greenberg's conceptualization of interactive matrix 203
Greenspan, S. I. 42–43, 47n1, 47n4
Guntrip, H. 45, 72

Hare-Mustin, R. T. 85
Harris, Adrienne 23, 86, 176, 227, 266
Hart, D. 165
Hartman, F. R. 190
Hartmann, H. 90, 189, 204
H. D. (Hilda Doolittl) 84
health-care industry 272
healthy femininity 57
healthy masculinity 57
heresy 219
Heschel, Abraham 90, 99, 102, 265
heternormative theories of psychic bisexuality 49
heterosexual intercourse 67
heterosexuality 49; marriage 78; naturalness 87; procreative 68; *see also* homosexuality
Hirsch, I. 161
historical continuity 26
Hoffman, I. Z. 123, 128, 136, 148, 155, 170, 173
Hoffmann, Y. 113
homophobia 245, 256, 258
homosexuality 77, 83, 233, 258

homosexual love 240n4
Hughes, A. W. 283n1
humanity 111, 267
hypersensitivity 172

I and the *me* 166, 170–171, 173
immune system 277
incompatible ideas 27
individual subjectivity 185n1
individuation 246
infancy: anxiety situations 62; sexuality 9
inhibitions 52
institutionalization 248
integration 26
intentionality 26
interactive matrix 202
intercourse 63
interdigitation of racism 258
internal copulating parents 64
internalization of relations 69–74
"The Internalized Primal Scene" (Aron, L.) 48–50; combined parent figure 62–68; fusion, splitting, and integration of gender 74–83; internalization of relations 69–74; primal scene 59–62; psychic bisexuality 53–58; psychoanalytic dialogues 51–53; psychoanalytic schools and splitting of gender 83–87
International Committee of Medical Journal Editors (ICMJE) 301
International Journal of Psychoanalysis 301–303, 310
interpersonal analysts 161
interpersonal difficulties 52
interpersonal participation 138
interpersonal psychoanalysis 241n9
interpersonal reality 121
interpretation as expression of the analyst's subjectivity 107–110, 138–139, 139n1; Aron, case illustrations from 134–138; Casement, case

illustrations from 130–131; complex relational event 138; countertransference, expressive uses of 121–123; data of interpretation 110–111; defined 109, 138–139; Etchegoyen, case illustrations from 132–134; explanation 110; Ferenczi's mutual/symmetrical analysis 111–113; Hoffman, case illustrations from 129–130; mutuality and symmetry in psychoanalysis 113–117; mutuality with asymmetry 123–124; relational perspectives on analyst's self-expression 124–128; and self-expression 120–121; Winnicott on interpretation 117–120

Interpretation of Dreams, The (Freud) 8, 279

intersubjective engagement 131, 136, 167, 180

intersubjective exchange 163

intersubjective recognition 117

intersubjectivity 26, 45–46, 71, 145, 169, 185n1

intrapsychic conflicts 34, 107, 167

introspection 45, 168

IPA Jerusalem institute 164

Irigaray, Lucy 256

Irma dream 6

Isakower, Otto 83, 260

Israeli Association of Psychotherapy 164

issue of idealization 209

I-Thou relationship 98

James, William 165, 169–170, 185n2

Jews 252

Josephs, L. 207

Journal of Clinical Psychoanalysis (JCP) 302

Journal of the American Psychoanalytic Association (JAPA) 303

Judaism 103–104, 246

Jung, C. G. 6, 142, 296; dream interpretation 14

Kabbalah, Lurianic 100, 104

Kabbalistic myth 100

Kaley, Harriette 3

Kalinkowitz, Bernard N. 186

Kantrowitz, Judy 303–304

Kaplan, Donald 87n2, 193

Kaplan, Louise J. 59

Kernberg, O. F. 69, 84, 145, 207

Kernbergians 84–85

Kernberg's analysis of primitive 207

Kernberg's narcissists 172

Kippur, Yom 268

Kirsch, James 296

Kirsch, Thomas 296

Klauber, J. 120

Klein, Melanie 27, 43, 52, 62–63, 67, 84, 107, 189; on birth and rebirth 219; Kleinian analysts 26

Kleinian theory 27, 64, 66; oedipal situation 62; part-object functions 75

Kleinian thinking 27

Kohut, H. 6–7, 22n1, 159, 171, 207; description of self-state dreams 6; innovations 13; Kohutians 84

Kohutian self-psychology 160–161

Kolbrener, W. 263

Kristeva, Julia 256

Kubie, L. S. 51, 84

Kuhn, Thomas 275

Lacan 145, 187, 223

Lacanian concept of the Third 191

Lachmann, F. M. 90

Laing, R. D. 45, 49, 69

Lapkin, Ben 3

Laplanche, J. 50

Lesser, R. C. 212–213

Levenson, E. A. 36–37, 126, 201

Levenson's models of technique 25

Lew, B. D. 165, 187, 246, 269, 271
Lewin, B. D. 79–80
Lewin's analogy of psychoanalysis and anesthesia 79
Litowitz, B. E. 221
Loew, Judah 263
Loewald, H. W. 53, 125, 142, 147–148
logical thinking 28
Lomas, P. 120
London Jungian approach 296

managed care 272
manifest content, value of 6
marital difficulties 17
Maroda, Karen 181
Marom, Daniel 283n1
masculinity 54, 78, 81, 83, 260
masochism 274
May, Rollo 3
Mayer, E. L. 205
McDougall, Joyce 59, 151, 218, 227, 230–232, 241n8, 242n10
McLaughlin, J. T. 82–83, 148
Mead, Margaret 61
Meltzer, D. 64, 67
mentalization 165, 179, 264
mental symptom formation 27
mentation 12
metapsychology 53
Michaels, Robert 185n3
Miller, J. -B. 85
mind-body problem 168
misogyny 253, 256, 258
Mitchell, Stephen 23, 60–61, 90, 138, 159, 164, 186, 190, 211, 265, 272, 280, 284n3
Mitchell's methodology 266
model scenes 222
Mol Levavenu 268
Morningstar, S. 240n5
mortality 267
mother-centered trend 86
mother-infant mutual influence 147
mother–infant relationship 83
mother transference 76, 83–84
Muller, J. P. 191–192
multigendered identifications 51
multi-gendered multiplicity 49
multiple self-states 264, 290
multiplicity 166, 176, 180, 273
mutuality and symmetry in psychoanalysis 113–117
mutuality-lack of mutuality 116, 128
mutuality with asymmetry 123–124
mutual participation in analytic understanding 120
mutual vulnerability 245–268
Mythology of the Soul (Fordham) 296

Nabokov, Vladimir 225
nachträglich 248
naive patient fallacy 155
naive realism 202
narcissism 52, 54, 61, 279
narcissistic neuroses 45, 72
narcissistics 171
narcissistic vulnerabilities 271
natural sexual differences 54
neurological processes 5–6
neuroses 8, 52
neurotic conflict 33
normotic illness 229
Nunberg, H. 27
Nussbaum, Martha 256–257

Obaid, F. P. 220
object constancy 144
objective self-awareness 171–172
object-relations theory 45–46, 296
obsessional symptoms 234
obsessive-compulsive illness 82
Oedipal law 261
oedipal triangle 44
Oedipus complex and intersubjectivity 42–47, 70, 87n1, 220, 246

Ofer, Gila 164
Ogden, Thomas 57, 64, 66, 90, 145, 170, 192
Olinick, S. L. 147
one-person psychology 116
Orange, Donna 185n1, 254–255
O'Shaughnessy, E. 74
own awareness 169

Pally, Regina 183
paradigm shifts 275
paranoid-schizoid mode 47n2, 65–66
paranoid-schizoid position 73
parental intercourse 82
parental sexual intercourse 59–60; internalization, basis of 64; privacy, secrecy, and exclusion 61
parental sexuality 223
parents' attitudes 150
parents' functioning together as couple 76
parents' personalities 150
participant-observer 125
passive-homosexual-love 77; *see also* homosexuality
paternal fecal-phallus 80
paternal oedipal transference 84
patient-analyst relationship 157
patient's experience of analyst's subjectivity 141–163
patient's rebirth in analysis 218
patriarchy 245
Pearce, J. 37
penitential liturgy 268
performance 38–40
persecution 248
Person, E. S. 221
personality integration 57
personal myths 222
person-to-person relationship 38
perspectivism 140n3
phallic-penetrating interpretations 81
phantasies of child 44

phantastic male—female relationships 58
phantasy systems 49–50, 52, 62–63
Phillips, Adam 118
Piaget, Jean 24
Piagetian principles 36
Piagetian theory and psychoanalytic method 23–27, 47; centering and decentering 29; competence, performance, and anxiety 38–40; egocentricity and decentering 33–38; egocentrism 28–29; interdependence of characteristics 30–31; intersubjectivity 42–47; Oedipus complex 42–47; preoperational thought, limitations 28, 32–33; reversibility and irreversibility 30; self and object relations 40–42; states and transformations 30
Piaget's cognitive approach 47n1
Piaget's complex relation to psychoanalysis 23
Pick, I. 150
Pies, Ronald 307
Pizer, Stuart 170, 298
pluralism 189, 271–276
Popper, Karl 274
Popper's theory 274
positivism 170
post-Bionian psychoanalytic thought 250
post-Freudian psychoanalysis 86
post-Freudian theoretical elaborations 54
postmodernism 58
postmodernists 57
post-Popperian approach 274
poststructuralism 57
poststructuralist 57
poverty 248
pragmatism 275
prayer 98
pre-birth 225

Precarious Life (Butler) 254
pregenital sexual activity 60–62
prejudice 248
preoedipal development 72
preoperational thought: centering and decentering 29; characteristics of 28; egocentrism 28–29; interdependence of characteristics 30–31; limitations of 28, 32–33; psychopathology 32–33; reversibility and irreversibility 30; states 30; transformation 30
primal phantasies 59
primal scene fantasy 59–60; developmental line 64; paranoid-schizoid mode 65; parental intercourse 64
primitive communications 161
primitive sensual experiences 225
primitivity 257
Principles of Psychology (James) 169
Productive Paradoxes of William James 170
professional facade 162
Prophets, The (Heschel) 265
pseudoscience 274
psyche-soma 122
psychic bisexuality 51, 53–58
psychic center of the interpersonal self 169
psychic reality 146
psychoanalysis 5–6, 15, 53, 83, 109, 253, 272–273, 289
Psychoanalysis 248, 272
Psychoanalysis in Israel 164
psycho-analysts-in-training 191
psychoanalytic affiliation 195
psychoanalytic dialogues 51–53
Psychoanalytic Dialogues 303
psychoanalytic dream theory 12
Psychoanalytic Electronic Publishing (PEP-web) Internet database 290
psychoanalytic pluralism 208
psychoanalytic process 7–8
psychoanalytic schools and splitting of gender 83–87
psychoanalytic theory 226
psychoanalytic thinkers 27
psychoanalytic training texts 6
psychoanalytic treatment 4–5
psychodynamics 42, 46, 72
psychological birth 221
psychologically oriented self-help books 5
psychopathology 32, 202
psychopharmacology 272
psychoses 52
psychosexual lexicon 247
psychosis 57
psycho-spiritual beings 89
Psychotherapy for the People, A (Aron & Starr) 248
psychotherapy/psychoanalysis binary 251
Pulver, S. E. 6

quintessential oedipal drama 62

rabbis 257
Rachamim, Kel Malei 99
racism 245
racism, interdigitation of 258
Racker, H. 148
radical relativism 273
Rangell, Leo 253
Rank, O. 83, 240n1
rape fantasies 300
rebirth 218–219
reciprocal communication 109
reflection in action 204
reflective self-awareness 45
reflexive awareness 184
reflexive self-awareness 172, 185
reflexive self-function 167
reflexive skepticism 269–274; chimera and like-enough subjects 277–278; critical pluralism 273–276; framework problem 276–277;

Freud as reflexive-skeptic 278–280; relational tradition 280–283
regulatory-systems conceptualization 147
Reiff, Philip 252
Reis, B. E. 185n1, 215
Relational Perspectives on the Body 183
relational-perspectivism 114, 140n3
relational-perspectivist approach 137–138
relational-perspectivist psychoanalysis 109
relational psychoanalysis 107, 141–163, 266, 282
relational psychoanalytic theory 166
relational theory 23
relational tradition 280–283
representations of representations 169
reproduction 223
resistance–counterresistance interactions 81
reversibility 24, 30
Rivera, M. 57
Rizzuto, A.-M. 90
role-responsiveness 127
Rorty, R. 275
Rosen, H. 47n1
Roustang, F. 237
Rudnytzky, Peter 304
Rycroft, C. 14

Sandler, J. 205
Sands, S. H. 182
Schafer, R. 81, 190
Schofer, Jonathan 257
Schon, D. 204
school of psychoanalysis 189
Schorsch, Ismar 90, 97
science and spirituality, psychoanalytic analysis 89–91; psychoanalytic psychology 91–104
Scylla of uncritical dogmatism 273

Searles, Harold 25, 42, 74, 136, 142
self-analysis 112, 167
self and object relations 40–42
self-as-knower 170
self-as-object 46, 184–185
self as story 15
self-as-subject 46, 170, 184–185
self as subjective-self 71
self-awareness: objective 167, 171–172; reflective 45–46, 71, 167, 185
self-blaming polarizations 264
self-criticism 270, 274–275, 280
self-denigration 26
self-destructiveness 225
self-disclosures 156, 209
self-doubt 274
self-effacement 274
self-esteem 26
self-examination 270, 280
self-expression and interpretation 120–121
self-expression with patient 137
"self-in-relation" school 88n7
self-observation 176, 275
self-psychological model 160
self-psychologists 7, 188
self-psychology 159–160, 279
self-reflection 176
self-reflective awareness 264
self-reflexive examination 157
self-reflexive functioning 173, 177
self-reflexive strategy 214
self-reflexivity 181
self-reflexivity and therapeutic action 164–185
self-revelation 117, 162–163
self-revelations 115
self-state dreams 6–7, 22n1
self-states 42
Selichot 268
sensori-motor intelligence 28
separation 246
sexual abuse 4
sexual fantasies 294

sexual intercourse 64
sexual intercourse, model of 67
sexuality: centrality of 60; child's knowledge and phantasy regarding 59; dark side of 68; *see also* internalization of relations; parental sexual intercourse
sexuality polarization 87
sexualized humiliation 246
sexual seduction 19
Shoshani, Michael 164
Sieck, Barbara 305
Singer, I. 133
Slap, J. W. 7
Smith, B. L. 127
social-constructivism 140n3, 213
social primal scene 49
Soloveitchik, J. B. 97, 102
Spezzano, Charles 181–182
Spielrein, Sabina 23, 25
Starr, Karen 248
Steiner, John 179
Stepansky, P. E. 237, 272
Sterba, R. 165, 175–176
Stern, B. 38, 145, 183
Stern, Donnel 264
Stoller, Robert 297
Stolorow, R. D. 14, 21, 145–146, 185n1, 203
Strachey, J. 131
structural-conflict dreams 6
structuralist philosophy 25
subjective awareness 171
subjective self 170
subjectivity 107, 111
subject-object knowledge 245
subject-relations theory 179
subject-to-subject relatedness 179
submissiveness 172
Suchet, Melanie 240n3
suicidal tendencies 225
Sullivan's interpersonal theory 161
Sullivan's therapeutic inquiry 36

surplus self-revelations 162
Sutherland, J. D. 69
symbolization 182
Symington, N. 121
symmetry-asymmetry 115
synthetic function of ego 27
systematic approach to psychoanalytic technique 215

Talbert, C. H. 226
Target, Mary 168–169, 178
Taylor, E. 169
Tel Aviv Institute of Contemporary Psychoanalysis 164
Tenzer, A. 38, 47n1
theory of development 202
theory of mind 202
theory of psychoanalytic technique 202
therapeutic action of psychoanalysis 177
thirdness 266
third-sex 252
Thompson, Clara 241n9
thought communities 275
three-variable psychology 193
Tif 'ereth Yisrael 263
Tirosh-Samuelson, H. 283n1
toilet-breast analyst 80–81
Trachtenberg, R. 250
transcendent function 184
transference 116, 147
transference-countertransference 125, 184; enactment 136; implications 35, 41; integrations 80, 138
transference cures 258
transformation 24
transitional phenomena 21
triangular space 44, 70–71
Trop, J. L. 203
Trunnell, E. E. 7
Tuckett, David 301, 310
two-person psychology 113

unconscious meaning of patient's thoughts 107
unconscious phantasy 78
uncritical dogmatism 273
unitary gender identity 54
unwelcome guests of the family 225

verbalizable latent content 6
verbalization 107
violent sexual intercourse 63
voyeurism 158
vulnerability 172

Wallerstein, R. S. 189, 194, 272
Wilner, W. 185n2
Winnicott, D. W. 21, 52, 108, 120, 122, 131, 145, 223, 277; analyst and patient 119–120; interpretation, attitude toward 117–120; on patient's greed 118
Winnicottian technique 120
Wolstein, Benjamin 148, 218, 227, 233, 241n9
Yalom, I. 225

Zeitgeist 187
Zucker, H. 37